In Exile from
the Land of Snows

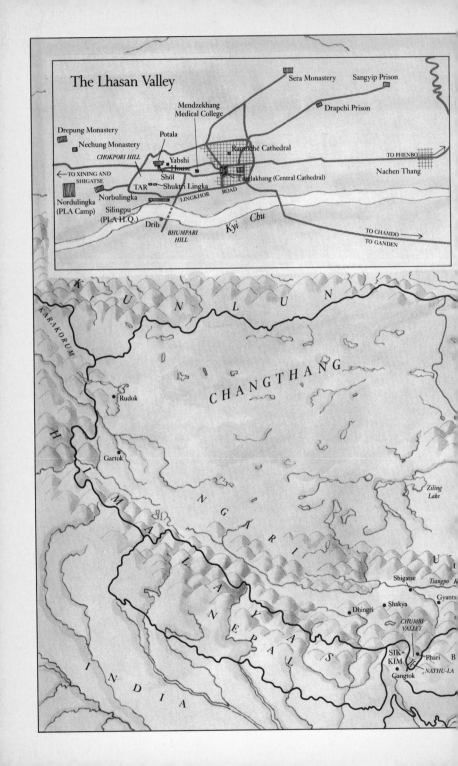

The Lhasan Valley

Sera Monastery
Sangyip Prison
Drapchi Prison
Mendzekhang
Medical College
Drepung Monastery
Nechung Monastery
Potala
Ramoché Cathedral
CHOKPORI HILL
Yabshi
House
TO PHENBO
TO XINING AND
SHIGATSE
Shöl
TAR
Shukteri Lingka
Tsuglakhang (Central Cathedral)
Nachen Thang
Nordulingka
(PLA Camp)
Norbulingka
LINGKHOR
ROAD
Silingpu
(PLA H.Q.)
Drib
Kyi Chu
BHUMPARI
HILL
TO CHAMDO
TO GANDEN

K U N L U N

KARAKORUM

CHANGTHANG

Rudok

Gartok

Ziling
Lake

N
G
A
R
I

H
I
M
A
L
A
Y
A
S

N
E
P
A
L

Shigatse
Tsangpo
Shakya
Gyants
Dhingri
CHUMBI
VALLEY
U
I

SIK-
KIM
Phari
B
NATHU-LA

I N D I A

Gangtok

Historic Tibet

TSAIDAM
BASIN

A M D O

Kokonor

Kumbum · Xining
· Taktser

Golmo

Langzhou

Tashikhiel

Ngoring
Lake

Charugon

Kyaring
Lake

MIN SHAN

Yangtze River (Drichu)

GOLOK

N G A P A

Jyekundo

K H A

Dengkog

Dergé Gonchen

M

Nagchuka

ENBO

N G

anden Monastery

Riwoché ·

Jomdha
Dzong

Chamdo

DRAYAB

Kanzé

NYARONG

C H I N A

Chendu

Po Tramo

PAYUL

Salween River

Mekong River (Ngachu)

Bathang

Markham
Gartok

Lhamo Lhatso

(Drichu)

n River (Brahmaputra)

Tsethang

DAKPO

Lhuntze
Dzong

sona

Tsakhalo

GYALTHANG

Mangmang

A S S A M

BURMA

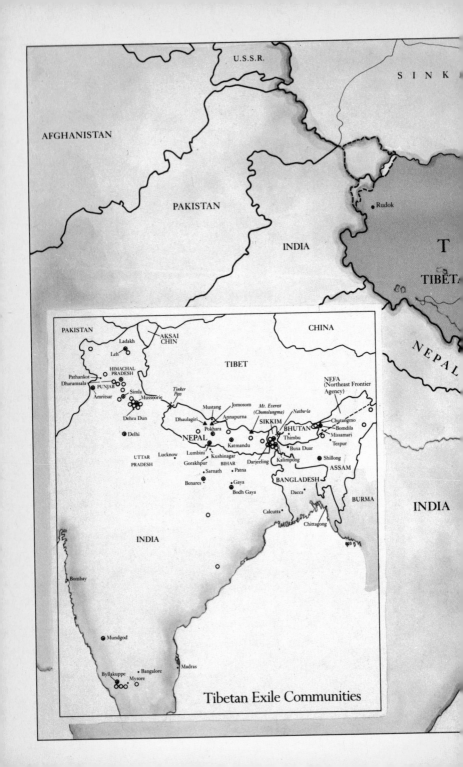

Tibetan Exile Communities

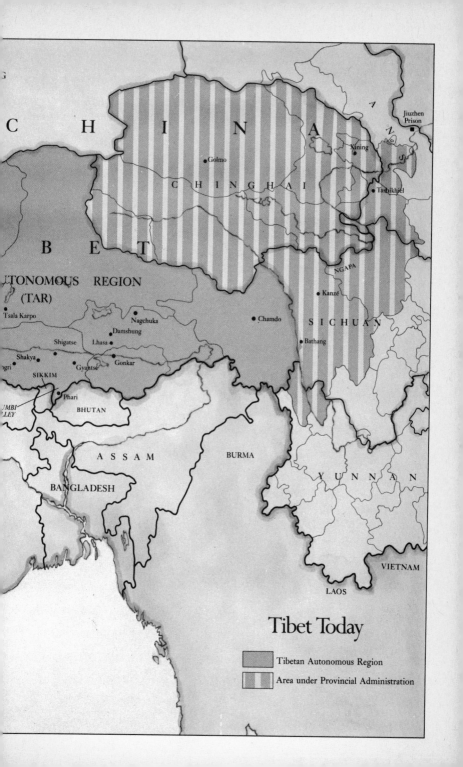

C H I N A

Jiuzhen
Prison

•Xining

•Golmo

C H I N G H A I

•Tashikhiel

T I B E T

NGAPA

AUTONOMOUS REGION

(TAR)

•Kanze

S I C H U A N

•Tsala Karpo

•Nagchuka

•Chamdo

•Damshung

Shigatse• •Lhasa

•Bathang

•Shakya

Gyantse• •Gonkar

ngri

SIKKIM

•Phari

BHUTAN

UMBI
LLEY

A S S A M

BURMA

Y U N N A N

BANGLADESH

VIETNAM

LAOS

Tibet Today

Tibetan Autonomous Region

Area under Provincial Administration

In Exile from the Land of Snows

The Dalai Lama and Tibet Since the Chinese Conquest

JOHN F. AVEDON

HarperPerennial
A Division of HarperCollins*Publishers*

This book was originally published in 1984 by Alfred A. Knopf, Inc. It is here reprinted by arrangement with Alfred A. Knopf, Inc. A paperback edition was published in 1986 by Vintage Books, a division of Random House. Portions of this work have previously appeared in Rolling Stone Press.

HarperCollins books may be purchased for educational, business, or sales promotional use. For information, please write: Special Markets Department, HarperCollins Publishers, Inc., 10 East 53rd Street, New York, NY 10022.

First HarperPerennial edition published 1994.

Library of Congress Cataloging-in-Publication Data
Avedon, John F.
  In exile from the land of snows / John F. Avedon. — 1st ed.
    p. cm.
  Includes bibliographical references and index.
  ISBN 0-06-097574-1
  1. Tibet (China) — History — 1951- I. Title.
DS786.A94 1994
951'.505—dc20   94-9866

96 97   **RRD H**   10 9 8 7 6 5 4 3

For the People of Tibet

Contents

Preface to the
HarperPerennial Edition

SINCE THIS BOOK was published a decade ago, Tibet's struggle has entered a pivotal phase. In January 1983, Beijing inaugurated a massive transfer of Chinese settlers—similar to earlier campaigns in Manchuria, Inner Mongolia, and Xinjiang—to absorb Tibet. Every facet of economic and domestic life has been affected, leading to a new round of Tibetan unrest, thirteen months of martial law, and a subsequent policy of repression under which a full 80 percent of the political prisoners arrested in China in 1993 were Tibetan. Despite ongoing resistance the Chinese influx may soon render hopes for Tibetan self-determination demographically irrelevant.

At the same time, the issue of Tibet has gained international attention. Following the Dalai Lama's receipt of the Nobel Peace Prize in 1989, numerous parliaments and the U.S. Congress and administration have supported the Tibetan cause, making it a significant factor in China's foreign relations. As a result, for the first time since the 1950 invasion, China's overall foreign policy goals have suffered from the occupation of Tibet and precisely at a time when systemic change is underway in its own government. With the growth of regionalism throughout China, it is possible that just at the moment when Beijing appears to have finally colonized Tibet, internal pressures could combine with external ones to undo its grip.

Whatever its outcome, Tibet's struggle no longer affects Tibet alone. Politically, Tibetan resistance to China's Communist regime has joined that of Chinese democrats to create significant momentum for reform. Strategically, the restoration of Tibet's historic role as a neutral buffer separating India and China has attracted increasing support as the most durable solution for long-term security in central Asia. Spiritually, Tibet's unique Buddhist culture—and above all the figure of the Dalai Lama—is poised to exert its moral authority on a China faced by the need to replace Communist ideology with indigenous ethical values. In short, Tibet's impact on both China and Asia as a whole contains broad potential to promote positive change.

Tibet's recent history is that of a holocaust in which ideological conquest took the lives of 1.2 million Tibetans, one-sixth of the population; destroyed 6,250 monasteries, the repositories of 1,300 years of higher Tibetan civilization; and decimated the forests and wildlife of a previously protected ecology the size of western Europe. However, it is also that of a nonviolent fight waged by the Dalai Lama and Tibetan people to preserve their culture and identity as a constructive refutation of Chinese claims on their homeland. There has been no Tibetan terrorism; no cycle of retributive violence to blight future generations. Instead, through peaceful, principled means, the Tibetan cause has slowly assembled world support in a formidable display of the efficacy of spiritual values in the arena of political strife. No matter how destructive the current Chinese influx continues to be—and no matter what harmful policies may still occur—Tibet's story already stands as one of this century's most inspiring examples of the power of compassion to resist and progressively undo aggression. It is my hope, shared by millions of people the world over, that the altruistic message of Tibetan religion and culture will be offered to the entire human family from a free Tibet in the near future.

John F. Avedon
New York City, 1994

Preface

TIBET'S STORY IS that of an ancient nation hurled into the twentieth century by the loss of its sovereignty, yet given a slim chance to regain its freedom and remake its identity. I came to write it as the result of a personal involvement growing over a period of eleven years.

In the summer of 1973 I undertook my first trip to Asia. On arriving in New Delhi I toured a Tibetan refugee camp and afterwards visited Tibet House, a library and museum in which blown-up photos of Tibet's great monasteries, the largest in the world, covered the walls. A week later I sat with thousands of Tibetans around an open tent on the outskirts of Katmandu, Nepal, watching a birthday celebration for their leader, the Dalai Lama. But it was not until I trekked up to the geographical, if no longer political, border of Tibet that I began to fully appreciate the country's present-day condition. The landscape was wild, the adjacent peaks of Annapurna and Dhaulagari loomed on either hand and down the narrow trail came an equally formidable middle-aged man, a long knife hanging from his belt and a heavy rifle slung over his back. Waving like an old friend, he stopped and within a few minutes of exchanged gestures revealed that he was a Tibetan guerrilla, whose headquarters, located less than two hours north in the principality of Mustang, was still waging a fierce fight for Tibet's freedom. Lifting his shirt, he pointed proudly to a long bayonet scar hewn across his belly and repeatedly said "Norbulingka." Thereafter he enacted the devastating massacre which had befallen soldiers of the Tibetan resistance fighting Chinese occupation troops at the Dalai Lama's summer palace outside of Lhasa. His barracks lay just across the seething brown waters of the Kali Gandaki river and it was clear from his spirit that despite Tibet's present fortunes, its people by no means considered the fate of their nation sealed.

Six years later Tenzin Gyatso, the Fourteenth Dalai Lama of Tibet, visited the United States. For much of his first American trip I accompanied the Tibetan leader to conduct a series of interviews. Following his departure I traveled to Asia once more, where I engaged in an extensive tour of the Tibetan communities in India. On a third journey, pursued over the winter of 1980–81, I continued to work with the Dalai Lama while living in the capital of the Tibetan diaspora and seat of the Tibetan government-in-exile, Dharamsala.

Research for this book was conducted primarily during the latter stay. In it, I have attempted to tell Tibet's tale through the lives of those who have both defined and been governed by the major developments of recent history. To further illuminate the narrative, I have added a section depicting some measure of Tibetan civilization, the spiritual underpinnings of which permeate every facet of the country's political life. Tibet's entry into the modern world has been unsought, painful and prolonged, but in many ways inspiring as well. It is my hope that the principles of faith and forbearance that have sustained the Tibetan people through their most difficult time will convey them to a new and self-determined era in the not too distant future.

John F. Avedon
New York City

I

I

Before the Fall

IN AUGUST of 1932, the Thirteenth Dalai Lama gazed out over the gardens of his summer palace, the Norbulingka or Jewel Park, and began to write his final testament to the Tibetan people. "It may happen," he warned, "that here, in the center of Tibet, religion and government will be attacked both from without and from within. Unless we can guard our own country, it will now happen that the Dalai and Panchen Lamas, the Father and the Son, and all the revered holders of the Faith, will disappear and become nameless. Monks and their monasteries will be destroyed. The rule of law will be weakened. The lands and property of government officials will be seized. They themselves will be forced to serve their enemies or wander the country like beggars. All beings will be sunk in great hardship and overpowering fear; the days and nights will drag on slowly in suffering." Though the Dalai Lama refrained from noting just who would inflict this devastating fate upon his country, the message was clear: Tibet, aloof and at peace for most of its 2,100 years, stood on the brink of disaster.

A year after his last words were circulated throughout the land, the Dalai Lama died. According to custom, his body was embalmed, dressed in gold brocade robes, placed in the lotus position and seated facing south —the direction of long life—on a throne in the Norbulingka. The golden rooftops of his winter palace, the Potala, and the Tsuglakhang or Central Cathedral in the heart of Lhasa, were draped in black banners. Prayer flags were lowered and butter lamps lit in the windows and on the roofs of every house in the capital. Stunned by their loss, the population of Lhasa filed in mourning past the deceased ruler's corpse, offering white scarves in the traditional gesture of respect. But even before government couriers could convey the news across the country, omens predicting the whereabouts of Thubten Gyatso's successor—believed to be the beloved leader himself returned in a new body—were occurring.

Checking the Dalai Lama's corpse one morning. attendant monks entered its sealed chamber, opened the salt-lined box in which it lay and found that the head had moved. No longer facing south, it had turned toward the northeast. Repositioned, it was again discovered facing east a short time later. In the ensuing months further signs appeared. The three state oracles turned eastward in trance and presented scarves; a patch of snapdragons sprouted from the east end of the platform used for public sermons in Lhasa's main square; overnight a giant star-shaped fungus grew on the east side of the northeast pillar of the shrine in the Potala where the Dalai Lama's jewel-inlaid tomb was under constructic n. And in one of the most time-honored occurrences marking the death of a high incarnate lama, the people of Lhasa beheld auspicious cloud formations, now and again pierced by rainbows, rising over the barren wall of mountains ringing the northeast end of the city.

In the spring of 1935, Tibet's newly appointed Regent, Reting Rinpoché,* joined by a senior minister of the old ruler's Cabinet, journeyed to the sacred lake of Lhamo Lhatso, seeking a vision. Located ninety miles southeast of Lhasa, Lhamo Lhatso was believed to be the foremost of Tibet's visionary lakes, bodies of water in which the future—individual as well as collective—could be seen. Oval-shaped and less than a mile in circumference, the lake lay at 17,000 feet in a basin surrounded by massive peaks, around which the weather was continually changing, from sun to rain, to hail and snow. The Thirteenth Dalai Lama himself had been discovered by means of a dramatic vision of his birthplace, seen by hundreds and lasting for a week, in the center of its waters. Now, more than half a century later, Reting Rinpoché had hopes for no less vivid a sign.

After spending some days in prayer at nearby Chokhorgyal Monastery, the Regent's party rode their ponies to the base of the rocky slope overlooking the lake. Proceeding upward on foot, they reached the top of a sheer ridge, whereupon they dispersed in different directions, each to seek his own vision. Alone among the group, Reting Rinpoché witnessed a remarkable sight. On staring at the clear alpine waters, he discerned three letters from the Tibetan alphabet float into view: Ah, Ka and Ma. The image of a great three-storied monastery, capped by gold and jade rooftops,

*Rinpoché is an honorific term given to revered teachers or incarnate lamas; it means "precious one."

followed. A white road led east from the monastery to a house before a small hill, its roof strikingly fringed in turquoise-colored tiles, a brown and white spotted dog in the courtyard. Later, the Regent dreamt of the same humble farmer's home, this time with oddly shaped gutter pipes emerging from the roof and a small boy standing in the yard.

Soon after the Regent's report was submitted to the National Assembly in Lhasa three search parties were dispatched across eastern Tibet, one southeast to Dakpo, another to Chamdo, capital of the eastern province of Kham, the last to the northeastern region of Amdo. The latter, departing in the autumn of 1936, consisted of forty members under the direction of one Kewtsang Rinpoché, a high lama of Sera Monastery. Riding over a thousand miles northeast, it chose as the center of its search Kumbum, the most important monastery in Amdo. Fifteen miles south of Xining, China's westernmost city, Kumbum had been built three and one half centuries before by the Third Dalai Lama to commemorate the birthplace of Tsongkhapa, founder of Tibet's largest sect, the Gelugpas or Followers of the Virtuous Way. As it came into view, set in low cedar-covered hills overlooking a fertile valley, the delegation saw that, just like the cloister in the vision, Kumbum's central temples were surmounted by brilliant gold and jade rooftops.

The party divided into four groups and proceeded to search the area for extraordinary children. A number of candidates were examined, all unsatisfactory. Six months into their stay, however, Kewtsang Rinpoché personally ventured forth to investigate the situation of a young boy living in a small farming village called Takster, two days east of Kumbum. The boy's existence had been brought to his attention by the Seventh Panchen Lama, Tibet's second-highest incarnation. While en route to Amdo, the delegation had encountered the Panchen Lama, then residing in Kham, and received from him a list—a product of his own inquiries—of three potential candidates for the Dalai Lama's rebirth. The boy in Takster was the last to be tested.

Early in the winter of 1937, Kewtsang Rinpoché, accompanied by a government official named Lobsang Tsewang and two attendants, set out for Takster. To avoid detection they disguised themselves as merchants on a business trip: Kewtsang Rinpoché donned an old sheepskin robe to play the role of servant; Lobsang Tsewang acted as the leader. Approaching Takster on the afternoon of the second day, they saw before them a typical Tibetan village: thirty or so stone farmhouses grouped together on a hillside, surrounded by lush fields of barley giving way to the foothills of spectacular snow-capped peaks, the most prominent, rising south of the village, called Kyeri. Covered with poplars and conifers, Kyeri's lower slopes were also home to two small monasteries, the upper, smaller one of which, Karma Shartsong Hermitage, had an especially renowned past. Perched atop a 500-foot sheer cliff face, its temples hewn from solid rock, Shartsong Hermitage was the very monastery in which Tsongkhapa had joined the company of monks and later taken novice vows. None of this was lost on the delegation as they rode up to a group of three flat-roofed buildings, each constructed around a central courtyard, occupying a spot somewhat up the hill from the rest of the village. Among them stood the house they sought, its single heavy wooden door, at the center of the windowless eastern wall, draped with a decorative cotton canopy above which rose a ten-foot-tall white prayer flag emblazoned with thousands of Buddhist mantras fluttering in the wind.

As the party dismounted, a brown and white spotted mastiff, chained to the entranceway, started to bark. The woman of the house emerged and Lobsang Tsewang, identifying himself as a trader, requested the use of her kitchen to make tea—a common practice of Tibetan travelers. While he was shown to the better rooms in the north wing, the others were directed to the kitchen which lay adjacent to the gate. Passing through the court-yard, Kewtsang Rinpoché noticed that the roof was fringed with turquoise tiles pierced by twisted waterspouts fashioned of gnarled juniper wood. Inside the kitchen he was directed to a wooden seating platform before a brick stove. A boy approached. Just two and a half, he had a bright, handsome face and was dressed in heavy Tibetan boots and wool overalls. Climbing into Kewtsang Rinpoché's lap, the child began playing with a rosary that had belonged to the Thirteenth Dalai Lama but now hung around the visitor's neck. According to the account of Amdo Kesang, the actual servant to the party, the little boy, whose name was Lhamo Dhon-drub, suddenly became agitated. Claiming that the rosary was his, he demanded that it be given to him immediately. "I'll give it to you," replied Kewtsang Rinpoché, "if you can guess who I am." "You are a lama of Sera," the boy said matter-of-factly. He then identified Lobsang Tsewang, to whom he had not been introduced, by his proper name and went on to mark the other visitors as having come from Sera monastery as well. Most astounding of all, Lhamo Dhondrub addressed the men in the dialect of Central Tibet, virtually unknown in his district.

Their interest roused, the delegation stayed the night, planning to leave unnoticed before dawn the next day. The following morning Lhamo Dhondrub had risen before them, and on seeing their preparations to depart pleaded in tears to be taken along. They succeeded in calming him down only by promising to return. When they did, it was to subject the boy to a battery of tests to determine if, in fact, this was the Dalai Lama.

When the party came again to Takster the monks offered gifts to the family and asked to be left alone with its smallest member. As night fell, they adjourned to the master bedroom at the center of the house, placed a low table on the *kang* or platform bed and arranged on it a series of articles some having belonged to the Thirteenth Dalai Lama, others, carefully crafted duplicates. The objects included the Dalai Lama's spectacles, silver pencil and eating bowl, as well as four items which the Oracle of Samye had ordered this delegation in particular to bring with it. They were a black rosary, a yellow rosary, two walking sticks and a small ivory hand drum used in religious devotions. The first stage of the examination centered on these.

Entering the bedroom, Lhamo Dhondrub was invited forward by Kewtsang Rinpoché, who sat with three officials on either side of the table. In his hand Kewtsang Rinpoché held the black rosary to which the boy had been drawn on the previous visit; beside it, a perfect duplicate. Asked to choose one, the child took the correct rosary without hesitating and placed it around his neck, a feat he repeated with the yellow rosary a few moments later. Next, the walking sticks were presented. At first Lhamo Dhondrub pulled gently at the wrong stick, but then let it go and took the correct one, happily holding it in front of him like a giant stave. This was considered particularly significant since the "wrong" stick had actually been used briefly by the Dalai Lama before he gave it to a friend. The final items, the drum, remained to be chosen. The false drum was beautifully decorated with floral brocade; the genuine one was less inviting. Once more, though, Lhamo Dhondrub took the correct object, twisting the drum quickly back and forth in his right hand so that it beat in the manner of tantric ritual.

A physical inspection was now undertaken. The boy was examined for eight bodily marks traditionally distinguishing the Dalai Lamas from all other men: among them, large ears, long eyes, eyebrows curving up at their ends, streaks like those of a tiger skin on the legs, and a print resembling a conch shell on the palm of one hand. Gently drawing back the child's clothing, the examiners found three indications resembling those they sought. As one of them, a monk named Sonam Wangdu, later recounted, they were overcome with "deep devotion, joy and gaiety." "Indeed we were so moved that tears of happiness filled our eyes," he recalled. "Scarcely able to breathe, we could neither sit properly on the mat nor speak a word." There was no longer any doubt. Here, halfway through his third year of life, was the Holy One himself, the Fourteenth Dalai Lama of Tibet.

Despite their success, a serious obstacle confronted the party. Ma Bufeng, the Moslem warlord of northwestern China, had learned of the child in Takster. Fearful of his intervention, the delegation sought to conceal their choice by examining dozens of children at the general's heavily fortified *yamen* or headquarters in Xining. When the very best managed to identify only two of four articles correctly, Ma Bufeng, undeceived, summoned Lhamo Dhondrub and his family to a private audience with a few other children. Here he became convinced, by the boy's precocious demeanor, that he was the most likely candidate for the Dalai Lama. As a result, when the delegation requested permission to take the child to Lhasa, Ma Bufeng refused to grant it. Unabashedly, he demanded 100,000 Chinese silver dollars (approximately $92,000) in ransom. With no other recourse, the officials paid. However, instead of releasing the boy, Ma Bufeng made further demands: 300,000 more dollars, a full set of the past Dalai Lama's robes and throne ornaments and a valuable gold-lettered edition of all 333 volumes of the Buddhist canon. Outraged but helpless, the Tibetans once more complied. While most of the money was being raised on loan from Moslem traders, Lhamo Dhondrub lived at Kumbum with his eldest brother, Taktser Rinpoché, himself already recognized as an incarnate lama.

The delegation's fear of losing the newly discovered Dalai Lama increased as additional proofs of his true identity were recorded. Besides the house, its odd waterspouts and dog, the letters Ah, Ka and Ma all fit the locale perfectly. Ah stood for Amdo, Ka for Kumbum and Ka and Ma together for the first word of the monastery on the nearby mountainside: Karma Shartsong Hermitage. It was now recalled that the Thirteenth Dalai Lama had stayed at the temple in 1909 on his return from five-and-a-half years of exile in Mongolia and China. He had left a pair of his boots as a blessing and in the memory of local people looked long and hard at the very house Lhamo Dhondrub was born in, commenting that it was a beautiful spot. More recently, crops in Taktser had failed for an unprecedented four years, causing the villagers to say that a high incarnation would be born among them, a notion grounded in the belief that an auspicious event had to be offset by one equally bad. Lhamo Dhondrub's family had undergone particularly severe troubles. A number of their livestock had died without apparent cause, and in the few months preceding the infant's birth, his father had fallen ill, again for no discernible reason. His mother, though, managed to carry out the household duties. On the day of the birth she retired to the cow shed, a small windowless room in the western wing of the house, lined with mangers and illuminated by a single mustard-oil lamp. At the break of dawn on July 6, 1935, the Fourteenth Dalai Lama was born, eyes wide open, a fact his mother noted as unusual. On the same day, his father recovered just as mysteriously as he had fallen ill, got out of bed, offered prayers at the family altar and on being informed that a son had been born to him, simply said, "Good. I would like to make him a monk."

Lhamo Dhondrub's parents had no inkling of their fifth child's remarkable identity. Within days of his birth, however, a pair of crows, believed by Tibetan Buddhists to be sacred to the protective deity Mahakala, came to the house in Takster and perched on its roof. Each morning they arrived at the same time, roosted for a while and then departed. It was now remembered that similar visitations had occurred at the birth of the First, Seventh, Eighth and Twelfth Dalai Lamas. As far back as 1391, Gendun Drub, the First Dalai Lama, had been protected by a crow on the day of his birth, when, during an attack by bandits, his nomad parents fled their tent, leaving their child behind. Returning that evening, they found the baby in a corner on the ground, a large black crow standing guard before him.

Prior to the search party's appearance in Takster, Lhamo Dhondrub's favorite game was to straddle a windowsill and pretend he was riding a horse to Lhasa. Following his arrival in Kumbum, the urge became so strong that the then three-year-old boy continually played alone at packing bags and setting off on a journey to the Holy City.

After eight months of waiting, on the first day of the sixth Tibetan month, mid-August 1939, the delegation, the prospective Dalai Lama and his family finally departed Kumbum. Joining the caravan of Moslem merchants who had put up the second part of the ransom (and were now en route to Mecca on pilgrimage), they left the monastery under a bright sun and light rain on the first stage of an arduous three-and-a-half-month trek over Tibet's barren northern plains. Lhamo Dhondrub rode with his six-year-old brother, Lobsang Samten, in a small palanquin suspended on poles between two mules. Though as yet not officially confirmed, he was already being treated with the respect accorded to a Dalai Lama. In the towns and nomad camps they passed through, he sat on a high throne receiving offerings and bestowing personal blessings to thousands of the faithful. Though he was outwardly at ease during the ceremonies, the sudden attention took its toll at first, those adults closest to the boy noticing, as one put it, that he was "fretful" and "occasionally wept." His spirits improved, though, as the caravan approached Central Tibet. When a cavalry detachment of the Tibetan army greeted the caravan north of Nagchuka, Lhamo Dhondrub was delighted by a display of trick riding put on for his benefit. Crossing the Thutoppchu River, he was equally pleased by a ride in a coracle, or yak-skin boat. On the far shore he was met by a delegation from the National Assembly in Lhasa, followed, a few days later, by a second group of emissaries bringing with them the Thirteenth Dalai Lama's yellow traveling tent and, with it, news of the government's decision to formally designate the child from Amdo as the reincarnation of the Dalai Lama. A proclamation to this effect, issued jointly by the Regent, the Cabinet and the National Assembly, was delivered by a third party of officials, who rode ten days out from the capital to greet their new ruler by torchlight one morning before dawn. As the first rays of the sun illuminated a large group of reception tents, the Dalai Lama was taken inside, dressed in the maroon and yellow robes of a monk and presented with the offering of the Mendel Tensum—an image of the Buddha, a reliquary and a scripture—the traditional homage paid to a high lama by his followers. Thereafter he rode in a golden palanquin, soon joined by the Regent and the Lord Chamberlain, through villages filled by exultant crowds. And as the entourage, now numbering in the hundreds, neared Lhasa, the Dalai Lama himself experienced a moment of profound joy when, in the midst of an audience for high government officials, an unfamiliar lama approached bearing in his hands a three-foot-long tube enclosed in heavy brocade. Sealed within lay one of the most sacred objects in Tibet, a *thanka* or scroll painting of Palden Lhamo, chief Protector of the Dalai Lamas. Believed to be a receptacle through which the Protector could communicate, it had been carried next to the person of every Dalai Lama since the 15th century. On seeing it, Lhamo Dhondrub was so ecstatic that many of those around him burst into tears.

On the morning of October 6, 1939, the Fourteenth Dalai Lama arrived in sight of Lhasa. Two miles east of the city on Doguthang Plain, a great tent encampment had been pitched in four concentric squares. In the center was a voluminous tent surmounted by a white and blue canopy known as the "Great Peacock." Fashioned of bright yellow satin with a silk lining and crown, it had been used over the centuries solely to greet the infant Dalai Lamas on their discovery and return to the capital. Flanked by leopard- and tiger-skin Mongolian yurts, the inner and smallest square was surrounded by an eight-foot-high wall, outside of which stood the hundreds of tents of Tibetan government and monastic officials gathered for the ceremonies.

Throughout the two days spent at Doguthang, Lhamo Dhondrub sat on a tall throne at the rear wall of the Great Peacock, holding a small yellow tassel in his right hand, individually blessing each of the 70,000 monks and lay people gathered. Pastries, dried fruit and yak meat were distributed to the crowd from giant troughs. Those not waiting in the endless line danced, sang and offered prayers, many weeping with joy.

Years later, the Dalai Lama recalled that, while the people's celebrations had been on an unprecedented scale, some had wished to ascertain for themselves that he was the correct choice. One venerable Geshé or Master of Metaphysics from Drepung Monastery went so far as to subject him to a brief but pointed questioning. As the Dalai Lama reflected, laughing, "So you see, though there were certain very proper old people who wanted to be sure, I apparently put on a good performance and convinced them."

As the sun rose on the morning of October 8, a crystal-clear day, a brilliant procession formed to escort the child into the city proper. Sixteen noblemen dressed in green satin robes and round red-tasseled hats carried the gilded palanquin in which the Dalai Lama sat. Before him marched the State Astrologer, musicians, monks and ministers of the Cabinet; behind, the Regent, the Prime Minister, the Dalai Lama's family and a long line of abbots and lay officials costumed according to rank. Clerics heralded the column's approach with ten-foot long horns blown from the roof of the Potala, rising on Red Hill in the middle of the Lhasan plain. Tens of thousands lined its route, which was demarcated with yellow and white chalk, incense braziers burning every thirty yards between a forest of rainbow-hued "victory banners" held aloft on tall poles. While Lhasans rang small hand bells, the regimental marching bands of the Tibetan army played "God Save the King," learned from their British instructors. Entering Lhasa, the procession circled the 1,300-year-old Central Cathedral, halting in the large square before it, where the ambassadors of India, China, Nepal and Bhutan waited to offer their respects. Also present was the medium of the chief State Oracle, surrounded by his attendants. As the Dalai Lama's palanquin arrived, the protective deity abruptly took possession. Dressed in thick silk robes, a polished silver mirror across his chest and a massive flag-festooned helmet weighing almost a hundred pounds on his head, the Protector rushed forward, hissing, cheeks puffed, eyes bulging, rhythmically kicking his legs in the air and bending them at the knees in the deity's honorific dance. In his hands he held a long white scarf or *kata* to offer the child. Bowing abruptly from the waist, he snapped his neck down with no difficulty, despite the helmet's weight, touched his forehead to the boy's and presented the scarf, which, calmly accepting, Lhamo Dhondrub then draped around the oracle's neck in blessing. The procession quickly moved on, entering the Central Cathedral, Tibet's most hallowed sanctum, where the Dalai Lama prayed. From there Lhamo Dhondrub was led past the foot of the Potala, through the city's western gate and two miles beyond, to the Norbulingka. Ushered into his predecessor's quarters at the end of the long parade, he pointed to a small box and nonchalantly declared, "My teeth are in there." Opening the case, attendants were astonished to find a set of the old ruler's dentures. But the amazement was not theirs alone. The Dalai Lama himself felt transported by all that had occurred. Years later he wrote of his entry to Lhasa: "As the people watched me passing, I could hear them crying, 'The day of our happiness has come.' I felt as though I were in a dream . . . as if I were in a great park covered with beautiful flowers while soft breezes blew across it and peacocks elegantly danced before me. There was an unforgettable scent of wildflowers, and a song of freedom and happiness in the air."

Within seven weeks, Lhamo Dhondrub was tonsured by the Regent in the Central Cathedral, given his novice vows and renamed Jetsun Jamphel Ngawang Lobsang Yeshi Tenzin Gyatso—Holy Lord, Gentle Glory, Eloquent, Compassionate, Learned Defender of the Faith, Ocean of Wisdom. Shortly thereafter, on February 22, 1940, Tenzin Gyatso—as he was now called—not yet five years old, was installed on the Lion Throne in an elaborate ceremony in the Potala's great eastern hall as, pending the attainment of his majority, supreme temporal and spiritual ruler of Tibet.

THE LAND over which young Tenzin Gyatso had been chosen to rule was, in its geography and people alike, a world apart. A plateau the size of western Europe at the heart of the Asian continent, Tibet was encircled by the earth's highest mountains—the Himalayas to the south, Karakorum, Kunlun, Min Shan, and Ta-hsueh Shan to the west, north and east. Only in the northeast, beside the shores of the great Blue Lake, Kokonor, did an unimpeded avenue, rising up like a long ramp through a portal in the mountains, give open access to the Tibetan Plateau. Once there, the world fell far below. Tibet's average altitude was 15,000 feet—three miles above sea level; more than half the density of the planet's atmosphere and three quarters of its moisture remained beneath. The country encompassed landscape of awesome beauty. At its center ranged the illimitable *changthang* or northern plains—an arid wasteland of salt and borax flats, pierced by glacial rivers and crystalline lakes rimmed with glaring white soda deposits. To the south, following the course of the Tsangpo or Brahmaputra River, lay the first of its three provinces—U-Tsang or Central Tibet. Like its geological extension, western Tibet, U-Tsang was dry and dusty, sheltered by the lee of the Himalayas and turning verdant only with the brief summer rains. A burning sun shone through an iridescent cobalt sky onto wide valleys sculpted from sweeping, 20,000-foot peaks, an occasional grove of willow, poplar or walnut trees gracing the riverbanks. Eastward, the plateau sliced into lower, less expansive valleys, compressed by the oblique, heavily forested slopes of Tibet's second province, Kham. Through Kham's dramatic mountain gorges ran the headwaters of Asia's great rivers: the Salween (Ngulchu), Mekong (Dzachu), and Yangtze (Drichu). Its vast forests of juniper, spruce and cypress inhabited by bear, wolf, monkey, leopard, panda, cuckoo, pheasant and eagle, Kham was the most rugged, inaccessible region of Tibet. To the north, Tibet's third province, Amdo, began. Running as far as the Kunlun Mountains and the Kokonor, it contained the country's most spectacular terrain. In Amdo, mountain and plain, forest and river, combined to produce a landscape similar to the American Northwest—expansive views over endless prairie, terminating in snow-capped mountains, along whose slopes grazed herds of antelope, yak, bhurrel and wild ass or kiang.

Tibet's seven million people were descended from nomadic tribes racially akin to the Mongols. According to their own legends, their land had once lain beneath a shallow sea, which indeed it had—the Sea of Tethys. With the water's disappearance, a monkey and an ogress had come to dwell in its immensity. The monkey, an emanation of the Bodhisattva of Infinite Compassion, Chenrezi, was peaceful and contemplative. He lived, absorbed in meditation, alone in a cave. The ogress, on the other hand, was wrathful and stubborn—a cannibal with an insatiable sexual appetite. Her lonely cries carried across the countryside, summoning a mate. Hearing them, the monkey was filled with pity and rushed to her side, where he remained long enough to father six children: the first Tibetans.

Born without tails and with few other simian traits, the offspring intermixed and multiplied. Those who took after their father were gentle and wise. Those who inherited their mother's disposition were cruel and given to excess. Abiding in the caves of the ogress, located on Gonpori Mountain in U-Tsang, they gradually disseminated to populate the land. By 127 B.C., the inhabitants of the Yarlung Valley, south of the caves, elevated the country's first king, Nyatri Tsenpo. From him descended a dynasty of forty-one monarchs spanning the first thousand years of Tibet's history.

A loose amalgam of competing chieftains and their respective clans, the early Tibetans were in continual conflict with one another. By the time of the thirty-third king, Songtsen Gampo (609–649), however, they had banded together to forge an empire which, brought to its zenith a century later, was the greatest in Asia, extending over two thousand miles from the captured Chinese capital of Chang'an in the east to the Pamirs and Samarkand in the west.

It was Tibet's thirty-seventh monarch, Trisong Detsen (741–798), who brought his nation's conquests to their height; paradoxically, he also ensured the empire's collapse. While previously the royal family had merely toyed with the alien faith of Buddhism, the new king firmly established its nonviolent tenets over Tibet's indigenous shamanism, known as Bon. Therein he laid the seeds for a political and cultural upheaval which, by the middle of the ninth century, had destroyed the monarchy itself. For more than four hundred years thereafter, Tibet was divided into feuding princely and monastic states. When centralized rule was finally achieved in the thirteenth century, it was at the price of Tibet's submission to Mongol dominion. Yet a unique understanding governed the bond, guaranteeing that it was purely nominal.

In 1207, apprised of the approach of Genghis Khan's armies, Tibet's chief rulers joined together to offer the Mongols tribute and thereby avoid invasion. Thirty-two years later, though, having failed to make annual payments, Tibet was invaded by Godan Khan, grandson of Genghis. Once he had burned Reting Monastery north of Lhasa and slaughtered five hundred monks and laymen in reprisal, the Mongol prince ironically sought religious instruction from Sakya Pandit, head of the Sakyas, the second of Tibet's four principal sects. Sakya Pandit assented and in return was given temporal authority over all of Central Tibet, a role which his nephew Phakpa inherited from Godan's successor, Kublai Khan. With this, the so-called Priest-Patron tie came into effect wherein the Mongols looked to Tibet's preeminent lama for spiritual authority, while considering the country itself to be within their own sphere of influence. Through it Tibet was loosely associated with China following Kublai Khan's capture of that nation's throne. With the waning, though, of both Sakya and Mongol authority one hundred years later, the bond broke. Three centuries of Tibetan independence followed, at the conclusion of which, in 1642, a new religious sect, the Gelugpas, led by their chief teachers the Dalai Lamas, established their rule over rival groups, once more using the fulcrum of Mongol support. Shortly afterwards China's second foreign dynasty, the Manchus, assumed the Mongols' role of lay patron. Symbolically aligned to them, the Dalai Lamas governed Tibet into the twentieth century, Lhasa considering its duties to Peking purely ceremonial; an effective means for deflecting a large, aggressive neighbor and little more. In the meantime, Tibet's unique civilization fully matured.

With the collapse of the early empire, the single-minded zeal Tibetans had shown for the pursuits of war turned to those of peace, transmuting the national character to that of the long-forgotten father of the race. The change resulted primarily from the Buddhist ideas themselves. Buddhism held worldly life in any form to be imbued with suffering. Only through realizing the ultimately illusory nature of existence could freedom—the state of Buddhahood—be obtained. Mahayana Buddhism, the school which came to Tibet, laid particular stress on attaining enlightenment for the sake of liberating all sentient beings from sorrow. Accordingly, the cultivation of compassion, matched by that of renunciation and wisdom, charged the Tibetan soul. Hunting, fishing and the killing of so much as an insect became anathema. Prayer wheels filled the rivers with mantras, prayer flags the sky; house-high piles of *mani* stones, inscribed with invocations, and the spire-topped reliquaries of Buddhist saints called *chortens* converted the landscape into a living web of sacred sites, linked by a constant flow of pilgrims. Where every valley had been dominated by the forbidding walls of a mountaintop *dzong* or fort, great city-like *gonpas*, or monasteries, now sprang up, centers of learning and culture, inhabited, in time, by a quarter of the male population.

It was in her cloisters that Tibet's culture flowered. Writing, literature, medicine, arts, architecture and the higher studies of the monastic colleges all derived from the great corpus of the Buddhist teaching or Dharma, which, alone among the nations of Asia, Tibet received in its entirety. While a rotating cadre of monks conducted its administration, the bulk of the monastic community, given to the *sangha* or clergy as young boys, rigorously pursued enlightenment through ritual, study and daily meditation. In Gelugpa monasteries scholars memorized and debated for up to twenty years before standing for their final exams in the Doctor of Divinity or Geshé degree. Their effort was matched only by the retreats of lifelong *gomchen* or hermits who, sealed in caves and isolated mountain huts, tended by a few disciples, practiced the most extreme mental and physical austerities. The preeminent religious practitioners, however, were the 4,000 or so *tulkus,* incarnate lamas believed able to choose the time and place of their rebirth. Recognized in infancy by their followers, they were returned to their monasteries to once more take up the great Buddhist work of leading all beings to liberation. Chief of these were the emanations of high Bodhisattvas or Buddhas, among whom, as the living incarnation of Tibet's patron saint, Chenrezi, the Dalai Lama stood out as the holiest presence in the land.

The lay society which supported such a temporally nonremunerative pursuit was feudal yet, owing to Tibet's severe terrain and the temporizing doctrines of the faith, imbued with an essentially democratic spirit. Tibetans themselves were naturally warm and pragmatic, accepting of their lot, socially conservative but individually tolerant. Their innate love of order had kept the various classes immutably defined for centuries.

Holding to the high, open country, Tibet's original inhabitants, her nomads, grazed vast herds of yak and sheep between summer and winter pasturage. Dwelling in low-slung black felt tents, speaking their own dialects, wearing heavy charm boxes, long swords and fleece-lined robes —though often stripped to the waist in even the harshest weather—they enlivened their existence by ambushing traders' caravans and, when the snows became too deep to move about, reciting for days on end Tibet's great epic poem *Gesar of Ling*. Wary of the sedentary lives of their neighbors, the nomadic tribes descended from the highlands only to trade meat and cheese in exchange for grain, guns and household goods. Here, along the protected valley floors and river basins, lived most of Tibet's population: farmers skillfully raising the staple crop, barley, out of a thin skin of easily depleted arable earth, beset by a dry climate, early frosts and devastating hailstorms. But within the limits of the land, Tibetans were prosperous. Famine was unknown; properly stored meat remained fresh for a year, grain for a century. Due to the germ-inhibiting altitude, disease was rare. Large families were the norm, polygamy, polyandry and monogamy all being practiced. The status of women was equal to that of men in both business and the household and, without doubt, the highest in Asia. The main repressive feature of Tibetan society was the system of taxation: since taxes were paid in kind or labor to whatever large monastic, noble or government estate dominated the area, peasants were tied to their property and social mobility was impeded.

The chance for economic betterment lay almost exclusively in trade. In autumn, following the harvest, one or two men from each family departed home on a trading expedition. Entering the ancient caravan ways, they joined the mule, yak and camel trains of the great merchant concerns, traveling south to India, east to China and north to Mongolia. Tea blocks, tools, tobacco, silver ingots, horses, Russian silks, Japanese matches and American perfume were all imported; musk, wool, salt, gold dust, furs, medicinal herbs and yak tails, used abroad for fly whisks and Santa Claus beards, were sent out. Camped behind stockades fashioned from bales of their goods, flintlocks and ferocious mastiffs at the ready, the traders broke their journey at midday, when afternoon dust storms scoured the land, and were afoot long before dawn. The greatest beneficiaries of their business were the small noble class, numbering no more than three hundred families, who, beside the monks, stood at the pinnacle of Tibetan society.

The oldest of Tibet's aristocrats traced their origin directly to the Yarlung kings. Like those ennobled more recently, they held ancestral estates by grant from the government, in exchange for which they rendered service to the bureaucracy. Their noble status was clear to all from their splendid silk robes (the sleeves worn a foot below the hands to denote leisure), pendant earrings and coteries of retainers who, as they rode forth from their homes, cleared the way. They ate off silver plates and jade bowls, had a passion for elaborate flower gardens, archery (using box-headed arrows that whistled in flight) and four-day picnics at which the guests were serenaded by exquisitely dressed *chang* or "beer" girls, who encouraged everyone to drink. The nobility, though, were not, by nature, opulent. All employed a staff of monks to say daily prayers before house-hold shrines, and their most compelling concern, beyond a strict adherence to their faith, lay in the business of governance. Though many had country estates in or around Shigatse and Gyantse, Tibet's second- and fourth-largest cities, the obligations of government work kept them in the capital for most of the year.

It was to Lhasa that all Tibet gravitated. At the hub of the city—and of Tibet itself—lay the Central Cathedral containing the country's most sacred image, Jowo Rinpoché, the Precious Lord. A statue of the Buddha believed to have been blessed by him, it was the magnet to which pilgrims would prostrate across the entire nation, an endeavor often years in the undertaking. Arriving at the Cathedral or Tsuglakhang, they turned the prayer wheels of the first of Lhasa's three circular roads, the Nangkhor, and entering the hallowed sanctum, beheld its golden face lit by the serene glow of colossal butter lamps. The Tsuglakhang epitomized Tibet's inex-tricable mix of the sacred and mundane. Within the more than 50 chapels on its ground floor lay an inestimable treasure of spiritual wealth, yet on the two floors above stood the offices of the Cabinet, the Foreign Bureau, the departments of Finance, Customs and Agriculture, the Mayor of Lhasa, the Regent and a score of others. Their documents, which included centuries-old treaties and tax records, were filed in bunches tied to red-lacquered pillars while much of their respective budgets were kept in the form of grain, material and fuel in adjoining storerooms. Between them all ranged more chapels and shrines, so that the seven grades of the civil bureaucracy were continually passing incense-shrouded images and de-vout worshippers as they conducted the various affairs of state.

Outside the Tsuglakhang ran Lhasa's second circular road, the Barkhor or marketplace. With the ship-like girth of the Potala looming in the distance, bakers, booksellers, rug and saddle merchants vied for the busi-ness of the huge crowds, among whom could be seen all of Tibetan society. Women of U and Tsang, Central Tibet's two provinces, wore their hair in great wood-framed headdresses, studded with coral, pearl and turquoise, bulky amber necklaces and multicolored aprons adorning their ankle-length *chubas* or robes. Towering Khampa men swaggered through the streets clad in thick wool garments and fox-fur hats, long, carved daggers in their belts. From Amdo came the nomadic Goloks, feared for banditry, the men wearing ivory bracelets and heavy red and black leather boots, their heads shaved save for a short lock left on the crown, the women's waist-long hair braided into 108 plaits bound with large silver discs and coins to show their wealth. Among the shoppers, monks stopped to buy snuff (their sole indulgence save for up to sixty cups of butter tea a day), children played at keeping a ribboned fly aloft with the kicks of one foot, while strolling drama troupes and traveling bards or *lama manis* regaled the people with tales from the lives of Tibet's great saints. Following New Year's the Cathedral and Barkhor became the nucleus of the three-week-long Monlam Chenmo or Great Prayer Festival. Thousands of monks swelled Lhasa's population; public sermons, doctrinal debates, parades, horse races and athletic events filled the city, spilling into its third and outermost circular road, the Lingkhor or Holy Walk.

Four miles long, the Lingkhor enclosed not just Lhasa but the vale's two major hills, on which stood the Potala and the government's chief medical college, Chokpori. Jammed by men and women performing prostrations, it passed through the numerous *lingkas* or parks to which Lhasans flocked in summer and early autumn for picnics and opera and, due to the preponderance of the faithful, was a principal haunt of beggars. Near it lived the Ragyapa, who, dwelling in curious shelters made of yak and goat horns, performed, along with Moslem butchers, the lesser tasks of life, such as conveying corpses to the great black rock east of the city where they were cut up to be fed, as a final act of altruism, to the vultures. Beyond the Lingkhor stood the Norbulingka as well as the world's largest monasteries, the "Three Pillars of the State," Drepung, Sera and Ganden, holding among them upwards of 22,000 monks. Further out, the valley was studded by dozens of ancient cloisters, all of which, in Tibet's theocracy, ensured the Place of the Gods, as Lhasa was known, to be the undisputed center of both secular and spiritual authority.

Since the advent of the Ganden Phodrang, the government of the Dalai Lamas, Tibet's administration had been equally split between the clergy and the nobility. Every key post was held jointly by a monk and a nobleman, both to share and to check power. Tibet's unique government worked so well that internal strife rarely emerged, save in the unavoidably weak regencies between the majorities of the Dalai Lamas. With the restraining hand of central authority removed, factionalism, which had plagued Tibet since the fall of the Yarlung Dynasty, inevitably cropped up. This and its corollary, the vague, potentially compromising tie to an outside power, most recently China, stood out as the nation's sole political liabilities. So long as Tibet remained hermetically sealed from the world, isolated behind impregnable mountains, the faults never threatened to destabilize it. Toward the close of the nineteenth century, however, more than two millennia of Central Asian solitude suddenly gave way to the encroachments of the modern world.

In 1904, concerned over Russian expansion—via Tibet—to the northern borders of its Indian realm, Great Britain dispatched an expeditionary force to Lhasa. After securing trade ties from the Tibetan government, the troops withdrew, not, however, before alerting China to the insubstantial nature of its claim on Tibet, described prior to the assault by Lord Curzon, the British viceroy of India, as a "constitutional fiction." To reassert their dominance, the Manchus sent an army of their own. After almost six years in exile, following the British attack, the Thirteenth Dalai Lama had been back in Lhasa only a few weeks when, in the winter of 1910, he was forced to flee once more, this time, ironically, to India and the protecting arms of the British. For the first time in history, Peking now ruled Tibet directly until, in the wake of the 1911 revolution, its forces were expelled and the Dalai Lama returned to formally reproclaim Tibetan independence. Ignoring the declaration, China's new republic, led by Yuan Shih-kai, announced a policy, based on Sun Yat-sen's doctrine of the five races of China, laying claim to most of the major regions with which the Chinese state, in its various forms, had had substantial contact over the centuries. Thus, not only Tibet but Manchuria, Mongolia and Xinjiang were held to be provinces of China proper, a belief subsequently adopted by both the Kuomintang or Nationalists and Communists as well. China, though, could not occupy these territories. By 1918 Tibet's small army had pushed the Chinese back through Kham to Dartsedo, the original border of the two nations. Nevertheless, the Thirteenth Dalai Lama recognized that a political solution must eventually be found. Enlisting Great Britain as mediator, he attempted, at the Simla Convention of 1914, to negotiate a compromise based on a British concept of Chinese suzerainty over a fully autonomous Tibet. When the Chinese refused to comply—holding out for complete control of Tibet—he began to modernize the country's antiquated army. As China's first republic collapsed, and the period of competing warlords followed by the Nationalists' long struggle with the Communists ensued, the issue faded. Tibet once more found itself fully independent, unassailed by outside pressures. For two decades peace descended on the country, aptly described by the Dalai Lama in his *kachem* or final testament, when he stated that under the latter part of his reign Tibet had become "happy and tranquil, like a land made new." Beside his sanguine portrait of the present, though, had been the ominous warning, drafted in such vivid detail, of a future Tibet eclipsed in oppression, the days and nights "dragging slowly on in suffering." Remote as such a fate seemed to be in the winter of 1933, its antecedents were to strike with shattering speed.

Three days after the Dalai Lama's death, Tsipon Lungshar, an ambitious Finance Minister, mounted a coup d'état. Hoping to capitalize on the delicate period of transition to a regency, he sought to displace the interim power of the Cabinet with that of the National Assembly, under his control. Inciting the thousand-man Drong Drak Magar Regiment to rebel, he succeeded in having his chief rival—a monk official named Kunphela, who had been supported by the regiment—banished by the Assembly to southern Tibet, charged with negligence in caring for the Dalai Lama during his final illness. It was not until the discovery of an assassination attempt, orchestrated by Lungshar against an intransigent minister, that both the Assembly and the Cabinet realized how close they had come to being superseded. (Documents in the possession of Lungshar's followers subsequently revealed a detailed plot to overthrow the government.) Convicted of high treason, Lungshar received Tibet's severest form of punishment—blinding. No sooner had the crisis been averted, however, than a second, less dramatic, if ultimately more dangerous threat developed. In the confusion following the Thirteenth Dalai Lama's death, a Chinese Nationalist general and two aides-de-camp were granted entry visas to Lhasa. In 1912, following the expulsion of the Manchu occupation force, the Tibetans had demonstrated their independence by refusing to accept Chinese representation in their country maintained, historically, by two Ambans, or Manchu officials, stationed in Lhasa—a convention that Peking had cited since the eighteenth century as proof of its own dominion. But now, unsure of itself, the government let just such a delegation in, under the guise of a condolence mission. Instead of departing after it had tendered official sympathies, the mission remained, opened up a liaison office and established a crucial foothold for the Nationalists in Tibet.

Thus, almost immediately following the Dalai Lama's demise, the two dangers foretold in his testament began to materialize—Tibet being threatened "both from without and from within." Under these inauspicious conditions Reting Rinpoché, a twenty-three-year-old lama of little political acumen, though greatly respected for his spiritual attainments, assumed the regency, having been selected by the National Assembly. Once more, Tibet turned away from worldly affairs, content to take up, in the evening of its seclusion, the pursuits of peace and meditation. Within this tranquil interregnum, the new Dalai Lama was to spend his childhood.

WHILE HIS FAMILY was quartered in a newly built residence called Yabshi House, below the eastern walls of the Potala, Tenzin Gyatso lived in four small rooms at the top of the enormous edifice. More than a quarter mile long, filled with over a thousand chambers, assembly halls, narrow corridors and dark, ancient chapels, the Potala was less a home than a living museum. In winter it was numbingly cold; in summer the stench from the sewers beneath its precipitous walls permeated the building. At its center stood the red or religious palace, containing the gold, jewel-encrusted tombs of nine previous Dalai Lamas, before which butter lamps burned and monks prayed. On either side rose the walls of the white palace, which housed the Dalai Lama's private monastery, the "Peak" school for monk officials, government offices and the meeting halls of the National Assembly. Halfway up the eastern wing, a large open square was overlooked by the Dalai Lama's quarters five stories above. With easy access to the Potala's roof the rooms commanded a breathtaking view of Lhasa, the Kyichu River and the 15,000-foot peaks surrounding the valley. Like miniature jewel boxes, their ceilings and doorways were ornately carved in gold and red lacquered filigree, the floors spread with bright Tibetan carpets, the walls and altars covered with silk brocade and *thankas*. Intricate frescoes depicting the life of the great Fifth Dalai Lama, who had built the Potala, adorned the walls of the sitting room, while the Dalai Lama's bedroom, with its modern night table and bed embellished with dragons, was no more than the size of a large closet. Thousands of religious and historical texts, many illuminated in gold, silver, turquoise and coral ink, filled the Potala's library; priceless works of art, tapestries, sculptures, metalwork and antique armor from the entire span of Tibet's history were scrupulously preserved in the many storerooms and treasuries.

Within this imposing setting, the young Dalai Lama was raised almost entirely in the company of monks. He was referred to as either the "Precious Protector," the "Wish-Fulfilling Gem" or simply the "Presence." Few were allowed to speak to him directly. He appeared in public only to preside over lengthy ceremonies of religion and state. But in spite of the constraints of his position, he seemed at home in the role. "From the earliest age, whatever my brother did, he did perfectly," recalled Taktser Rinpoché, the Dalai Lama's eldest brother. "We all saw this. He never complained or rebelled. Everyone was greatly impressed." The Dalai Lama himself remembered: "When I was very young, everything came easily to me, as if I was used to all of it. I just enjoyed the spectacle."

At the age of six, Tenzin Gyatso's education began. Arriving early in the morning for the day's first lesson, his tutors commenced what was to be an eighteen-year course of studies. Learning to read and write on chalk-covered boards, he also spent long hours memorizing, the principal means of study for young monks in Tibet. Facing his teachers, the Dalai Lama was required to recite without pause increasingly longer sections of scripture, a skill which, later employed in dialectical debate, drew on thousands of pages of abstruse metaphysics, philosophical terms and prayers. The Dalai Lama's tutors soon noted their charge's natural gift for study.

Nevertheless, there were times when the role proved daunting. When, at the age of seven, Tenzin Gyatso was required to intone a prayer before 20,000 monks gathered in the Central Cathedral, he almost fainted from anxiety. Later, he often dreamt of escaping the Potala and leading a less stultified life. "When I was ten or eleven," the Dalai Lama recounted, "I would read on religious retreat with my elder tutor. We always sat in a small, dark room at the top of the Potala, with one window facing north. Beneath us lay a road where boys and girls led their families' cattle to pasture. Each evening the children would return home, herding the animals, and they would always be singing Tibetan opera songs. Then I often wished that I was with them. If I were there, I used to imagine, that would be something truly fantastic."

At winter's end, the Dalai Lama departed from the Potala for the Norbulingka, his procession marking the official start of summer. On the day of the parade the entire government set aside their heavy winter costumes and put on lighter equivalents, transforming the look of the capital for the new season. They then marched together with the Regent, Cabinet ministers and Commander-in-Chief of the Army, sword drawn in salute before the Dalai Lama's palanquin, through hushed crowds kept in place by the long whips of the bodyguards, who, all over six-and-a-half feet tall, padded their shoulders for further effect. To the people's delight, the young ruler's nightingales and parrots called out from their cages while his brilliantly caparisoned horses, decked in yellow saddles, bridles and bits of gold, pranced behind their grooms; monks blew shrill, high-pitched *gyalings* or short horns and the regimental bands played "It's a Long Way to Tipperary." From behind the palanquin's silk-fringed windows, though, it was the sight of nature that pleased the young Dalai Lama most. "The season was most beautiful," he remembered. "All the lawns were turning green, the apricot trees flowering and the birds singing. I used to love that day going from the Potala to the Norbulingka."

Founded in the eighteenth century by the Eighth Dalai Lama, the

Norbulingka, two miles west of Potala, had grown from a favored bathing and picnic ground into a walled park of temples and two-story palaces almost a mile square. Though the government transferred its work to the summer quarters as well, the enclosure remained permeated by an atmosphere of peace and tranquillity. Tame musk deer, pheasant and peacocks wandered freely between its pavilions; pet fish filled its ponds, rising to the water's surface to be fed when they heard the Dalai Lama's footsteps approach. While large sections of the park remained densely wooded, each morning the palace lawns were neatly laid out with hundreds of earthenware pots filled with flowers and rare plants. More ambitious gardening reaped the rewards of the Norbulingka's astonishingly fertile earth. Radishes weighing up to twenty pounds and cabbages more than three feet wide were routinely produced. Peach, pear, cherry, apple and walnut trees were also grown.

Within the Jewel Park the Dalai Lama spent the happiest times of his childhood. Rummaging through the Thirteenth Dalai Lama's collection of old *National Geographic* and *Life* magazines, he conceived a passion for modern inventions, encouraged by the gifts of a Meccano set and a telescope. Growing older he began to disassemble watches and a few treasured but generally inoperative movie projectors, reconstructing them from memory. His attentions then turned to Tibet's sole cars, two baby Austins and an orange Dodge, which had belonged to the previous Dalai Lama and had lain idle since his death. In the company of a young Tibetan trained in India to drive, Tenzin Gyatso repaired two of the vehicles, teaching himself in the process the workings of the combustion engine. When the driver departed for the day he secretly raced the cars across the lawns of the inner garden, occasionally crashing into gates or trees. Breaking a headlight on one such foray, he endeavored to conceal the damage with a specially cut piece of glass fogged by repeated applications of sugar syrup. He also spent long hours poring over the mysteries of AC and DC current produced by a somewhat faulty generator, an enterprise that met with continual harassment from the Lord Chamberlain and his tutors who feared the Dalai Lama would be electrocuted. Returning to the Thirteenth Dalai Lama's foreign books and periodicals, the young ruler grew interested in maps, history and world affairs. As he entered adolescence he requested two officials who spoke English to translate a set of volumes he had ordered on the recently concluded Second World War. Simultaneously he began to study the alphabet and increased his vocabulary. The Dalai Lama pursued these unprecedented interests entirely on his own, until a much-needed comrade emerged in the person of Heinrich Harrer, an Austrian mountaineer then living in Lhasa.

"He seemed to me like a person who had for years brooded in solitude over different problems, and now that he had at last someone to talk to, wanted to know all the answers at once," wrote Harrer, recalling his first meeting with the then fourteen-year-old Dalai Lama. Through an intermediary, the Dalai Lama had requested Harrer to construct a film hall in the Norbulingka. On its completion, he unexpectedly invited the Austrian to meet with him in person. "I went towards the cinema, but before I could enter the door opened from the inside and I was standing before the Living Buddha," Harrer recounted. "Come, let us see the capitulation of Japan," said the Dalai Lama, pushing his guest into the projection booth. Nervously Harrer started to thread the projector, but was "nudged aside" by the Dalai Lama, who completed the task in a moment. Following the film showing, Tenzin Gyatso dismissed his rather distraught abbots, and ushering Harrer into the now sun-filled theater, pulled him down by the sleeve onto the maroon carpet. Confessing that he had long planned a meeting, as he could think of no other way to become acquainted with the outside world, the Dalai Lama poured forth a flood of questions. "Do you like it here in the Holy City? Can you operate an army tank? An airplane? How do jet airplanes fly? Why do you have hair on your hands like a monkey?" Feeling the "attraction of his personality," Harrer stared at the young man. He sat cross-legged before him, hands folded peacefully in his lap, cheeks glowing with excitement, his whole body swaying from side to side. His complexion was considerably lighter than that of most Tibetans. He was tall and well formed, with "beautiful aristocratic hands" and eyes full of "expression, charm and vivacity." Rather bashfully, the Dalai Lama took out his notebook of English words and said, "Heinrich. You will teach me this language. We will start now."

Their lessons continued for months. Mathematics, geography and natural science were studied, including topics ranging from the structure of the atom to why Lhasa was eleven hours behind New York. Much time was also spent in the new movie theater watching films, the Dalai Lama's favorites being a documentary on the life of Gandhi, Castle newsreels and *Henry V*, painstakingly translated by Harrer from Shakespearean English into Tibetan. "He continually astonished me by his powers of comprehension, his pertinacity and his industry," observed Harrer. "When I gave him for homework ten sentences to translate, he usually showed up with twenty." The Austrian was also taken by the Dalai Lama's unusual character. He described his native modesty as a "source of perpetual wonder," the "average child of a rich tradesman being far more spoiled than he was." Decisiveness emerged as another distinguishing trait, the Dalai Lama possessing "a clear-cut individual will capable of imposing itself on others."

He sensed in him—and was confirmed in this by the ruler's mother—an inner loneliness. Yet, as their friendship grew, the young Dalai Lama continually brought up the subject closest to his heart: religion. Confiding that he was practicing techniques by which consciousness could be separated from the body, he told Harrer that, on completing them, he intended to send him seven hundred miles west to Gartok, from where he would guide his actions directly from the Potala. "When you can do that," said Harrer to his student, "I will become a Buddhist too." Unfortunately, the experiment, and along with it the burgeoning friendship, was abruptly brought to an end.

ON THE EVENING of August 15, 1950, while Tenzin Gyatso was taking a small meal of tea, yogurt and homemade bread delivered once a week by his mother, an earth tremor suddenly shook the Norbulingka. It was followed by forty tremendous reports resounding in rapid succession across the sky. The Dalai Lama and his attendants ran out into the garden of his residence, looking east toward Sera Monastery, from where the explosions had come. At the time they imagined them to be artillery fired near Sera, but shortly afterwards people arrived from Lhasa saying that the blasts had originated even farther east. A day later it was heard over All India Radio that a massive earthquake had rumbled across southeastern Tibet; a quake so powerful that while moviegoers in Calcutta fled theaters in terror, the sound of the aftershocks traveled twelve hundred miles across Tibet, all the way to its western borders.

"This was no ordinary earthquake; it felt like the end of the world," wrote Robert Ford, an English radio operator working for the Tibetan government in Chamdo, the provincial capital of Kham. In fact, it was the fifth-largest quake in history; mountains and valleys exchanged places in an instant, hundreds of villages were swallowed up, the Brahmaputra River was completely rerouted and for hours afterwards the sky over southeastern Tibet glowed with an infernal red light, suffused with the pungent scent of sulfur.

Coming when it did, the quake was viewed by all Tibetans, the Dalai Lama included, as something more than just a geological phenomenon. In its devastating destruction, they saw a harbinger of their nation's fate.

As early as 1945, four years before the end of China's civil war and with it the inevitable renewal of aggression against Tibet by the victor, the State Oracle had faced eastward in a trance, wildly shaking his head in warning. In 1947, he had prophesied that in the Year of the Iron Tiger—1950—Tibet would face "great difficulty." Two years later, in 1949, his caution had been accented by the appearance of a bright horse-tailed comet. Hanging in the heavens day and night for several weeks, it was viewed by older Tibetans in particular as an indubitable omen of war, the 1910 invasion by China having been preceded by just such a comet. The next summer, the unfavorable signs turned from the natural to the uncanny. On a bright, cloudless summer's day, in full view of downtown Lhasa, water poured from one of the golden gargoyles inaccessibly located on the roof of the Central Cathedral. The capital of a tall stone column, erected in A.D. 763 to commemorate Tibet's conquest of China, was found shattered one morning at the foot of the Potala.

Just as the Thirteenth Dalai Lama had prophesied, once more the external threat was matched by signs of internal decay. In 1941, Reting Rinpoché had given the Regency to the senior tutor of the Dalai Lama, Taktra Rinpoché, a mutual pact ensuring that on completion of the religious retreat for which he had retired, Reting Rinpoché would return to power. Six years later, in the spring of 1947, Taktra Rinpoché's entourage was all but ready to relinquish control. During their rule, bribery and bureaucratic negligence had run rampant. To restore Tibet's government to more capable hands, Reting Rinpoché's followers attempted a coup. Requesting support from Generalissimo Chiang Kai-shek, Nyungne Lama, the ex-Regent's private secretary, dispatched a hand grenade concealed in a package addressed to Taktra Rinpoché. The grenade exploded prematurely, the plot was uncovered and Nyungne Lama shot himself in the bathroom of a friend's house in Lhasa. Reting Rinpoché was then arrested and detained in the Potala, an act which, in turn, sparked a revolt by the monks of the Je College of Sera Monastery, to which he belonged. In twelve days of fighting with government troops, two hundred monks perished before the rest surrendered. Little more than a week later Reting Rinpoché died mysteriously in prison, a small collection of blue marks on his buttocks the only abnormal sign.

The brief civil war left Tibet profoundly demoralized. In addition, fifteen years after the arrival of the Kuomintang mission, their attempts at subterfuge had grown to include Tibetans in all segments of society. It was not until July 1949 that the Tibetan government realized the extent of the infiltration and, fearful that the newly victorious Communists would take advantage of it, closed the "liaison" office, deporting its staff, along with some twenty-five known agents and their Tibetan accomplices. Banishing the Chinese from Lhasa, however, could not extinguish their irredentist claims.

On New Year's Day 1950, three months after the creation of the new People's Republic of China, Radio Peking announced to its people and the world that "the tasks for the People's Liberation Army for 1950 are to liberate Taiwan, Hainan and Tibet." A slew of broadcasts from Xining and Chengdu, capital of Sichuan, followed, each asserting that Tibet was "an integral part of Chinese territory." Tibet had fallen under the "influence of foreign imperialists," the announcements stated. As a result, it required "liberation" to "secure China's western borders."

Though the language was novel, the implications were clear. With four decades in which to have prepared defenses now lost, Lhasa finally moved to protect itself. The Tibetan government turned first to the army. Since the Thirteenth Dalai Lama's death its improvement had been ignored. No more than a glorified border patrol, the 8,500 troops possessed fifty pieces of artillery and only a few hundred mortars and machine guns. Enlisted men often traveled in the company of their wives and children; officers, primarily noble officials on brief tours of duty, had no prior military training. Nevertheless, fresh troops and ammunition were soon deployed to a thin chain of garrison towns lining the western bank of the Upper Yangtze River, Tibet's de facto border with China. Both the men and their commanders were confident that, with the aid of the country's greatest natural asset, its lofty ranges, they could hold off the seasoned troops of the PLA.

Diplomatic expectations were not so sanguine. Aware that there was no possibility of a lasting self-defense against China, the government telegraphed India, Nepal, Great Britain and the United States requesting them to receive missions seeking support. Lacking official relations with all but India—Tibet never having deemed it necessary to establish ties to a world with which it had no contact—it received, in the main, polite but negative replies. India, for whom Tibet served as a vital buffer state, proved the greatest disappointment. By the terms of the 1914 Simla Agreement, which had devolved on him, India's Prime Minister Jawaharlal Nehru, was required to deny recognition of Chinese suzerainty over Tibet until China itself acknowledged Tibet's strictly defined autonomy. Instead, he repeatedly spoke of this suzerainty, though "vague and shadowy" as being a generally recognized fact, thereby signaling Peking that India's new government would not, as its British predecessor had, come to the aid of Tibet. On hearing of Tibet's request, China immediately warned New Delhi that receiving "an illegal delegation" would be tantamount to "entertaining hostile intentions against the Chinese People's Republic." A few months later, the Chinese government offered assurances to the Indian ambassador in Peking that China had no intention of using force against Tibet. Thereafter, Nehru encouraged Lhasa to negotiate alone on the basis of the Simla Convention. Compelled thus to deal directly with the Communists,

Tibet's government dispatched a delegation to Peking to secure, as its instructions stated, "an assurance that the territorial integrity of Tibet will not be violated" and to "inform the government of China that the people and government of Tibet . . . will maintain their independence." En route the delegation contacted Chinese officials in New Delhi, who suggested they wait for the arrival of the newly appointed ambassador to India. They did; but in the furtherance of their own designs, the Chinese did not.

By early spring, advance units of the PLA had climbed up from the plain of China deep into the highland gorges of eastern Kham, until then nominally controlled by the Nationalists. Similar moves occurring in late 1949 had already secured much of Amdo. On April 16, Lin Biao, China's famed "Red Marshal," led his Fourth Field Army across the narrow strait separating mainland China from the island of Hainan in the Gulf of Tongking, and within a few days defeated its Kuomintang command, thereby fulfilling the second of the PLA's "goals" for 1950. Radio Peking's May Day message now mentioned only Taiwan and Tibet as remaining to be "liberated." Broadcasts three weeks later proposed "regional auton- omy" and "religious freedom" if the Tibetans would agree to "peaceful liberation." Within a few days of the message, however, the PLA launched a probing attack across the Yangtze and took the poorly defended town of Dengkog. Two weeks later seven hundred Tibetan troops, led by the capable Muja Dapon, recaptured Dengkog, their overzealous Khampa recruits slaughtering to a man the Chinese force of around six hundred soldiers. Though victorious, the outcome of this first and bloodiest engage- ment of the burgeoning conflict—taking place little more than a week before the onset of the Korean War—could not dispel the confusion that plagued Tibet's outnumbered and disparate ranks.

Even before news of the attack on Dengkog reached Chamdo, head- quarters of Tibet's eastern front, the city had been plunged into chaos. A Central Tibetan soldier had forced his affections on a Khampa girl, result- ing in a demonstration by hundreds of Khampa irregulars before the army barracks. Distinguished by their robust stature and independent bearing, the men of Kham had always, despite their Buddhist convictions, been quick to avenge a wrong—a trait that had kept Kham embroiled in clan rivalries and bitter vendettas for much of its history. Brandishing their long swords and rifles, they now demanded that the army come out and settle the issue en masse. The two colonels in command had actually ordered bayonets fixed in preparation for a melee when a senior government official, in the good graces of the Khampas, arrived to defuse the crisis. Dispersing for the time being, the Khampa recruits nonetheless redoubled their daily habit, as Ford described it, of galloping through Chamdo "firing shots into the air, flourishing their swords and letting out bloodcurdling screams. The girls were kept indoors, and some of the Lhasa officials also kept out of the way."

Regional rivalry threatened more than just the municipal peace of Chamdo. The very roots of Tibet's defense were precariously pinioned on it. Nowhere was this more evident than in the choice of the city itself for the army's headquarters. Roughly one hundred miles from the border-of Sikang, the eastern portion of Kham (appended to China as a province in 1939), Chamdo lay on a promontory at the confluence of the Dzachu and Womchu rivers which, joining at the town's base, formed the headwaters of the Mekong. Chinese forces had been driven from it in October of 1917; since then, Kham's taxes to Lhasa had paid for the presence of regular troops—the principal service received from the central government. Politically, therefore, Chamdo's defense was indispensable, being intimately linked with the allegiance of Kham. Yet strategically it was a useless point for resistance. Outflanked from the north, it could easily be cut off from Lhasa. To deal with this dilemma, Kham's Governor-General, Lhalu Shapé, resolved to hold Chamdo until the last moment. Then, assuming that at first the Chinese would not attack in substantial numbers, he would withdraw—the Khampa allegiance held intact—to the high, easily defended passes by Riwoché, fifty miles to Chamdo's rear on a tributary of the upper Salween.

In theory, the plan made the best of a bad situation. However, being solely defensive, it failed to utilize Tibet's most effective option: guerrilla warfare. Ironically, the possibility had already been offered in the person of Rapga Pomdatsang, a powerful Khampa leader regarded warily by Lhasa for his attempts at making Kham independent. While Rapga arrived in Chamdo in June to offer his private army for hit-and-run attacks east of the Yangtze, his brother Topgye was already in Dartsedo, the Chinese base of operations, proffering the same troops as guides in return for the same assurances of freedom. Because Lhasa would not undercut its authority with such an arrangement, it failed to recruit the Pomdatsangs, sending their ferocious fighters into the arms of the Communists and with them Tibet's only real military hope. As one Tibetan summarized the situation in hindsight: "If we Tibetans had fought together from the first day of the Chinese attack, we could never have lost. Our mountains are impregnable. There were no roads. The Chinese had no supply lines. Their soldiers were helpless for days, marching snow-blind one behind another. No army on earth could have conquered that country with the people united against it, but because of our own confusion, they just walked in."

Peace was finally lost on the morning of October 7. Rowing across the

Yangtze in small skin coracles, 84,000 troops of the First and Second Field Armies, under the overall command of General Liu Bating, invaded at dawn, assailing six locations from Tsakhalo in the south to Dengkog in the north. There having been no substantial contact since the previous raid on Dengkog four months earlier, the attack took Tibet's four *Dapons*, or "Lords of the Arrow" commanding the army's forward line, by surprise.

At the center of Tibet's defensive arc, Khatang Dapon remained unaware of the onslaught until, having wiped out the frontier ferry post of Kamthog Druka, the PLA assaulted his unfortified headquarters at Rangsum. Routed, the Tibetans retreated to the sole viable defensive position, a high pass west of the town. Night fell and, rather than pressing on, they decided to camp behind a hastily dug earthwork defile on a plain at its base. During the night the Chinese, who had not paused for sleep, attacked. The battle was soon over, Khatang Dapon captured, literally without his boots on.

Although Tsakhalo, the southernmost town, held out, its defenders lost one of three key passes to the north, permitting the PLA to cut it off. Markham Gartok, the large town southwest of Rangsum fell with equal speed. Its commander, the Prince of Dergé (posted there by Lhasa from his semi-autonomous kingdom further north), heroically rode out to surrender himself to the advancing Chinese in an attempt to save his now vastly outnumbered troops. Thus, within a few days the PLA had gained an unobstructed approach to Chamdo, from both the south and the east. Two hundred and fifty miles north, however, Dengkog held. Having maintained strict discipline among his troops, Muja Dapon, the general in command, was able to throw the Chinese back across the Yangtze, inflicting heavy losses. When finally forced to withdraw, outflanked by units who had crossed the river farther north, he did so fighting each step of the way, bent on protecting Riwoché, the key garrison guarding Chamdo's rear. For the first week of the war, Riwoché, indeed, remained quiet, but it was known that Jyekundo, just north of it, had been occupied, making an assault—and with its success the fall of Kham—inevitable.

It took four days for news of the invasion to reach Chamdo. When it did, the city was hurled into disarray. Throughout the summer Lhalu Shapé had dutifully continued to arm and recruit Khampa levies. At the end of August, though, his three-year tenure as Governor-General expired. Incredibly, given the knowledge that the Chinese attack must come before winter, the Cabinet in Lhasa went ahead, according to routine procedure, and replaced him with a second of its ministers. Ngabo Ngawang Jigme arrived in Chamdo to assume command of an unfamiliar situation, only a few weeks before the invasion struck. Compounding the error, he spent the entire month of September attending the customary reception parties. Ngabo himself was a poor choice for such a delicate task. Though he had served one tour of duty in Kham already, he was regarded by many as more of a showman than an able leader. Described by Ford as a "tall and stately man, long-jawed and with a dignified but cheerful face," he benignly assured all on his arrival, "There will be no local surrender as long as I am in Chamdo."

Few, it seemed, believed him. As word of the invasion spread through the city a long procession wound down from Chamdo's monastery to the shore of the Womchu. There, amidst a cacophony of cymbals, horns, conch shells and Khampa warriors firing their ancient muzzle-loading rifles, the monks cast fearsome effigies into a pyramidal pyre, exorcising the Chinese evil. In the next few days, a growing line stretched along the street from the door of Chamdo's most prominent fortune-teller, rooftops were freshly strung with prayer flags and thousands turned out to circumambulate Chamdo's Lingkhor or Holy Walk, fervently turning prayer wheels and prostrating. The agitation of the inhabitants was such that three vowed to undertake the five-hundred-mile pilgrimage to Lhasa prostrating every foot of the way—and set out immediately to do it. "In general, we Tibetans are very religious-minded and there are many who are good practitioners as well," commented the Dalai Lama. "But believing the country would be saved without human effort, through prayers alone, resulted from limited knowledge. From this point of view religious sentiment actually became an obstacle."

A more serious hindrance was the central government's inefficiency. On receiving news of the invasion, Ngabo immediately wired a coded message to the Cabinet. All of Lhasa's senior officials were attending a five-day-long party at the time, offered annually by the cabinet to the bureaucracy. Dice, mah-jong, drinking *chang* or barley beer and dressing in one's finest silks were temporarily uppermost in people's minds—not the PLA. Accordingly, there was no immediate reply to the cable, and though one eventually was sent out, the invasion itself was kept secret for nine days while the Cabinet deliberated on what course to pursue.

In Chamdo time ran out. Receiving word that the Chinese were only a day away in the east, while to the rear Riwoché was being surrounded, Ngabo lost his nerve. He radioed Lhasa for permission to surrender. When it was denied, he packed his belongings, took off the long gold and turquoise pendant earring hanging from his left ear, changed his yellow silk robes for the plain gray serge of a junior official and decamped in the middle of the night. With the discovery, soon after dawn on October 17, that the Governor had fled, Chamdo erupted in panic. Ngabo had neglected to secure transport from nearby villages so that his troops could undertake an orderly retreat. He had, therefore, simply abandoned them, not even bothering to divvy out the existing animals with his own body-guard. His sole order, issued to one of the garrison's two colonels, was to destroy the ammunition dump—shells and cartridges of inestimable value to the Khampas, who were compelled to remain and defend their homes. As a result, while great explosions rent the air and officials from Lhasa, their army and families fled the city on foot, Khampa tribesmen went on a rampage, looting and rioting, in a vain search for someone upon whom to vent their rage at betrayal.

Ngabo's capitulation did not end there. Fleeing west down the trail to Lhasa, desperately hoping to outdistance the Chinese advance from the north, he encountered a column of reinforcements, armed with artillery, dispatched from the capital weeks before. To their utter astonishment, he ordered the men to throw their arms into a deep ravine and join the flight. Soon scouts reported that a small party of Khampas working for the Chinese had already cut the route. Rather than fight his way through—which, with the entire garrison of Chamdo at his command, would not have been difficult—Ngabo sought refuge in a nearby monastery, believing that within its hallowed precincts he would be safe from the Khampas. Following his arrival on the afternoon of the eighteenth, Muja Dapon, falling back from Dengkog with his entire force of almost five hundred battle-tried and well-armed cavalry—without doubt, the best soldiers in the eastern command—rode in. Hearing that an advance party of one hundred Chinese was not far behind, Ngabo ordered Muja's troops to lay down their arms and surrender. While the soldiers' wives set up camp, unloading yaks and mules, pitching tents, preparing cooking fires and tending their babies, the men watched incredulously as a small contingent of PLA set up field artillery and then, in the company of Khampa guides and translators, walked in to accept surrender from a force twenty times their number. With that, eleven days after the war between China and Tibet had begun, it ended.

One week later, on October 25, the People's Republic of China announced for the first time that its troops had entered Tibet, "to free," as Radio Peking stated, Tibetans from "imperialist oppression." Protesting the invasion the following day, India was met with a stern reply in which the PRC maintained that "the problem of Tibet is entirely the domestic problem of China. No foreign interference will be tolerated." Twelve days later Tibet's Cabinet cabled an impassioned appeal to the United Nations, pleading for intercession to "restrain Chinese aggression." Nothing of China's intent was actually known in Lhasa, however, until two officials, dispatched by Ngabo, arrived to say that he had been imprisoned—along with his four generals—in Chamdo. He wished to be empowered to discuss peace terms, the Chinese commanders having assured him that, for the time being, their advance would be confined to Kham. With the reality of defeat finally at hand, the government in Lhasa made its most important decision to date in the crisis.

Calling the medium of the Gadong Oracle to the Norbulingka, an official trance was conducted. As the protective deity took possession, the medium's body reared up from its seated position, hissing loudly and shuddering with tremendous force. Quickly attendants placed the ritual helmet on his head and fastened it tightly beneath his chin. The Oracle then approached the Dalai Lama's throne to present a long white scarf in offering after which he resumed his seat. When the time came to submit questions to the deity, the Cabinet ministers humbly sought guidance, a secretary reading their formal request from a scroll. Once more the Oracle came before the Dalai Lama. "Make him King," he clearly said, and collapsed, the trance concluded.

Tenzin Gyatso was filled with anxiety. He knew little of government and less of international affairs. Toward the end of that summer the National Assembly had moved from the Potala to the Jewel Park to facilitate communications with the young ruler. During this time the Dalai Lama had undertaken his first brief try at policymaking, one which had greatly impressed his advisers. At age fifteen, however, he was still three years short of the accepted point for a Dalai Lama's ascension to secular power. Nevertheless, he had no choice. Despite Chinese assurances, the Red Army could move on Lhasa at any moment. The people themselves had already begged him to lead, posters all over the capital demanding that "the Dalai Lama be given the power." Demurring at first, Tenzin Gyatso finally agreed. On November 17, 1950, in a stately ceremony enacted in the Potala, the Dalai Lama was invested as supreme temporal ruler of Tibet. Whatever his own reactions, history had forced itself upon him. "I could not refuse my responsibilities," he later wrote. "I had to shoulder them, put my boyhood behind me and immediately prepare myself to lead my country."

2

Occupation

1950–1959

Early in November 1950 the Dalai Lama's eldest brother, Taktser Rinpoché, unexpectedly arrived in Lhasa. Since the Communist occupation of Amdo a year before, he had been held under duress, compelled to witness the dismantling of Kumbum Monastery and the centuries-old lifestyle of its surrounding villages. As China prepared to invade Kham, the new Communist Governor of Xining attempted to enlist his support in a scheme to overthrow the Dalai Lama. Takster Rinpoché was to persuade Tibet's ruler not to resist the PLA's entry; failing that, he was to assassinate him. In return, the Chinese promised him the governor-generalship of all Tibet.

Pretending to comply, the Dalai Lama's brother secured his freedom and left Kumbum for the capital. Once there, he informed the Dalai Lama of Chinese intentions and filed a detailed report to the Cabinet, revealing for the first time the full scope of Peking's plans, not only to annex Tibet but gradually to dismember both its secular and religious life, replacing them with a Marxist state. Soon after, even more discouraging news arrived. On the recommendation of India's delegate, whose clear concern was to minimize friction with China, the United Nations had declined to consider Tibet's case, deeming, moreover, as Great Britain's ambassador maintained, that its international legal status was unclear. With the decision, all of Tibet's options were exhausted. Fearing the Dalai Lama's capture by the PLA, the National Assembly requested him to flee to the border town of Yatung, from where, if need arose, he could escape to India.

At 2:00 a.m. on the night of December 19, 1950, Tenzin Gyatso slipped from the Potala. Accompanied by forty nobles and two hundred select troops of his bodyguard armed with machine guns and howitzers, he mounted a gray horse and rode south down the Lhasan Valley toward the Indian border. At the column's center flew the personal banner of the Dalai Lama, beside it the flag of Tibet: two snow lions holding the three jewels of the Buddha, Dharma and Sangha (clergy) before a twelve-rayed sun rising above a snow-capped peak. By morning 1,500 pack animals and a host of retainers followed behind.

The National Assembly had insisted that the Dalai Lama's departure be secret in the belief that, once informed, the public, unaware of the great risk in his remaining, would try to prevent the flight. Less than a day's ride from the capital, just such an obstacle arose. As the column approached the retreat center of Jang, thousands of monks, convened from Drepung, Sera and Ganden for their winter debate session, streamed onto the road to block its way. A tense standoff ensued, broken only when the Dalai Lama himself interceded to persuade the monks to let him pass. Once through, the procession continued on to Gyantse and then Phari, Tibet's highest town, from where the route dropped rapidly down into the heavily wooded Chumbi Valley, for centuries the principal trade conduit between India and Tibet. At the valley's far end, just below the border passes, stood the prosperous town of Yatung. With military checkpoints established throughout the area, the Dalai Lama took up residence in the picturesque Dungkhar Monastery, while in the town below his officials and followers, including Taktser Rinpoché and the fleeing Heinrich Harrer, made shift among the houses of local farmers and merchants. In the meantime, the Cabinet empowered Ngabo Ngawang Jigme, along with four other officials dispatched from Lhasa and Yatung, to negotiate directly with China for whatever measure of freedom Tibet could still hope to gain.

In the last week of April 1951, Tibet's delegation arrived in Peking. After a courteous reception by China's Prime Minister Zhou Enlai, they were presented with a ten-point plan specifying terms of capitulation or, as it was phrased, Tibet's "peaceful liberation." Because the proposal maintained that Tibet was an "integral" part of China, the delegation refused to sign. A stalemate followed, until a second, Seventeen-Point Agreement was put forth. This time no discussion was allowed. The delegates were cut off from their government and thereafter threatened with both personal violence and large-scale military retaliation against Tibet. On May

23 they yielded—unauthorized by the Dalai Lama and Cabinet. In a formal ceremony enacted in Tun-nen-hai, the living compound of China's leading officials, and later publicized throughout China and the world, they certified the document with duplicate seals of the Tibetan government already forged for the purpose in Peking.

On the basis of the Seventeen-Point Agreement, Tibet lost its identity as a nation-state. Ngabo Ngawang Jigme went on Radio Peking and announced the settlement—the very first time the Tibetan government, still based in Yatung, heard of it. "The Tibetan people shall unite and drive out imperialist aggressive forces from Tibet," stated clause one. "The Tibetan people shall return to the big family of the Motherland—the People's Republic of China." Clause two outlined precisely how this was to be accomplished, the now "local government of Tibet" "actively" assisting the PLA to "enter Tibet and consolidate the national defense." The remaining points mixed stipulations to uphold Tibet's indigenous government—including the position of the Dalai Lama—with others designed to render it impotent, such as eliminating the authority to conduct foreign affairs and absorbing the army into the PLA. Stunned by the so-called agreement, the Dalai Lama ordered Taktser Rinpoché to cross the Indian border and, via private channels, make a final appeal for support—this time from Harry Truman and the United States.

Surprisingly, America agreed. Through intermediaries in Calcutta, a secret pact was drawn up wherein the Dalai Lama promised to seek asylum in India and publicly repudiate the Seventeen-Point Agreement. For its part, the United States pledged to support him and his government abroad, reintroduce Tibet's cause to the UN, and finance its struggle against China, including, if it developed, a military option. July 12 was fixed for the Dalai Lama's arrival in India, Prime Minister Nehru having already agreed to grant sanctuary.

The plan never ripened. A short time before the scheduled departure, the abbots of Drepung, Sera and Ganden monasteries arrived in Yatung. In repeated meetings with the Dalai Lama, they pleaded for him to return to Lhasa. The State Oracle was consulted and on two occasions instructed Tibet's ruler to return. Deciding that some scope for a compromise with China still existed, Tenzin Gyatso canceled his flight abroad and on July 16, looking out apprehensively from the upper rooms of Dungkhar monastery, caught his first glimpse of a Communist leader as, accompanied by two aides dressed in gray, high-collared suits, General Zhang Jinwu, chief of the newly coined Military and Administrative Committee of Tibet, was received by the splendid silk-clad figures of the Tibetan Cabinet. In a brief meeting over tea the general delivered a letter from Mao Zedong welcoming Tibet into the People's Republic. He then proceeded on to Lhasa. The Dalai Lama followed a week later, returning home after an eight-month absence, in August 1951. Just sixteen years old, Tenzin Gyatso set forth on the delicate task of coexisting with Tibet's new rulers.

On September 9, 3,000 troops of the 18th Route Army marched into Lhasa, tubas and drums blaring, portraits of Mao and Zhou Enlai held aloft, between phalanxes of China's red flag, one of whose four small orbs, circling the great yellow star at its center, was now Tibet. Within three months two more contingents arrived, bringing the occupation force to 20,000 troops—almost half of the city's population—backed by 30,000 camels and horses requisitioned en route. Whereas the Tibetans had watched in dazed silence at first, they now lined the streets spitting and clapping, their age-old practice for driving out evil. Children threw stones and monks tied the ends of their outer robes, to whip, as they passed, the "Tendra Gyamar"—"Red Chinese Enemies of the Faith." Setting up camp on Lhasa's cherished picnic grounds by the shores of the Kyichu River, the Chinese took over the nobles' larger homes, the roofs of which soon sprouted bright red signboards adorned with colossal black slogans proclaiming the "unity" of all races in "the motherland." Groups of soldiers, dressed in drab khaki uniforms, their sole distinguishing emblem the red star on their caps, moved warily through Lhasa's busy streets. While the day dawned to the blunt commands of parade-ground maneuvers, breaking the smooth litany of prayers rising from every household, the Holy City now sat under an offending fog of putrid smoke from the burning bones of dead animals.

Unlike the Chinese incursion forty years before, the present occupation left most Tibetans puzzled. Assurances of religious freedom, mixed with lavish gifts to the nobility, promises of new hospitals, schools, roads, and, as it was later learned, official prohibition of the common Chinese term for Tibetan—*man-tze*, meaning "barbarian"—all confounded popular expectation. The precedent for such largess, however, had been set a year before in Kham. Tibetan soldiers captured in the wake of the invasion had been called "brothers" by their counterparts, given packets of food and money and then released, Chinese cameras filming their relieved expressions as evidence of the people's joy on being "liberated." One Khampa warrior summed up the general reaction by observing, "They are strange people, these Chinese. I cut off eight of their heads with my sword and they just let me go." Stranger still was the content of propaganda pamphlets. The claim that China wished to help Tibet modernize made some sense, but that of "uniting to drive out imperialist forces"—there having been only six Westerners in Tibet prior to the invasion, all of whom had now left—was incomprehensible. Being "welcomed back" to the "big family of the motherland" amounted to a blatant non sequitur. "In the beginning," commented Takster Rinpoché, who found a new home in America, "they put their words like honey on a knife. But we could see, if you lick the honey your tongue will be cut."

Within nine months of occupation, the first crisis occurred. True to its name, the People's Liberation Army lived off the land, taking from the civilian population whatever it required. On their arrival in Lhasa, the Chinese had demanded a "loan" of two thousand tons of barley from the Tibetan government. When a second order for an additional two thousand tons was issued, the back of the capital's delicate economy broke. The price of grain spiraled to a tenfold increase, that of meat, vegetables and household goods close behind. For the first time in history famine hung over Lhasa and with it the people revolted. Songs and posters denouncing the Chinese filled the streets, public meetings were held and Tibet's first major resistance group, called the Mimang Tsongdu or People's Assembly, formed to dispatch a six-point petition to both the Tibetan government and the Chinese military command demanding the PLA's withdrawal.

The Chinese reacted swiftly. They insisted that the Tibetan Army be integrated into the PLA without delay. When Lukhwanga, the Dalai Lama's outspoken lay Prime Minister, defied them, his resignation was called for as well as the imprisonment of five of the Mimang Tsongdu's leaders. To forestall further confrontation, the Dalai Lama accepted the resignations of both his lay and religious Prime Ministers in the spring of 1952, determining henceforth that he would deal directly with the Chinese generals.

Tenzin Gyatso now viewed himself as the sole buffer between his people and China's armies. Recognizing that a future impasse in relations would severely jeopardize Tibet's remaining freedom, he resolved to pursue a strict course of nonviolent resistance. Though politically expedient, the approach was ultimately rooted in the Dalai Lama's religious conviction, shared by the entire clergy. As Kyhongla Rato Rinpoché, a lama of Drepung Monastery, explained: "We could not hate the Chinese because it was their own ignorance that motivated them to harm us. A true practitioner of religion considers his enemy to be his greatest friend, because only he can help you develop patience and compassion." "Basically everyone exists in the very nature of suffering," the Dalai Lama later wrote of his decision, "so to abuse or mistreat each other is futile."

Tibet's compliance, however, was far less than what China hoped for. By the end of 1953, Peking determined that its attempt to create a puppet government, through which it could both control the country and mute international condemnation of its invasion, had failed. Accordingly, the Politburo of the Chinese Communist Party decided to supersede the Seventeen-Point Agreement by intervening directly in the administration of Tibet. The Dalai Lama was invited to China, where Mao Zedong planned to impose a new arrangement on him. Against the strong opposition of the Tibetan people, Tenzin Gyatso accepted. Ostensibly, he was merely being invited to attend the first Chinese People's National Assembly, which was to adopt a constitution for the new republic.

On the morning of July 11, 1954, all Lhasa gathered around a large tent on the north shore of the Kyichu River to bid the Dalai Lama farewell. Thousands wept as, the ceremonies concluded, the nineteen-year-old leader walked down a white carpet to the river's shore, boarded a group of skin co:acles lashed together and, a yellow silk parasol held above his head, set out across the water. On either side clouds of incense billowed across the Kyichu, revealing in clear spots hundreds of Chinese and Tibetan troops lining the banks to restrain the people, many of whom had threatened to throw themselves in after the Dalai Lama. While Tenzin Gyatso waved farewell, huge mounds of water swelling the river's summer course appeared to swallow his diminishing figure, leaving Lhasans, as they returned to their city, feeling bereft of all hope.

Five hundred of Tibet's chief noble and religious dignitaries and their servants, however, accompanied the Dalai Lama. For twelve days the cavalcade rode east, camping nightly until, penetrating the beautiful juniper and pine forests of Poyul in southern Tibet, they entered one of two roads China was constructing to link Lhasa with the mother country. Here travel became increasingly difficult. The new road ran above shaftlike river gorges and in many places was washed out by rain, forcing the party to walk for hours on end through deep mud, boulders crashing down in their midst from the mountainside above. Many mules and three people died, yet the Chinese refused to divert to the old Tibetan trade route. The Tibetans' spirits were further depressed by the inauspicious news that Gyantse, Tibet's fourth-largest city, had been destroyed by flood.

On the twenty-fourth day the party transferred to a fleet of slope-backed Russian jeeps and trucks which, in two more days, brought them to Chamdo. Here the Dalai Lama got his first look at the harsher face of the Chinese occupation. Under military control since the invasion, Chamdo had been rigged with loudspeakers which, as in cities in China proper, marshaled the population to work and delivered constant propaganda tomes throughout the day. Greeted under a welcome gate decked in fir boughs, by an accordion orchestra, and a line of brightly smiling Chinese women cadres holding flowers, the Dalai Lama gave his customary blessings to the city's inhabitants backed by a PLA honor guard, an incongruity which was now routinely required as tens of thousands flocked to see him in the remaining towns of Kham. Passing through Dartsedo toward the close of August, the high pass of Arleng Hren was crossed and China entered. "On the Tibetan side the ascent was gradual," recalled the Dalai Lama, describing his first moments beyond Tibet's borders. "But going down the route was long and steep. Reaching the plain of China, I thought: Oh, this is something really different. Rice paddies, water buffalo—it made a most vivid impression on my mind." In Chengdu, capital of Sichuan, Tenzin Gyatso boarded an airplane and flew to Xian, where he was joined by the sixteen-year-old Panchen Lama and his party of two hundred. Both men proceeded on by private train, and though it was the Dalai Lama's first experience of the machines that had fascinated him for so long, he felt little joy. Arriving beneath the tall buildings of China's capital, the Dalai and Panchen Lamas alighted in gold brocade robes and pith helmets—a legacy of Tibetan ties with the Mongol Khans—and carrying bouquets, strode down the platform to the vigorous applause of hundreds of workers and students marshaled by Prime Minister Zhou Enlai and Vice-Chairman Zhu De, Chief of the Army. That evening a sumptuous banquet was held in the Purple Light Pavilion in central Peking, officially welcoming the Tibetans "back to the motherland." Two days later the Dalai Lama met Mao Zedong.

The Dalai Lama's reaction to Mao was not unfavorable. He found him forthright, kind and dedicated. Among other details he observed that the leader of the revolution and Chairman of the Party never wore polished shoes, dressed in frayed cuffs, smoked incessantly and panted a lot. He seemed to be in poor health, but when he spoke, his unusual powers of analysis shone through. "Chairman Mao did not look too intelligent," noted the Dalai Lama. "Something like an old farmer from the countryside. Yet his bearing indicated a real leader. His self-confidence was firm, he had a sincere feeling for the nation and people, and also, I believe, he demonstrated genuine concern for myself."

Mao, in fact, was quite taken with the young leader. He spent long hours offering advice on how to govern, going so far as to admit that Buddhism was a good religion—the Buddha having cared considerably for the common people. Invariably, though, political conviction outweighed personal taste. On one occasion, in the middle of an intimate talk, Mao leaned over and whispered in the Dalai Lama's ear, "I understand you very well, but of course religion is poison." During a New Year's celebration given by the Tibetans, he watched his hosts throw small pieces of pastry in the air as an offering to the Buddha, whereupon, taking two pinches himself, he threw one upward and then, with a mischievous smile, dropped the other onto the floor.

In their first private meeting together, Chairman Mao informed the Dalai Lama that a new committee was to govern Tibet. Known as PCART —Preparatory Committee for the Autonomous Region of Tibet—it would be comprised of five groups—four Tibetan, one Chinese—whose task it was to prepare the country for assimilation into the administrative framework of the People's Republic. Ironically, the news came as a blessing. As Mao disclosed, until meeting the Dalai Lama he had intended to govern Tibet directly from Peking. The Tibetan's conciliatory attitude, he indicated, had softened his stance. This had been Tenzin Gyatso's prime goal: creating sufficient trust in himself to deflect unconditional Chinese rule. "We had to realize that our country was backward, it needed progress," related the Dalai Lama. "The Chinese claimed that the very purpose of their coming to Tibet was to develop it. So here, you see, there was no need for argument; we enjoyed a common principle."

During his remaining seven months in China, the Dalai Lama's optimism was dampened by what he learned of Peking's deeper intent. Taking copious notes at political meetings, touring factories and schools, he and his Cabinet finally comprehended the full array of motives underlying the invasion of Tibet.

China's foremost objective was strategic. Since the days of the Tibetan invasions a millennia and a half before, all Chinese governments had looked warily to their western border. The Communists, fearful of losing their newly acquired hold on the country, saw, in the 1904 British incursion to Lhasa and its resulting ties, the basis of a new threat. Despite New Delhi's apparent refusal to fulfill the terms of the 1914 Simla Convention, the spirit of which clearly placed it as broker in relations between China and Tibet, Peking was convinced of an "imperialist" menace in the west. Defensively then, China, by annexing Tibet, desired to permanently shut its "back door." But no less important were offensive considerations. In possession of the Tibetan Plateau the People's Republic stood at the apex of the Orient. In the event of conflict with either of Asia's other giants— India and the Soviet Union—Tibet, as the central and highest ground, would prove an invaluable platform from which to launch an assault. Economically, the outlook was no less inviting. Known in Chinese as *Xizang* or "The Western Treasure House," Tibet possessed everything China lacked: vast, underpopulated tracts of land, their mineral, forest and animal reserves virtually unexploited. Politically, still in the first ideological flush of victory, the Chinese Communist Party felt mandated to "liberate" all "oppressed" peoples, its historical justification for absorbing not only Tibet but fifty-three other so-called Minority Nationalities occupying 60 percent of its territory but comprising only 6 percent of the Republic's population. It was the CCP's ultimate aim, through its long-held Minorities Policy, to meld the disparate groups—despite talk of "regional autonomy"—both politically and culturally into the Han mold. And it was this policy which both the Dalai Lama and the vast entourage accompanying him found most daunting.

In China, the Tibetans had their first look at the modern world, one carefully orchestrated to elicit their approval. Housed in amply staffed bungalows around Peking, high lamas and Cabinet ministers each received a limousine, chauffeur and private cook, lesser officials sharing graded levels of kitchen and transport. Packets of money were handed out on a weekly basis—the higher one's rank, the more money received—and as winter approached, new warmer clothing was provided for all. Though political meetings were required of senior officials, the majority of the Tibetans spent their time sightseeing, shopping, attending theater, ballet, acrobatic shows and dancing parties. But beneath China's efficient, industrial facade, they found the human climate unappealing, the submission of self to the state contrary to their own individualistic nature. An even deeper gulf separated the philosophies of the two peoples. While the Communists believed that socialism, properly applied, offered a panacea for life's ills, as Buddhists, the Tibetans felt that earthly existence in any form could never be satisfactory. Liberation, to them, meant freedom gained by enlightenment from the inevitable sufferings of birth, old age, disease and death. Mere physical well-being had never been an ideal in Tibetan culture.

Returning to Lhasa on June 29, 1955, the Dalai Lama found Tibet's capital already changed by the new world he had visited. Two roads, one emanating from Xining in the north, the other from Chengdu in the east, had been opened the previous December, bringing with them to Tibet the first trappings of the twentieth century. Military trucks now coursed through Lhasa's ancient streets, traffic soon becoming so heavy that a concrete island, manned by a white-jacketed policeman, had to be installed at the main intersection. The Tibetans themselves had begun to electrify the city prior to 1950, but the Chinese now extended the work, along with telephones and—to their growing bases in Shigatse, Gyantse and Yatung —telegraph. A pylon-supported bridge extended across the Kyichu River where the Dalai Lama had ridden in a coracle less than a year before. A bank, hospital, movie theater, secondary school, newspaper, youth and women's leagues were all being founded, but not, ironically, for the masses. The innovations were primarily to win the collaboration of the upper classes or "Patriotic Upper Strata," as they were known, on whom the CCP hoped to rely for support in the initial stages of its work. Socialist reforms were to be introduced gingerly; the Tibetan government's own role was to be proportionately decreased. Both were the tasks of PCART, which opened with much fanfare on April 22, 1956, in the newly built Lhasa Hall, holding Tibet's first auditorium, directly across from the Potala.

Rather than serving as a vehicle for compromise, as the Dalai Lama desired, the preparatory committee directly subverted Tibet's government. In the manner of political maneuvering to which they were bred, the Communists had tailored the committee to appear indigenous—only five of the fifty-one members being Chinese—while, in fact, dividing the Tibetans against themselves, so that PCART could function solely as a mouthpiece for the CCP working committee, the highest authority in the land. The Dalai Lama was Chairman, the Panchen Lama and General Zhang Guohua Vice-Chairmen, Ngabo Ngawang Jigme, now in open collaboration, Secretary-General. The Tibetan government was permitted only fifteen members. A second group of eleven Tibetans was comprised of prominent monks and laymen picked by the Chinese. The third and fourth Tibetan groups, however, were far more insidious. Containing twenty members between them, they were the so-called Chamdo Liberation Committee, founded in Chamdo after the invasion, and the Panchen Lama's Committee. As political bodies, they divided Tibet into three regions and directly challenged the authority of the central government in Lhasa. Thus, in the thirteen departments into which PCART was divided to govern Tibet, the country's own administration was not only displaced but outvoted by a minimum of a two-thirds majority on every issue. "Sometimes it was almost laughable to see how the proceedings were controlled," wrote the Dalai Lama. "But often I felt embarrassed at these meetings. I saw that the Chinese had only made me Chairman in order to give an added appearance of Tibetan authority to their schemes."

Inversely, Peking also hoped to erode the Dalai Lama's prestige by elevating that of the Panchen Lama. Since the 17th century, the elder of the two had served as tutor to the younger. In 1923, however, the Seventh Panchen Lama, convinced that the Thirteenth Dalai Lama was persecuting him for complicity with China during the 1910 invasion, fled his ancestral seat—Tashilhunpo Monastery in Shigatse—for Peking. The Panchen Lama never returned home, dying in Jyekundo in eastern Tibet in 1937. Finding the breach advantageous, the Nationalists influenced the selection of the new Panchen Lama themselves, certifying him in Xining in 1949 without the approval of the National Assembly in Lhasa. Soon after, the then eleven-year-old boy fell into Communist hands, from which time he was utilized as the PRC's principal Tibetan collaborator. His claim to the position was validated by Lhasa only under duress as part of the Seventeen-Point Agreement. Given virtually equal status with the Dalai Lama, the Panchen Lama came, through PCART, to embody the cutting edge of Peking's subversion. But elsewhere an even greater threat emerged.

The changes China pursued by stealth in Central Tibet it chose to impose by force in Kham and Amdo. Within a year of the invasion the transformation of Tibetan society began. Progressing gradually at first, it gained an implacable momentum until early in 1955 PLA contingents, accompanied by party workers and small numbers of newly recruited beggars—ironically entitled *hurtsun chenpos* or "diligent ones"—fanned out across the countryside to disarm the population, relieve them of their personal possessions and execute the first stages of collectivization, leading eventually to full-fledged communes. The culmination of five years of softening up, the Democratic Reforms, as they were called, were met by stiff resistance in virtually every village. The PLA responded by singling out prominent families, bringing them bound to the center of their community and, before the full population assembled at gunpoint, conducting *thamzing* or "struggle session." It was the duty of the *hurtsun chenpos* to carry out this facet of the Democratic Reforms, in which they beat and denounced their "oppressors," who, if unable to render a suitable confession of "crimes against the people," were forthwith executed. Violent intimidation and enforced socialization were abetted by the abduction of thousands of young children to be raised, not as Tibetans in their own homes, but as wards of the state in a newly created network of minority schools. Simultaneously, China began infiltrating the first of what it hoped would eventually be millions of settlers to colonize the "Roof of the World."

The Khampas' reaction was unequivocal. Following their clan leaders, they assembled by the thousands, mounted their sturdy ponies and, swords and rifles in hand, descended on PLA camps throughout the east. Overwhelmed by the onslaught, Chinese garrisons in Dergé, Kanzé, Nyarong, Po, Lithang and many of Kham's lesser districts were forced to retreat, suffering massive losses. Yet until the Chinese committed a further indiscretion the majority of the Khampas' senior *pons* or tribal chieftains remained at peace.

Six months after the fighting broke out, early in the summer of 1956, General Wang Jimei, Chamdo's PLA commander, summoned 350 prominent men to the city and asked for their endorsement of the Democratic Reforms. "No reforms" was the overwhelming vote. Four subsequent meetings yielded the same result until 210 leaders from Dergé, the largest region in Kham, were convened at the local fortress of Jomdha Dzong, forty miles east of Chamdo. When they were all inside, 5,000 Chinese troops surrounded the fort. For two weeks the Tibetans were held prisoner. On the fifteenth day of detention, they finally assented. After three more days Jomdha Dzong's guard was relaxed and that same night all 210 men escaped into the mountains. In this manner, Tibet's formal guerrilla resistance was born, the Chinese themselves having turned much of the Khampa establishment into outlaws.

In Lhasa, news of the revolt placed the Dalai Lama in an irreconcilable dilemma. His six-year effort at compromise thwarted, his own people no longer under his control, Tenzin Gyatso considered withdrawing from political office. During June of 1956, however, the Crown Prince of Sikkim brought an invitation to the 2,500th anniversary of the Buddha's birth, to be celebrated in India. With it, the Dalai Lama found a new source of hope. Not only was India the Holy Land from which Tibet's higher culture had come; more recently it had given birth to Mahatma Gandhi, who was deeply revered by all Tibetans for his nonviolent precepts. In the company of Gandhi's associates, Tenzin Gyatso hoped for advice on Tibet's predicament. Under the British at least, India had been Tibet's most powerful ally, a role, perhaps, it could be relied on once more to fulfill.

For "reasons of security," China denied the Dalai Lama permission to attend the celebration. On October 1, Prime Minister Nehru himself telegraphed Peking, resubmitting the invitation, this time revised to include the Panchen Lama. It became clear that a second denial would severely damage the facade of Sino-Tibetan cooperation, making it appear as though the Dalai Lama was being held against his will. Nevertheless, a full month passed until, on November 1, following queries pressed by the Indian consul general in Lhasa, China conceded to the Dalai Lama that a second invitation had been sent, which he would now be permitted to accept. Tenzin Gyatso quickly prepared to go, viewing the trip as "a lifeline to the world of tolerance and freedom."

Departing Lhasa in late November, the Dalai Lama drove south to Yatung. Leaving their Chinese escorts for the first time in years, the Tibetans rode upward through thick forests of fir and rhododendron to the 15,500-foot Nathu-la Pass. Before a giant cairn surmounted by scores of weather-beaten prayer flags, they paused in a low cloud to throw stones, crying with traditional high spirits, "*Lha Gyal Lo!*" ("The Gods are victorious!") At the border of the tiny Himalayan kingdom of Sikkim, the Tibetans were greeted by a guard of honor and a small group of dignitaries bearing scarves and garlands, huddled together in the mist. Then, as night fell and a heavy snow descended, they rode down the mountainside, the bells of their horses tingling in the dark, and halted at a group of tents and bungalows beside a frozen lake. The following day, the Choegyal of Sikkim met his revered guest outside Gangtok, the capital, from where the Dalai Lama proceeded to Bagdogra Airfield inside the Indian border. After flying by special plane to New Delhi, the Dalai Lama was met on the tarmac of Palam Airport by Prime Minister Nehru and much of the capital's diplomatic corps. Believing that now he could best serve his people by remaining in the free world to promote their cause, Tenzin Gyatso broached the topic to Nehru at their first meeting alone.

The Prime Minister's response was emphatic: he must return to Tibet and once more seek compromise within the much-despoiled Seventeen-Point Agreement. Before 1950, Nehru pointed out, not a single nation had formally recognized Tibet's independence; it was out of the question for India to give the appearance of doing so now. Its relations with China were strictly governed by the spirit of Panch Sheel, the five principles of mutual coexistence, articulated in the preamble to a 1954 trade pact between the two new republics. Though strongly criticized by Indian opposition leaders as an act of appeasement, Panch Sheel was, for Nehru, the expression of one of his highest and most cherished ideals: the peace and unity of the world's two largest emerging nations and therein Asia. As such, it not only evinced Nehru's admiration for Chinese anticolonialism, but served as a crucial safeguard for the limitations of India's army, which was already committed against Pakistan. Although Nehru refused to lend the Dalai Lama substantial support, he did agree to represent the Tibetan position to Zhou Enlai, who en route to Europe stopped off in New Delhi on a sudden visit. In a subsequent meeting with the Dalai Lama, Nehru—as he later reported to the Indian Parliament—assured the Tibetan leader that Zhou Enlai had personally told him that it was "absurd for anyone to imagine that China was going to force Communism on Tibet."

In his own discussions with China's premier, the Dalai Lama forcefully detailed the PLA's repressive actions in Kham. In return, he received a pledge—as did two of his brothers at a later meeting—that inequities, if they existed, would be corrected and that Mao himself would be apprised of all the Tibetans' complaints. Strangely, Zhou Enlai seemed unaware of the Democratic Reforms in eastern Tibet, though well informed about the uprising, which had been their result. The meeting ended on cordial terms. A few weeks later, though, Zhou was back in Delhi, greatly concerned about the Dalai Lama's plans. At a tense second conference, he made clear the PRC's willingness to use the utmost force in suppressing the first significant challenge to its seven-year-old rule. He then bluntly asked Tenzin Gyatso if it was true that he was planning not to return home. "It was a bit dirty," stated the Dalai Lama. "Zhou Enlai tried to manipulate me but I also manipulated him. We each feigned sincerity, in reality not meaning the words we spoke. When he asked if I was planning to remain in India I indicated that nothing of the sort was going on—that things were absolutely normal. He threatened and warned but in the end, despite this and the indecisiveness among our own people, I decided to go back. Thus my discussions with the Prime Minister turned out true after all."

In the first week of February 1957, while the Dalai Lama was still in New Delhi, Mao Zedong publicly stated that Tibet was not yet ready for reforms: they were to be postponed for a minimum of six years. Subsequently, cadres in Tibet assured the people that if they themselves did not request them, reforms would not be imposed for a further "fifteen or even fifty years." It was also announced that a number of Han personnel would be withdrawn, and PCART's departments reduced by half. Bolstered by the initial of these Chinese concessions, given out of fear of losing him and the veneer of Tibetan compliance, Tenzin Gyatso returned to Lhasa on April 1, seeking once more to stave off the erosion of Tibet's freedom.

During his absence, the situation had greatly deteriorated. In the aftermath of the Khampas' first victories, Chushi Gangdruk had been formed: "Four Rivers, Six Ranges"—a traditional epithet for Kham and Amdo, now used by the newly allied Tibetan chieftains as the name of their joint guerrilla organization. Gompo Tashi Angdrugtsang, an important trader from Lithang, took charge in the field, while Gyalo Thondup, the Dalai Lama's second-eldest brother, who lived in Darjeeling, upgraded an intelligence-gathering operation he had established with the CIA in 1951. A small number of guerrillas were smuggled to Guam via India and Thailand, where they were introduced to modern weaponry and commando techniques. Parachuting back into Tibet at night, they took up the task of organizing the resistance on a more efficient course, aided by periodic airdrops of light arms. By then, however, the fighting had escalated, the PLA having counterattacked with a full fourteen divisions—over 150,000 troops.

By mid-1957, a ruthless pattern of attack and reprisal developed, turning much of Kham into a wasteland. The guerrillas, clad in shirts of parachute silk, wearing heavy charm boxes to protect against bullets and living on dried meat and *tsampa* or parched barley, operated on horseback from mountain strongholds, ambushing—with flintlocks, swords and the occasional grenade—small PLA outposts and convoys coursing between the large, heavily garrisoned towns. China responded by attempting to cut off Chushi Gangdruk's base of popular support. From their fields in Kanzé and Chengdu waves of Ilyushin-28 bombers flew sorties across Kham, while huge mechanized columns moved overland shelling into rubble scores of villages, inhabited mainly by old men, women and children. Though by some accounts the Chinese lost 40,000 soldiers between 1956 and 1958, their own campaign in Kham, as attested to in two reports (issued in 1959 and 1960) by the International Commission of Jurists, a Geneva-based human rights monitoring group comprised of lawyers and judges from fifty nations, let loose a series of atrocities unparalleled in Tibet's history. The obliteration of entire villages was compounded by hundreds of public executions, carried out to intimidate the surviving population. The methods employed included crucifixion, dismemberment, vivisection, beheading, burying, burning and scalding alive, dragging the victims to death behind galloping horses and pushing them from airplanes; children were forced to shoot their parents, disciples their religious teachers. Everywhere monasteries were prime targets. Monks were compelled to publicly copulate with nuns and desecrate sacred images before being sent to a growing string of labor camps in Amdo and Gansu. In the face of such acts, the guerrillas found their ranks swollen by thousands of dependents, bringing with them triple or more their number in livestock. So enlarged, they became easy targets for Chinese air strikes. Simultaneously, the PLA threw wide loops around Tibetan-held districts, attempting to bottle them up and annihilate one pocket at a time. The tide of battle turning against them, a mass exodus comprised of hundreds of scattered bands fled westward, seeking respite within the precincts of the Dalai Lama.

Soon after the Tibetan leader's return to Lhasa, the Holy City was engulfed by the tents of over 10,000 refugees. Aware now that Mao's promises of respite had been disingenuous, Tenzin Gyatso witnessed the inevitable result when, on June 16, 1958, the revolt finally penetrated to Central Tibet with the founding of the Tensung Tangla Magar or National Volunteer Defense Army. A natural union of Chushi Gangdruk and the original Mimang Tsongdu, Central Tibet's own resistance group, the NVDA first raised its flag to the cheers of 5,000 cavalry drawn up on an open plain before an incense-shrouded portrait of the Dalai Lama, less than a hundred miles from Lhasa. Establishing a secretariat, a finance department and a twenty-seven-point code of conduct, the new force received support from Tibetan government officials throughout the central district of Lhoka, thus directly compromising the Cabinet. Under Chinese pressure the government sent a five-man delegation to the guerrillas to offer a promise of no reprisals if they laid down their arms. Instead, the mission joined the resistance. Fighting now reached—with an estimated 80,000

Khampa horsemen in U-Tsang alone—to within thirty miles of Lhasa, where, in the autumn of 1958, the 3,000-man PLA garrison at Tsethang was overrun. While hastily reinforcing their central Tibetan troops, the Chinese ordered the Tibetan army itself to put down the uprising. The Dalai Lama's Cabinet promptly refused, citing the obvious fact that Tibet's army, though loosely integrated with the PLA, was only waiting for an opportunity to join the guerrillas. Thwarted, the PLA deployed special detachments, disguised in Khampa garb, to pillage local villages, hoping in this way to arouse Central Tibetans' age-old fear of Khampa banditry and turn them against the freedom fighters. Concurrently, the Dalai Lama found that virtually every effort at mediation had been exhausted. "There was a particular room in the Norbulingka used for meeting the Chinese generals," he recounted. "It got to the point where I was reluctant even to enter that room. I just became tired and fed up. It was a sad experience. Their attitude, you see, was one full of contradiction. One day they would say, 'This is white,' the next, 'It's black.' It was mad, and actually foolish. If you have to lie, you should at least do so in a manner that won't be exposed too soon. But they didn't even bother about that. And when you disagreed they resorted immediately to force to impose their argument."

On March 1, 1959, while the Dalai Lama was residing in the Central Cathedral, two junior officers from the PLA's headquarters, a brick-walled camp called Silingpu built between the Potala and the Kyichu River, came to call. They conveyed an invitation from General Dan Guansan, then in command, to attend a theatrical show. Somewhat surprised that the request had not been transmitted through the proper channel of the Cabinet, Tenzin Gyatso nonetheless replied that he would be happy to come but could not fix a date until his final examinations, then underway, were completed. The Chinese soon withdrew and the Dalai Lama turned his attention to the task at hand.

By all standards, the tests for the Geshé Lharampa, the highest grade of the Doctor of Divinity degree, were the most rigorous in Tibet's ancient academic system. They had begun the previous year, when for three months the Dalai Lama had toured Sera, Drepung and Ganden monasteries to stand for preliminary exams. In day-long sessions he had debated fifteen monastic scholars—three for each of the five topics studied—before thousands of onlookers. His performance had been accounted uncanny, given the fact that throughout the eleven most intense years of his preparation, from age thirteen to twenty-four, the requirements of daily debate, memorization and seven levels of courses had been conducted under the great weight of political office. On the day of his final exam, the Dalai Lama was questioned by a rotating team of eighty scholars before 20,000 monks crammed into every niche of the Central Cathedral's inner sanctum. With two breaks only, the test proceeded from early in the morning until ten at night, hours of debate seeming "like an instant," as the Dalai Lama recalled. His performance convinced the assembled abbots and scholars that he was indeed the incarnation of Chenrezi.

On March 7, General Dan Guansan again asked the Dalai Lama to set a date for attending the theatrical show. March 10 was reluctantly agreed on, the event to be held inside Silingpu itself, an unprecedented location for the Dalai Lama's presence. On the morning of March 9, P. T. Takla, general of the 500-man Kusung Magar, the Dalai Lama's bodyguard, was hurriedly summoned before one Brigadier Fu at Chinese headquarters. The brigadier informed Takla that on the following day Tibet's ruler was not to be accompanied by his customary contingent of twenty-five soldiers, his route was not to be lined with troops, as was normally the case, nor were the two or three bodyguards permitted to join him inside the Chinese camp to be armed. When Takla requested the reason for such extraordinary conditions, the brigadier mysteriously asked, "Will you be responsible if somebody pulls the trigger?" He further insisted that the occasion be kept secret from the public. It could not be. Within hours of the meeting, Lhasa was swept by the rumor of a Chinese plan to kidnap the Precious Protector. Serving only to reinforce the people's suspicions, Radio Peking had just announced that the Dalai Lama would attend an upcoming meeting of the Chinese National Assembly, though, in fact, he had not yet agreed to go. Three planes were known to be standing by at Damshung Airport, seventy miles northwest of the capital, giving further credence to the idea. Moreover, similar deceptions had occurred before. In the east, at least four high lamas had been invited to cultural performances without their retinues, whereupon they were imprisoned and all save one executed. No one besides the Dalai Lama's personal staff had been invited to the performance, not even the Cabinet. Apprised of the people's feelings, however, the PLA command issued last-minute invitations to prominent Tibetans on the evening of the ninth, an act which appeared so transparent as to confirm the population's worst fears.

Soon after dawn on March 10, crowds began pouring out of Lhasa. By nine o'clock almost 30,000 people had gathered before the two giant stone lions flanking the Norbulingka's front gate. Their mood was explosive. Shouting that the Dalai Lama must be protected, they sealed off the Jewel Park. Two longtime Cabinet ministers were belatedly permitted entry, but a third, newly appointed official, driving in the company of a Chinese officer, was attacked. When a known collaborator, named Phakpala Khenchung, rode up on a bicycle firing two shots from his revolver to warn the crowd back, he was stoned to death, his body tied to a horse and dragged through the city's streets.

As the morning progressed, seventy of Lhasa's chief citizens were elected to be popular spokesmen. By noon they had obtained the crowd's initial objective: a Cabinet minister announcing over the gate's loudspeakers that the Dalai Lama had decided to forgo the performance as well as to decline—as the leaders had requested—future invitations to the PLA headquarters. Encouraged rather than placated, the people mustered a large volunteer force to guard the Norbulingka. Then thousands returned to Lhasa to mount mass demonstrations demanding that the Chinese quit Tibet. Meanwhile, three Cabinet ministers drove to Silingpu hoping to mollify General Dan Guansan. Pacing up and down the room in which he, ten officers and Ngabo Ngawang Jigme—already in the Chinese camp —received the news, the general was outraged. He accused the Tibetan government of acting in complicity with "reactionary rebels" and threatened severe reprisals if their "scheming" continued. Storming out of the meeting, he led the way to the camp's auditorium to introduce the theatrical show, which, despite the day's unscheduled events, was to proceed as planned.

At five o'clock, after having seen the show, Ngari Rinpoché, the Dalai Lama's thirteen-year-old brother, left PLA headquarters and walked east past the Potala toward his family's residence, Yabshi House. "It was the end of dusk, the sun was big and yellow and the shadows were long," he recalled. "But the road was completely deserted. Where it branched off to Lhasa there stood a large Chinese pillbox. On top of it soldiers were patrolling back and forth carrying submachine guns. I had never seen anything like that before. Normally, the Chinese kept their troops unarmed. Then, when I reached my mother's house, I found the outer gate locked. It should have been closed only at night, but now even the gate to the inner courtyard was shut. As I walked through, I looked up at the house and there was my mother anxiously staring out of a window. When she saw me, she clapped, she was so happy."

As the eleventh of March dawned, the Norbulingka readied itself for battle. The previous night, government officials and members of the bodyguard had joined the popular leaders in declaring an end to the Seventeen-Point Agreement, following which the entire Kusung Magar openly revolted, casting off the Chinese uniforms they had been compelled to wear and donning their own Tibetan ones. Taking up positions alongside the volunteer guard, they surrounded the Jewel Park, while dispatching a force northeast to barricade the Xining road against Chinese reinforcements. As a precaution, the Dalai Lama's family moved from Yabshi House to a small pavilion in the Norbulingka. Following their arrival, Ngari Rinpoché went on a tour of inspection. By each gate in the outer white wall, and again by those in the inner yellow wall demarcating the Dalai Lama's private enclosure, contingents of armed men had camped, their ponies left tethered in long lines outside the park. "I remember them sitting around their campfires," recounted Ngari Rinpoché, "resting against their saddles and taking snuff. There was a chill in the air and during the next few days it was overcast, so you could smell the smoke from a distance. Every so often those guarding the walls would descend to drink tea and rest in the old tents they had pitched. They wore big boots, fur-lined hats and robes and they had stuffed the barrels of their rifles with red, green and blue tassels to keep out the dirt. Everyone was always engaged in very vigorous conversation."

Outside the Norbulingka, Lhasa continued in a state of turmoil. A series of popular meetings took place inside the large government printing house in the village of Shöl beneath the Potala. Here, formal resolutions were signed by the government, representatives of guild associations and monasteries, calling for *rangzen* or independence. Concurrently, the city fortified itself. All of the larger houses and even the Central Cathedral were transformed into heavily manned stockades. The Chinese also prepared for what appeared to be an inevitable showdown. Withdrawing personnel into their own houses, they strengthened the exteriors with sandbags, lined the roofs with barbed wire and, from in between the numerous red flags, mortar and machine-gun nests marking their positions, photographed the constant marches which coursed through the capital's streets. But their key preparations were considerably more subtle. While the Tibetan people hoped to rout the Communists in the convulsive manner of the 1912 expulsion of Manchu troops, the PLA was busy emplacing heavy artillery around the entire Lhasan Valley, with which, without directly confronting the revolt, they could swiftly suppress it.

"I felt as if I were standing between two volcanoes, each likely to erupt at any moment," wrote the Dalai Lama, adding that his "most urgent moral duty . . . was to prevent a totally disastrous clash between my unarmed people and the Chinese army." The likelihood of such a calamity had long been clear to Tenzin Gyatso. Though reluctant to discuss it, the Dalai Lama had dreamt a year earlier of the Norbulingka becoming "a killing ground." Other dreams concerned his impending flight to India, an event which the Nechung Oracle had alluded to as well many months before. The crisis itself now confirmed the portents. Once freed from the political constraints which had bound them for nine years, the 40,000 or so PLA troops occupying Lhasa would undoubtedly unleash a devastating reprisal.

In an attempt to avert the confrontation, the Dalai Lama urged the large crowd still before the Norbulingka to disperse. In addition, he sought to buy time, replying encouragingly to three letters sent over the next six days by General Dan Guansan. In them, the general offered protection from what he termed the "reactionary clique" surrounding the palace. He also pressed his request for the Dalai Lama to come to the PLA headquarters. Replying to the first note, Tenzin Gyatso maintained that under the pretext of protecting him, those outside the Norbulingka were actually endangering his safety. In his next response he said that he had ordered the "immediate dissolution" of the "illegal people's conference"; in the last, that he was attempting to separate the "progressive people" from "those opposing the revolution," at which point he would, under protection of the former, make his way secretly to Chinese headquarters. Five days were thus gained, yet no appreciable slackening of tension occurred. Early on March 16, after seventeen pieces of artillery had been trained on the major strong points in and outside the city, a final letter from the general arrived, accompanied, in the same envelope, by one from Ngabo. The latter plainly conveyed the PLA's true intentions. It entreated the Dalai Lama to take up a secure position inside the yellow wall—safe from the "evil reactionaries"—and to notify the general of his location, so that, as the letter ominously promised, "this building will not be damaged." Whether or not Tenzin Gyatso complied, it was now clear, the PLA intended to shell the Jewel Park.

On March 15, a platoon of Chinese soldiers suddenly appeared within fifty yards of the Norbulingka's long southern wall. Hundreds of Tibetan troops ran to their positions and took aim. "They were so close we could see their faces," recollected Ngari Rinpoché, who, against his mother's orders, manned the defense. "Everyone held their breath waiting for the first shot to be fired, but they just kept marching. It was only a reconnaissance mission to draw out our numbers." Shortly afterwards, Dr. Tenzin Choedrak, the Dalai Lama's personal physician, arrived in the Jewel Park with news from Lhasa. On the morning of March 12, he informed the Dalai Lama's mother, the women of the city—young girls and grandmothers alike—had massed at the foot of the Potala. Following the meeting, they had taken to the streets around the Barkhor or marketplace, daring the Chinese to open fire on them and shouting, "From now on Tibet is independent." In a more sober step their leaders had requested the Indian consulate—unsuccessfully—to assist in restraining the Chinese. "I knew this year would bring trouble," commented Dr. Choedrak, concluding his tidings with a nod to Ngari Rinpoché. "On the very morning of New Year's Day, I remember you set off a firecracker in the house and let out a loud war cry. When children are playing at war, it's a sure sign the adults will be fighting soon."

Two days later, at four o'clock in the afternoon of March 17, the first shots were fired. While the Dalai Lama and his Cabinet sat in session inside the Chensel Phodrang, one of his predecessor's palaces, two mortar shells shattered the tranquillity of the inner garden. One fell in a marsh outside the northern wall, the other in a pond not far from the residence. Inexplicably, none followed. Yet this first bombardment yielded a swift result. One of the Kalons or Cabinet ministers raced to the Norbulingka's front gate to restrain the volunteer guard from attacking PLA positions at a nearby transport center, the rest, consulting with the Dalai Lama, took the momentous decision to flee Lhasa that very night.

"At around six-thirty in the evening of the seventeenth, my mother called me into her room," related Ngari Rinpoché. "Her voice was trembling a bit. She said, 'You'd better change into layperson's clothes. We might have to leave soon.' Straightaway I said, 'For India?' She said, 'No. Just to a nunnery across the river. But don't tell anyone.' I promised I wouldn't, but I knew we were going to India. Lhoka was clear of Chinese and once you passed through it you reached the North-East Frontier Agency—NEFA—in India. And of course I could see how frightened my mother was. There was so much tension."

Ngari Rinpoché, though, felt exultant. Shedding his maroon monk's robes, he buckled on an old Luger inside a plain *chuba* and, "bursting to tell someone the news," ran down the pavilion's front steps to a small room on its ground floor. "I went to see what my fat uncle was doing," he continued. "There he was sitting alone stitching bags like mad from a pile of white cotton curtains. When I saw him, I realized that nothing had been planned. It was all an emergency. I poked my nose in and he yelled, 'Go away! I'm busy!' So I ran back upstairs to my mother's maid and said, 'Acha, you know what? We're going to India.' She snapped, 'Keep quiet!' very sternly. Then I decided to see my mother. It was just nighttime and when I entered her room the lights were so bright that everything looked exaggerated, like a stage. There were my mother and elder sister in pants, being dressed up like men by their servants. Now I thought, 'We're really in business!' It was too much. I started to laugh and they started laughing. Then my sister gave me a beautiful pink mohair scarf and a wool cap called a monkey cap that you can pull down over your face."

At eight-thirty, Gyapon Lobsang Tashi, a captain in the bodyguard, arrived, accompanied by a soldier armed with a tommy gun, to inform the

Dalai Lama's mother that it was time to leave. While he was inside, Ngari Rinpoché stood on the front porch saying goodbye to two attendants. "There was a cool breeze blowing, the stars had come out and it was very peaceful," he remarked. "Then suddenly a burst of Bren-gun fire came from the direction of the river. The soldiers dashed out of the house and we all looked from the porch, but couldn't see a thing. Later we heard that a hundred of our troops guarding the Ramagan ferry had run into a Chinese patrol. Luckily our fire scared them off, keeping the way to the river clear."

At nine, the Dalai Lama's family—his mother, sister, brother and uncle —and the women's maid departed, the first of three groups to do so. Descending the building's steps in the dark, they moved silently beneath the trees toward the Jewel Park's southern wall. Ironically, not only did the Chinese have to be avoided but the Tibetan fighters as well. For days they had checked everyone who passed in or out of the Norbulingka, worried that by some plot the Dalai Lama would fall into Chinese hands. Their vigilance was based, in large part, on a profound distrust of the Cabinet, who, due to its years of compromise, was believed by many Tibetans, and particularly those from the east, to be capable of the worst treachery. Accordingly, disguised as a volunteer guard, Lobsang Tashi ordered the gate to be opened for a "patrol" which, he claimed, had been dispatched to inspect the riverside. "I think I was the misfit because of my height," said Ngari Rinpoché, laughing, "but they let us through any-way." Continuing over an open plain dotted with bushes, the party met a lone man and pony waiting for the Dalai Lama's mother, who had difficulty walking on account of a weak knee. Once mounted, she was led forward, the rest proceeding on foot, spread out like a genuine patrol, one of the soldiers carrying the uncle's two bags, which, filled with *tsamba*, butter and meat, were the only provisions he had been able to bring. On the Kyichu's stony bank twenty soldiers stood silent vigil by two coracles. Ushered in, the party was rowed to the far shore, where thirty Khampa guerrillas waited with their horses in the night. While the coracles headed back for the next group, that of the Dalai Lama, Ngari Rinpoché took a short walk downstream, gazing across the Kyichu at the electric lights of a massive PLA camp two hundred yards west of the Norbulingka. Beyond it, backed into the mountains on the north end of the valley, stood Dre-pung, the world's largest monastery. "When I saw Drepung, I felt a strong urge to prostrate three times, in farewell," he remembered. "May I see you again," I prayed, and then went back to the horses to wait for His Holi-ness."

In the Dalai Lama's palace, Tenzin Gyatso prepared for the ten o'clock departure of his group. During his final hours in the Norbulingka he had written a letter formally certifying the people's leaders. He had then instructed the militia not to make a stand, but in the event of conflict to retreat south of the Kyichu. Alone, he now changed into a layman's maroon robe and fur hat and, for the last time, walked slowly to his prayer room. Seated on his meditation cushion, the Dalai Lama read through the scripture before it, stopping at a line in which the Buddha advised a disciple to be courageous. Rising, he took hold of the sacred painting of the Protectress Palden Lhamo, kept always by his person, and slinging its special container across his shoulder, departed from his home, completing his disguise by shedding his glasses and borrowing a rifle from one of the guards at a gate in the yellow wall. Joined by the bodyguard's general, the Master of Religious Ceremonies and the Lord Chamberlain, he proceeded out of the Norbulingka through the same gate his family had used forty-five minutes before. No one recognized him.

"All of a sudden I heard a lot of people and horses passing in the dark," said Ngari Rinpoché. "Then I heard Mr. Phala, the Lord Chamberlain, saying in a hushed voice, 'Tashidelek, tashidelek,' which means 'Good luck,' an expression we use only on auspicious occasions like New Year's." Joined by the third contingent, consisting of the Cabinet, the Dalai Lama's two tutors and the medium of the Gadong Oracle, all of whom had been smuggled from the Norbulingka hidden under a tarpaulin in a truck, the parties rode down on a narrow track clinging to the hillside just above the riverbank. Undetected, they passed the PLA's sprawling Nordulingka camp, and with some 700 Khampas guarding their rear, headed for the Tsangpo River and the guerrilla-held mountains of Lhoka beyond.

"We rode all night in small groups," related Ngari Rinpoché. "Before dawn it got so cold that I thought my legs would freeze, but when the sun came up it was crisp and clear, so we all felt a bit refreshed." By midmorning Ngari Rinpoché's group reached the base of the Che-la or Sandy Pass. "The whole way up Che-la," he continued, "my fat uncle's saddle kept slipping off and he was desperately clutching his horse's neck. I couldn't stop laughing until we dismounted on the other side, where it's sand, and everyone ran down." Two hours ahead, the Dalai Lama's party hurriedly covered the ten miles remaining before the Tsangpo. As they rode, an early-spring sandstorm fortuitously whipped up, concealing their flight from any pursuers. Reaching the river safely, they crossed in coracles to the far shore, where the people of a small village, alerted by the National Volunteer Defense Army, whose territory they had now entered, waited to greet them, many in tears, their hands clasped in prayer around sticks of burning incense. After another half hour of riding the first halt was made at the small monastery of Ramé. By sunset, after more than twenty hours in the saddle, Tenzin Gyatso's family arrived.

"Just after we rode up, I was called to see His Holiness," said Ngari Rinpoché. "I walked into a small room on the monastery's second floor. There was one window across from the door with a little light filtering through and His Holiness was standing before it in high leather boots and layman's clothes. I had never seen him dressed like that before but he actually looked quite natural. He just asked me, 'How are you feeling today?' I said, 'Nothing special. Everything went well, except the sandstorm was a little rough and Mother had some problem with her leg from riding.' Then he looked at me quietly for some time and finally said, 'Choegyal'—my personal name—'now we are refugees.' "

"The day after I escaped from Lhasa," related the Dalai Lama, "I felt a tremendous sense of relief. Actually the danger was still very much alive. But despite this we were moving freely, on our own, and we had finally come to the point of openly criticizing the Chinese. 'I have the right to say bad things about them,' I remember thinking. That feeling of freedom was very vivid: my strongest reaction following the escape."

"It was very funny," observed Ngari Rinpoché of the company's mood. "After our first ride everything was done in such a relaxed, happy manner. Really Tibetan style. As if we were only out for a picnic in the countryside." The route, however, was tiring. Skirting Yamdrok, the great multi-limbed Turquoise Lake, the party rode south. The treeless landscape on either side was broken only by ancient traders' tracks resembling shallow wrinkles traced across the vast empty valleys and by the occasional village or monastary. To avoid detection by air they traveled in separate groups, struggling, one after another, up 18,000-foot passes still laden with the bulk of the winter's snow. Each day small guerrilla bands materialized, seemingly from nowhere, to check the party's progress. "It was reassuring to see them," said Ngari Rinpoché, now riding in the Dalai Lama's contingent. "They were all big men—real Khampas, draped with pistols, rifles, swords, daggers and charm boxes—a very colorful, tough-looking bunch. Every night after we'd stopped large bands rode in. They'd disarm, then come before His Holiness, to prostrate and receive his blessing. His Holiness would talk briefly with them, asking where they came from and which unit they were serving in. Then they would disappear back into the night and resume their positions."

During evening halts the Dalai Lama and eight advisers met to discuss plans. At first they decided to establish a temporary base behind the lines of the National Volunteer Defense Army at Lhuntse Dzong, a large district fort commanding a hilltop sixty miles north of the Indian border.

From there Tenzin Gyatso intended to negotiate with the Chinese, hoping that so long as he remained in Tibet, and could be of use, the PLA might be prevented from reprisals. But the hope was ill-founded. On March 24, the Dalai Lama received word that little more than two days after he had fled, at two o'clock in the morning on March 20, the Norbulingka had been shelled. Four days later, on March 28, the Dalai Lama listened over a small transistor radio as Zhou Enlai announced China's dissolution of the Tibetan government. With a dialogue no longer possible, Tenzin Gyatso chose to reestablish his administration, doing so in a brief ceremony in Lhuntze Dzong soon thereafter. But Lhuntze Dzong was not safe. The PLA had already crossed the Tsangpo in force and was advancing on the party. A Chinese radio message had been intercepted ordering troops along the Bhutanese border to move east, blocking all avenues of escape from southern Tibet to India. Realizing that the border would shortly be sealed, the Dalai Lama decided to seek asylum in India. Messengers were sent ahead to request entry permission while the party followed behind, with two of the highest, most difficult passes still to be crossed.

On the Lagoe-la Pass, leading to the small town of Jhora, a fierce storm descended. Hands and faces frozen, the Tibetans led their ponies through a violent snowfall and emerged exhausted, only to arrive the following day at the Karpo-la or White Pass. Here blinding snow glare forced the 350-troop escort to shield their eyes by letting down their long braids while the Dalai Lama pulled his scarf, like a surgeon's mask, over his face. "I was riding with Mr. Liushar—the Foreign Minister," recounted Ngari Rinpoché, "when just on the other side of the pass, we heard a plane. Liushar looked completely bewildered, then a big transport, with no markings, flew right above us, just two hundred yards overhead." Men and horses scattered across the gleaming snow. The Dalai Lama dismounted and stood alone on a bare patch of windswept ground. Word rapidly passed down the column not to fire, though the transport was an easy target for Bren guns and semiautomatics. "They weren't blind. They had to see us," continued Ngari Rinpoché. "After that we were sure the Chinese would be on us in no time."

Breaking into smaller groups, the company moved forward for two more days, descending from treeless wastes through alpine terrain into the jungle-covered hills occupied by Monpas, a Tibetan tribal people whose dialect was barely intelligible to those from Lhasa. Here, in Mangmang, the last village in Tibet, the messengers returned with word that preparations for their arrival were underway at Chutangmo, on the Indian side of the border. Further details of the fighting in Lhasa, reported by eyewitnesses who were now escaping along the same route, were also heard.

"When the suppression finally took place, the majority of our people were asleep," stated the Dalai Lama. "In the dark, surrounded by noise and smoke, they didn't know where the projectiles were coming from. When dawn broke there wasn't a single Chinese soldier visible. Therefore, I think the Chinese inflicted a psychological defeat at the very first stage of the fight."

On the morning of March 20, hundreds of dead and wounded lay amidst the burning ruins of the Norbulingka's palaces and temples. Following renewed shelling, the PLA attacked in force. By four o'clock in the afternoon, the Tibetans were thrown into a disorderly retreat to the Kyichu River, shooting their wounded rather than have them captured. Caught in a crossfire from the Nordulingka camp to the west and the PLA's Shuktri Lingka position to the east, those who did make it to the Kyichu were faced with a torrential spring current so swift that many were swept away and drowned. By linking arms in long chains the survivors emerged on the far side, their clothing ripped from their backs, yet for the time being safe. Meanwhile, as the PLA assumed control of the Jewel Park, a massive search was mounted for the Dalai Lama—whose flight remained unknown—the multitude of corpses being examined one by one.

In Lhasa, the fight lasted three days. Beginning on the morning of March 20, while artillery pounded the Potala, Sera Monastery and Chokpori Hill, site of the medical college, the city exploded in street-to-street fighting. Lhasans, armed only with light weapons, petrol bombs, axes and knives, impulsively rushed Chinese buildings from behind haphazard barricades of cobblestones, furniture and telephone poles. They were slaughtered by the thousands, the PLA refusing to be lured out. Desperate to confront the enemy, they dug tunnels between the centuries-old stone buildings, many of which, by sunset, were in flames, illuminating the city throughout the night.

Early on the morning of the twenty-first the conflict resumed in a more beleaguered vein. As thick clouds of incense rose alongside prayers from rooftops across the city, a company of Khampas crept through the still streets to storm the Happy Light cinema. Overwhelming its 100 PLA defenders they achieved the Tibetans' sole victory. In its wake dozens of pitched battles erupted. The Ramoché Cathedral, Lhasa's second most hallowed temple and home of the Upper Tantric College, soon fell, its millennia-old walls set aflame by Chinese shells. A half mile to the west the Tibetan artillery post on Chokpori Hill also succumbed, its defenders killed to the man, the entire medical college, in which it had stood, obliterated by incoming rounds. Beneath its rocky slopes, thousands of noncombatants who had camped at the Norbulingka for the full eleven days of the emergency poured into Lhasa, all heading for the Tsuglakhang, convinced that there, in Tibet's most sacred shrine, they would be safe from Chinese attack. By nightfall more than 10,000 people filled the Cathedral's courtyards and myriad chapels—a chaotic press of men, women, children, mortar-bearing guerrillas and hundreds of monks fervently praying before the feet of colossal images.

Just after dawn on Sunday, the twenty-second, the PLA started to shell the Tsuglakhang. While mortars pocked its ornate roofs, thousands of civilians camped in the large square before the southeastern walls came under heavy machine-gun fire from adjacent buildings. Three tanks slowly converged on the square, Chinese soldiers abandoning their defensive bulwarks to attack under their cover. Though the entire Drapchi Regiment had been pinned down in their barracks east of Lhasa, a detachment of Tibetan cavalry managed to gallop in from outside the city to help sustain the battle for three hours. Hundreds of Tibetans and Chinese soon lay in piles around the tanks while flames leapt from the cathedral behind. But by noon the fighting was over. Reinforced by armored cars, the PLA rammed down the Tsuglakhang's front gates and stormed its interior. Two hours later Ngabo Ngawang Jigme's voice came over Chinese loudspeakers around the city. Claiming that the Tibetan government had reached a settlement Ngabo ordered the remaining pockets of resistance to surrender. Civilians holding white scarves above their heads filled the streets, while members of the NVDA slipped away to join the resistance in Lhoka. Above the blackened, shell-pierced Potala, five red flags now blew in the warm breeze of an early spring afternoon. On the corpse-littered road below, long lines of prisoners marched toward the Norbulingka. Inside Lhasa tens of thousands more were detained, as the first hours of the unimpeded rule China had for so long sought over Tibet finally dawned.

In Mangmang, the Dalai Lama lay ill. The snowstorms of the high passes had turned, at a lower altitude, to torrential rain, inundating the frail tent in which he had tried to sleep. On the morning of March 30, Tenzin Gyatso succumbed to dysentery. Moved to a nearby house, he spent a feverish day in bed and a second sleepless night. As the next morning in Mangmang began, word arrived that Chinese troops were closing on Tsona, a village within striking distance of the camp. Despite his condition, the Dalai Lama decided to cross the border immediately, a party of eighty officials, lamas and family members comprising his retinue. Mounted on a black *dzo* or hybrid yak, Tenzin Gyatso departed Mangmang, as he later described, "in a daze of sickness and weariness and unhappiness deeper than I can express."

At four o'clock in the afternoon of March 31, he entered a large clearing.

On its far end stood a newly built bamboo welcome gate beside which six Gurkha soldiers, in heavy British ammunition boots, and floppy jungle hats, waited at attention. As the Gurkhas presented arms, their commander stepped forward to offer a scarf in greeting. The Dalai Lama dismounted, accepted the scarf and slowly walked across the border into India and exile.

II

3

In Exile from
the Land of Snows

'1959–1960

FOR EIGHTEEN DAYS the Dalai Lama rode down through the jungle-covered hills of Assam. Led by Gurkhas, the various groups in the entourage camped in the midst of lush rain forest, the sight of tropical birds, insects, monkeys and great flowering trees contrasting vividly with the arid plateau of Tibet just a few miles behind. Reaching Tawang, forward headquarters for the Kameng Division of the North-East Frontier Agency (NEFA), they settled temporarily in bungalows, where the outside world made its first contacts. On the day of their arrival an Indian air force transport flew in low over the large meadow below the town, dropped half-filled sacks of flour, shoes and fedora hats and then circled higher to unload heavier cargo by parachute. For three days the planes came, while below the Tibetans watched glumly, incapacitated by malaria, cholera and typhoid vaccines. Pressing on to Bomdila, a major town up to which roads had been dug and electricity laid, the Dalai Lama received a telegram from Prime Minister Nehru welcoming him and extending all "facilities" for his residence in India. Heartened by the official greeting he halted once more, recuperated from the last traces of his illness and prepared to meet the world press, which was gathered at nearby Tezpur, a tea-planting center on the Brahmaputra River.

Little more than two weeks before, Nehru had announced the Dalai Lama's safe arrival to a standing ovation from the Indian Parliament. A week earlier, however, Peking had already issued a detailed communiqué presenting its view of the turmoil in Tibet. In it, the revolt was portrayed as a minor insurrection engineered by an "upper-strata reactionary clique" seeking to reestablish its rule over "the darkest feudal serfdom in the world." "The spirit of these reactionaries soared to the clouds and they were ready to take over the whole universe," stated the New China News Agency on March 28. "With the aid of the patriotic Tibetan monks and laymen," it continued, "the People's Liberation Army completely crushed the rebellion. Primarily this is because the Tibetan people are patriotic, support the Central People's Government, ardently love the People's Liberation Army and oppose the imperialists and traitors." The communiqué declared that the Dalai Lama had been "blatantly abducted" and "held under duress by the rebels," who, it implied, were acting under orders not just from Taiwan and the United States but from India as well. The small Himalayan trading town of Kalimpong, populated by Tibetan expatriates during the 1950s, was identified as "the command center of the rebellion" and the fact that India's Parliament had recently discussed Tibet was referred to as an "impolite and improper" interference in the "internal affairs of a friendly country."

Nehru responded mildly to Peking's indictments. Conceding in Parliament that Kalimpong was indeed the focus of "a complicated game of chess by various nationalities," he nonetheless dismissed the notion that India had played a role in Tibet's revolt. He further sought to reassure China by citing his firm adherence to Panch Sheel, which precluded involvement by either nation in the internal affairs of the other. The Prime Minister's position, though, as he himself termed it, was "difficult, delicate and embarrassing." A ground swell of popular sympathy for Tibet had swept India, compelling its government to offer some gesture of support. Nehru accomplished this by granting the Dalai Lama asylum. Yet, as he was acutely aware, such an act left India open not only to accusations of violating Panch Sheel but also to the considerably more damaging charge of having fallen into the anti-Communist camp of the Cold War and thereby lost its nonaligned stance, the cornerstone of the Republic's foreign policy. To forestall such criticism, Nehru stressed that his support of the Dalai Lama was humanitarian only, based on a "tremendous bond" growing out of centuries of spiritual and cultural exchange between India and Tibet. The Dalai Lama was not to be permitted to use India as a base for a Tibetan independence movement or to engage in politics of any kind. Above all, he was to be isolated from the press and public in an effort to soften Peking's increasingly inflammatory posture. But the latter was not simply achieved.

Since the first word of fighting in Lhasa had appeared late in March, news of a revolt in remote Tibet had leaped into world headlines. Over a hundred correspondents flew in from Paris, London, New York, Africa and East Asia seeking what was already billed as the "story of the year." Choosing Kalimpong as the best spot to begin their search, they converged on the Himalayan Hotel, run by David Macdonald, a former British trade agent in Tibet and an acquaintance of the Thirteenth Dalai Lama. While "Daddy" Macdonald took to his bed from worry on hearing of the Fourteenth Dalai Lama's flight, the press scoured the surrounding peaks with binoculars, accosted the town's more prominent Tibetan citizens, drove a hundred miles a day back and forth to Gangtok in search of leads and, under increasing pressure from their editors to provide front-page news on the whereabouts of the mysterious "God-King," began issuing fabricated reports over Kalimpong's antiquated Morse-key telegraph. Competition for a scoop was so stiff and genuine news so scarce that much of the reporters' time was spent surreptitiously tailing one another for sources. With word of the Dalai Lama's crossing into the NEFA, however, they could, just by looking at the map, infer that he would eventually emerge at Tezpur. Thereupon the press corps decamped en masse, first to Shillong, the capital of Assam, and then to Tezpur itself. Sleeping on the couches and billiard tables of the local Planter's Club, they clogged the town's tiny airstrip with single-engine planes hired to race exclusive photos of the "God-King's" arrival to Calcutta's Dum Dum Airport and the presses of the world's periodicals beyond.

In the early hours of April 18, Indian officials lifted a travel ban previously imposed on a small road camp called Foothills, thirty miles from Tezpur, where, shortly after dawn, the Dalai Lama was due to arrive. Those able to acquire transport caught their first glimpse of the exiled leader as, followed by his mother, sister, Ngari Rinpoché and the seventy-man remnant of the Tibetan government, he stepped from a jeep, walked down an impromptu carpet of tarpaulins laid between facing rows of Indian troops and entered an overseer's cottage for a breakfast of cornflakes, poached eggs and toast. Emerging, the Dalai Lama was met by a shiny red Plymouth, the Tibetan and Indian flags mounted on bamboo splints above its headlights. An hour and a half later batteries of microphones and television cameras came to life before Tezpur's Circuit House as once more he walked smiling, but silent, inside. While Tenzin Gyatso looked through hundreds of letters and cables sent by leaders and well-wishers from around the world, an Indian and a Tibetan official appeared before the press to read a statement composed by the Dalai Lama in the third person. Giving a capsule history of the key events leading up to his flight, the document revealed for the first time that the Seventeen-Point Agreement of 1951 had been signed "under pressure from the Chinese government" and that from the day of the PLA's arrival in Lhasa "the Tibetan government did not enjoy any measure of autonomy." It then denied Chinese claims that the Dalai Lama had been abducted, stating that he had come to India "of his own free will and not under duress." "His country and people have passed through an extremely difficult period," the statement summed up, "and all that the Dalai Lama wishes to say at the moment is to express his sincere regret at the tragedy which has overtaken Tibet and to fervently hope that these troubles will be over soon without any more bloodshed."

China reacted harshly. "The so-called statement of the Dalai Lama . . . is a crude document, lame in reasoning, full of lies and loopholes," declared the New China News Agency two days later. "Actually, Tibet's political and religious systems were all laid down by the Central Government in Peking. . . . Not even the title, position and powers of the Dalai Lama were laid down by the Tibetans themselves. In modern history the so-called Tibetan independence has always been a scheme of the British imperialists for carrying out aggression against China and first of all against Tibet. . . . Indian expansionist elements inherited this shameful legacy. . . . " Citing as evidence of his abduction the fact that the Dalai Lama's statement had not been written in the first person and that an Indian official had passed out copies of it to reporters, the dispatch upgraded Peking's earlier accusations in what was perceived in New Delhi as an unwarranted and bellicose reversal of the facts. "The publication at the present moment of this so-called statement of the Dalai Lama, which harps on so-called Tibetan independence, will naturally cause people to ask: Is this not an attempt to place the Dalai Lama in a position of hostility to his motherland, thus blocking the road for him to return to it? What is meant by independence here," it stated, "is in fact to turn Tibet into a colony or protectorate of a foreign country."

At one o'clock in the afternoon of April 18, a few hours after his arrival in Tezpur, the Dalai Lama boarded a special train for the three-day ride to his newly designated residence, the former British hill station of Mussoorie in the mountains north of New Delhi. Riding in a private saloon, behind the long, black barrel-nosed steam engine of Indian Railways, a pilot train clearing the tracks in advance, the Tibetans headed west across the dusty northern edge of the subcontinent, traversing Assam, Bengal, Bihar, and finally Uttar Pradesh, where, turning due north, they approached Dehra Dun, the railhead eighteen miles from Mussoorie. Tens of thousands of white-clad Indian students and laborers lined the train's route, choking the stations it passed through, chanting *"Dalai Lama Ki Jai —Dalai Lama Zindabad."* ("Hail to the Dalai Lama—Long live the Dalai Lama.") Along the empty tracks between towns, farmers waited for hours on the edges of their fields, palms pressed together in reverence, for a glimpse of the holy presence. At the major stops of Siliguri, Benares and Lucknow, Tenzin Gyatso left the saloon to address mass gatherings. It was not until early in the morning on April 21, as the Dalai Lama drove into the cool, pine-covered slopes of Mussoorie, the snow-capped peak of Nanda Devi visible in the distance, that his month-long, 1,500-mile journey concluded at Birla House, a summer resort owned by the powerful Birla family.

Located on a pine-and-oak-covered promontory overlooking Happy Valley on the outskirts of Mussoorie, Birla House was built in the style of an English country home: two stories marked by steep dormers above a prominent veranda and a terraced garden filled with irises, lilies and blue and white violets. Inside, it was furnished in deep-backed chairs and couches, portraits of Gandhi and Nehru interspersed with paintings of Hindu gods and goddesses on the walls. There was a large radio in the drawing room before which the Dalai Lama and his Cabinet soon began listening to news bulletins while a chamber next to the Dalai Lama's bedroom on the second floor was converted into a shrine for meditation. With Tenzin Gyatso and his family isolated behind Birla House's new fourteen-foot-high barbed-wire fence and the Tibetan government quartered mainly at the Happy Valley Club, headquarters of the Provincial Armed Constabulary, a thick security screen of roadblocks and undercover agents effectively sealed the Tibetans from all contact with the press or other visitors.

On April 24, three days after the Dalai Lama's arrival at Birla House, Prime Minister Nehru drove through the streets of Mussoorie, dressed in his traditional tight white pants, black knee-length coat, buttonholed rose and Congress Party cap, to loud cheers from thousands of hill folk and vacationers. Stopping to address a convention of travel agents, his ostensible reason for making the trip, Nehru commented that he had come to fulfill "an old engagement," not realizing he would "meet a big traveler." In response to a reporter's question he pointed out that India's interest in Tibet was "historical, sentimental and religious and not essentially political." "Our entire policy," Nehru said, his words clearly directed to Peking, "whether it relates to cooperative farming, community development or industrial expansion, is based on cooperation." After inviting the Panchen Lama and other Chinese officials to visit the Dalai Lama and see for themselves that he was not held "under duress," Nehru drove past the police tent pitched at the gate of Birla House and posed with the Tibetan leader for a brief round of photographs on the lawn. The two men then retired inside, where they conferred for almost four hours, assisted only by an interpreter. "I explained the full situation to Nehru," recounted the Dalai Lama. "His advice was to rest and consider things well without being hasty. Like a true, old friend he showed every sign of sympathy. It gave me happiness and hope. Yet at the same time, he cautioned me in line with reality. So because of this I felt a little discouraged, somewhat helpless, in fact." The "reality," Nehru made clear, was that, although offering "sympathy," India would never substantially support the cause of Tibetan independence. "I mentioned casually to Pandit Nehru," continued the Dalai Lama, "that we had established a temporary government in southern Tibet. He became slightly agitated. 'We are not going to recognize your government,' he said immediately. You see, I think we came from Tibet with some blind, unreasonable hope that with support we could still make a stand. But after discussing these matters with the Indian government we realized that, in reality, it was not so easy. Despite their sympathy they had to follow their policy of complete nonalignment. Of course, Pandit Nehru was a very knowledgeable and a greatly experienced person. But I think because of the Tibetan crisis he must have gotten a lot of headaches."

Nehru indeed found himself in an increasingly complex situation. The initial discussion of Tibet in the Indian Parliament took place in late March and early April and gave way, in May, to a lively, often acrimonious debate. While India's Communist Party articulated China's view of the crisis, accusing the government of entertaining designs on Tibet, virtually all of the other opposition parties labeled Nehru's stand as one of appeasement. The previous year, Acharya Kripalani, leader of the Praja Socialists, had condemned Panch Sheel as "born in sin to put the seal of our approval on the destruction of an ancient nation." Now India's leading politicians castigated their Prime Minister for failing to stand up to Peking, whose successful conquest of Tibet paved the way for a direct attack on the country's northern regions, parts of which China already claimed as properly belonging to itself. "I cannot understand how it is possible to be friendly with this nation with this mentality," said Kripalani. "Yet our efforts to save it [friendship] will only result in this: They will not give us credit for good intentions. They will only give us credit for cowardice." "The tragedy of Tibet hangs heavily on our conscience," asserted K. M. Munshi. "For a young independent nation like ours, with its spiritual heritage, our handling of the Tibetan situation has been a crime in history."

While admitting shock "beyond measure" at Peking's charges, Nehru refused to alter his position, insisting it was of "the greatest consequence" that India and China get along. Indispensable to this was the Dalai Lama's good behavior. Given the current atmosphere, a Sino-Indian war could be sparked by the slightest provocation—a conflict India was utterly unprepared to fight. Recognizing that as a guest in India his position, and with it Tibet's sole hope for an independent future, hung in the balance, Tenzin Gyatso temporarily took Nehru's advice to "rest" and "consider things well" and set about adjusting to his new state in life.

The great changes in the Dalai Lama's circumstances soon became apparent. By public demand, he commenced giving a weekly *darshan* or blessing from a silk-draped chair on a rickety wooden stage at one end of the Birla House lawn. As summer began, Tibet's exiled "God-King" turned into Mussoorie's greatest tourist attraction until, on June 3, after being showered with rose petals by an audience of five thousand well-wishers and called to reappear twice on a balcony by latecomers chanting "*Darshan! Darshan!*" his ministers, already in a storm over many Indians' attempts to shake hands with "the Presence," canceled all future appearances. Tenzin Gyatso, though, took eagerly not only to shaking hands but also to abolishing almost all of the centuries-old protocol surrounding him. "In the past there was too much formality. You couldn't talk, you couldn't even breathe freely," he commented. "I hate being formal. Now, the new circumstances made it easier for me to change things. In this way, you see, becoming a refugee was actually useful. It brought me much closer to reality. And also it deepened my understanding of religion, particularly impermanence. Although the world is always changing one never notices it. Then suddenly your home, friends and country all are gone. It showed how futile it is to hold on to such things."

While the Dalai Lama adapted, Indian officials paradoxically did their best to maintain past protocol. Three years after his arrival confusion still reigned, demonstrated by the experience of one journalist who having been instructed not to touch or to turn away from the Dalai Lama, stumbled backwards toward the door at the conclusion of his audience. For a moment the Dalai Lama looked on amused. Then he strode quickly after the reporter, took him by his shoulders, turned him around and gave a friendly push.

Within two months the Dalai Lama's self-imposed silence ended. Since early April thousands of refugees had begun streaming over the Himalayan passes leading into Bhutan, Sikkim, Nepal and India. With them came news of a wholesale effort on the part of China to uproot Tibetan society and culture. As they had been in Kham, "democratic reforms" were about to be imposed: collectivization of property and labor, class division, daily political "reeducation," dismantling of the clergy, as well as plans for an influx of Han settlers to begin the Sinicization of Tibet. In addition, there were reports not just of mass imprisonment and execution but of repeated atrocities, torture, rape and dismemberment, carried out directly by the newly established Military Control Committees in each region. The full dimension of Tibet's tragedy now compelled the Dalai Lama, against Nehru's admonishments, to launch a campaign for international support.

On June 20, Tenzin Gyatso held his first news conference. Under a large shamiana or open-sided tent, pitched on the lawn of Birla House, scores of reporters listened to the Dalai Lama read a lengthy statement cataloguing the destruction in Tibet, while identifying China's ultimate aim as "the extermination of the religion and culture and even the absorption of the Tibetan race." He called for an international commission to investigate the reports of atrocities, made clear that the Seventeen-Point Agreement was abrogated and stated: "Where I am, accompanied by my government, the Tibetan people recognize us as the government of Tibet. I will return to Lhasa," he added, "when I obtain the rights and powers which Tibet enjoyed and exercised prior to 1950."

The Dalai Lama's most immediate concern, however, was the problem of refugees. By the end of June almost 20,000 Tibetans had fled their homeland, the first of repeated waves of exodus, eventually totaling 100,000. While those closest to the border had been compelled to scale the world's highest and least frequented passes, others, traveling inland from Kham and Amdo, had fought their way free in running battles lasting three and four months. These saw their ranks drastically reduced; a typical group of 125 survivors, who reached Assam in June, reported that they had set out 4,000 strong. Most of the refugees were starving or wounded, ill from the low altitude and stunned by a profound culture shock on descending to an alien world. "During the summer of 1959 my immediate task was to somehow save the refugees," said the Dalai Lama. "They came just as the hot season started, wearing heavy boots and long robes which had to be burned, as they were completely useless. It was necessary to take very close care of their health. Then, with the little knowledge we possessed, we took it as our duty to tell these 'fresh' refugees that it was not so easy to return to Tibet. 'We will have to remain in India for a longer period than expected,' we said. 'We will have to settle mentally as well as physically.' "

Two large transit camps had been established to handle the influx: one called Missamari, located ten miles from Tezpur; the other, Buxa Duar, a former British prisoner-of-war camp situated near the Bhutanese border in West Bengal. The camps represented an effort not only of the Indian government but also of the opposition parties, who, led by Acharya Kripalani, united to create a Central Relief Committee that was instrumental in obtaining food, medical supplies and international aid. Disinfected, fingerprinted, interrogated by Indian intelligence, issued blue-green trousers and brown bush shirts, the mixture of monks, guerrillas and families waited in barracks to be dispersed for road work to the cooler regions of northern India, a plan the Dalai Lama and New Delhi had jointly devised to check the growing number of fatalities. As July began, the first group left Buxa, to be followed shortly by hundreds more, deployed over a twelve-hundred-mile arc across the Himalayas. With their own limited chances for survival lay the sole hope for Tibet's eventual self-determination.

AFTER THREE DAYS of tramping over the 25,000-foot mountains dividing Tibet and Bhutan, Tempa Tsering, his parents and two younger sisters faced their goal. Beneath them stretched the heavily wooded slopes of the southern Himalayas, breaking for the first time in days the uncharted wilderness of brilliant snow-capped summits, ridges and defiles that they had struggled through. Six months earlier, the revolt had been crushed. Tempa's father, Chopel Dhondub,* together with all the able-bodied men in the village of Drumpa, had been imprisoned by the PLA. Released, he was rearrested after only a few weeks, and then freed again, just in time to see his wife beaten and denounced in *thamzing* or public "struggle session." He then received notice that Tempa, though only ten years old, was to be sent away with thousands of other Tibetan children for education in China. Frightened of losing their only son, Tempa's parents decided to flee.

In the middle of October 1959, Chopel Dhondub led his family out of Drumpa. Departing after midnight, his wife and their five- and eight-year-old daughters hurried from the village in silence. A short while later, he and Tempa followed, leaving the door of their home unbolted so as not to arouse suspicion. Trailed by their dog, who refused to be turned back, the family walked east, carrying a few bags of food and clothing, before heading south, off the track, into the mountains separating Lhoka from Bhutan. Climbing all night, they ascended to 18,000 feet. The two girls clung to their parents' backs, Tempa walked between, holding their hands. With each step forward the adults sank waist deep into freshly fallen powder that rendered the ascent extremely difficult. As dawn broke, they stopped to sleep behind a boulder, huddled together on a blanket on the

*Most Tibetans lack a shared family name and are known by personal names only.

snow. Only then did they realize that their dog had disappeared, stuck, most likely, in a drift and unable to free himself.

On waking at sunset, Tempa's family gazed out over a vaulted world of jagged peaks and indigo sky, the sere umber-colored hills of Tibet beginning to glow in the fading light far below. After a brief meal of melted snow, dried meat and roasted barley, they moved upward again, the moonlight so bright on the snow and ice that their eyes had to be shielded every few steps. By dawn all were exhausted. Tempa's youngest sister had started vomiting from the thin air and altitude; the others had lost their appetites. Without eating, they fell asleep under an overhang in a depression between spires. The next night the trek continued. At three in the morning a needle-thin ridge suddenly loomed ahead. One at a time, Chopel Dhondub led his children and wife carefully across an invisible chasm dropping away in the darkness to either side. Once the ridge had been safely negotiated, however, the incline gradually descended. Camping again in the snow, they awoke the following afternoon and, less fearful of capture, traversed a wide, saddleback slope until, with the sun setting and the wall of mountains they had passed through now rising behind them, the foothills of Bhutan came into view. The family would have been greatly relieved if it was not for the condition of their youngest child. For two days she had refused to eat or drink. Throughout the last march she had lain limply on her mother's back, unresponsive to attempts at reviving her. Listening anxiously to her daughter's labored breathing, Tempa's mother called out toward four o'clock that the child was "not keeping well at all." The group came to a halt about an hour above the tree line. Sitting down, Tempa's mother lifted her daughter from her back and began to rock her. At that moment, while the others looked on, the little girl stopped breathing. "It was a shock," recalled Tempa. "One moment she was alive and the next, just when the worst of the climb was over, she died."

As the sun sank below the last ranges, Tempa and his family wept over the corpse. Finally, Chopel Dhondub took his youngest daughter's extra clothes from one of the bags they had brought, dressed her small body in them, and scooped out a shallow grave. He then buried his child, covering her face with packed snow. Still weeping, the family set off down the mountain. Four hours later, among boulders and waist-high shrubs, they laid out their blanket, made their first hot tea in three days and fell asleep.

Tempa and his family now lay on the edge of a world that in every respect was unknown to them. Once before Chopel Dhondub had traded in Bhutan. He, at least, had seen a forest. The others never had. As with many of the refugees coming from Tibet, their knowledge of the globe consisted of a vague image of China and India, beyond both of which, they thought, stretched only the great ocean. Unaware that the Dalai Lama had escaped—the Chinese having kept his departure secret—the family, now that its flight was complete, had no further goal. As a result, on the following day they simply took the first path they found, which, after another night's camping in the forest, led to a village.

To the Tibetans, the local Bhutanese, wearing knee-length checkerboard robes and short, braidless hair, looked like fellow countrymen who, lost for generations, had fallen into an odd, half-remembered mimicry of their ancestors' ways. To the Bhutanese, however, the refugees were anything but strange. Since early spring thousands had already come this way, disoriented and sick, not a few of them starving. In the immediate aftermath of the uprising, the Bhutanese government had closed the main passes, fearful that China would exact reprisals if the refugees were permitted to enter. But with the great influx of religious and political figures, some of whom were related to the royal family itself, they finally modified their policy. Tibetans were subsequently permitted to pass through the kingdom on condition that they proceed to India. Although some 4,000 refugees eventually remained in Bhutan, the rest were forced to beg their way across the country, bartering the few pieces of jewelry, images and *thankas* they possessed, so that, on their egress a month later, most were destitute. Following the pattern, Tempa, his parents and sister traversed Bhutan, camping in the woods by night, begging in hamlets each day.

Within a week a routine emerged. Arriving at the outskirts of a village, the family divided into two teams, mother and daughter in one, father and son in the other. Passing from house to house, they appealed for whatever leftover food, mainly rice and vegetables, the inhabitants would spare. Returning to their camp outside the town, they ate and then continued traveling. Discovering that people were more generous to the children, Chopel Dhondub instructed his son to beg alone, but this, though profitable, only increased Tempa's already persistent fear of getting lost, an anxiety they all shared. Unlike Tibet's limitless vistas, the abundant forest, so thick that it often blocked out the sky, created intense claustrophobia worsened by the constant fear of separation. Dread of what lay hidden among the trees increased the Tibetans' unease. Tigers, wild boars and poisonous insects were all present. Tempa's father warned the children about snakes, describing them as creatures who resembled the black and white ropes used by Tibetan traders but who moved. No vigilance, however, was sufficient to guard against the omnipresent leeches. Each day they would latch on unnoticed and gradually swell with blood up to two inches in length. Salt and fire were the sole antidotes. Preserving their few matches for campfires, Tempa and his family begged for salt for the leeches and wrapped themselves in their hot Tibetan clothing. Through it all, Tempa's mother wept continually over the loss of her daughter. In the few words they exchanged before sleep each night, the others never mentioned the tragedy for fear of upsetting her more.

As the family's trek across Bhutan progressed, they met other refugees, flowing like so many rivulets down through Thimbu, the capital, and thence to India. Finally, after five weeks of walking, they entered a large meadow in the woods filled with Tibetans preparing to cross the Indian border two days beyond. Among them, Tempa's father found a family he knew. He joined their cooking fire, and the two groups exchanged accounts. Entering India together, they arrived a few days later at Buxa.

Located in an airless pocket between three jungle-covered hills, Buxa's thirty concrete barracks, enclosed by a high barbed-wire perimeter, presented a dismal setting. At the time of Tempa's admittance, thousands of refugees were bivouacked inside and outside the camp's gates, the majority incapacitated from the heat and low altitude. To relieve overcrowding, the Indian government had begun shipping out sizable contingents, either for road work or to the more spacious transit camp at Missamari, where, after two weeks, Tempa and his family themselves were transferred. "We left Buxa in a large group and walked about two miles to the railroad," recalled Tempa. "Everyone was discussing the train. No one had ever seen one; we had only heard its new Tibetan name, *rili,* from the English word 'rail.' I was very excited listening to people talk about big houses that moved, but when we first arrived there was so much rushing that I had no chance to look." Herded by Indian police into a narrow passage dividing two stacks of triple-level wooden bunks, Tempa managed to get a window seat, from which vantage point he soon received a terrific shock. "It was so funny," he remembered. "When the train started I actually thought the mountains were moving out, not us. I was staring through the window and thinking, 'How do these mountains move so quickly?' I just couldn't understand it." By nightfall, though, as the train turned south and the Himalayas vanished, he had begun to adjust. Then, after a second night, they arrived at a town called Rangapari from where the refugees were driven in trucks to the new camp.

Externally, Missamari was larger and less depressing than Buxa. Built on a sandy flat by a river in the jungle, the camp comprised 150 bamboo barracks laid out in neat rows. Up to 100 people lived in each. Around them grew a profusion of kitchen vegetables; cucumber vines, which had blanketed many of the buildings' roofs in only a few months, offering a modicum of shade against the tropical sun. Up until the arrival of Tempa's family, Missamari's almost 15,000 inhabitants had been predominantly men: Khampa fighters and monks who had fled Lhasa in the midst of the uprising. They had already experienced the worst of camp life. At Missamari, erected for the Tibetans in little more than two weeks, the water supply was contaminated, sanitation was inadequate and the rations of potato curry, rice and lentils, though plentiful, were detrimental to a people accustomed solely to a diet of barley, butter and meat. The result had been an epidemic of deadly amoebic dysentery. Smoke from the cremation ground on the riverbank five hundred yards away drifted over the barracks daily. Old and young died first, unable to resist the infection, succumbing usually in a day or two. Weeping was the most noticeable sound in the campground, occasionally mixed with the rapid hum of a sutra, recited by a lone monk now dressed in government-issue clothing like all the rest.

Tempa spent almost three months in Missamari. Each day his family sat listlessly on their beds, hearing of a new death. Their sole consolation was the hope that soon, led by the Dalai Lama, they would return to Tibet. Constantly, illogically, they spoke of it. There seemed little doubt that their stay in India could only be temporary. By late winter of 1960, however, a Tibetan official in the camp announced that they would soon be sent north for road work. Chopel Dhondub deduced that a return to Tibet was far less likely from a road gang than from Missamari itself. With this realization the family lost their resolve. Unaffected till now, both Tempa and his remaining sister contracted dysentery. In spite of the small white tablets given to her at the camp's dispensary, the little girl's health failed rapidly. Her periodic outdoor playing—from which she often ran inside, frightened on seeing a dark-skinned Indian—ceased. She stayed in bed all day, too weak to move or eat. A short while before the family was to leave for road work, Tempa's second sister died.

Two days later, Tempa and his parents were put on a train, their destination unknown. During the ride Tempa's mother refused to let go of him. Too distraught to eat, she wept continually, repeating over and over, "We escaped the Chinese only to bury our bodies in a foreign land." Tempa's father sat listlessly beside his wife, speechless from the loss. After three days on the train, the 160 refugees on board disembarked at a small town before the foothills of the western Himalayas. A Tibetan government official greeted them at the railway station, but his Indian counterpart had failed to show up. For three days more the travelers camped on the platform, during which time their first Tibetan New Year's in exile came and went without celebration. When their presence was eventually discovered, they were taken by truck to a group of old army tents, torn and patched after years of use, pitched in uneven lines on a rocky slope near an Indian village called Bawarna. A few hundred yards distant, down a path through pine trees, lay the head of the road construction.

Work began a week later. A whistle blew at 7:45 each morning and the refugees proceeded through the woods to the road. Standing for roll call taken by Indian overseers, they were divided into groups of ten; men were given axes and crowbars to cut and clear trees, women shovels to dig the roadbed, children baskets to remove dirt and stones. With an hour's break for lunch, they labored until 5:00 p.m., receiving little more than a rupee, or 10 cents, a day, just enough to purchase rice and once a week some meat and vegetables. Shopping in the village after work, the refugees had their first unofficial contact with Indians.

As they discovered, in common with one road group after another, contact with the local people, though necessary, was often hazardous. Whatever infectious diseases were present among the inhabitants—tuberculosis in particular—passed indiscriminately to the Tibetans, who, lacking the proper antibodies, most often died. Within a few months of the exiles' arrival in India it became clear that the task of transition was not only more threatening than that of escape, but so universally destructive, affecting virtually every family, that the survival of the refugees as a coherent group was itself called into question. In many cases, a visible illness could not even be found as the cause of death. The Tibetans themselves attributed such fatalities simply to heartbreak and the shock of exile. Tempa's mother now appeared afflicted by just such a malaise. After two weeks on the road she lacked the strength to work and took to the straw and blanket the family used for a bed in their tent. Compelled to labor in order to eat, Tempa and his father were unable to tend to her. In the evenings they carried her to Bawarna's small clinic, but the medical worker in charge could find no specific symptoms to treat. Still devastated by the loss of her two daughters, she lingered alone until, one Sunday, the Tibetan official in charge of the road camp arranged for a visit to nearby Dharamsala, the Dalai Lama's new residence, to which he had shifted from Mussoorie a few months before.

After driving for two hours, the road workers were let off in a small hillside hamlet called McLeod Ganj just above the main town of Dharamsala. From there, Chopel Dhondub carried his wife on his back up the steep cobblestone path leading to the Dalai Lama's residence. At its entrance, the group passed through a security check and then were directed onto a narrow strip of lawn before a veranda on the south side of a large house. The Dalai Lama appeared and they all prostrated. The young leader spoke of plans and improvements underway, after which they filed by to receive his blessing. Then the brief audience ended. Two days later, back in

Bawarna, Tempa's mother looked up at her husband and son from bed and said, "Now that I have seen His Holiness I feel relieved. If I die, that is my fate. I'm satisfied." The next day Tempa's father sent him to work alone. That night his mother held his hand and remarked, "Now you must take care of your father. One day, I know, you will go back to Tibet." When Tempa returned from work the following day, his mother was dead.

Two weeks later Chopel Dhondub began vomiting. As with the children, his state quickly deteriorated. He was taken to a hospital in Palampur, an hour's drive away. Tempa, just approaching his eleventh birthday, was left alone in the tent his mother had died in. In the mornings, the Tibetan government official collected him for work, telling the Indian overseers not to demand too much labor from him. In the evenings, he walked the boy into Bawarna to buy him sweets. Each night Tempa lay alone crying, terrified that his father would die as well and leave him orphaned. Miraculously, Chopel Dhondub returned a week later, enervated but alive.

Yet another separation was in store. There were forty children in Tempa's road gang, all of whom, it was decided, were to be sent to the newly established nursery in Dharamsala, set up in the spring of 1960 to care for the hundreds of young people left bereaved on the roads. On hearing the news, Tempa refused to leave his father. Even when Chopel Dhondub assured his son that he was out of danger, insisting that there was no future for him carrying dirt and stones on a road gang, Tempa remained obdurate. But the adults were not dissuaded. Distraught, Tempa was packed onto a bus and driven in tears to Dharamsala, separated, finally, from everything he had known. It was a year before he heard from his father again. In the interim, a new life, pieced together by the Dalai Lama and the Tibetan government-in-exile, began to take shape for him and the others of his generation.

WHILE REFUGEES CONTINUED to descend throughout the summer and autumn of 1959, the Dalai Lama pushed forward his effort to obtain international support for Tibet. Responding to his call for an impartial inquiry, the International Commission of Jurists launched an investigation into the manifold accounts of Chinese atrocities as well as Tibet's international legal status. After compiling an initial document by the end of July, a full report was issued one year later. In it, the commission concluded that, despite the ambiguity shrouding its legal status, Tibet had, in reality, been a fully sovereign state, independent in both fact and law of Chinese dominion. Regarding violations of human rights, the commission determined that Red China was guilty of "the gravest crime of which any person or nation can be accused—the intent to destroy, in whole or in part, a national, ethnic, racial or religious group as such"—genocide.

Bolstered by the International Commission of Jurists' preliminary findings, the Dalai Lama left Mussoorie by train on September 8. Arriving at the Old Delhi station by six o'clock the next morning, he was greeted by thousands of Indian supporters, driven to Hyderabad House, the Indian State Guest House, and then on to confer with Nehru at the Prime Minister's residence Teen Murti. There, he disclosed the reason for his trip. "It was my decision, despite strong opposition from India, to approach the United Nations," recounted the Dalai Lama. "To begin with, I personally met with the Prime Minister to explain our stand. After listening, Nehru said, 'Now that you've decided to appeal, all right, go ahead.' At that moment, I really felt how beautiful freedom is. Our right was accepted although we had been discouraged against this whole idea of approaching the UN. Because of my past experience with the Chinese it was almost unthinkable; an extraordinary surprise within my lifetime."

Having obtained Nehru's assent, Tenzin Gyatso cabled the United Nations Secretary-General, Dag Hammarskjöld, the same day, prepared a delegation to follow and then embarked on an unprecedented round of diplomatic calls, attempting to raise support for the appeal. "Compared to the Dalai Lama of today, I myself was a bit confused," said the Dalai Lama, reflecting on his visits to New Delhi's diplomatic corps. "It's always more useful to talk person to person, but sometimes it was hard to know how to start. Then, gradually, my own style grew. I had more courage to express myself and was less concerned about diplomatic formalities. During 1959, though, I lacked this confidence in myself. Therefore it was very difficult sometimes. I used to be quite anxious."

His efforts, nevertheless, proved out. As a result of them, Ireland and Malaya co-sponsored Tibet's case to the Steering Committee of the General Assembly, where, unlike its cursory dismissal in 1950, the issue was now debated in depth. In many respects the discussion reflected that of India's Parliament. As introduced by the sponsoring nations, Tibet's plight was depicted primarily as one involving human rights; the underlying issue of its nationhood was ignored, as the Chinese Nationalists on Taiwan, though not in occupation, also claimed sovereignty. In his opening comments, Dato Ismail Kamil, Malaya's representative, cited the conclusions of the International Commission of Jurists' initial report, which maintained that "almost all the rights which together allow the full and legitimate expression of human personality appear to be denied to the Tibetans at the present time, and in most cases for some time past." "On the basis of the available evidence," the report concluded, "it would seem difficult to recall a case in which ruthless oppression of man's essential dignity has been more systematically and efficiently carried out." In his rebuttal, Vasily Kuznetsov, the Soviet Union's representative, dismissed the report's validity, accused the appeal's sponsors of attempting to "utilize the United Nations in order to intensify the Cold War," and maintained that "a nonexistent Tibetan question has been fabricated in order to worsen the international situation and the atmosphere in the Assembly." Like India's own Marxists, the entire Communist bloc, following Russia's lead, voiced Peking's view of the Tibetan issue as a matter "wholly and completely within the domestic competence of the Chinese People's Republic," even the discussion of which "would constitute a gross and wholly unjustified interference" into China's internal affairs. Thus, Tibet's case—just as Nehru had predicted—fell immediate victim to the broader global conflict. Nonetheless, by meeting's end a large majority voted to include the issue on the agenda of the 14th General Assembly, where many Third World countries joined Western democracies in passing a resolution in Tibet's favor by a vote of 45 to 9 (with 26 abstentions). Though not identifying the People's Republic of China by name, it called for "respect for the fundamental human rights of the Tibetan people and for their distinctive cultural and religious life." As continued reports of atrocities and wholesale destruction were brought out by repeated waves of refugees from Tibet, two more resolutions were passed in 1961 and 1965. In these the United Nations considerably stiffened its language. It not only registered, as in the second resolution, "grave concern" and "deep anxiety" over the "severe hardships" imposed on the Tibetans through the "suppression of their distinctive cultural and religious life," but "solemnly" renewed its call "for the cessation of practices which deprive the Tibetan people of their fundamental human rights and freedoms, including most importantly their right to self-determination."

In December 1959, with the initial UN appeal behind him and the end of his first year in exile drawing near, Tenzin Gyatso went on pilgrimage. At Bodh Gaya, site of the Buddha's enlightenment, he stayed in the Tibetan monastery within sight of the great second-century Mahabodhi Temple next to the Bodhi Tree, under which the Buddha had attained nirvana. Here the Dalai Lama met with some sixty representatives of the refugeees, who pledged their continued efforts to fight for Tibet's freedom. Afterwards, for the first time in his life, he ordained a group of 162 monks. Then, traveling on to the Deer Park at Sarnath, where the Buddha's first sermon had been delivered, the Dalai Lama drove with a typically reduced entourage of sixteen through a crowd of 2,000 weeping Tibetans who were camped around tea stalls beneath the trees, selling old clothes and a few of the valuables that they had managed to retain. Remaining for two weeks, he gave religious teachings in the traditional Tibetan style, seated on a high brocade-draped throne before the crowd. At their conclusion, Tenzin Gyatso spoke for an hour in the advisory manner he would address his people with from now on, presenting a long-range plan he had conceived, in which the exiles' reconstruction and their struggle for Tibet's independence would be combined. "For the moment Tibet's sun and moon have suffered an eclipse," said the Dalai Lama, "but one day we will regain our country. You should not lose heart. The great job ahead of us now," he revealed, "is to preserve our religion and culture."

4

Reconstruction

1960–1974

THE DALAI LAMA'S vision of exile society took root in his new headquarters, an abandoned British hill station called Dharamsala, located a day west of New Delhi on the northern margin of the Punjab. Perched across the lower ridges of the Dhauladar Range, a plumb barrier of snow-capped peaks fencing in the Kangra Valley, Dharamsala had been established by the British in the early 1860s as the summer seat of the Jullundur Division. Beginning with a military cantonment on the shoulder of the tallest crest, Mun Peak, they had gone on to found a small town, McLeod Ganj, on a slender ridge facing the plains below. A colonnade was erected to house shops, fronted by a genteel park of cedar trees, a birdbath and stone benches. Down the hill rose the rusticated belfry of St. John's in the Wilderness, an Anglican church, while, scattered well apart over the slopes, more than a hundred bungalows sprang up, sporting turrets and gingerbread woodwork, vaulted ceilings and multiple wings, and dubbed with a bevy of romantic names such as Ivanhoe, Eagle's Nest, Chestnut Villa, Wargrave and Retreat.

By the turn of the century, McLeod Ganj supported one of the most vigorous societies, outside the cities, of any in the Raj. With the rail line put through to Pathankot, seven miles from the foothills, bureaucrats from both Delhi and Lahore flocked to the mountains. In the spring the woods were blanketed with primrose, mistletoe and red and mauve rhododendron, followed in June, after the onset of the monsoon, by an explosion of buttercups, violets and honeysuckle. Wildlife abounded: leopards, panthers, porcupines, foxes, jackals, hyenas, red-faced monkeys and huge white-maned langurs roamed the lower hills, joined in the colder months, when they descended to forage, by black and brown bears. Above McLeod Ganj hawks and white-bellied vultures wheeled in wide gyres on all sides. Partridges, pigeons, ravens and snow pheasants flew tamely into town. Slated to become the summer capital of the Raj, Dharamsala's future seemed secure until an earthquake struck in 1905. The British picked Simla instead and those local officials who remained relocated their offices 1,500 feet down the hillside to the less exposed Lower Dharamsala. On August 15, 1947—India's independence day—they departed as well.

Only one man remained to preside over the spectral life of McLeod Ganj: N. N. Nowrojee. As proprietors of a general merchandise "Oilman" or "Europe Store" as they were called, the Nowrojee family had lived in Dharamsala since its inception. Parsees, they had journeyed to India themselves as refugees, fleeing religious persecution in Persia over a thousand years before. The family line had remained intact and, with the founding of their own business in McLeod Ganj, become, to generations of British bureaucrats, something of the hamlet's guardian spirit. Entrusted now with dozens of abandoned bungalows, N. N. Nowrojee, fifth proprietor of Nowrojee and Sons, unsuccessfully sought to bring the village back to life. For twelve years he offered the buildings free of charge to schools and as tourist lodges to the state government, but there were no takers. Finally, on hearing through friends of the central government's hunt for a permanent residence for the Dalai Lama, he approached New Delhi directly. His tale of a forgotten ghost town wasting in the woods proved intriguing enough to warrant inspection, following which, to his surprise, Delhi deemed it ideal. First, however, the Tibetans had to agree. "Pandit Nehru personally chose Dharamsala for us, based on what he called its 'peace and tranquillity,'" recounted the Dalai Lama. "From our viewpoint, though, it had good as well as bad sides. Delhi is the nerve center. The nearer to Delhi, the better the communication. Dharamsala's disadvantages, then, were clear. But we also saw its potential. It was open and there was more room to expand. Thus, after complaining at first that we were reluctant to move, once our officials visited and formed a good opinion, we decided to shift."

On April 29, 1960, after a little more than a year's stay, the Dalai Lama left Mussoorie. Traveling by overnight train to Pathankot, he was met at the station the following afternoon by state and municipal authorities, as well as a few thousand Tibetan refugees en route to Dalhousie for road work. Pausing to console the crowd, many of whom were weeping uncontrollably at the sight of their leader in such reduced circumstances, Tenzin Gyatso admonished them not to lose courage, promising that "one day we will go back to Tibet." Then, led by an escort of police jeeps, he began the two-hour drive up the narrow, boulder-strewn valleys leading to Dharamsala, the shining white summits of the Dhauladar Range rising ahead.

"It was a very small town," recalled the Dalai Lama of his first sight of Lower Dharamsala, "but the local people gave me a hearty welcome—all they had to offer." Driving slowly past the old British post office, police station and district headquarters, Tenzin Gyatso's motorcade entered the tumbling warren of fruit and vegetable stalls, open-air barbershops, tailors, cobblers and sweet-sellers cluttered around the main street bisecting Katwali Bazaar. Three thousand people, hill folk in their bright embroidered mountain caps, Sikhs in scarlet and blue turbans, bureaucrats and businessmen wearing black suits, their wives clad in diaphanous saris, and even Gurkhas, descended from the still-active army cantonment, lined the route showering their new neighbor with flowers, one of which carried a small caterpillar, which, as the Dalai Lama reminisced, rather ungraciously bit him on the leg. With the sun tinting the adjacent dome of Mun Peak violet, the column drove five miles more up steep switchbacks through the cantonment to McLeod Ganj, where at 5:00 p.m. it passed beneath a freshly hewn bamboo gate dressed in fir boughs and colored streamers, a big golden WELCOME written across its top. Behind it, 250 Tibetan refugees who had arrived a week before began performing full-length prostrations, while khaki-clad Indian police frantically urged them back. N.N. Nowrojee stepped forward, introduced himself and directed the Dalai Lama to a waiting jeep for the drive up the hair-raising track leading to his new home, Swarg Ashram. "When I arrived at Swarg Ashram it had become quite late, so I didn't see much," remarked the Dalai Lama. "The next morning I woke up at my normal time of five and the first thing I heard was a bird, peculiar to this place, chirping very loudly. Karakjok. Karakjok. Like that. Later I was told that one of our senior officials had been kept awake all night by this bird. Then I didn't engage in a meditation session, but just looked out at the mountains and the view. It was the first day of May 1960. A very nice day and quite hot."

Under Nowrojee's direction four bungalows had been renovated to accommodate the Tibetans. The original seat of the District Commissioner, Highcroft House, renamed Swarg Ashram or "The Heavenly Abode," had been chosen as the Dalai Lama's residence. Roughly a quarter of a mile above McLeod Ganj, the building occupied a small flat on the western edge of the mountainside. The view was astounding, the entire enclosure seemingly anchored on a buttress of rock flung into space, yet the house itself was almost windowless, a thirty-two-room behemoth, one-storied, with cavernous chambers lit by trap-like dormers and heated in winter by only a few diminutive fireplaces. On its front end—turned sideways, for lack of room, to the vista—two giant bay windows jutted into a covered porch overlooking a narrow walkway, beyond which a stone wall dropped twenty feet to a grass lawn, previously used as a tennis court but soon to become an audience ground. Behind, three outbuildings, including the kitchen, rose on progressively higher and smaller levels up the mountain. While the three villas prepared to house the eighty government officials, the Dalai Lama's senior and junior tutors and New Delhi's liaison officer were even more removed, Swarg Ashram received the benefit of guard huts, barbed-wire fencing and, in time, a tall concrete gate, standing incongruously amidst the dark green pine groves cloaking the hillside, the sole emblem of the hidden compound's prestigious occupant.

From his first day in Dharamsala the Dalai Lama realized that he was very much alone in the woods. With the departure of the 250 refugees for road work a few weeks later, only Nowrojee remained in McLeod Ganj. Constantly on call, he supplied the Tibetans with everything from blankets, toiletries and thermoses to cooking oil and umbrellas. Life in Swarg Ashram itself was crowded. Behind the Dalai Lama's monastic bedroom, prayer room and office—all at the front of the house—lived his mother, his two sisters, his brother-in-law P.T. Takla, the Masters of Robes, Ceremonies and Food, the Lord Chamberlain and an assortment of secretaries and translators. Both Tibetan and Indian guards patrolled the grounds, leaving the only free space beyond the gate. Soon after his arrival the Dalai Lama began trekking up the mountains, sometimes climbing as high as 16,000 feet to a pass below the pinnacle of Mun Peak, from where he would descend for the night to a hikers' lodge called Triund. Only a few companions accompanied him. "We used to climb very steep hills," remembered the Dalai Lama. "It would have been very difficult for the Indian guards to follow us. Poor fellows, they wore heavy boots, which had slippery nails in their soles, and they also carried large guns. So instead we had them put their rifles down and just wait below for our return. We were all very friendly. We often drank tea and ate together in a good meadow that I found in the woods. I really enjoyed it. That was one of my new experiences in Dharamsala and it had its own special beauty."

The Dalai Lama's life in Swarg Ashram was altogether different than that in Tibet. Its rigors included two to three buckets of water a day dripping during the monsoon from an unrepairable ceiling around his bed; its pleasures, snowmen and snowball fights the first winter, table tennis in the main sitting room, where Tenzin Gyatso took meals with his mother and, after office hours at five, a regular badminton game on the lawn before the porch. A novel series of pets including a young deer and a number of independent-minded Lhasa Apsos, added to the household's informal atmosphere.

Though the Dalai Lama found more time in Swarg Ashram for spiritual matters, the bulk of his day focused on the refugees' plight. By waging a constructive fight for Tibet, through the re-creation of Tibetan culture abroad, he was convinced that Peking's efforts to legitimize its rule over his homeland would fail. Moreover, such an effort not only would prevent the collapse of the refugee community but would offer the chance to modernize, if in embryo, Tibetan society, fashioning a template of sorts for the Tibet of the future, once its freedom was regained.

As a first step, the government had to be reconstituted. Using Mortimer Hall for a Secretariat, the Cabinet divided its ministers and workers among six portfolios: Home Affairs, Foreign Affairs, Religion and Culture, Education, Finance, and Security. A bureau was established in New Delhi to serve as the Tibetan link with the Indian government and the various international relief agencies that were coming to the refugees' aid. It was followed by four offices, in New York, Geneva, Tokyo and Katmandu, each in its way acting as an unofficial embassy for the government-in-exile. Ten civil service ranks, scaled up from the seven in Tibet, were created, while the Dalai Lama, assisted by Indian lawyers, set about drafting a democratic constitution upon which to found the first elected government in Tibet's history. Rehabilitation, however, was the immediate task at hand. "At the beginning of our work," related the Dalai Lama, "two factions existed among the community of our responsible people. One thought we Tibetans must concentrate in northern India; the other— including myself—felt that it didn't matter where we lived. The important thing was to find a place and settle properly so that we could preserve the Tibetan identity, culture and race." The Dalai Lama's view eventually won out, as northern India, despite its desirable proximity to Tibet's border, lacked large tracts of unused land. Once apprised of the Tibetans' wishes, Prime Minister Nehru canvassed the chief ministers of India's less populated southern states for vacant countryside. Karnataka responded affirmatively, offering an uninhabited stretch of jungle situated in gently rolling hills fifty-two miles west of Mysore. As a joint investigating team from Dharamsala and New Delhi soon discovered, the available land was wilderness, save for a single road running down from Mysore along which lay a few primitive villages. Regardless, its potential was equivalent to that of Dharamsala; whatever success the Tibetans managed to wrest from the land would be their own.

In the second week of December 1960, almost two years after their arrival in India, the first group of 666 Tibetan refugees left their camps along the northern thoroughfares to build permanent homes in the south. "No one had the slightest idea where we were going," recalled Lobsang Chonzin, a sturdy, aquiline-featured farmer who became leader of the settlement's first village. "A Tibetan government official told us that we had been chosen to pioneer new land. Then a few weeks later he came to put us on a special train that traveled south for three days. At the end, buses were waiting at a station in a big city. They took us straight into the countryside, further and further, until we finally saw our destination, a group of tents in a clearing in the middle of the jungle."

Unlike the subtropical rain forests of Bhutan and Assam, through which most of the refugees had passed, this new jungle, at the very heart of the Indian subcontinent, was psychologically as well as physically remote. The few mud-and-wattle villages the refugees had glimpsed from the buses as they drove through, hung with brilliant clusters of red peppers, bananas and mangoes, sheltered a small, dark race of semi-aboriginal people who looked altogether alien. The Tibetans' sense of displacement gave way to disorientation after the buses had gone and only a few Indian police stayed on to help organize homesteading. Aware that the primeval expanse surrounding them was the natural abode of elephants, tigers, wild boars and other dangerous animals, the settlers' first act was to fashion tall bamboo stakes into a protective rampart around one of the larger tents. Inside, they built a makeshift altar upon which to place a precious image of the Buddha given to them by the Dalai Lama. As night fell they dug pits, lined them with stones and cooked their first dinner. "We forced ourselves to eat," continued Chonzin, "but we all felt so frightened and forlorn that no one could speak. Many people sat helplessly on the ground crying to themselves. We could hear the calls of wild animals in the jungle and, unlike in Tibet, you couldn't see a thing. Wherever you looked there was nothing but trees."

Soon after dawn the following morning, a group of monks, seated before the sacred image in the tent, began praying for success. They continued for a week, after which the work of felling and burning the forest began. An ax, a saw and a machete were given to each family of five, and two rupees or twenty cents a day were paid out as salary by the Indian government. With new groups of 500 sent down from the north at six-month intervals the settlement, known as Byllakuppe, struggled into existence. "The heat was the worst," said Chonzin, shaking his head. "For two years, day and night, smoke and fire covered everything—even during the monsoon. Then we would work all day in the pouring rain and come home at night to find our tents blown down. Under these conditions many people died. They would recall Tibet, look at where they were and just give up." As fresh ground was broken a new danger appeared. Workers felling trees farthest from the tent camps repeatedly met and were often trampled to death by enraged elephants. A chain of guard huts had to be built around each clearing; these were manned day and night by sentries equipped with tin cans, gongs and firecrackers both to sound the alarm and to scare off intruders. The fight against the elephants took on almost mythic dimensions; settlers, armed with slingshots and other homemade weapons, walked warily through newly cut roads in the jungle, while those caught alone by an elephant not infrequently returned to their tents a day or two later, having spent the interim up a tree. In the midst of the besieged colony's travail, the Dalai Lama arrived on a tour of inspection. "During my first visit to Byllakuppe," he recalled, "the people made a special tent for me of bamboo walls and a canvas roof. Still, it could not keep out the tremendous dust produced by clearing the forest. Because of such circum-stances, the Tibetans were quite low-spirited. The death rate was high and due to the heat of the sun and burning trees all of them had become quite dark and thin." Confronted by a pervasive sense of hopelessness, the Dalai Lama offered the only encouragement he could—assurance of eventual prosperity. "Whenever I visited our larger settlements I always promised that we would prevail," he observed. "I pushed and pushed and pushed and finally, year by year, the picture completely changed. Then, when things got better I teased the people about their once dark, thin faces, which now had become quite healthy and smiling. I told them that in the past I was only making empty promises, because I myself, poor things, could offer them nothing. But those Tibetans always followed my word without the slightest doubt. As a result, we succeeded. It was just like watering an old flower about to wilt. If you water it with some hope it will immediately become fresh and enthusiastic."

Early in 1962, the first group of settlers moved into more than a hundred brick-walled, tile-roofed homes, taking their prized butter lamps, offering bowls and scarf-draped photos of the Dalai Lama with them. The first of Byllakuppe's eventual twenty villages, housing 10,000 people on 5,500 acres, camp No. 1 served as the prototype for virtually every refugee settlement developed over the next two decades. Little more than a year after its establishment, the inhabitants watched, along with those of camp No. 2, as their names were randomly pulled from a container and they were allotted an acre of land apiece. Thereafter, the attempt to transform Byllakuppe into a full-fledged farming community began.

Despite the fertile soil, it was not easy. A crop of lentils, cotton, tobacco and coriander sown on twenty-eight acres in 1961 had not done well. Then almost fifty times as much cotton and tobacco was sown, all of which failed dismally. Farming in southern India was so different from Tibet's unique high-altitude agronomy that it seemed the settlement would founder, until an agricultural adviser from a relief organization called Swiss Technical Co-operation arrived to offer guidance. Conducting soil tests, he determined that maize should be planted, sustained by fertilizer and farmed by tractors rather than the bullock plows the Tibetans were using. The new methods and crop worked. Maize proved so successful that by 1966, six years after its founding, the settlement was self-supporting. Three years after that, with 77,000 fruit trees planted, a dairy and poultry farm and a second crop of ragi (a cereal grass) raised to diversify the harvest, Byllakuppe was making a substantial profit on its produce.

By then 38 settlements harboring almost 60,000 people had sprung up throughout India, Nepal and Bhutan, all starting out on land too remote or inhospitable for local people to care for. After houses were built, farming often proved so recalcitrant that many settlements had to rely on traditional Tibetan handicrafts, such as carpet weaving, for their income. Yet by the early 1980s only 3,000 refugees remained on road gangs, while some 44 settlements, linked by commercial, political and religious ties, looking to Dharamsala as their capital, housed almost 100,000 refugees, the remnant having emigrated to twenty-four countries around the world.

The refugees' rehabilitation was further enhanced by what many international relief agencies working closely with the Tibetans came to consider an economic miracle. While a number of industrial efforts, including a woolen mill, lime plant, limestone quarry and fiberglass factory, all failed, the exiles found that collective marketing and purchasing, carried out through agricultural cooperatives, had an immense potential in India's chaotic economy. Once more Byllakuppe led the way. In 1964, the settlement's first six camps inaugurated a co-op, Luksum Samdup Ling ("Preserving Tradition-Fulfilling Wishes"). Sixteen years later, Byllakuppe's fourteen "new" camps founded a second co-op, Dickey Larso ("Revival of Happiness"). With funds from the Swiss Technical Co-operation and, later, from the Mysore Rehabilitation and Agriculture Development Agency, the co-ops transformed the settlement. Restaurants and stores were added to its villages; seed, fertilizer, trucks, a flour mill and dehusking machine purchased to boost production; and a large workshop built to fashion furniture, carts, knives, axes, and farming tools in the quest for self-sufficiency. Young men were sent to Norway, Denmark and Iran to be trained as tractor mechanics. On their return they expanded the settlement's motley fleet of Escorts, Soviet Zetors and Ford tractors, creating in the process a repair and machine shop that soon took over all the business for fifty miles around.

While the co-ops marketed the settlement's produce as far away as Bombay and Calcutta, individual settlers continued to ply a trade that came to account for the livelihood of almost a quarter of the refugee population: selling sweaters. Capitalizing on the success of a Tibetan hand-knit sweater business in Kalimpong, thousands of refugees began to sell gaudy green, purple, yellow and red machine-made products purchased from previously unpatronized Punjabi factories. Each winter they set up shop out of tin trunks on the sidewalks of bazaars and marketplaces all across India. Their success was such that by the latter half of the sixties a Tibetan sweater fad was sweeping the subcontinent. The sudden popularity of "Tibetan" sweaters enabled an average worker to earn up to 5,000 rupees or $626— seven times more than his or her wages on the road. The nomadic business of sweater-selling not only improved their diets, but also fulfilled the traditional Tibetan's love of trade and travel. Introduced through it to their host country, they used the opportunity to promote their cause; every sweater, stocking-cap, or scarf sold contained a small card that explained how the refugees had been forced down "from the roof of the world" to the "hot plains of the subcontinent."

A further resource came from the Dalai Lama's personal funds. Over a thousand pack animals had followed the Tibetan ruler's 1950 flight from Lhasa to Yatung, each laden with 120 pounds of treasure. Sent to Sikkim as a precaution in case Tenzin Gyatso would be forced to flee Tibet, forty mules bore gold, six hundred carried silver and the remaining animals, sacks of centuries-old coins. Though the Dalai Lama returned to the Potala, this relatively small share of his *labrang* or household treasure did not. Guarded by a single unknowing Lepcha sentry, it remained hidden for nine years in the Choegyal of Sikkim's abandoned stables located on the hillside below the palace in Gangtok. When before dawn one morning in 1960 a long convoy of trucks departed the capital for Calcutta, half the population of Sikkim awoke to what most imagined was the sight of their king fleeing his own country. Only after the treasure was safely deposited in the underground vault of a Calcutta bank did the truth emerge, spawning rampant speculation in India's press over the "God-King's fabulous fortune." In fact, after its conversion into currency and subsequent investment, only $987,500 materialized to form His Holiness the Dalai Lama's Charitable Trust, the resource from which virtually every exile project found seed money.

With economic security, the refugees' cultural reconstruction was assured. The Dalai Lama had begun the work of preservation from his first days in Swarg Ashram. "We divided our culture into two types," he explained. "In the first category we placed that which, we determined, needed to be retained only in books as past history. The second category included whatever could bring actual benefit in the present. These things, we resolved, must be kept alive. Therefore, many of our old ceremonial traditions I discarded—no matter, I decided, let them go. However, our performing arts, our literature, science and religion as well as those crafts from which we could earn a livelihood—painting, metalcraft, architecture, woodworking and carpetmaking—these, we took special pains to safeguard. To achieve this we employed modern methods although they were altogether new to us and posed many difficulties."

As the wellspring of Tibetan civilization, religion had first priority. Unlike other Asian nations to which Buddhism had spread, Tibet alone contained the entire corpus of the Buddhist Dharma; the full scope of sutras, tantras, their accompanying liturgy and most critically the guru-disciple lineages, founded on oral transmission, which served as unbroken links to the origin of the oldest of the three world faiths. Only 7,000 of Tibet's more than 600,000 monks and a few hundred or so of its 4,000 incarnate lamas had escaped. Those left behind had been defrocked, while new refugees brought word of the country's 6,524 monasteries being gutted by Chinese teams specially assigned to ship their valuable artifacts to the homeland, either to be melted into bullion or sold via Hong Kong on the international antiques market. For each scholar who died on a road gang, centuries of learning were lost, causing the Dalai Lama to take emergency steps to remove them from the deadly labor, even before their lay compatriots.

By August of 1959, as its last inmates were shipped out to road camps, Buxa Duar began receiving groups of refugee monks, assembled to salvage the Dharma. By the following year, almost 1,500 monks were living in the barracks of the newly named Buxa Lama Ashram, rising at 5:00 a.m. for congregational prayers in its central courtyard, then breaking into their monastic colleges to conduct memorization, debate and tutorials with senior scholars and incarnate lamas. Scouring road camps, the monks collected as many scriptures as could be found, from which they began lithographing with stone and ink over 200 volumes of major works—only a small fraction, however, of Tibet's 1,200 years of philosophic writing. With members of the Gelugpa sect predominating (those of the other three orders more often finding refuge at monasteries in Sikkim, Bhutan and Nepal), examinations for the Geshé degree continued after only a year's hiatus and it seemed as though the religion would rapidly mend. Then monks began to die. With their occupants sleeping sixty-six to a barracks and the bamboo beds only six inches apart, tuberculosis ran rampant. Each morning following prayers, 200 to 300 men would queue up behind the twenty-foot barbed-wire fence, waiting for hours in the broiling sun to be checked by the camp's single medical worker. "We were eager to save our religion," recalled Khentrul Rinpoché, a lama from Sera Monastery, who lived in the camp from its inception. "But after just a few years the number of monks dying increased to the point that the rest couldn't help wondering whether or not we'd ever escape from that place alive. Watching our friends become dark and thin and their teeth turn black, we constantly had depressed, suffocated feelings. We could only endure this hardship because we knew that the religious tradition of Tibet depended on us alone."

By 1968, the large settlements of Byllakuppe and Mundgod were finally ready to begin receiving survivors. Once moved south, the monks took up farming and started to gradually build over 150 new monasteries, filling them with young novices and creating the most vivid emblems of Tibetan life in exile. The monasteries in turn complemented a series of cultural institutes, primarily based in Dharamsala.

The first institute to be founded, three months after the Dalai Lama's arrival in Swarg Ashram, was the Tibetan Dance and Drama Society. Its seventy-four members—only twenty of whom had been performing artists in Tibet—managed to conserve in their repertoire four abridged Lhamo operas (the often week-long spectacles performed in Tibet's larger cities), two historical plays, numerous *cham* or monastic dances and even a reconstituted marching band which often played for the annual March 10 rally in Dharamsala, convened to commemorate the Lhasa uprising.

A year later, in October of 1961, the Tibetan Medical Center was founded under Dr. Yeshi Dhonden, one of only three Lhasa-trained physicians to escape. Tibet's unique medical science, developed indigenously over 2,100 years, was salvaged in a small hospital, pharmacy, astrology department and school, which by the late 1970s had graduated enough Tibetan doctors to staff the larger settlements. The third major institute to be opened was the Library of Tibetan Works and Archives, started in November 1971, in an imposing Tibetan-style building situated in the midst of the government's new Secretariat compound, Gangchen Kyishong. Located halfway between Lower Dharamsala and McLeod Ganj it soon became a magnet for hundreds of Asian and Western scholars who previously had scant access to Tibetan culture. By 1984, the library's numerous teaching and collection projects had amassed over 50,000 volumes, an estimated 40 percent of Tibet's literature—the remainder having been destroyed both before and during the Cultural Revolution in Tibet. In New Delhi, Tibet House, founded in 1965, supplemented much of the

library's work, while the Tibetan section of All India Radio was enlarged
and a number of refugee publications appeared. But by far the most extensive and critical of the cultural projects lay in the school system. Created
by the Dalai Lama to preserve the Tibetan identity while introducing the
"exile generation" to the modern world, it was looked on by all the
refugees, monks and laymen alike, as the most fundamental hope for the
future of their cause.

THE BUS on which Tempa Tsering left the road camp in Bawarna for
the Nursery in Dharamsala arrived in McLeod Ganj early in the afternoon.
Discharged into the hands of Mrs. Tsering Dolma, the Dalai Lama's elder
sister, and the Nursery's principal, a monk named Thubten Nyingee, the
children were led up a winding dirt road through the woods to Conium
House, a barnlike building of whitewashed stone walls and zinc roofing
inhabited for five months now by almost 200 orphaned and semi-orphaned
youngsters.

The Nursery for Tibetan Refugee Children, as Conium House was
formally known, had been founded by the Dalai Lama less than three
weeks after his own arrival in Dharamsala. Its immediate catalyst was a
report of children dying among a refugee group delayed by heavy snows
en route from Missamari to work sites in Ladakh. Fifty-one children were
taken from the group and housed with Tibetan government workers in
their bungalows until, under the direction of the Dalai Lama's sister, the
Nursery opened on May 17, 1960. Removed from road work, few of the
children died, though the majority were afflicted by a wide range of
ailments from tuberculosis to dysentery, influenza, scabies and severe malnutrition.

Tempa's own dysentery had long gone, yet he remained withdrawn
and uncommunicative. Deloused and with a newly shaved head, he was
issued his first Western clothes, a pair of shorts and two shirts, and seated
in a long line of children for a dinner of rice and boiled lentils dished into
beaten-tin bowls. Afterward, he and thirty others unrolled their blankets
on the floor of a room in Conium House and prepared to sleep, the sick
mixed in with the healthy, as there were too many to isolate. The next
morning the day began with prayers, exercise and a class in the Tibetan
and English alphabets, followed by an afternoon of unsupervised play.
Throughout, Tempa refused to participate. A month later, however, with
his room packed each night with 120 children, so crowded that no one
could move, he finally began to focus on the present. One day a ball was
kicked toward him during a game of soccer in the courtyard. Returning

it, he joined the other boys, from which time his incapacitating depression slowly began to lift.

Tempa's interest in life was restimulated most by three encounters he now had with the Dalai Lama. One morning, the older children were taken through the forest to witness a prayer session at Swarg Ashram. It was Tempa's first religious ceremony. As he sat on the steps of the Heavenly Abode's porch, gazing at the Dalai Lama on a throne surrounded by monks enacting the graceful *mudras* or hand gestures of tantric ritual while they recited scripture, he experienced an unusual feeling of reverence that, far more than the modicum of physical well-being afforded by the Nursery, gave him a sense of security.

On a second less formal occasion he made contact with the Dalai Lama himself. At that time Tenzin Gyatso walked from Swarg Ashram to Conium House to share a traditional Tibetan dinner of *thukpa* or noodle soup with the children. Before his arrival, the Nursery was thrown into a state of high excitement, few of its adult teachers having had such close contact with their leader in Tibet. Marshaled like a regiment on a parade ground, the children greeted the Dalai Lama, who immediately asked to be shown what they were studying. Tempa was singled out before the gathering to write the letters *A*, *B* and *C* on a slate. The Dalai Lama watched carefully and, giving him a warm pat on the shoulder, said, "Very good." "Of course," recalled Tempa laughing, "I liked him from that moment on."

A third meeting with the Dalai Lama marked Tempa's departure from the Nursery. One hundred sixty of the oldest children had been chosen to attend the Mussoorie School, the first educational institute to be created in exile, founded one year before. In their company, Tempa hiked to Swarg Ashram, where the Dalai Lama, seated on the porch with the children gathered around, advised them to study hard so that later they could help those who would not have the same opportunity. At the conclusion of his remarks, Tempa led the group in reciting the eleven-verse Long Life Prayer of the Fourteenth Dalai Lama. "My friends said I was so nervous that I was shivering and forgot whole parts," he recalled. "But I think I got the chorus right, at least where it says, 'Bless Tenzin Gyatso, Protector of the Land of Snows. May his life not fail, but last a hundred eons, and may his will be effortlessly accomplished.' "

"In Tibet I had a great desire to establish a modern school," said the Dalai Lama. "From the early fifties on, I felt the need very strongly. Without any knowledge of how such a school functions I just thought over and over, 'We must have a modern school. We must have a school.' But I didn't even know how many classes to have." Returning to Mussoorie after his 1959 pilgrimage, the Dalai Lama scouted the town for a suitable building in which to begin his project. Eventually he found an old home called Kildare House, belonging to an Indian army officer who, convinced the building was haunted by the ghosts of Moslems killed there during the riots at India's partition, was glad to sell at a low price. Located in a rocky clearing not far from Birla House, its eight decaying rooms opened on March 3, 1960, to fifty young men—monks, Khampa guerrillas and government officials—aged eighteen to twenty-five. Although the Dalai Lama was not versed in modern education, two recent expatriates were: Mary and Jigme Taring, among the first Tibetans to have been educated in India, to whose guidance the Mussoorie School was fully entrusted.

The Tarings were a pioneering couple. Jigme Taring was a prince, the nephew of the Choegyal of Sikkim; Mary was the daughter of Wangchuk Gyalpo Tsarong, a senior Cabinet minister under the Thirteenth Dalai Lama and a descendant of Tibet's famous eighth-century physician, Yuthok Yonten Gonpo. With their background as surety against criticism from Tibet's xenophobic establishment, the Tarings were the foremost proponents of modernization in their generation. In exile, they represented an invaluable asset to the fledgling government.

After arriving at the new school Tempa found in their guidance the first substantial explanation of his situation. "All of us children called them Mother and Father and they really acted like that," he recalled. "After a while there were three or four hundred kids, but the Tarings took an interest in each and every one. They explained over and over, in classes, in meetings and alone, what had happened to us. Above all they said that we were Tibetans. We had been driven out by the Chinese, and somehow we had to get back, to regain our country. This was the responsibility children like us had. We had to work for all the Tibetan people, not just ourselves. From hearing this again and again I stopped being completely absorbed in my own tragedy. I began to see that I had a greater duty. The Tarings made sense of it all to us. They gave that to the children."

Following the Tarings' lead, two more residential schools, one in Simla, the other in Darjeeling, were begun. The Dalai Lama then approached the Indian government to propose a long-range plan. Consulting with Nehru at a private luncheon in New Delhi in May 1961, he received the Prime Minister's support for the founding of an autonomous body within the Indian Ministry of Education, called the Tibetan Schools Society; its purpose would be to run a network of residential and day schools staffed jointly by Indian and Tibetan teachers. Education being one area in which Nehru could freely aid the Tibetans without political consequences, his support was so generous that by 1964 the system included seven residential schools housing, in the main, over 500 children each, four day schools in the settlements, three transit schools at road-construction sites and a number of grant-in-aid schools indirectly supported by the Society. Nevertheless, there were obstacles. In organizing the large residential schools, the dearth of such basic necessities as flat land caused immense difficulty. Situated in mountainous regions that offered few buildings with surrounding grounds, the schools were compelled to adopt whatever facility was available, while the children themselves, for the most part, converted it: in Darjeeling, an old barracks of the North Bengal Mounted Rifles; at Mount Abu, the abandoned palace of the Maharaja of Bikaner; in Panchmari, the defunct Royal Hotel; at Kalimpong, a woolen warehouse unused since the heyday of Tibetan trade. By 1966, almost 7,000 young people had been saved from road gangs. Half, however, were over-age, and many of those who would have failed to complete high school by the age of 20 were forced to withdraw. There were also troubles with the faculty. Because the TSS was not a full-fledged component of India's school system, teachers were concerned over tenure, reluctant to work in remote settlements and as only university-level faculty could instruct in English—the medium chosen by the Dalai Lama—hard to find to begin with. Those finally hired could not even talk to their Tibetan counterparts until a vocabulary list of 500 Hindi and Tibetan words was circulated from New Delhi.

The children, though, were learning, and they were the first generation in Tibet's history to see maps of the world and hear of other nations. As Tempa reflected, "When we were first taught geography, it was almost unbelievable. The teacher showed us a globe and pictures of different peoples, but until it was thoroughly explained, I found it hard to accept that the world was really so large. I just couldn't comprehend it. In Tibet, India had always been the end of the earth for us." The young Tibetans' curiosity was particularly stimulated by the bizarre objects represented by the Western aid workers, who, as the first Caucasians they had seen, were jokingly nicknamed "yellow heads" for their blond hair. Meanwhile, their own Tibetan instructors were now being systematically readied in a Teachers Training School established in Dharamsala, and a textbook committee and a printing press were soon issuing a syllabus covering Tibetan language, history, literature and religion from first grade through the end of high school. By the time the Tibetan Schools Society changed its name to the Central Tibetan Schools Administration in the early seventies, 9,000 children were attending its thirty-two institutions; ten years later 15,000 studied in fifty-two schools, the majority of whom chose to continue on to a university. Advanced studies in Tibet's own academic tradition were provided by the Institute of Higher Tibetan Studies, founded in January 1968 in Benares, as well as the Buddhist School of Dialectics, begun in Dharamsala five years later. To continue care for orphaned children, a system of Tibetan foster homes was created, beginning in 1962 with the Mussoorie Homes run by Mary Taring. By the end of the decade, with 600 children in twenty-five Tibetan-style households staffed by live-in parents, Mussoorie was outdone only by the Nursery in Dharamsala, which changed its name to the Tibetan Children's Village. Placed under the direction of the Dalai Lama's younger sister, Pema Gyalpo, it relocated to Egerton Hall above the military cantonment and began rapidly expanding over the hillside. At the close of the seventies its city-like campus housing over 1,000 destitute children six months to eighteen years old was regarded by UN agencies and others as a paradigm for rehabilitating refugee children and was indisputably the most successful enterprise in exile.

At the age of fourteen, after two years in Mussoorie, Tempa was accepted at St. Gabriel's Academy, a secondary school outside Dehra Dun. In company with many of the older refugee children, whose age made them ineligible for the Tibetans' burgeoning institutions, he was compelled to spend the next decade in the alien environment of Indian schools. "After arriving at St. Gabriel's," he recounted, "even though there were six Tibetans, the sense of being an outsider just grew deeper and deeper. The more contact we had, the more we felt removed. Only a handful of people had heard of Tibet. The rest kept asking, 'Where is your father? What does he do? Who are your brothers and sisters?' Each time they asked, you couldn't help but recall your past—that you are a refugee and you have no country—but still these people remained very ignorant of what we were. Overall it inculcated in me a further awareness of being Tibetan. My desire to have Tibet back, to regain my own country, just increased."

After he was transferred to Dr. Graham's Homes, a missionary school in Kalimpong, Tempa's anger at what he perceived to be a popular disregard for Tibetans, the notion that they were "backward and uncivilized," manifested itself in competitive drive. Excelling in academic work, he became, during his five and a half years at Dr. Graham's, head of virtually every sports team, earning the titles of proctor, vice-captain and finally captain of the school, under whom the entire student body was administered. With his name inscribed on the school's commemorative plaque listing outstanding students, Tempa's success was such that a special convocation—the first in Dr. Graham's history—was convened after graduation to honor him. "I had to be independent," he commented, appraising the reversal in his character following the shock of his sisters' and mother's deaths. "Deep down I realized that I didn't have anything unless I created it for myself. And I think that kept pushing me; the loss of Tibet, of my parents, the breakdown of the family—all of it. For my own good as well as the Tibetan people's—there was so much personal as well as national loss—I just had to succeed in building it back up."

When he arrived at Madras Christian College, however, one of India's most prestigious schools, Tempa found himself, as the first Tibetan in the city, the object of constant racial harassment. Within a week the taunts became so frequent that he contemplated withdrawing. Instead, he walked into the principal's office and requested permission to address the college. "I just told him that I was so disappointed and embarrassed," stated Tempa. "Not only the students but even the teachers hardly knew the first thing about Tibet. 'I can't continue explaining to people where I come from,' I said, 'so I'd like to address the whole school at once.' " A few days later, Tempa walked alone onto an empty stage, a packed auditorium of amused undergraduates seated before him. Nervously he read a speech outlining Tibet's recent history until, reaching the uprising in Lhasa and the subsequent flight of the refugees, he suddenly found himself departing from the text and relating the events of his own life. Save for a brief account he had given to a close teacher two years before, it was the first time that Tempa had spoken publicly of his personal tragedy. Overwhelmed by a standing ovation at the talk's conclusion, Tempa went on to duplicate his success at Dr. Graham's, studying now to become a doctor, there being at that time only three or four Western-trained Tibetan physicians. Despite three years of applying to aid organizations, though, he was unable to locate a sponsor for medical school. As a result, irrespective of his long record of outstanding academic work, Tempa Tsering faced the world with no prospects. It seemed a great defeat. The only option remaining was to join his father, now living in Byllakuppe, and become a farmer.

Tempa traveled inland by train, journeying from India's eastern seaboard to Mysore. Boarding a battered country bus, he rode fifty miles south to the Cauvery Valley. On either side the country turned increasingly wild, until even the roadside fields gave way permanently to jungle. At the small town of Cauvery, he disembarked and set out on foot for the settlement. Crossing the Cauvery River, he saw men and women from Byllakuppe spreading their washing to dry on wide boulders painted in bright, primary colors with the national mantra of Tibet, *Om Mani Padme Hum.* Turning off the main road by the settlement workshop, he entered a wholly Tibetan atmosphere. Lush, undulating fields stretched to the horizon, crisscrossed by neat rows of haystacks crowned by prayer flags. At high points rose the maroon and white walls of Byllakuppe's six monasteries, including the rebuilt Sera and Tashilhunpo, interspersed by villages, schools, the old settlement office and a hospital. On the long roads uniting the camps, fringed in brilliant mauve and yellow flowering bushes, a cavalcade of monks, farm workers and women with babies tied to their backs, rosaries in hand, passed by. Only the heat and the jungle-covered hills circling the settlement's perimeter remained as evidence of Byllakuppe's un-Tibetan locale.

Tempa had visited Byllakuppe often since taking up his studies in Madras. Before, he had seen his father on only three occasions in the eight years subsequent to departing the road camp at Bawarna. Now, for the first time since leaving Tibet, father and son lived together. The changes in both were instantly apparent. Chopel Dhondub, like most of the elder refugees, had clung to all the old Tibetan views. Physically, he had altered by turning smaller and darker; emotionally, due to the strain of work, by becoming more temperamental—a trait usually suppressed in Tibetan society. Tempa, on the other hand, was now a hybrid, the product of circumstances and learning beyond his father's understanding. Their differences reflected a threshold in the refugee experience: the maturation of the first generation in exile, and with it, a change in the Tibetan character. "As soon as I started living with my father again he immediately pressed for an arranged marriage," said Tempa. "In Tibet this was normal, but I told my father that it was none of his business. It wasn't his marriage but mine." Though Chopel Dhondub couldn't prevail, other families continued to arrange marriages for their children, life in the settlements, far more so than that of Dharamsala or other urban centers, clinging to conservative ideals even, on occasion, to the point of violence. As Tempa related, "When long hair and bell-bottoms came to India all the young Tibetans naturally took them up. The elders couldn't understand it. They thought it looked disrespectful. In Byllakuppe, when we danced to the Beatles, our parents actually came out and threw stones at us. But we never reacted. We never said even a word to them. We just took it. Then, when things cooled down, we explained, 'You have to change. We're living in the world now. This is the way things are.' Gradually, after lots of patient discussion, they began to accept it."

A more fundamental shift concerned religion. Under the demands of exile life Buddhism's all-pervasive influence was naturally reduced. Though they had studied the Dharma in their TSS syllabus, the younger generation found little occasion for its practice and they grew critical of Buddhism's social function in a heretofore inconceivable manner. As a monk from Byllakuppe observed, "Many of these young Tibetans won't return my smile on the street. They see that I am a fellow Tibetan but these robes are just like a prison suit. The monks, they think, are the reason we lost Tibet." "Too much religion, too little politics," remarked Tempa, describing the widespread belief among his peers that religion, carried to the extreme it was in Tibet, had undermined the organization of the state. "Basically the younger generation is more political than religious. For my father, religion came first, politics second. But I think this generation, for the first time in centuries, feels the opposite."

Young and old never differed, though, in their commitment to Tibet's cause. "When I first began to visit my father in Byllakuppe," said Tempa, "every time we met he would say, 'I was born and bred in Tibet and I want to die in Tibet. I want my body buried there—not in India.' I learned a lot from this. After my mother saw His Holiness she said, 'That's good enough for me. Now let me die peacefully.' Then she gave up. But not my father. He's never stopped fighting. All those that lived—the survivors —they're all like that."

Tempa remained in Byllakuppe for a year. In search of a more stimulating pursuit than farming, he volunteered to work part-time at the settlement office, while joining the local branch of the Tibetan Youth Congress. Founded in 1970 by a small group of young Tibetans, the Congress had quickly grown into the largest political party in the exile community. At its week-long inaugural conference in Dharamsala, Tempa had discussed for the first time his long-held thoughts on Tibet's political struggle. Now, given the chance to work for the Congress, he enthusiastically took over its local adult education program, lecturing in the evenings on health care, still a major problem among the refugees. He obtained a film projector to show documentaries on Gandhi's nonviolent fight for national liberation, the Satyagraha movement. Next, he requested books from the schools he had attended, assembling, a parcel at a time, the settlement's only library. Within a few months his disappointment at failing to become a doctor passed as he was elected general secretary of the Byllakuppe chapter, the largest of the Youth Congress's forty branches, containing between them 10,000 members.

Not long after Tempa's election, the Dalai Lama came to Byllakuppe to offer the Kalachakra Initiation, a religious event attended by the entire settlement. At an audience with the Youth Congress, Tempa once more encountered the Tibetan leader: the first time he had met him in person since his childhood days at the Nursery in Dharamsala. "The example of His Holiness had the strongest effect on me," said Tempa. "As the leader of his people he was so uplifting and farsighted. We all know how simply he lives and how hard he works and cares for the Tibetans, but when I actually saw this in practice, I felt personally inspired to do something more for my country."

A few months later, the entire government-in-exile appeared in Byl-lakuppe to hold its annual report meeting in the settlers' presence. Attend-ing the event as a Youth Congress observer, Tempa was captivated by the proceedings, conducted according to the democratic constitution promul-gated by the Dalai Lama in 1963. During a break one day he was ap-proached by Mr. Kundeling, a Cabinet minister whom he had known slightly in the past. On hearing that Tempa had graduated from college only to be a farmer, Mr. Kundeling insisted he leave Byllakuppe and join the government in Dharamsala. He then instructed the secretary of the Information and Publicity Office to give him a job. A few weeks later, a letter arrived from the office offering him a position as an assistant secre-tary. "After receiving the letter I discussed it with my father," Tempa related. "I had just finished school and I felt a responsiblity to look after him. I told him this. I also told him that the Byllakuppe settlement office would not be happy if I left. Then I said, 'This time you make the decision. So far, I've made almost every decision in my life without your knowledge. Now this is up to you.' He replied immediately, 'From our point of view Dharamsala is the central government, whereas here it's just one office, looking after three thousand people in the old camps. So obviously, if you go to Dharamsala, you'll be of more service to all the Tibetan people. For myself, if I know you are sincerely working for His Holiness, then, even if I have to die alone, with no one to pour cold water in my mouth in the last days, I won't have a single regret.' When he said that, everything was clear. I said, 'O.K.', and I went to Dharamsala."

A few weeks later, still, after fourteen years in India, with few more possessions than his own clothing, Tempa said farewell to his father for what would be another six years. Taking a bus from Cauvery to Mysore, he boarded a northbound train to Pathankot in the Punjab, from where another bus deposited him on the fringe of Katwali Bazaar, Lower Dha-ramsala. There, he caught the local bus for the half-hour ride five miles farther up the hill to McLeod Ganj. On the way he watched intently through the barred windows as the road zigzagged up the pine-covered slopes leading to the military cantonment and the Tibetan Children's Village above. After driving through Forsythe Ganj, another hamlet in the hills, the spindle-like ridge on which McLeod Ganj sat drew into view. In a few minutes more, St. John's in the Wilderness passed, alone in the woods, and then the galvanized canopy of Nowrojee's front porch hove in sight, a characteristic press of Tibetan monks, gaddis, or hill folk, and a few local tourists from lower in the valley beneath it, idly watching the commotion at the head of town. As the bus halted, Tempa jumped off, retrieved his bag from its roof and entered the energetic press of "Little Lhasa," as Upper Dharamsala had rather wistfully come to be known.

Since the first days of the Dalai Lama's tenure, McLeod Ganj had shuddered through an onslaught of development. Its permanent population now approached 4,000, with hundreds of pilgrims, traders, government officials and foreign visitors in periodic residence. The serene colonial park at its center had been obliterated without a thought by the Tibetans. Three rows of buildings housing shops, restaurants and hotels had replaced it. At their center rose a tall gold-crowned *chorten*, dedicated, as its plaque explained, to the memory of all those suffering under Chinese occupation in Tibet. Day and night it was circled by a stream of faithful, spinning two lines of prayer wheels and reciting mantras. Outside of town stood their homes: an impromptu jumble of tin and stone shanties, ascending floor over roof like a ziggurat up the hill, graced by marigolds in the windows and hundreds of faded prayer flags strung between the trees overhead. The people of Little Lhasa were mainly sweater sellers who left their unheated huts in the cold winter months to ride the rails between Indian cities in search of commerce. When in Dharamsala, they made full use of their closeness to the "Precious Protector" by each day circumambulating a reconstituted Lingkhor or Holy Walk, similar to the one in Lhasa, surrounding his new residence, Thekchen Chöling. It was toward this that Tempa proceeded, walking out of the far side of town and turning down a narrow road to the knoll-like crest capping the farthest of the ridges surrounding McLeod Ganj.

Built in 1968, Thekchen Chöling or "Island of the Mahayana Teaching" enclosed a great expanse of forest and hillside through which the Dalai Lama could stroll, tend his flower gardens, look after wild birds and meditate. The green corrugated roofing of his modest private cottage dominated a kitchen complex, office building, security and secretarial quarters all located at progressively lower levels leading to the front gate.

Across a flagstone *chöra* or debating courtyard, used by the young monks of the Dialectical School and flanked along its southern end by the cells of Namgyal Dratsang, the Dalai Lama's personal monastery, stood the new Central Cathedral, a three-story lemon-yellow hall topped by gold pinnacles and designed by the Dalai Lama himself in a modern idiom. Turning the battery of prayer wheels that lined its outer walls, Tempa entered the bright interior to offer prayers before its giant images of the Buddha and Tibet's patron saints. Then, continuing down the hill via a rocky shortcut through the trees, he approached the new Secretariat compound of the government-in-exile, Gangchen Kyishong or "Abode of

Snow-Happy Valley." Halfway to Lower Dharamsala, Gangchen Kyishong had been built out of the same necessity as Thekchen Chöling: to
replace the cramped, perennially leaking quarters of the old British bungalows. On the white pillars that framed its front gate the government's
emblem—two turquoise-maned snow lions holding the eight-spoked
wheel of the Dharma before snow-capped peaks, the sun and moon—
proclaimed its identity. To maintain congenial relations with New Delhi,
no Tibetan flag was flown. Within, on a long flat, surrounded by the more
temperate foliage of the lesser slopes, rose the monumental edifices of the
Library of Tibetan Works and Archives and the Cabinet building, its
ground floor an assembly hall for government meetings. The library was
flanked by an amphitheater of dormitories for its hundred resident scholars
and the Cabinet, by tiers of buildings lodging the government departments, on the uppermost of which, set back in typically Tibetan style with
a wide roofscape before it, were the two rooms of the Information Office.
Tempa's quarters, which he was shown after reporting to his new superior,
lay in a chalet-like log building facing the secretarial mess, not far away.
With the knowledge that he had arrived at the very heart of the political
struggle for Tibet, he settled in his first night, eager to begin work the
following day as an active member of his government.

5

The Fight for Tibet

1959–1984

THE GOVERNMENT-IN-EXILE that Tempa found in the summer of 1974 was an odd mix of innovation, bureaucracy and the hierarchic vestiges of the Ganden Phodrang of Tibet, the religious rule formed under the Fifth Dalai Lama in 1642. Recognized by no one save its own people—all of whom refused to accept Indian citizenship—Dharamsala's powers were circumscribed, its resources scant; yet the government's poverty surprised even Tempa. Its offices operated in a clutter of semi-audible phone lines, secondhand typewriters and formal portraits of the Dalai Lama, and the living quarters for the then 141 Secretariat workers, cramped together on the hillside around Gangchen Kyishong, were barely functional. The building in which Tempa lived had no heat or running water; his room, which he shared with another young man, lay in complete disrepair. Each day a shower of old Indian newspapers, mud patches and beaten-tin cans fell from the rotting walls onto his narrow cot, so worn that its wicker body sank beneath his weight to touch the concrete floor. Meals were taken in the spartan Secretariat mess and came out of Tempa's salary which, hovering around fifty dollars a month, provided for only the barest essentials.

The Information Office was the most political of Dharamsala's departments. To promote Tibet's cause it consulted closely with the four offices established abroad as well as the large bureau in New Delhi. It maintained a listening room to monitor Radio Lhasa's daily broadcasts and screened recently escaped refugees for the latest information on China's occupation—a job to which Tempa was assigned. At the same time, he was put in charge of answering the inquiries addressed to Gangchen Kyishong from around the world. He also cut clippings on political, scientific and cultural developments for translation in *She Ja* or *Knowledge,* a current affairs magazine published to keep the refugee community informed of global events. Meanwhile, as his first weeks passed, Tempa acquainted himself with the structure of the exile government.

At the head of government stood the Dalai Lama and his Cabinet, the Kashag. Below them, six major departments and two subdepartments (to which those of Health and General Audit were added in the early eighties) were divided among the ministers. Here the resemblance to Tibet's former government ended. Just up the hill, behind Tempa's own quarters, were the homes and office of the seventeen-member Commission of Tibetan People's Deputies, the body of elected representatives who, in exile, acted as a parliament. Unlike the Tsongdu, Tibet's old National Assembly, the deputies were popularly elected to three-year terms—three men and one woman from each province, a cleric from each of the four religious sects, including one for Bon, Tibet's indigenous religion, and an additional final member appointed by the Dalai Lama for distinguished service in art, science or literature. Their most important task was shared with the Cabinet; together they comprised the Tibetan National Working Committee, the highest policy-making organ of the government. They also conducted the Annual General Meeting, in which each department head was publicly questioned on his section's performance during the past year. Although the deputies' ability to redress Tibet's plight directly was limited by the constraints of refugee life, the Dalai Lama believed that engaging in a democratic experiment in itself constituted an essential ingredient in his nation's struggle. "Just to criticize China was not sufficient," he explained. "We had to have a definite alternative of our own. So for this reason we created a representative government and to do this, we discussed and prepared a draft constitution."

In framing the constitution, the Dalai Lama adopted a blend of socialist guidelines, to ensure the equal distribution of wealth, and democratic procedures for conducting representative government. He also drew heavily on his own personal beliefs. "From a very young age I always felt how all-important the people are," he related. "Therefore, any ideology that stands for the benefit of the poor, the downtrodden, the lowest people, I feel is sacred. The very thought of democracy, though I couldn't put it in words, was with me in Tibet. Now, theoretically, Marxism also stands for the majority—the working class. This touches me, yet there is something wrong with its implementation in the present Communist states. Their excessively rigid atmosphere actually spoils the value of human life. On the other hand, while freedom is necessary, one must have an equal economic opportunity with which to exercise it. So it seems portions of both systems are needed."

On March 10, 1963, the fourth anniversary of the Lhasa uprising, the constitution was promulgated, carefully labeled as a "draft" pending approval by the six million majority in Tibet. In exile, save for a few noble families and Khampa chieftains, who thought that their power would be eroded, the majority of the refugees greeted the document as a momentous, if puzzling, step into the modern world. Among its seventy-seven articles, provisions were made to balance the immense powers of the executive branch, in the person of the Dalai Lama, with a strong legislature and supreme court. Renouncing war "as an instrument of offensive policy," it declared the fundamental rights of all Tibetans to include those of universal suffrage, equality before the law, life, liberty and property, as well as freedom of religion, speech and assembly. Fulfilling socialist ideals, state ownership of the land was provided for as well as a prohibition against the amassing of wealth and the means of production "to the common detriment." Once passed by popular referendum, the exile government set about supplying the constitution, as best it could, with a representative framework, one, however, which had already been in place for three years.

Impatient to begin Tibet's experiment in democracy, the Dalai Lama pushed through the refugees' first elections as early as the summer of 1960 —only months after his arrival in Dharamsala and more than a year before the constitution's outline was even announced in the autumn of 1961. The election had been an extremely informal affair. Most Tibetans had never imagined participating in government, much less heard of voting; politics had been the business of monks and noblemen for centuries. As a result, there were no candidates. Assembled in their various road camps, people simply wrote on slips of paper the names of those they respected most. The sole requirement was to vote for a representative from one's own region or, in the case of the clergy, one's sect. Naturally, all of the thirteen men whose names appeared most frequently were either important lamas, aristocrats or tribal chieftains from Kham and Amdo. By September 1960, they had joined the Dalai Lama in Dharamsala to begin an undertaking as peculiar in its way as their election.

Unfamiliar with administrative procedure, the first group of people's deputies decided that, rather than oversee policy, they should gain experience by working in the various government departments as deputy directors. The second assembly of representatives, elected in 1963, continued in the same capacity. Those who were not reelected easily found new jobs with the understaffed administration. It was not until the third group of deputies was sent to Dharamsala in May 1966 that the government's legislature and administration were finally separated, it having developed that, once trained, the deputies' participation in the bureaucracy necessarily compromised their ability to regulate it.

Despite the improvement, the electoral process itself continued to be run by the administration. In 1963, the second elections saw the introduction of election committees, ballot boxes and female representatives (to comply with the constitutional article ensuring equality of the sexes). In 1966, the third elections included actual candidates, mounted by the election committee at Dharamsala and not by political parties as campaigning, in exile, was considered a potentially destabilizing activity. It was not until 1975 that the fifth Commission of People's Deputies finally instituted a two-tier vote whereby candidates could be popularly chosen in primary elections. However, even after fifteen years of refining the electoral process, many people—particularly older Tibetans—still found the concept of a popular vote obscure. As Lodi Gyari, chairman of the seventh assembly of deputies, noted, "A lot of people go into the election tent and just pray to His Holiness. 'I don't know any of these candidates, but please let me choose the right one to help the Dalai Lama and the people.' Then they close their eyes, put their finger down and ask the election officer, 'Would you see whose name is here.' When they hear it they reply, 'Oh, it's so-and-so. I'll vote for him.' "

Resistance, not to representative government, but to its fundamental prerequisite, that of individuals declaring themselves as candidates, also hampered acceptance of democratic procedure. "If I go and ask someone to vote for me," continued Lodi Gyari, "it would be considered an act of great shamelessness. It's very funny, you find this in many Oriental cultures, but we are raised to always say, 'I am very unable and uneducated.' If someone does not behave like this, it's considered a clear indication that he has personal motives and is not out for the common good." As a result, some deputies found themselves elected against their will, unaware even that the committee in Dharamsala had nominated them as candidates until they were summoned to be sworn in. On the opposite end of the spectrum, even those willingly elected were subject to disqualification by either the Dalai Lama or the National Working Committee, who could judge them unfit to hold office.

The issue of how much authority the Dalai Lama should command lay at the very heart of the struggle to create a genuine democracy. The Dalai Lama had used the constitution to weaken his position, ironically against the wishes of his own people. In its final draft, Article 36, section (e), provided, "in the highest interests of the state," for the Dalai Lama's impeachment by a two-thirds majority of the National Assembly in consultation with the Supreme Court. Resistance was such that over 150 representatives had gathered in Dharamsala to refuse to approve the constitution unless the clause was deleted. "Of course this was my idea," the Dalai Lama related. "If we were to have a true democracy there had to be provisions whereby the Dalai Lama's powers could also be changed. But at the time people complained, mainly, I think, out of an emotional feeling and also because it was something new and difficult to understand. I had to convince them that it was absolutely necessary not just for the present but for the future of all the Tibetan people. This point was one of the most important issues of the early sixties."

"After working in the government for some time, I could see that just holding elections does not create a democracy," observed Tempa Tsering. "Even in office, many of the deputies were very apathetic. They were more comfortable with the idea of an all-powerful executive than they were with a free legislature. So for this reason, I believe, democracy has yet to take hold. It's only among the younger generation that people have a real understanding of the democratic spirit." In the Tibetan Youth Congress, Tempa found a truly contemporary political climate. Becoming acquainted with its leaders, who, though they still lacked an office, all lived in Dharamsala, he realized that they, not the government, represented the vanguard of the Dalai Lama's aspirations for a politically open society.

From its start, the Youth Congress had captured the commanding role in the Tibetans' political life. Dedicated to struggling for the independence of Tibet, it had been created by four young men, all from upper-class backgrounds and most educated in the best British-based schools in India.

"In 1970 things were still pretty bleak in Dharamsala," recalled Jamyang Norbu, a Youth Congress convener, describing the organization's birth. "There were no Westerners, only the Peace Corps people who came around at Christmastime to sing carols. Among the Tibetans there were a lot of idealistic youth. It was very bohemian, not intentionally, but just because the life was so hard. Each night five or six people would crush into your room to sleep. No one had any money, so nobody gave a damn. Whatever you got, you would just spend in a few days. A group of us used to get together and drink barley beer and, if we could afford it, rum. Then we'd always start talking about Tibet. It was a bit sentimental, I suppose. We'd say, 'So what are we going to do? What is our dream?' Then someone would declare, 'One of these days I'm going to get across that pass with my tank and see the Potala.' That sort of talk. After a while we'd make tea on a kerosene stove, but we never had enough glasses or spoons, so we'd always have to stir it with a toothbrush."

Enough late-night talks produced a consensus. Not only were young Tibetans in exile not in touch with one another; many felt that the refugee government had continued, despite its efforts at reform, in the lesser traditions of its predecessor in Lhasa. "There was too much mediocrity. It had become the fashion to play it safe," continued Norbu. "It's always the same old story. The people with conviction and talent stayed behind and fought in Tibet to the last, and a lot of second-level people, bureaucrats, made it out. In India, the whole establishment always kept quiet. It was not particularly the Indian government who clamped down on them, but their own selves. No one was pushing."

To unite exile youth in a more aggressive struggle for Tibetan freedom, the group decided to hold a small conference. Once informed, the Dalai Lama offered to cover the meeting's cost on the condition that it be expanded to include representatives of the younger generation from among all the refugees. "His Holiness didn't impose any terms on us. He just took a very sympathetic, laissez-faire attitude of 'Let it grow and let's see what these kids can do.' Everyone was thrilled," said Norbu.

A month later, on October 7, 1970, 300 young Tibetans sat before a pennant-lined table outside Conium House, a large green map of Tibet draped behind them. At the conclusion of the national anthem, the Dalai Lama, flanked by his two tutors and the Cabinet, rose to give the opening address. There followed a week-long debate, unlike anything that had taken place before, either in exile or in Tibet. "No one had anticipated how outspoken the proceedings would be," related Norbu. "People asked the Cabinet point-blank about the past. How could the Chinese get into our country just like that? Why didn't the army put up a good fight? What really happened at Chamdo when it fell? Then there were very probing questions about favoritism in the present administration and misuse of funds. One of the ministers was really shivering. The tablecloth wasn't long enough, and you could see the folds in his Tibetan *chuba* trembling. So because of all this our relationship with the government started right off on a little note of tension."

With the Tibetan Youth Congress officially inaugurated midway through the conference, the role of loyal opposition was effectively filled in the exile community. Yet it was an odd situation. Heavily dependent on the younger, better-educated English-speaking refugees, the government counted almost 40 percent of its employees among the Congress, a figure which grew to 75 percent by 1984. An awkward combination of the establishment and its chief critics was thus created. When Youth Congress members in the government criticized bureaucratic errors and corruption, the Cabinet saw disloyalty in its ranks and reacted by attempting to undermine the TYC Central Executive Committee, or Centrex. "Centrex repeatedly made clear to the Kashag that we always considered them the rightful government of Tibet," said Jamyang Norbu. "Our loyalty was beyond question. But just because of this, we maintained, the Congress was not obliged to behave in a servile way or agree with all their decisions. When we challenged the Cabinet we felt that we were acting out of idealism, but they only saw us as a threat to their power."

Two years after the founding of the Youth Congress, in July 1972, a second popular organization called Struggle for the Restoration of Tibet's Rightful Independence was inaugurated in Dharamsala. Its leadership, though, was given over to the Commission of Tibetan People's Deputies, who primarily employed it to collect the refugees' voluntary tax, consisting of up to 2% of their monthly wages, and accounting for almost a third of the exile government's revenue. Simultaneously, trouble between the Cabinet and the Youth Congress continued to grow, climaxing in the Tibetans' first real test of democracy, produced by a dramatic confrontation during the spring of 1977.

The engagement evolved from a chain of events beginning on March 10, 1977, the eighteenth anniversary of the Lhasa uprising, celebrated that year, among other gatherings, by a TYC-organized demonstration at the Chinese embassy in New Delhi. There had been many Tibetan demonstrations at the embassy previously, some of them violent. This time, plans were drawn up to break into the compound and disrupt it. The Intelligence Bureau or IB, India's internal secret service, however, got word of the arrangements. Early on the morning of the tenth, as hundreds of demonstrators massed near Majna-ka-Tilla, the Tibetan refugee camp on the banks of the Jumna River in Old Delhi, police cordoned off the area. The few hundred Tibetans who managed to get through were all subsequently arrested after a pitched battle at the embassy. They were released without being charged, but not before the protest had been joined by a thousand more refugees. Putting their gathering to a new purpose, the demonstrators decided to hold a hunger strike calling for the implementation of the United Nations' three resolutions on Tibet. A Coordinating Committee for the newly formed Tibetan People's Freedom Movement was created and a large tent, equipped with beds for the strikers to rest on and a medical unit to monitor their condition, erected across from the UN Information Office near the Lodi Gardens. From eighty-three volunteers three teams were selected, their members to fill in one at a time as each

person died. The strike, it was decided, would only be called off if the
United Nations agreed to once more take up the question of Tibet. "We
put the fear of God into them," recalled Norbu. "We called in the volunteers one at a time and said, 'This is for keeps. We are going to live, but
you will die. It's going to be very difficult. You'll be lying there starving
to death and we won't be paying any attention to you. We'll be laughing
and talking. So you better pull out now.' That reduced the numbers right
away. Finally, we came up with three guerrillas, a woman and three other
men for the first group. Then we put them all under the charge of a real
tough character, an ex-guerrilla who didn't give a damn about death. This
was our insurance to guarantee that no one would weaken their will with
false sympathies."

The strike started at 10:00 a.m. on March 20, 1977. Within a few days
the Tibetans received more press and television coverage than at any other
time since the Dalai Lama's arrival eighteen years before. There could not
have been a more opportune moment. India was in the midst of elections
following Indira Gandhi's twenty-month-long emergency. Within a
week, the Janata Party was voted into power on a dramatic wave of
popular libertarian sentiment. The coincidence was astonishing. The
Janata leaders, who had been relegated to the opposition for decades, were
the same men who had championed Tibet's cause most vociferously. Now,
given power, they were finally in a position to recognize the exile government, and at the very time when the Tibetans, encouraged by widespread
support for the strikers throughout the diaspora, had mustered their most
unified political effort to date.

Recognizing the moment's potential, Lodi Gyari (then president of the
Youth Congress) decided to speak directly to the Janata Party leaders,
many of whom he knew. With the dual pressure of their past commitments
to Tibet and the hunger strike—whose massive publicity was clearly detrimental on the eve of their inauguration—he hoped to obtain formal
pledges of support for Tibetan independence. Without notifying the Cabinet in Dharamsala, who undoubtedly would have suppressed the plan,
Gyari, joined by Jamyang Norbu and a heavy monk nicknamed Gosey or
the "Blond Lama" (from his skin being slightly yellow), went immediately
to Janata Party headquarters. " 'How the hell are we going to get in?' I
asked Lodi," recalled Norbu. "They were choosing the Prime Minister
and the building was packed with people and press. Besides, we looked a
mess. I had come down from Dharamsala in a hurry with just a toothbrush.
I was wearing shorts, a blue jean shirt and flip-flop sandals. Lodi was in
his white Indian pajamas with his briefcase and then we had this portly
monk. But the three of us just got a taxi and drove over anyway."

When they arrived, the young men pushed ahead of the journalists and managed to catch the attention of the secretary of J. P. Narayan, the Janata Party's most respected elder statesman and kingmaker. The secretary, however, promptly denied them permission for a meeting. " 'Just tell J.P. we're Tibetans. He's never refused a Tibetan.' That was Lodi's line," said Norbu. "I told him, 'Lodi, all your bullshit is not going to get us anywhere this time.' But the next minute the secretary came out and said, 'Gentlemen, please come this way.' Then all the reporters started bawling, 'How come these low characters are getting in?' and we just walked through."

Offering Narayan a white scarf, Lodi Gyari congratulated him on the Janata Party's victory and appealed for support for the hunger strike. Narayan instantly agreed. Furthermore, he promised to secure the backing of Morarji Desai, the Prime Minister-to-be. Somewhat stunned by their success, the three left a few minutes later. Over the next days an unprecedented series of letters and politicians about to be appointed to the new cabinet arrived at the tent. One and all pledged to back Tibet's cause: the first time that the refugees' struggle had been publicly condoned by their host country. In exchange for its unique gesture, the Janata Party secured the cessation of the hunger strike and the fast was broken on its tenth day as Acharya Kripalani offered orange juice to the seven Tibetans. Elated, Gyari and Norbu returned to Dharamsala, in the wake of the strikers' tumultuous welcome, bringing with them the Janata Party letters to present to the Cabinet.

The result was chaos. Preempted by the youth in contacting the new Indian government, the Kashag condemned the entire affair. It accused the strikers of recklessly endangering all the refugees' efforts, there being no way of knowing what, once in office, the government's final stand on the Tibetan issue would be. To repair the damage, the Cabinet demanded the resignation of the leaders of the Tibetan People's Freedom Movement, whose key members also headed the Youth Congress. For days Dharamsala was filled with angry crowds denouncing the government. Both the Cabinet ministers and the people's deputies (who, it was assumed, were in collusion with the Kashag) were accosted in public, few of the refugees comprehending why they had turned against the triumph. Finally, to defuse the crisis, the Coordinating Committee of the Tibetan People's Freedom Movement disbanded and, as an act of protest, the four founding members of the Youth Congress resigned from its Central Executive Committee. Not long after its inauguration, the Janata Party reneged on all of its promises, preferring, like its predecessor governments, to keep the Tibetans from impeding a still-hoped-for peaceful coexistence with China.

The limits of political freedom in exile had been vividly drawn by the confrontation. Yet, as evidence of democracy's strength, within a few years all of the youth leaders were not only back in politics but working in the very posts they had previously attacked—as a Cabinet minister, as directors of the Information Office and of the Drama Society, and, in Lodi Gyari's case, Chairman of the Commission of Tibetan People's Deputies. Meanwhile, the Youth Congress received new leadership, at the head of which stood Tempa Tsering. Not long after his arrival in Dharamsala, Tempa had found his name put up among thirty other candidates for election to Centrex. On the basis of his reputation as general secretary of the Byllakuppe branch, he was voted in 1974 to be the Congress's treasurer. Four years later, he was elected to be an adviser to Centrex, among the highest posts in the Congress and one of the most powerful positions in exile society. Under Tempa the Congress initiated a new militant course of action. Its leaders decided, in strict secrecy, that the time had come to employ terrorism in the fight for Tibet. Though the idea had been discussed for years, its adoption now seemed inevitable, made so not just by the failed attempt to win public backing from India's new government, but by the outcome of a clandestine martial struggle already underway since 1959.

EARLY IN 1961, the leader of Gendun Thargay's 500-man road gang called him aside for a private talk. "You've been chosen to go for training," said the foreman. "You'll need an X ray and a photograph of yourself." Obtaining the two items in Tezpur, Gendun returned to the camp a few days later and was introduced to another young man, who, like himself, was also from Kham, tall and ruggedly built. "Tell your friends that you are going to work in Darjeeling," said the foreman. "From now on, whatever happens you are sworn to secrecy." Vowing to neither ask questions nor divulge what had already occurred, the two men received packets of money, an address in Darjeeling and a six-digit number which, presented at their destination, would gain them access. Uncertain as to the type of training they were to receive, they departed, all the while fearful of capture by IB agents who, searching for Chinese spies among the refugees, had banned unapproved travel by Tibetans. On the train the next day, though, Gendun noticed two other men, like him and his partner strikingly robust and undoubtedly from eastern Tibet. When they exited one stop before Darjeeling, Gendun hurriedly followed and on a hunch sought their aid. Inquiring whether they knew of a good restaurant in the vicinity, he received a subdued assent and was guided to a small café. There, after a brief meal, a truck arrived. Without a word concerning the

The future Fourteenth Dalai Lama with his parents and elder brother, Gyalo Thondup, shortly after his birth in 1935.

Farmers ploughing barley fields in Central Tibet, 1930.

*Thubten Gyatso, the
Thirteenth Dalai Lama,
in Darjeeling, ca. 1910–1912.*

*The Chensel Phodrang,
the Thirteenth
Dalai Lama's favorite
residence in the
Norbulingka, or Jewel Park, 1937.*

Lhamo Lhatso, the sacred lake in which the vision of the Fourteenth Dalai Lama's birthplace was seen.

Lhamo Dhondrub, the Fourteenth Dalai Lama, at the time of his discovery by a government search party.

Tibetan noblemen gathered before the Potala to officiate at the New Year's celebrations, 1924.

Tibetan noble ladies from the provinces of U (left and right) and Tsang (center).

The Dalai Lama on his throne at the time of the Chinese invasion in the autumn of 1950.

Soldiers of the Tibetan Army on parade in Lhasa; later, in 1950, these troops fought the Chinese.

*Commanders of the People's
Liberation Army, accompanied
by officials of the Tibetan
government, inspect troops
in front of the Potala.*

The Tibetan delegation signs
the Seventeen-Point Agreement
in Peking, May 23, 1951.

Ngabo Ngawang Jigme
(exteme left) toasts the
signing of the Seventeen-Point
Agreement with Zhu De,
Commander-in-Chief of
the People's Liberation Army.

Mao Zedong hosts a banquet for the Panchen Lama (left) and Dalai Lama (right) on their arrival in Peking, August 1954.

Prime Minister Nehru with the Dalai Lama and Zhou Enlai in New Delhi, November 1956.

*Chinese trucks arrive for
the first time in Lhasa on the
newly completed Chinghai-
Tibet Highway, January 1955.*

Nechung Monastery, home of Tibet's State Oracle; Drepung, the world's largest monastery, in the background, late 1950s.

One of the many anti-Chinese demonstrations held in and around Lhasa in March 1959.

*The Dalai Lama delivers
his New Year's sermon to
50,000 monks in front of
the Tsuglhakang, Lhasa's
Central Cathedral.*

The Dalai Lama
(second from left) *and his
bodyguard on horseback.*

The Dalai Lama with his
younger brother, Ngari Rinpoché
(front row, extreme right) and
Khampa guerrillas during
their escape from Tibet.

*The Dalai Lama
escorted by Gurkhas
after his arrival in India.*

*Officers of Chushi Gangdruk,
Tibet's guerrilla resistance.*

*One of the first groups
of Tibetan refugees
to reach India.*

A class of refugee schoolchildren in Mussoorie, early 1960s.

Guerrillas from
Mustang on a
foray into Tibet.

apparently shared mission, the men instructed their companions to lie on the truck's floor. When it eventually stopped, Gendun looked out at the exact address he had sought in Darjeeling. Presenting his number at the door, he was ushered in, and henceforth permitted to leave only for short walks or an occasional meal. Though the people who ran the house never so much as mentioned their work, in the interim, Gendun clearly realized that he had come under the auspices of Chushi Gangdruk, Tibet's still-active guerrilla resistance.

After three weeks in Darjeeling, Gendun Thargay was told to store away his few belongings. Given money, he was then released to the nearby market to purchase a single pair of sneakers. Returning to the house, he waited through the day with four other men—all from Kham and Amdo —his only remaining possession a *tung-wa* or cloth bundle worn around the neck, containing red protection cords and barley grains blessed by the State Oracle. At five o'clock, Lhamo Tsering, a high-ranking officer in Chushi Gangdruk, arrived with a document in hand. He instructed the men either to leave or to sign the paper, which, as a recruitment form for the National Volunteer Defense Army, bound them to obey to the death any order given by a superior. All five signed and at six o'clock sharp under cover of darkness, a canvas-roofed jeep picked them up at the bottom of the hillside street on which the house stood. At a second stop, six more men crammed into the jeep, compelling Gendun to hang out the back as it drove south from Darjeeling, heading directly, it seemed, for the border of East Pakistan.

"You don't have to think about what's under you—mud, water or shit," said the man in charge three hours later. "When we arrive in a minute, do only what I say, just like in war." Pulling onto the shoulder of the road, the jeep stopped and the men were ordered to sprint in silence across an open field. They started running, but a pair of headlights appeared, followed by the leader's abrupt command to drop. The car passed and they ran again. The bank of a wide river loomed in the darkness. Arriving, they regrouped and for the next few hours wandered back and forth along the shoreline until, plainly lost, their leader asked a member of the company who spoke Hindi to enter a nearby village and cautiously inquire whether or not it lay in Pakistan. A half hour later the man returned surrounded by a mob of angry villagers carrying sticks and rifles. Outnumbered, the luckless Tibetans were promptly hustled to a nearby police station where, they were convinced, a jail cell would be waiting. On entering, however, they were surprised to witness the commanding officer dismiss the villagers and once they had gone offer a cordial reception. He then explained that not only were they in Pakistan but that the special agent whose presence they had fruitlessly sought on the riverbank had already alerted authorities throughout the region to look for their group. A short while later the contact showed up in a Pakistani army truck. The Tibetans were put inside, driven to a small house and left for the remainder of the night.

Early the next morning, at the first hint of dawn, Gendun was roused from sleep and ordered to run to an adjacent building. From here he watched the rest of his group race over, one at a time, followed by the agent, who was clearly concerned that there be no further sighting by local people. Given food and blankets to sit on, the Tibetans spent the day indoors waiting for nightfall when the army truck once more picked them up. Driven into a forest, they were placed in groups of threes and told to sprint again. Across a clearing lay a railroad track. On it stood a solitary car. As he ran, Gendun glimpsed a station farther down the line. Reaching the car, he paused to look at it more closely, but was quickly pulled inside by a squad of Pakistani soldiers armed with submachine guns. Escorted to a locked compartment, the metal blinds of its windows firmly shut, he soon heard a train arrive, couple with the car and begin pulling it in what he judged to be a southerly direction. One day later, the sounds of a large terminal became audible. Unhooked, the car jolted loose from the train and was drawn some distance away. The door of Gendun's compartment then flew back and a Pakistani soldier gestured for him to follow. Outside the train, the Tibetans were rushed into a waiting troop truck, which, led by a military jeep, exited the station and drove swiftly through a large city —Dacca, as Gendun learned years later. On the outskirts of the city, the truck halted before a lone building standing at the far end of an airstrip. Within a few minutes, a gray unmarked two-propeller craft landed and taxied directly over. Though some of the Khampas had seen Chinese planes from below as they flew bombing missions over Kham, none had glimpsed a *namdu* or "skyboat" at close quarters. An even greater surprise followed, however, when a small door near the tail of the plane opened, a ladder descended and out stepped a tall, sharp-featured white man smoking a pipe.

A single row of seats ran down the right side of the plane's interior. On the left, a small photo of the Dalai Lama was taped to the fuselage. Gendun watched closely while three Caucasian men demonstrated how to fasten a seat belt. As the plane's propellers revved, they drew the curtains. Then, returning from the front cabin after takeoff, they opened them and passed out paper cups containing a cold brown drink. "What is this, rum?" Gendun asked the Tibetan interpreter in the group. The translator spoke to one of the white men in an unfamiliar language. "This is a foreign drink," he momentarily announced to his compatriots. "It is called Coca-

Cola." After sipping Coca-Cola, the passengers were each given a tray of food. Grappling with roast beef sandwiches, pickles, salt and pepper shakers, a few of the Tibetans, wondering if it too was some strange new food, unwrapped the small bars of soap beside their plates and ate them as well. Following dinner, they relaxed for the first time since their journey had begun two days before. In typical Khampa style, they left the odd chairs and, indifferent to their surroundings, sat cross-legged on the floor. A pair of ivory dice materialized and a raucous session of *shö*, Tibet's most popular game of chance, was shortly underway, each player shouting at the top of his lungs as his turn came to hurl the dice down. After a brief fuel stop late in the night the men eventually went to sleep, waking the next morning to behold a brilliant expanse of sunlit water shimmering below—their first sight of an ocean.

After a day in the air, the small plane landed. An army transport backed directly up to the steps in its rear and drove the Tibetans off. The climate was cool and a heavy rain pummeled the roof. Finding a small hole in the canvas, Gendun pried it larger and bending down, was able to look outside. Orientals, holding umbrellas against the downpour, walked past stores with Chinese characters on their signs. Gendun assumed that he was in Taiwan. The truck passed through a checkpoint in a wire fence and then stopped by two small buildings hidden behind a thick stand of trees. Inside, the Tibetans were shown to a row of cots in a barren room in which they were to spend the next twenty-eight days, forbidden, when outside, to go beyond the immediate surroundings.

The men soon realized that they were quartered in a remote corner of a vast military base—not in Taiwan, but on Okinawa, as was subsequently revealed. One day the man with the pipe spoke to them through their interpreter. He said that they had been waiting for a second group of Tibetans. It now appeared that the entire contingent had been apprehended by India's IB while crossing the Pakistan border. As a result, they were to proceed alone. "Each of your backgrounds has been closely checked to ensure that you are not a Chinese spy," he stated. "You are going to receive new names in my language and from now on you must respond only to them." To the Tibetans' great amusement, they were forthwith dubbed Doug, Bob, Willy, Jack, Rocky, Martin and Lee, confirming what many of them had already surmised, to wit, that the Communists' worst enemy had finally seen fit to become the Tibetans' best friend—a distant country called America.

Once more the gray airplane, its curtains, fastened, rose noisily into the sky. An odd comradeship between the white men and their charges had developed. While the Tibetans gambled on the floor, drank Coca-Cola, shouted and laughed, the Westerners, clearly taken by their unrestrained spirits, walked up and down the wide aisle, periodically placing their hands in prayer before the Dalai Lama's photo and grinning broadly. Though they repeatedly order their passengers to go to sleep—going so far as to hustle them into their seats and turn the overhead lights out—the Khampas, accustomed to taking orders only from their own tribal chieftains, persisted in returning to the floor to gamble in the dark. In the morning a large island appeared in the sea below. After they landed, the men rested for a day, in the course of which the American with the pipe insisted on having his picture taken with Gendun. They got back on board and the aircraft took off, flying through a second night until, looking out toward sunset the following day, Gendun noticed a long coastline below, with a large city sprawled across low-lying hills in its midst. As they crossed a range of dun-colored mountains, he saw the lights of another great city, among which the plane soon landed. Once more army trucks were waiting. This time, though, the temperature was extremely cold. After driving upward for three hours, a rest stop was taken by the side of the road. Stepping from the trucks, the Tibetans were astonished to see towering, snow-covered peaks under a brilliant starry sky. The mountains looked so familiar that for a moment some thought that they had returned to Tibet. Others, after five weeks in tight quarters, ran wildly through the fresh-fallen snow oblivious of their wet sneakers and were only boarded once more with a good deal of effort by their escorts. Three hours farther into the mountains, they passed a checkpoint in a barbed-wire fence and drove up a long valley. At its end stood a cluster of single-story buildings. Inside one each man was assigned a bed, beside which stood a small table neatly stacked with pencil, pad and towels. The barracks was bare and immaculate, but Gendun found a single telltale item which had eluded the keepers, an old pencil, its eraser end covered by toothmarks. In Tibet, when writing, it was the normal procedure to hold one's pen between the teeth while using both hands to fold the paper into lines. The toothmarks convinced Gendun that Tibetans had been there before. From then on he was sure that he was in America.

The second island in the sea had been Hawaii; the city on the coastline, San Francisco; the one landed at, Denver; the mountain base the Tibetans had been taken to, Camp Hale, eighteen miles north of Leadville, Colorado. Used during the World War II for high-altitude combat training, Camp Hale had been redesigned for the creation of a clandestine Tibetan army under the direct administration of the CIA.

The decision to train Tibetans in the United States was made little more than a month after the March uprising. On April 21, 1959, three weeks after the Dalai Lama's escape, General Gompo Tashi Andrugtsang, field commander of the National Volunteer Defense Army, confronted with overwhelming Chinese forces, gave orders for his Lhoka-based headquarters to be abandoned. While guerrillas continued to function in separate units throughout Lhoka, the NVDA's chief officers sought refuge in the NEFA, Gompo Tashi himself suffering from debilitating wounds. Proceeding to Darjeeling, he met with the organization's leader, the Dalai Lama's elder brother, Gyalo Thondup, and together with their advisers, the two men laid plans for the next stage of the NVDA's fight, which, now that China stood in outright possession of Tibet, was to be based on a substantially closer involvement with the CIA.

To date, the CIA's training of Khampas had been limited. On Guam and Okinawa (the agency's forward station for monitoring its Tibetan operation), recruits had received four months of instruction, after which, armed with a tommy gun, a radio and poison, to be self-administered in the event of capture, they were flown from Bangkok and dropped by parachute into Tibet to organize cells. While only *pons* or tribal chieftains and their sons had been used, the new project, begun in May 1959, called for the instruction of five groups totaling almost 500 men, selected both for their physical stature and to represent each district in Tibet's three provinces. As in the past, once training was complete, they were to be dropped into their native regions to organize a resistance that eventually would be linked to the broad body of NVDA troops, who hoped to relocate to a new base somewhere on Tibet's borders.

The utmost secrecy shrouded the operation. The Tibetans were never told that they were in the United States. Thus, if any man was captured, American involvement could not be proved. Meanwhile, training a covert army of Asians in the middle of the Rocky Mountains warranted the greatest care. By mid-July 1959, the CIA had planted a front page story in the Denver *Post* reporting that atomic testing—though not bomb detonation—was to be conducted at Camp Hale. The vast area of 14,000-foot peaks and valleys covered by the camp was henceforth strictly off bounds to the civilian population. People who were near Peterson Air Force Base, outside of Colorado Springs, when a subsequent group of Tibetans was flown out, found themselves detained. Up to forty-seven at a time were held at gunpoint behind army roadblocks until mysterious buses, their windows painted black, had passed by. When news of unidentified Orientals in Colorado reached the New York *Times*, Secretary of Defense Robert McNamara personally had the story suppressed. As a final resort, soldiers guarding the most sensitive areas of the base—as well as the Tibetans themselves—were given explicit instructions to shoot to kill anyone found within the perimeters.

Gendun's group was the fourth to arrive at Camp Hale. On their first day the men were issued black combat boots and green army fatigues. After breakfast, they were taken on a tour of the camp's immediate area, which consisted of ten buildings near the bank of a small river. All around, heavily forested mountains screened off the outside world, but even within the camp restrictions were imposed. Their barracks, the dining hall, the classrooms and a large room with odd-looking tables called "pool" and "Ping-Pong" were the only areas Tibetans were permitted in. They were told as much at their first lecture given by a large instructor in combat fatigues. Informing the group that training would last for six months, the American concluded by asking two questions: "Will you jump from an airplane? If so, raise your hands." Pleased with the response, he smiled and said, "Who wants to fight the Chinese?"

Camp Hale's curriculum covered a wide variety of topics. Addressed by their English names, stamped on plastic panels pinned to visored caps, the Tibetans were taught weaponry, survival techniques, radio operations, coding, how to organize an underground network, make letter drops and chart contact points. Morning classes began with a twenty-six-letter, ten-number code used in wireless transmission, map reading, and compass work. One-of-a-kind equipment had been manufactured by the CIA specially for the Tibetans' use, including radios no larger than a hand yet powerful enough to transmit clearly over vast distances. M-1 rifles, mortars, bazookas and silencers were among the weapons employed. The men were taught parachuting, rock climbing and river crossing and went through exercises in which deer had to be killed and butchered on the run, the meat eaten raw for a week, while instructors (often pursuing with live ammunition) hunted their pupils. They were also introduced to the more refined arts of espionage. Gendun was told that on being sent into Tibet, he must spend days in hiding, observing the daily patterns of his parents and relatives to be certain, before making contact, that they were not working with, or being observed by the Chinese. He was then taught to establish resistance cells which would report regularly to him on Chinese troop movements. They were to be ready at all times for the signal to rise up in revolt as part of a coordinated effort across the whole country. He learned how to move by night through hostile territory, how to pass, disguised, through checkposts if forced to move by day, and if captured, how to resist interrogation. Holding to a fixed story for as long as possible, he was gradually to lead the Chinese to believe that he was breaking, choosing the most credible moment to stage a collapse, after which he would present them with the supposedly true account of his identity, itself also a fabrication, prepared long before.

After a few months at Camp Hale, 125 more Tibetans arrived. A short while later Gendun completed his training and was chosen, among eighty of the most proficient men, to be dropped into Tibet. Though each man's assignment was kept secret from the others, the Tibetans learned, through a bit of their own spying, that their group was only the latest strand in a web already woven around the entire countryside. One day, while sweeping a normally guarded staff building, a Tibetan trainee found himself alone. Looking behind the large white sheets that covered a wall in the main room, he discovered a detailed map of Tibet. All across it red pins marked the location of agents. Rummaging about further, he found prepacked parachute bags, with the names of his own group stenciled on them. Their contents included radios, lightweight pistols and silencers. A short while later, Gendun was taken under cover of darkness out of Camp Hale to embark on the long journey home. In the course of his stay, however, much had changed, altering not only the CIA-Tibetan link but the entire balance of power in Central Asia.

At 5:00 a.m. on the morning of October 20, 1962, Chinese artillery opened fire on a small Indian border garrison guarding the Kameng Division of the NEFA. An hour later, 20,000 Chinese troops poured over the Thagla Ridge while 1,500 miles away a simultaneous attack in Ladakh was launched. The PLA pushed all the way to Bomdila in the east and captured 14,500 square miles of the Aksai Chin in the west before, on November 21, withdrawing to the original McMahon line separating India and Tibet in the NEFA. Only four months after the expiration of Panch Sheel, Nehru's decade-long effort at amicable relations with the People's Republic had abruptly collapsed, the victim of Chinese border claims and a plainly expansionist policy. New Delhi's humiliating defeat forced him to admit that: "We have been living in a fool's paradise of our own making"; whereafter he turned directly to the United States for support against future aggression.

At the core of India's belated effort to arm its northern border lay the formation, under CIA tutelage, of a new clandestine commando group, known as the Special Frontier Force and code-named Establishment 22, after its chief base. Raised on November 13, 1962, under the command of the Research and Analysis Wing of Indian Intelligence (RAW), the SFF was to be an entirely Tibetan force charged with the mission of guarding the world's highest border. Though its existence was staunchly denied by the Tibetan government-in-exile, Indian sources portrayed its critical role in easing the difficult CIA-Khampa connection through Pakistan with a new, direct channel via New Delhi. According to the same sources, much of the NVDA's activities were henceforth administered under 22's auspices directly from the Indian capital. A special communications base was set up south of Calcutta in Orissa, from which, in an area free of dense radio traffic, weekly communication with the operatives in Tibet could easily be maintained.

Returning to Asia, Gendun was taken off combat status and assigned, instead, to the staff of the Orissa center. Here, two large receivers, attached to special antennas able to pick up the most remote signals emanating from north of the Himalayas provided a steady stream of information. Recorded by Gendun and ten co-workers, the data were transmitted in numerical code by teletype to the NVDA's headquarters in New Delhi. After a time, Gendun was transferred to work in New Delhi itself. There he decoded messages in the company of three other wireless men and two file clerks in an innocuous-looking one-story building, traveling to and from work each day, for eleven years, hidden under blankets in a station wagon. Each Monday night a joint meeting of senior officers in the NVDA, RAW and CIA representatives was convened, at which cyclostyled copies of the week's transcripts from Tibet were analyzed and directives given. Concurrently the most visible of all efforts to fight for Tibet freedom took shape in the NVDA's new forward base.

In the middle of 1960, with CIA training well underway, leaders of Tibet's resistance chose the 750-square-mile kingdom of Mustang as the best seat for re-forming their operations. Jutting at 15,000 feet, like an elevated wedge, into western Tibet, Mustang had been appended to Nepal as a vassal state since the early nineteenth century. Over a month's trek from Katmandu, however, it was so isolated as to have no contact with the government of Nepal beyond paying an annual tax of little more than $100. The kingdom's principal approach from the south lay through the needle-thin Kali Gandaki Gorge, the deepest gorge in the world (by virtue of its lying between two of the planet's highest peaks, Annapurna and Dhaulagiri), and virtually impassable if defended. But Mustang's chief value lay in its strategic proximity to the Xinjiang-Lhasa road. As one of Tibet's two main arteries, the highway originated in Kham and ran along the entire northern scarp of the Himalayas through to the Aksai Chin region of Ladakh, from where it looped northwest into Xinjiang and the Sino-Soviet front beyond. Its dirt roadbed and single telegraph line united Chinese garrisons over 1,500 miles of sensitive border. Mustang also had the advantage of being one of the few remnant pockets of indigenous Tibetan culture. As such, it was home ground for the Khampas: both a haven from which to raid Chinese columns and nearby camps with impunity and a vital rear base for guerrillas still active in southern and eastern Tibet.

Late in 1960, NVDA troops began arriving in Mustang. Though subsequently joined by guerrilla bands coming directly from Tibet, the project was spearheaded by men who had retreated from Lhoka with General Gompo Tashi. Collected from road gangs, they proceeded to Darjeeling and Gangtok, from where, organized in groups of forty, they proceeded westward, crossed secretly into the thick jungle of southern Nepal and trekking up through the alpine terrain of the Kali Gandaki Gorge, emerged finally onto the arid, windswept Tibetan Plateau, at Mustang's border. Welcomed by the kingdom's twenty-third monarch—whose fear of the nearby PLA exceeded only that of an independent army on his own ground—they established a network of interlocking bases. Some were forward tent camps manned by only a hundred to two hundred troops; others were supply depots built around preexistent towns and monasteries. Headquarters was placed to the rear, on Mustang's southern rim, an hour and a half north of Jomosom, the last Nepalese town. In time, twenty-five buildings housing five departments—supply, transport, ammunition, intelligence and internal discipline—rose between a deep gorge and the foot of the heavily wooded Nilgiri Mountain. At their center stood the office of General Baba Yeshi—Mustang's commander—a three-storied building surrounded by a wall with a parapet; a huge Tibetan mastiff was chained to the main gate, the flag of Tibet flew in its courtyard. Besides the locale, Tibetan ponies tethered hitching posts and Khampa troops clad in captured PLA jackets and bandoliers, all gave, as one veteran recalled, a "Wild West flavor" to the place. But it was precisely the dry, rocky environment that made creating the Mustang base extremely difficult in the beginning. Before sufficient supplies could be parachuted in, most of the initial 4,000 men were reduced to boiling their boots and saddles for food, with some, according to one account, carrying out raids across the border into Tibet, not to attack the Chinese, but to steal livestock for their own survival.

With the airdrops came almost forty graduates of Camp Hale. From them, the National Volunteer Defense Army received a badly needed education in modern combat. They brought M-1's and Springfields, heavy 80-millimeter recoilless guns and 2-inch mortars as well as solar batteries to run hidden radio hookups, scramblers for coding messages, machine-gun silencers, "death pills" and miniature cameras for espionage. Under their instruction, khaki uniforms were adopted and daily life became more regimented with a 5:00 a.m. rising followed by calisthenics, singing of the Tibetan national anthem, farming, survival training and maneuvers in the hills. Their presence gave Tibet its first substantial military hope since the height of the revolt in 1958.

Resuscitated, the NVDA struck out east, north and west from Mustang's high plateau. An average raid consisted of a few dozen men penetrating Tibet for up to a month, ambushing a PLA convoy and then retreating. The country was so wild that, given a reasonable troop parity, the guerrillas were guaranteed success whenever they attacked. Some forays, though, were luckier than others. In 1966 a small party sent to disrupt transport along the Xinjiang-Lhasa road annihilated a Chinese convoy. It was not until the battle was over that the guerrillas discovered the head of the PLA's western command in Tibet and his entire staff among the corpses. The party had been traveling with all of their records, which now proved a treasure trove, not just for the Tibetans but for the CIA as well. Through these, invaluable information on the recently begun Cultural Revolution was obtained as well as a remarkable document revealing that by China's own count some 87,000 Tibetans had been killed in the 1959 revolt, an event which Peking had continued to portray as only a minor disturbance.

Mustang's greatest achievement lay in its espionage network. Within a short time the NVDA had succeeded in establishing underground links throughout Tibet, not only the scope but the quality of information retrieved making the operation immensely profitable. Though the Chinese were suspicious of all Tibetans, the regional CCP was compelled to employ a number of minority cadres for administrative tasks. Among these were many "sleepers," Tibetans who appeared to be collaborators but in reality were, as they slowly ascended the local hierarchy, supplying the NVDA with information. NVDA couriers, traveling from place to place by night collected information from agents and were responsible for documenting not only China's massive military buildup along the Himalayas but also the critical shifting of the PRC's principal nuclear base from Lop Nor in Xinjiang to Nagchuka, 165 miles north of Lhasa.

For all of its advantages Mustang proved to have one critical flaw. It was too remote from the main theater of Chinese operations—"an isolated army in an isolated territory," as one guerrilla described the second stage of Tibetan resistance. In addition, Khampa fighters, raised for millennia as cavalry, were now denied the use of their mounts. Due to the difficulty of retreating up the treacherous passes which enclosed the plateau, only sixty Tibetan ponies were kept for the entire corps. Retreat itself inflicted the highest number of casualties. The wounded were generally left to die, Mustang's headquarters, much less its front-line camps, had little medicine and no surgical equipment. Nevertheless, in time, age, not battle, caused the greatest loss of life. "It was pathetic," recalled one of the younger guerrillas, a TYC recruit who was sent to Mustang to replace men entering their forties and fifties. "People didn't die from bullets, but just by walking to a fight and back. Once they knew a raid was on, the Chinese would send patrols to cut off its retreat. The PLA were fresh and our men had been literally jogging night after night. So the old-timers would give out. They'd take a whole tin of coffee, mix it together with water and soup in their bowls and drink it. That kept them going. But after doing this kind of thing two or three times, their hearts would just pop."

As the 1970s began, a combination of external and internal pressures placed Mustang's continued existence in jeopardy. Following Henry Kissinger's secret flight to Peking, paving the way, in July of 1971, for a U.S.-Chinese rapprochement, the CIA suddenly cut off support to the Tibetan guerrillas. With the Special Frontier Force grown into a mature unit, India had no need to maintain on its own the previous level of aid. Even worse, Nepal, no longer fearful, as it had been in the early 1960s, of a Chinese attack, now wished to counter New Delhi's influence in the region by furthering ties with Peking. Hence, in 1972 Katmandu, which had feigned ignorance of the Khampas' presence for twelve years, took the first step toward expelling them by launching a propaganda attack accusing the Tibetans of banditry, rape, and murder.

Internal disarray as well plagued the National Volunteer Defense Army. In 1969 Gyalo Thondup, acting on long-standing complaints of younger CIA-educated officers, had withdrawn General Baba Yeshi as commander, replacing him with a nephew of the late Gompo Tashi Andrugtsang, the sole survivor of the first group of Tibetans to be trained by the United States, General Gyato Wangdu. Baba Yeshi went peacefully at first, journeying to Dharamsala where he was offered as reparation the prestigious post of Chief of Security, holding a rank equivalent to that of deputy Cabinet minister. He declined the position, however, and within a short time was back in Mustang. Rallying almost two hundred of his tribesmen, Baba Yeshi broke from the NVDA, publicly accused Gyalo Thondup of misappropriating funds and occupied a guerrilla camp called Mamang east of Mustang from which he openly attacked the main body of soldiers, now, in effect, a rival faction. In return, General Wangdu laid siege to the splinter group's holdout, until Katmandu, apprised of the internecine strife, compelled Baba Yeshi to present himself at the capital. Three months of personal negotiations, led by Nepal's Home Secretary, followed. At their climax Baba Yeshi, according to one witness, burst into tears, pleaded for protection and then, in exchange for a grant of political asylum, gave the Nepalese a detailed account of the NVDA's troop strength, supplies, weaponry and positions.

By then, the trouble had already spread to the Tibetan communities in India. Prominent leaders in thirteen settlements, populated mainly by refugees from Kham and Amdo, sided with Baba Yeshi in the dispute, believing that his dismissal by Gyalo Thondup had been the result of a concerted effort on the part of the primarily Central Tibetan government in Dharamsala to disenfranchise them.

In large part the opening of a regional fault line—always Tibet's greatest internal threat—resulted from Kuomintang agitation. From the Tibetans' earliest days in exile, KMT agents had attempted to win a faction of the refugees to their own cause. Their greatest success had been with some of the easterners in the so-called 13 camps, who, though they had no pro-Taiwanese sympathies, were happy to accept large financial contributions as an alternative to Dharamsala's support. Exploiting the NVDA split, the KMT now sought to draw the 13 group further from Dharamsala and closer to itself by successfully fueling separatist sentiment. After a failed attempt at redress in Dharamsala, the 13 group's relations with the exile administration soured and some of its members ceased to submit the one rupee a month contribution given by most refugees to their government.

Early in 1974 the various pressures combined to destroy Mustang. In a November 1973 meeting in Peking, Mao Zedong personally threatened King Birendra of Nepal with direct action unless he shut down the Tibetan guerrilla base. Complying, Birendra declared all of northwestern Nepal a restricted zone and began flooding the area with 10,000 troops of the Royal Army, police and Gurkhas, summoned from duty abroad with UN peacekeeping forces. Given the single narrow track, carved into the sheer western face of the Kali Gandaki Gorge, leading north from Pokhara to Jomosom, it was a phenomenal exercise just to reach Mustang. Yet even though they outnumbered the Khampas two to one, the Nepalese, once in place, still had only a small hope of victory. After a decade and a half the Tibetans' knowledge of the terrain was unsurpassable, their stores capable of supporting them for up to two years. Accordingly, Nepal secretly coordinated plans with China for a PLA drive on the Khampas' northern flank should they attempt a retreat into Tibet.

While the military geared up for a fight, the Nepalese government took its first political step in March 1974. Sending emissaries to General Wangdu, Katmandu offered a trade-off: almost half a million dollars in "rehabilitation" aid and the rights to land and buildings already developed in exchange for a full surrender and disbanding of the various camps. When the Khampas refused, Nepal attempted to force their hand. On April 19, Lhamo Tsering, the NVDA's chief officer in New Delhi, was arrested in Pokhara while en route to Mustang. He was then held hostage to force a surrender. It was, however, a tentative move. Because the Nepalese were frightened that any greater show of force would provoke the Khampas (who were a week's trek away) to descend and, as one observer put it, "massacre everyone," Lhamo Tsering was only placed under house arrest. In addition, he was able to smuggle a message north, ordering that under no condition should the Mustang base yield to Nepalese demands. Nepal reluctantly completed positioning its troops and called for the Tibetans to agree to five-point surrender terms by July 30 or face expulsion. As the situation rapidly escalated to a confrontation, the Dalai Lama himself intervened. Tape-recording a twenty-minute message in which he requested the NVDA to disarm peacefully, he dispatched the Minister of Dharamsala's Security Department, P. T. Takla, to Katmandu. Once there, Takla requested Nepal to free Lhamo Tsering and permit both him and the guerrilla leader to bring the tape to General Wangdu and his officers. Acceding in part to the proposal, the Nepalese allowed Takla to pick up Lhamo Tsering in Pokhara. From there the two flew in a helicopter to the Stol airstrip in Jomosom. Across from the strip stood a one-story Nepalese army post, around which thousands of troops were now massed. While Lhamo Tsering was held in a nearby building, Takla rode an hour and a half north to the NVDA command, where, apprised of his mission, a large coterie of Khampa officers was waiting.

The scene that followed was tragic. P. T. Takla began his appeal for surrender by saying that the Nepalese had Lhamo Tsering in Jomosom; if the guerrillas wished him released they would have to disarm. After two decades of waging a forlorn guerrilla war against the largest nation on earth, the Khampa commanders greeted this line of reasoning as laughable. They joked that Takla had brought good, not bad news, as that very night they would raid the post and free their comrade. Only then did Takla play the Dalai Lama's tape. There was immediate and anguished disorder. Pachen, head of the internal discipline department and one of the most respected and impassioned leaders, rose to speak, "How can I surrender to the Nepalese when I have never surrendered to the Chinese?" he said. "I'll never give them my weapon. But at the same time I cannot disobey my lama's orders. We should all return to Tibet this minute and die there fighting rather than live in shame." Wangdu, though, in concert with other senior officers, decided to obey the Dalai Lama's orders and surrender. A few days later Pachen slit his own throat. Two other officers followed his lead, preferring to take their own lives rather than accede to the contradictory terms of their failure.

As the Dalai Lama's message traveled from camp to camp, played over loudspeakers, columns of pack animals laden with weapons began heading south. Nonetheless, once apprised of the Khampas' decision, Nepal reneged on its promise of a trade-off. Entering Mustang, it launched a "search and seizure" operation. All those guerrillas who had voluntarily disarmed were apprehended and marched into Jomosom while their land and property were confiscated. Word of the duplicity swiftly passed to General Wangdu.

With an escort of forty select troops and the guerrillas' documents, Wangdu fled. Riding west, he leapfrogged back and forth between Nepal and Tibet, attempting an end run for the Indian border 200 miles away. The PLA was already waiting for him. Over the course of a fortnight Chinese attacks twice pushed the Khampas into Nepal, while a Nepalese ambush sent them back to Tibet. And then, once more, treachery undermined the guerrillas. Early in the flight, during a night march, a mule carrying food was lost. General Wangdu sent two men to retrieve it, one of whom failed to return. Instead he went to Jomosom, and in an exchange for a reprieve reported the Tibetans' escape route. Forty men of Baba Yeshi's rival faction, already recruited by Nepal to guide its army into Mustang, were hurriedly put on Wangdu's rear, while the Nepalese themselves set up a massive ambush twenty miles from the Indian border, at the guerrilla leader's goal, a 17,800-foot pass in the Jumla District called Tinker.

Arriving at Tinker toward the end of August, Wangdu called a halt. Exhausted, his men dismounted and sat on a hillside within sight of a nearby PLA camp. When none volunteered to seek out forage and water for the horses, Wangdu personally led a party of five to reconnoiter up the track. In a short while, the general and his patrol disappeared into a small draw before the pass. A moment later those left behind heard a storm of rapid fire erupt from all directions. As they ran to their mounts, they beheld the advance group's five ponies galloping, riderless, back toward them. Racing up to join the fight, they arrived just in time to see Wangdu gunned down while single-handedly charging Nepalese positions on an adjacent slope, the other men, save one, already dead. A fire fight then broke out, lasting the entire day and, according to one account, taking the lives of hundreds of Nepalese troops. Outnumbered, the Tibetans finally abandoned their horses and using ropes scaled the surrounding cliffs, outflanked the pass and escaped a few hours later over the border into the waiting arms of the Indian army.

A day after the fight at Tinker Pass, Baba Yeshi flew by helicopter from Katmandu to identify Wangdu's body. Following the confirmation, an official ceremony was held in the Royal Palace. King Birendra himself distributed prizes, promotions and cash rewards to scores of Nepalese soldiers who had taken part in the destruction of Mustang. Under a large tent in the Thundikhel field, at the city's center, Wangdu's amulet, wristwatch, rings, rifle and tea bowl were displayed to crowds of curious Nepalese who queued up for days to see the guerrilla leader's remains. Beside them were exhibited a vast assortment of binoculars, radios and light arms from Mustang's various camps. At the south side of the field, just beyond the central post office, Lhamo Tsering and the six Khampa leaders who had heeded the Dalai Lama's order to surrender sat in Katmandu's central jail, wherre they languished for seven years until, in a 1981 amnesty granted by the King, they were finally set free. While the NVDA's New Delhi office survived the guerrilla's rout, its clandestine network in Tibet, painstakingly built up since the late 1950s, was now blown by the Nepalese, who forwarded Baba Yeshi's disclosures to the Chinese. A quarter century after China's invasion, the fight for Tibet seemed to have collapsed overnight in a tragic debacle.

But the Special Frontier Force remained. Informed that a secret regiment, independent of the guerrillas, was being created to fight for Tibetan independence, male refugees had flocked from road gangs to assembly points at train stations throughout the early sixties. Taken to Dehra Dun, the groups were ferried by army trucks to Establishment 22, 100 kilometers away at the Chakrata military base. Here they were inducted and put through six months of basic training. At first Americans conducted operations; then, after a disagreement over procedure, Indian officers took full charge. Regardless, below the highest ranks, an entirely Tibetan officer corps was developed, thus making 22—with a troop strength of 10,500— to all practical purposes a fully Tibetan army—the embryo, it was hoped, of the future army of a free Tibet.

The first—and standing—objective of the Special Frontier Force was to scout the inhospitable terrain on "the Roof of the World." Not only could Tibetans survive in the cold with far greater facility than the Indian Jawan; they proved immune to altitude sickness no matter how many years they had lived on the subcontinent. With them India was able to develop a network of bases spanning its Himalayan territories from Ladakh to Assam. The Frontier Force's second objective was less docile than guard duty. Having determined that an independent Tibet, serving along the lines of an Asian Switzerland, as a neutral buffer state, would afford the best protection against China, New Delhi secretly decided that, in the event of war, an attempt to wrest Tibet's liberty could be made, 22 taking the lead. As such, the Frontier Force was trained not just to scout but also as high-altitude paratroops—commandos versed in the arts of ambush, demolition, survival and sabotage. Given the existence of numerous underground groups in Tibet, sustained by a virtually universal hatred of the Chinese, the men and women of 22 (two companies of female medics and communications specialists were enlisted to demonstrate Tibetan women's willingness to fight for their country) were designated to be dropped behind Chinese lines. While India's regular army would engage the Chinese head-on, the Tibetans would link up with the underground, raise pockets of resistance and disrupt the PLA's flanks and rear.

War with China, though, was not forthcoming. Impatient for contact, entire companies of Tibetan commandos periodically disobeyed Indian orders and crossed the border in secret to attack PLA outposts. Restraining 22 became such a problem that all of its bases had to be relocated twenty miles behind the front, and Indian troops posted between the Tibetans and their homeland. Not until a decade after its founding did the SFF have a chance to prove itself in sanctioned action—as the spearhead of India's assault, late in October 1971, in the Bangladesh war.

Wishing to assist East Pakistan in a bid for secession from its western twin, New Delhi settled on 22 as the perfect unit for the job. It was not a part of the regular army, and its shadowy existence and unique racial makeup provided perfect cover for a covert attack. Roughly 5,000 troops —half the force—were committed to the operation, an elite corps which opened the Bangladesh war with a surprise attack on a key Pakistani base. Labeled by the Indian press Mukti Bahini or Freedom Fighters, 22 went on to capture the city of Chittagong, Pakistan's main forward position, earning a reputation in the upper echelons of India's defense establishment as being among the country's best troops. Thereafter, 22 returned to its bases. During the 1977 election that ended the Republic's state of emergency, it received a new notoriety as Indira Gandhi's "own force." As was later revealed, the Congress Party leader planned to rely on its troops to suppress opposition party riots if they developed. She also kept an AN12 aircraft on constant alert at the SFF paratrooper base, Sarsawa, with instructions to fly her to Mauritius if her life was threatened. Following the Janata Party victory, 22's prize anti-terrorist squad was posted to duty at Palam Airport in New Delhi. The rest of the Special Frontier Force, however, remained on its high-altitude bases helpless as before, unable to fulfill its ultimate mission.

The guerrillas' demise, combined with 22's ineffectuality, reinforced the exile youths' conviction that the fight for Tibet had devolved on them. "We realized that independence wouldn't come on a plate," said Tempa Tsering, describing the Youth Congress's projected turn to terrorism. "It had to be fought for and won. In a fight, whether we would succeed or not was a different question. But at least we had to be prepared. If you aren't ready, even if an opportunity arises, you can't seize it." In a series of meetings Tempa and the other members of Centrex discussed two potential scenarios, either of which, they believed, could serve as a suitable platform for regaining Tibet: war between China and India or the Soviet Union, or an internal collapse on the mainland itself, such as had occurred in 1911. The potential for the first existed almost daily, there having been numerous volatile incidents on both the Sino-Soviet and Sino-Indian borders. With Moscow tied to New Delhi against Peking and Islamabad in the current Central Asian power configuration, there was a direct link between the struggle of the two Communist giants, that of India and Pakistan and the question of Tibetan independence. The PRC's collapse from internal division was equally plausible as China's Communists were apparently helplessly bound to a cycle of devastating power struggles such as those that had erupted following the Hundred Flowers Movement, the Great Leap Forward and during the decade-long Cultural Revolution.

Late in 1977, the Youth Congress laid plans to develop a freedom-fighting wing. While encouraging all graduates of the Tibetan schools to enlist for a tour of duty in the Special Frontier Force, it resolved that an elite group of Congress militants should engage directly in terrorist activities against Chinese embassies and personnel abroad. Arrangements for their training, to be conducted under the guise of a mountaineering institute, were explored. "From the moment Yasir Arafat was invited to the UN and given a standing ovation, we had begun debating the use of terrorism," said Tempa. "It was clear the world had come to this: you kill and commit destruction and you are listened to. You appeal for justice for your people and you are ignored. When we finally went ahead with the plans, though, it was only on a very selective basis. This type of action is contrary to the Tibetan character. So to begin with, we carefully sought to determine whether or not even the training itself would produce negative results among our young people."

TYC instruction in guerrilla warfare, using wooden guns manufactured in settlement workshops, got underway by early 1978. Morning calisthenics programs were organized, bringing young men and women alike into the fields, wearing "Fight for Tibet" T-shirts. Carefully screened groups were given more sophisticated instruction for extended periods in the jungles surrounding the larger settlements. The Youth Congress also expanded its existing ties with the underground groups in Tibet, while publicly, at least, welcoming the possibility of non-binding support from Moscow, whose overtures to Tibetan exiles had increased since the mid-sixties. But the question of violence, outside the setting of an actual war, remained a delicate point for most Tibetans, putting a brake on the Congress's efforts. As the Dalai Lama, whose leadership the Youth Congress charter swore to uphold, stated: "In theory violence and religious views can be combined, but only if a person's motivation, as well as the result of his actions, are solely for the benefit of the majority of the people. Under these circumstances and if there is no other alternative, then it is permissible. Now, regarding Tibet, I believe that a militant attitude is helpful for maintaining morale among our youth, but a military movement itself is not feasible. It would be suicidal."

By the late 1970s the Dalai Lama's own plans for Tibetan independence had in many respects already ripened. Refugee society was thriving. Economically, culturally and politically—it had matured into a cohesive whole, precisely the situation he had hoped to create two decades earlier. No longer able to count on the exiles' disintegration, Peking, he was confident, would soon be forced to terms. Convinced that success was near, the Dalai Lama set about reawakening international interest in Tibet through a series of trips across Asia and the West. Undertaken for religious purposes (hundreds of Tibetan Buddhist center having cropped up around the world during the 1970s), the trips were also guaranteed to affect China which, since the early 1960s had been demonstrably sensitive to international opinion on the legitimacy of its occupation. And as the liberalization following Mao Zedong's death took root and developed novel Chinese initiatives in foreign affairs, Dharamsala became—if as yet for no concrete reason—newly optimistic.

Tempa's beliefs also underwent change. In 1978, after four years in the Information Office, he was promoted to the post of deputy secretary. Three years later, in the spring of 1981, he suddenly received word to report for duty at Thekchen Chöling, the Dalai Lama's residence. The chief secretary of the foreign wing of the Dalai Lama's private office had to leave his post temporarily and Tempa had been chosen to fill it. "When I first heard this news I was worried that I was too inexperienced to work in such a high position. I didn't have the confidence," said Tempa. "But then I considered carefully. For my whole life my only hope has been to one day go back to an independent Tibet. This is the one thing for which I've struggled. Naturally, the closer you are to His Holiness, the better you'd feel. But whatever I'm doing I know I am serving him and my people. So in this respect I decided it doesn't make very much difference, and I could take the change in a normal way. But about my inexperience, I was quite concerned."

Within the year Tempa was wholly absorbed in being one of the Dalai

Lama's closest assistants. Placed in charge of all correspondence between the private office and non-Tibetan world, he also translated each afternoon at the Dalai Lama's regular round of audiences with foreigners, while overseeing numerous projects with the government's Foreign Offices. At the age of 32 he looked back from his new position on his time in India. Recalling the death of his younger sister in the mountains above Bhutan, his second sister's demise from dysentery at Missamari and his mother's death in the tent by the road camp at Bawarna, he recognized how much his own survival, as well as that of the nation, had been the product of the Dalai Lama's peaceful efforts at reconstruction. Traveling with the Tibetan leader through Asia, Europe, the Soviet Union, Mongolia and the United States, Tempa, and through him many of his colleagues in the Youth Congress, became convinced that Tibet's unique hope lay not where the guerrillas had failed, but in the strength of the traditional society, now rebuilt and entering the world at large.

III

6

Tibetan Medicine

THE SCIENCE OF HEALING

DR. YESHI DHONDEN pressed the three middle fingers of his right hand gently along the inside of William Schneider's left wrist, bowed his head and listened. The fifty-two-year-old patient smiled, perplexed. The physician before him wore neither a white coat nor a name tag. He asked no questions and carried no charts or instruments. Dressed in maroon robes, head shaved, a turquoise-studded charm box bulging beneath his orange shirt, Dr. Dhonden remained motionless, deep in concentration. A minute later, he took the patient's right arm and briefly pressed the radial artery as if to confirm his findings. Ushering Mr. Schneider into an adjacent room, the doctor gestured for him to undress, whereupon he pressed selected points along his spine. With each touch, Mr. Schneider cried out in pain. Dr. Dhonden nodded sympathetically and told him to get dressed.

In his guest suite at the University of Virginia, Dr. Yeshi Dhonden offered his diagnosis of William Schneider, a man he knew nothing of and had met only minutes before. "Many years ago you lifted a heavy object," he said, speaking through an interpreter. "At that time you damaged a channel in the vicinity of your right kidney, blocking the normal flow of wind through your back. The wind has accumulated outside the channel, there is bone deterioration and the disease has become quite severe." Mr. Schneider was stunned. For three years, he confirmed, he had suffered from acute arthritis along the neck and lower back. The illness had caused incapacitating pain, and he had been forced to give up his job. But he was even more astonished at Dr. Dhonden's ability to reconstruct his past. "In

1946," he recalled, "I injured my back lifting a milk can out of a cooler. I was in bed a week, and as soon as I got up I reinjured it and was bed-ridden again. That must have been the start of the whole problem."

It was a diagnosis that Western physicians could arrive at simply by using an X ray, but Dr. Yeshi Dhonden, the Dalai Lama's personal physician, sent by him in the winter of 1980 to introduce Tibetan medicine to the West, enthralled American doctors and patients alike with his unique skills. "It's quite conceivable that in our attempt to be scientific, some of our powers of observation have atrophied," said Dr. Gerald Goldstein, a professor at the University of Virginia's Medical Oncology Department, who worked closely with the Tibetan physician during his stay. "Dr. Dhonden, on the other hand, is totally attuned to everything that is going on. He uses all of his senses as his medical instrument. Our patients have been very impressed." Dr. Richard Selzer, assistant professor of surgery at Yale University, met Yeshi Dhonden in 1974 on his first visit to the United States. "I went to observe Dr. Dhonden with some healthy skepticism," he recounted. "I was surprised and elated by what I found. It was as if he was a human electrocardiogram machine interpreting the component parts of the pulse. We have nothing like it in the West. It's a dimension of medicine that we have not yet realized." "Western scientific documentation of Tibetan claims is nonexistent," observed Dr. Herbert Benson, leader of a team of Harvard researchers that visited the Tibetan Medical Center in 1981. "It would be nice, though, to discover the worth of what they have developed over thousands of years. If their claims are only partly true they would be worthy of investigation. Therefore, can we really afford to ignore this?"

To test the efficacy of Tibetan drugs by laboratory standards, Yeshi Dhonden agreed, while in Virginia, to engage in an experiment with cancerous mice. On the basis of a visual examination alone, he prescribed a general Tibetan cancer drug, comprised of over sixty ingredients, for nine tumor-implanted mice in a lab in the University of Virginia's vivarium. Six mice refused the medicine and died within thirty-five days. Three mice accepted it and survived up to fifty-three days. A second experiment involving sixteen animals confirmed the findings, producing the most successful results since work with the particular tumor involved began in 1967. Of even greater interest, though, was the fact that Dr. Dhonden had no knowledge of the nature of the cancer he was dealing with. "There are literally hundreds of kinds of tumors," commented Dr. Donald Baker, the researcher in charge of the experiment. "How often has Dr. Dhonden encountered a KHT anaplastic sarcoma growing in a highly inbred strain of 3CH/HEJ female mice? It would be utterly unreasonable to ask him to decide what would be the best treatment. If he had been familiar with these conditions he might well have effected a complete cure." "There is no question that this is a very fertile area for cancer quacks," added Dr. Goldstein. "In the end, though, things either work or they don't work. Dr. Dhonden has things that work."

Sitting cross-legged over a cup of butter tea in his Virginia apartment, Dr. Dhonden offered a brief description of cancer in Tibetan terms. "I've treated perhaps one thousand cancer patients of which sixty to seventy percent have been cured," he maintained. "Our medical texts specify fifty-four types of tumors which appear at eighteen places in the body in one of three forms. We consider cancer to be a disease of the blood. It begins with pollutants in the environment. These, in turn, affect seven types of sentient beings in the body, two of which are most susceptible. They are extremely minute, but if you could see them, they would be round, red and flat. They can travel through the bloodstream in an instant, are formed with the embryo in the womb and normally function to maintain strength. In general the Buddha predicted that eighteen diseases would become prevalent in our time due to two causes, low moral conduct and pollution. Cancer is one of the eighteen."

Based on the results of his first experiment those physicians working with Yeshi Dhonden hoped to initiate a broader study of Tibetan medicine in the West. Dr. Dhonden, too, was eager to undertake an in-depth exchange of medical lore. "If Western medicine can come to understand the Tibetan view of the human organism," he commented toward the close of his stay in Virginia, "I feel it will be of inestimable value. Our medicine has many cures for diseases which Western doctors currently don't understand or have incorrectly identified. We successfully treat diabetes, various forms of coronary disease, arthritis, hepatitis, Parkinson's disease, cancers, ulcers and the common cold. We have difficulty treating epilepsy and paralysis. But because the Tibetan system is scientific, Western physicians, as scientists, will see what is of value and what is not." To illuminate an ancient science hidden behind the Himalayas for over two thousand years, Yeshi Dhonden described his own life and training as a Tibetan doctor.

Dr. Dhonden was born in 1929 into a wealthy family of farmers living in the small village of Namro, south of the Tsangpo River, one day's ride from Lhasa. Much of the land surrounding Namro belonged to the Dhonden family and their relatives. Five thousand sheep, yaks and horses and many fields of *chingko* or mountain barley were owned by Yeshi Dhonden's aunt and uncle, who, not having a male child, assumed he would grow up to run the estate. Dr. Dhonden's parents, however, felt differently. As their only child, they decided that Yeshi Dhonden should devote his life to the Dharma. Accordingly, at the age of six, their son left his home and traveled a short way up the mountain behind Nanıro, to be accepted as a novice monk in the local monastery of Shedrup Ling. "I remember it all," recollected Dr. Dhonden. "Becoming a monk, entering into the comfort of the group, living with my teacher. I had a strong wish to learn quickly and my mind was very clear. I could memorize four of our long pages in a single day." Yeshi Dhonden's facility for memorization earned him a high position among his peers, on the basis of which he was selected at the age of eleven to represent Shedrup Ling at Mendzekhang, the larger of Lhasa's two state-run medical colleges. Like all monasteries, district headquarters and military camps, Shedrup Ling was required by the government to send medical students to Lhasa. Upon the completion of their training, they would then return to practice in their region. But while the monastery's superiors were not averse to receiving the government salary paid to them for their students' attendance, the four hundred monks were less than enthusiastic at the prospect of medical studies. "Everyone in the monastery was afraid that he would be selected," recalled Dr. Dhonden, laughing. "No one wanted to become a doctor. You have to spend at least eleven years in classes and there is a tremendous amount of memorization. But because I liked to memorize, when my parents told me that I had been chosen, I was eager to go."

The medical system Yeshi Dhonden was to study had begun as one of the ten branches of learning originally pursued by all Mahayana Buddhist monks. It flourished for over a thousand years in the great monastic universities of northern India, from whence it was taken to Tibet by two Indian pandits in the first century B.C. Thereafter, it was the province for almost seven hundred years of a single family of physicians attendant on the Royal Tibetan Court. With the introduction of over a hundred Buddhist medical texts in the sixth century, however, it grew into a widespread practice and was ultimately acclaimed by a conference of physicians from nine nations convened in Tibet, as the preeminent medical science of its time. Subsequently, Tibet's first medical college, called Melung or "Country of Medicine," was built in the eighth century by King Trisong Detsen in Kongpo, south of Lhasa. Melung inspired the founding of scores of medical schools, most contained in *dratsangs* or colleges appended to the country's larger monasteries. In the mid-seventeenth century, the Fifth Dalai Lama built Tibet's second medical college, called Chokpori, atop Iron Hill, just across from the Potala. There, doctors from all across Tibet and Mongolia were trained to practice a composite of the various schools of medicine that had developed over the years. The need for more physicians in modern times resulted in the Thirteenth Dalai Lama's construction of Tibet's most recent central medical college, Mendzekhang or "Medicine House," in 1916.

Mendzekhang lay on the west side of Lhasa, next to the Tibetan government's newly built post and telegraph office. It was centered on a flagstone courtyard, with dormitories for students, both lay and monk, occupying two long wings, at the head of which, facing the main gate, stood the classrooms, assembly hall and the Master's quarters. Outside, the college walls were lined with display beds of frequently used medicinal plants. Inside, life at Mendzekhang followed a spartan schedule. At four each morning a bell sounded in the main temple at the head of the courtyard. Yeshi Dhonden had a few minutes to wash and roll up his bedding before hurrying to his classroom to begin memorizing by the soft light of butter lamps. As the mind was believed to be most fresh on waking, the first three hours before sunrise were given over to the memorization of the 1,140 pages of the four medical tantras, the root texts, preached by the Buddha, which, together with hundreds of commentaries and pharmacological catalogues, were the basis of Tibetan medicine. At seven o'clock instructors quizzed their students on the morning's work, after which they would return to their rooms for the day's first bowl of tea. A second bell then rang, and the whole college gathered to pray in long seated rows running the length of the pillared assembly hall, its walls hung with *thankas* illustrating herbs, anatomy, embryonic development and surgical instruments. On the way back to his room, Yeshi Dhonden would pass patients lined up for treatment beneath the apartments of Kenrab Norbu, the Master of Mendzekhang. Under their instructors' observation, senior students examined the sick while other professors, along with all the doctors of Chokpori, fanned out into the city on morning house calls, visiting those too ill to come to the colleges. As always in Tibet, medical treatment was free, only the medicines themselves having to be paid for.

Although Yeshi Dhonden's day was spent mainly in memorization, he often looked in on Mendzekhang's chief pharmacist and his staff. Two doors east of the front gate, they carried out the first step in the preparation of medicines, pounding into a fine powder the various roots, stems, leaves and branches as well as the numerous gems, minerals and animal products used in the 2,000 drugs routinely made by the college. The demands of their work were so great that Mendzekhang was covered with the raw materials of the trade. Hundreds of pungent medicinal plants, collected on expeditions into the mountains, were laid out to dry throughout the school's hallways, classrooms and rooftops. Subsequently they were administered either in powder form or as shiny black and brown pills.

Following an early dinner at five o'clock, the student body once again assembled, this time to practice debate. Seated by class in the courtyard, the college would, on the Master's signal, break into a cacophony of shouts, claps and loud retorts as attackers queried their respondents on the correct interpretation of the tantras' description of the causes, conditions and treatments of various illnesses. Often debates became so heated that when the five-hour session had concluded, individual pairs, a small group of entranced onlookers seated around them, their *sens* or outer robes wrapped tightly against the chill, continued debating far into the night.

After two years and four months, Yeshi Dhonden completed memorizing the medical tantras. He then recited for a full day before his teacher, declining to divide his first test over a period of time, as was customary. Promoted, despite his youth, to be senior student among the five in his room, he went on to take his official examination. The mornings of four days were set aside. His parents came from Namro to attend, while his home monastery, Shedrup Ling, offered a tea service at each session. Yeshi Dhonden, aged thirteen and a half, then appeared in the Assembly Hall before the Master of Mendzekhang, the faculty and the entire student body and after prostrating three times to the images of the Medicine Buddha and Tibet's most famous doctor, Yuthok Yonten Gonpo, on the main altar, recited verbatim the one hundred fifty-six chapters of the four tantras—in and out of sequence—as he was requested. Only minor mistakes were accepted—a lapse of any kind being considered grounds for failure. On the afternoon of the fourth day Yeshi Dhonden was informed that he had passed in good standing. Rewarded with a white scarf and a set of brocade book covers, he was admitted into the college to commence his formal education.

Dr. Dhonden spent the next four years absorbed in eleven divisions of study. To provide an overview of the medical system, Mendzekhang's curriculum began with the Illustrated Tree of Medicine, a diagram wherein each field of learning found its proper place in relation to the whole. Yeshi Dhonden and his fellow students spent long hours laying out on the large flagstones before their rooms the three roots, nine trunks, forty-two branches, two hundred twenty-four leaves, three fruits and two flowers of the tree, using colored thread, sticks and bright plastic buttons from the Barkhor or marketplace. After they had mastered the diagram, they were taught how to collate the appropriate chapters of the tantras with the various parts of the tree, following which they entered into the study of root one, trunk one, branch one, explaining the most important topic in Tibetan medicine, the theoretical basis for the entire system, that of the three bodily humors.

As explained by the Buddha in the First or Root Tantra, three humors govern the condition of all sentient beings: wind, bile and phlegm. Wind is described as rough, hard, cold, subtle and motile in nature; bile as light, oily, acrid and hot; phlegm as sticky, cool, heavy and gentle. Five kinds of each orchestrate the human organism. The five winds control movement, respiration, circulation, secretions and the joining of consciousness to the body; the five biles, digestion, sight and skin tone; the five phlegms, among other functions, the body's cohesiveness. The quantity of wind in an average adult is said to fill a bladder, that of bile a scrotum, that of phlegm, three double handfuls. Although active throughout the body, wind predominates in the pelvis, bile in the middle torso and phlegm in the upper torso. Wind moves through the skeleton, bile in the blood, phlegm in the chyle, flesh, fat and regenerative fluid. Phlegm prevails in youth, bile in adulthood, wind in old age. When all the humors are in balance, health exists. The smallest imbalance, however, produces disease. Every illness—of which the tantras account for 84,000 in 1,616 divisions—owes its cure to the correction of a humoral imbalance. Equipped with such an all-inclusive theory, the medical system could address itself to any disease, known or unknown, including mental illness, as not just the body but also the personality of each individual was said to be governed by the balance of humors in his makeup.

With a working knowledge of the humors, Dr. Dhonden went on to study embryology, anatomy, metabolic function, signs of death, pathology, treatment and diagnosis. In embryology, conception, followed by the weekly growth of the embryo (including the nature of its consciousness at critical stages of development), was described in texts predating Western medicine's own findings by 2,000 years. Techniques for determining the sex of the child prior to birth were demonstrated, along with medicines which would reduce labor to between two and four hours, guard against postpartum infection and ease pain. Anatomy was the next subject. As autopsies were performed only if attending physicians disagreed on the cause of death, Mendzekhang's students obtained their anatomical knowledge from detailed charts first drawn up late in the eighth century when the practice of surgery in Tibetan medicine was at its height. At that time Tibetan surgeons had routinely performed heart and brain surgery until the mother of King Muni Tsenpo, Tibet's thirty-eighth monarch, died during an operation to lessen swelling from water retention around the heart. Following her death, surgery was officially banned. Nevertheless, minor operations continued to be performed and the use of surgical instruments as well as that of anesthetizing drugs remained part of the Mendze-khang program. While metabolic function and signs of death were relatively brief topics, pathology, treatment and diagnosis were immense undertakings, requiring Yeshi Dhonden's greatest efforts. Pathology alone, dealt with in the ninety-two chapters of the Third or Oral Tradition Tantra, entailed individual descriptions of the categories, causes, symptoms and complications of thousands of diseases, supplemented by their treatments under varying conditions. It was here that memorization of the tantras proved invaluable as, equipped with commentaries written by Tibet's long line of physicians, Yeshi Dhonden gradually built up an intricate picture of the entire range of human illness through its expression in single, double and triple humoral imbalances. The study of diagnostic procedure, though, was even more difficult. Unlike academic topics, the three trunks, eight branches and thirty-eight leaves of the Diagnostic Root of the Tree of Medicine could be thoroughly understood only through actual practice. Questioning the patient and analyzing nine aspects of his urine were essential to diagnosis. But it was mastery of the third trunk, pulse diagnosis, that was the hallmark of a leading physician.

Although pulse diagnosis was taught for an entire year in Mendze-khang, it was believed to take a decade or more to fully comprehend. The basics were laid out in thirteen sections of the Last Tantra. The first four detail eight guidelines for the evening before an examination. To prepare themselves, both patient and doctor should refrain from the consumption of tea, alcohol and overly nutritious food, also avoiding exercise, sex and any anxiety-producing encounter. The following morning, after the sun has risen but, as the Tantra says, before "its rays have fallen on the mountaintop," the pulse should be read. In this brief period, two definitive factors characterizing every pulse, disease and medicine—the forces of hot and cold—are believed to be most in equilibrium. Prior to dawn, lunar influences, manifested in an enhanced cold or negative pulse, accentuate wind and phlegm; after dawn, solar influences augment the hot or positive pulse of bile and blood (sometimes spoken of as the fourth humor). Because the patient has not yet eaten, digestion does not obscure other functions, while all the winds have subsided during sleep into the heart of the central channel, where, according to tantric theory, the mind and body are joined.

The best place to read the pulse is said to be on the patient's wrist, just over the radial artery. The Last Tantra queries itself: "Why is the radial artery used?" It replies that listening to arteries close to the vital organs "is like talking to someone by a waterfall," whereas using those in the extremities is like receiving "messages brought by distant merchants." The radial artery is the optimum position and is likened to "a voice in summer shouting across an open field." "How is it possible to read the quality of the twelve organs at the radial artery?" the tantra continues. "Just as a successful businessman can discern the place of origin and make of wares at a marketplace, so the pulse if read at the radial artery can exhibit the condition of the hollow and solid organs." Only in children below the age of eight and terminally ill patients is the pulse to be read elsewhere: in the former, on the blood vessels in the lobe of the ear; in the latter, to determine how many days of life remain, at the posterior tibial artery behind the ankle.

The doctor is now instructed in the technique for taking the pulse. If the patient is male, the left arm is examined first; if female, the right. Switching hands, the physician then examines the patient's other arm. In both cases he uses the three middle fingers of either hand spaced apart the width "of a grain," while to overcome the thickness of the forearm's muscle, his index finger presses the skin, his middle finger the flesh and his ring finger the bone. The essential ingredient of pulse diagnosis is explained next. Each of the six fingers used is to be divided into an "inner" and "outer" half. These twelve positions monitor the organs; hollow organs are read on the outer half, solid on the inner. For example, the outside of the physician's right index finger reads the heart; the inside, the small intestine; the outside of his middle finger, the spleen; the inside, the stomach. The correspondence of all six fingers is the same for both men and women save for one instance. In a male patient the doctor's right index finger registers the heart; his left, the lung. With a female patient the reverse applies. They are switched because the consciousness of a woman is believed to enter the center of the ovum and sperm at a slightly different position than that of a man at the time of conception. The text then admonishes the doctor to always keep his fingertips "smooth, sensitive, without scars and pliable."

There is one final consideration before the pulse can be read. One of three "constitutional pulses," corresponding to the three humors, is said to dominate every person. The male pulse, similar to wind, is bulky and prominent; the female, similar to bile, subtle and rapid; the neuter, similar to phlegm, slow and smooth. Unless the patient's particular type—any of which can be had by either a man or a woman—is known to the physician (either by examining the patient when healthy or by being told), a diagnostic error can easily be made. Furthermore, once the constitutional pulse is known, it is crucial to factor in the "seasonal pulse"—each season manifesting an influence on the characteristic pulse imprint of a particular organ, such as heat in summer, which affects the heart, and cold in winter, which affects the kidneys.

The doctor begins by ascertaining whether the illness is hot or cold in nature. He does so by using his own respiratory cycle, to determine the rate of the patient's pulse. If the pulse beats five times per breath, the person is in perfect health. More than five beats denotes a hot disorder; less than five, a cold. Above eight in a hot disorder or below three in a cold disease means an extremely severe, usually incurable problem.

One of twelve general pulse types is now sought. The six hot beats are strong, ample, rolling, swift, tight and hard. The six cold beats are weak, deep, declining, slow, loose and hollow. If the moment all his fingers touch the radial artery a hot beat is superficially felt, the physician knows that the disorder is new and minor. If, after pressure is applied, they are felt deeply, the illness is chronic and complex. The reverse holds true for cold disorders; superficial pulses reveal old, serious ailments; deep ones indicate new, minor imbalances. From this second step the history of an ailment is known.

The state of the three humors in the body is now explored. Each humor, as well as its combinations, possesses a characteristic pulse type. When it has been identified, the individual pulse of one of a huge number of conditions is sought. If the patient is pregnant, the "pregnancy pulse" will reveal it, as well as, after the sixth week, the sex of the child. If worms are present, the pulse is "flat" and seems to knot as it beats; if bacteria, it is incomplete, with "sudden, irregular and unpredictable cessation in the rhythm of the beat." In leprosy, the pulsebeat is "quivering," and contracting at its conclusion "like a person who limps." Wounds manifest a "bulky, hard and quick" pulse. A bullet lodged in the body produces a "limping and double" pulse as if there were two arteries, not one, being read. After describing tests to distinguish pulse types, the tantra instructs the physician to investigate the individual organs through the twelve positions on the fingertips. His exam complete, over a period of roughly one hundred breaths, the doctor knows what the humoral imbalance is, its severity, which organs are affected and in what manner.

As Yeshi Dhonden and his classmates discovered, however, the topic of pulse diagnosis was far from exhausted. In the remaining sections numerous exceptions to the rules were cited as well as the uses of the pulse in determining lifespan, spirit possession and, in an extremely complex section known as the "Seven Amazing Pulses," the future course of an illness. In the eleventh section, those pulses which reveal that a disease will be terminal are described, showing how vivid the tantra's descriptions can be.

The "changing" death pulse is said to "flutter like a flag in the wind"; while the "irregular" death pulse appears "like a vulture attacking a bird, who stops, plunges, beats its wings quickly, stops again and then resumes flight." In a combined wind-bile disorder, the patient's pulse will resemble "a fish leaping out of water to catch a fly, who quickly shimmers back." Accumulation of phlegm and wind producing death are like "the pecking of a hen eating grain"; that of a triple humoral imbalance, like "the saliva of a drooling cow, moving in the wind." The text then enumerates death pulses unrelated to the humors. If a healthy person who has had an accident has a thin pulse, he will die shortly. If in a person who has been sick for some time the pulse suddenly turns strong or violent, death is imminent. The amount of time left to live, within a period of eight days, is shown by the absence of pulse. Death will occur in three days if the liver or gallbladder pulse is missing; in two if the lung or large intestine pulse is absent; in one if the tongue is black, the eyes are in a fixed stare and the pulse of either the heart or the small intestine is gone.

Dr. Dhonden's true education in pulse diagnosis came only after his studies were completed. At the age of eighteen he was sent by Kenrab Norbu, Mendzekhang's principal, to undertake a four-year internship with a master physician practicing in Lhoka, who was already surrounded by many disciples. During this second stage in his training, Dr. Dhonden rose before dawn each day to take pulse, analyze urine and present his diagnosis of patients' ailments to his new teacher. While his understanding of the myriad pulse types grew, he came to have a profound regard for the efficacy of the entire medical system. Although patients in advanced states of illness could not be cured, others, afflicted by a number of usually fatal degenerative diseases, such as cancer and diabetes, responded with complete remission. In the case of diabetes, seen in one out of every two to three hundred patients, he witnessed many cures occurring within six to nine months. When medicine proved ineffective, he and his teacher used accessory treatments: emetics, purgatives, moxabustion, cauterization, bloodletting and acupuncture or "Golden Needle" therapy, which, according to Tibetan medical histories, originated in Tibet and spread to China via Mongolia. Among the most successful treatments Yeshi Dhonden found were those for senility (employing memory pills), those included in the divisions covering women's and children's diseases as well as those in the eight branches of infertility, itself an entire category of medical practice. Although rarely prescribed, due to Buddhist ethics, two types of birth-control pill existed. One had to be taken for a few consecutive days, whereafter its effect lasted for a year; the other eliminated fertility for life.

A related specialty known as *chu-len* or "Extracting the Essence" dealt with rejuvenation. By using its medicines, religious practitioners on three-, nine- or twelve-year retreats were able to survive, it was believed, on a single seed or flower a day. For lay people *chu-len* could restore hair and teeth while increasing lifespan by many decades. As Dr. Dhonden explained, "Each of us breathes 21,000 times a day; 500 of these breaths are associated with lifespan. *Chu-len* medicines, taken in conjunction with the correct meditation practices, increase the number of these breaths. From my own experience I can definitely say they work. I've known people in their hundreds who have undergone the full course of treatment, beginning at the age of fifty, and been restored to a state of middle age. I met one lama when he was 170 years old. He had gray hair but the face of a forty-year-old."

Having administered rejuvenation treatment for two millennia, Tibetan physicians considered it a normal component of their medical practice. However, one group of drugs, as venerable as those of *chu-len*, excited particular interest—*rinchen ribus* or "Precious Pills." Whenever Dr. Dhonden returned to Mendzekhang to replenish his professor's medicines, he made sure to inquire which Precious Pills had most recently been manufactured in the college's pharmacy. Seven types existed, the weakest composed of eighteen ingredients, the strongest, known as the King of Medicines, of one hundred sixty-five. Wrapped in colored cotton, tied with rainbow-hued thread and sealed with wax, the Precious Pills received their name for two reasons: for their contents—gold, silver, mercury, pearl, ruby, sapphire and diamond, specially treated and then mixed with various medicinal plants—and for their function—as panaceas for the entire body. Precious Pills, it was believed, could cure the most intractable ailments. As their manufacture sometimes took up to three months of around-the-clock labor by a team of twenty druggists, they were extremely potent and administered only under strict conditions. The stronger ones often incapacitated the patient for a day, while toxins were eliminated and imbalances in the body corrected. Though Yeshi Dhonden was familiar with their ingredients, his internship was primarily geared toward expanding his knowledge of Tibetan medicine's vast pharmacopoeia. To check his progress, Kenrab Norbu required Dr. Dhonden to accompany the college each year on its annual outing to pick herbs in the mountains.

The journey commenced at the start of July and was attended by those who had completed memorization, generally 300 students and faculty in all. As a rule, each traveler brought three changes of clothing, the Buddha having stressed the importance of cleanliness while collecting medicinal substances. With one pack animal and a groom serving every two students, the caravan left Mendzekhang and, skirting Lhasa, proceeded a day north to Dhakyaba, a region of peaks and alpine meadows considered ideal for herb gathering. A large tent camp provided by the government, staffed with cooks and fully provisioned, already awaited the college. For seven weeks, changing location every three days, small groups of students and teachers set off at eight o'clock each morning to collect herbs just below the snow line. While harvesting, they recited prayers to the Medicine Buddha, intent on keeping the mind as well as the body pure. Thirty classes of plants, subdivided into fifty-nine categories, with each plant having nine divisions, were initially sought. Hundreds of herbs with less universal value were also taken. With the waxing of vegetative processes and the onset of pollination, barks and plant secretions received less attention; flowers, fruits, seeds and leaves, more.

Halfway through the summer, large wooden crates began arriving from Lhasa. Ordered from district governors months in advance, the crates contained dozens of medicinal plants that were unavailable in Central Tibet. They had been carefully picked with earth still around their roots and immediately packed in snow and ice. By the end of August, when all had arrived, the students had completed their own collections and were ready to take the year-end test on the identification of plants.

The exam took place inside a large tent surrounded by a high cloth wall. Within, stacks of wood covered with white cotton lined the enclosure, two hundred selected plants laid out haphazardly on top. With Kenrab Norbu presiding from a high seat at the far end, three faculty members, each assisted by a secretary, escorted students past the tables. While the secretaries recorded their replies, the students were asked to describe each specimen by type, species and the medicinal power of the active part. Guided out the tent's rear, they were separated from those yet to be examined, and the next group of three took their places. While they did, the scores were tabulated and given to the Master, who had them announced to the whole gathering—a procedure guaranteed to increase the tremendous tension the students already felt. The test completed, students once more were taken around, this time to have their mistakes pointed out.

Most of Mendzekhang's aspiring physicians took up to five exams before they could correctly identify a majority of each year's plants. In his first and second attempts, Yeshi Dhonden placed sixty-second, then forty-fifth in the ranking. By the age of twenty, though, with his internship completed, he captured third place. By coincidence his old roommates took first and second, giving the three friends a clean sweep of the top positions. Because their scores were so close, Kenrab Norbu ordered a retest. This time the young men were taken around the tables blindfolded. One by one their examiners held up plants, requesting that they be identified by odor and taste alone. As Yeshi Dhonden recalled, "This was very difficult, but fortunately all of us were able to answer correctly. When the test was over, it was announced that I had come in number one. Later, though," he added, laughing, "I found out there had been a catch. Because I was graduating, my friends had pretended to make little mistakes. In reality I was number three, but thanks to their trick I was chosen as the best student in the college."

Following the exam, a large celebration, equivalent to graduation day, was held. Hundreds of people came from Lhasa and the surrounding villages to watch as the students were publicly ranked. Those who took first and second places received long silk scarves embroidered with the words "Luck in the Day. Luck in the Night." Those who came in last didn't fare so well. The fifth from last was pronounced "Carrier of the Medicines"—a barb equivalent to "nurse"—and given a blue doctor's bag to hold, of the kind used by every physician's assistant. The fourth from last, called "The Doorman," was dressed in the black robes of a government servant and placed at the entrance to the tent; the third from last, costumed as a muleteer, escorted the second from last and the last— banished not just from the race of physicians but that of men—known, respectively, as the "White" and "Black Donkeys." With bells, reins and halters on their necks and medicines loaded across their backs, the "donkeys" were driven around the camp, bellowing and braying, to the great amusement of the crowd, after which a picnic was shared by all. The next day the college returned to Lhasa, where a ceremony at the Central Cathedral took place and the year ended for a week's vacation.

After graduating, Dr. Dhonden served as Kenrab Norbu's special assistant for three years. In the evenings he continued to debate with Mendzekhang's senior students and faculty members. Once a month he went to the Lingkhor, Lhasa's Holy Walk, to treat the hundreds of poor pilgrims and beggars who rarely came on their own for help. In conjunction with this, he paid special attention to cultivating the eleven vows of the physicians' code which attempted to instill an altruistic motive as the basis of a doctor's practice. As Yeshi Dhonden commented, concerning his own application of the ancient code, "I am just an ordinary person afflicted by desire, hatred and ignorance. But through contemplating the suffering I see in my work, I have tried to increase my compassion. As doctors we are expected to put kindness before all else." Out of his own curiosity, Dr. Dhonden also went, two hours a day, to the British Legation, to acquaint himself with Western medicine. Finally, in 1951, Kenrab Norbu sent Yeshi

Dhonden's diploma to the office of the Cabinet, where it was officially confirmed. The Kashag then dispatched letters to district officials in Lhoka, as well as the government transport center, from which Yeshi Dhonden received free passage home. Thirteen years after his education began, Dr. Dhonden left Lhasa, looking forward to taking up practice on his own.

He didn't have long to wait. An epidemic had broken out along the Bhutanese border, imported—along with chocolate, batteries, silks and the beloved fedora hats—by traders returning from India. In Tibet's high, germ-scarce environment, those who contracted the disease—a form of intestinal influenza—died quickly. Scores of doctors had already flocked to the area.

Traveling to a monastery called Sungroling Gonpa, Dr. Dhonden joined three physicians who had been attempting, unsuccessfully, to check the epidemic. Nine of the monastery's 300 monks had already died, as well as many of the inhabitants of the village below its walls. Arriving just before nightfall, Dr. Dhonden was shown to a private room, where, after his regular evening meditation session, he went to sleep, expecting to see his first patients in the morning. During the night, however, he experienced an unusual dream, one which, though seemingly inexplicable by Western standards, demonstrated the close relationship of religion to science in Tibetan medicine. "In the night I dreamt that a naked woman came before me, a *khadroma*," said Dr. Dhonden, referring to a spiritual being believed, in a manner similar to that of an angel, to aid practitioners in meditation. "In her right hand she held a tantric drum; in her left hand she held a skull. She carried a bag of medicine under her left arm. A white tin cup with a red design and a slight crack on its rim, filled with urine, appeared before her. Then the woman asked me, 'After examining this urine can you tell me the disease of the patient? What is your diagnosis?' In the dream I looked at the urine and replied, 'This is today's epidemic, one of sixty-five types of the eighteen new diseases predicted in the tantras for this era.' 'What is its cause?' she asked. I responded that it was due, as the tantras state, to environmental pollution and that it was a hot disease. 'You said that externally it is a fever, but are you sure that internally it's not cold?' she said. At that time, because my memory was fresh from constant study, I recalled that the thirteenth and fourteenth chapters of the third Tantra address the topic of cold and hot diseases together. I answered her in debate form, quoting the text as proof, stating that there was no hidden cold fever, but that the ailment was hot both inside and out. We debated back and forth for some time and finally she said, 'What treatment will you give?' I replied, 'Because the bacteria causing the disease have mixed the blood and bile, medicine should be given to separate them.' Then she asked what the patient's behavior and diet should be—two aspects of treatment that always accompany medicine. I answered and she said, 'Tell me again. How will you cut the tail of this disease?' Once more we debated vigorously and then she laughed and suddenly disappeared. There was complete silence and I woke up."

In a short while, as the day began, Dr. Dhonden was brought tea. Afterwards he was asked to visit his first patient, a twenty-three-year-old monk, infected by the illness, languishing in his room. "I went to see the young man," continued Dr. Dhonden. "It was a very serious case. The room he lay in stank. Diarrhea mixed with blood was pouring from him onto the bed and he was semi-comatose; he couldn't talk. I asked for his urine specimen and it was brought to me in a tin cup. All of a sudden I remembered my dream. It was the exact cup, even with the crack on the rim. 'Oh, I have already examined this before,' I thought. I was amazed. Then the whole dream came back. I recalled the debate and the treatment and immediately I prepared the correct medicines. The man recovered and after that, the epidemic in the village was completely stopped. Now when I look back on it," Dr. Dhonden said, "I feel that whoever came to me in the form of a *khadroma* that night was actually administering my true final examination."

As Dr. Dhonden's reputation spread, he spent the remainder of the 1950s traveling from one district to another. "Each day I rode from village to village, returning periodically to Lhasa to obtain medicines," he recounted. "I was able to cure three quarters of my patients. And because I gave penicillin injections for skin disease—a great novelty among Tibetans—my reputation continued to increase. I never had a free day." A group of young relations began to study with him, but before long the uprising against the nine-year-old Chinese occupation broke out in Lhasa and the Dalai Lama fled. "I saw His Holiness when his party came through my area," recalled Dr. Dhonden. "Those who weren't following him had joined the guerrillas to put up a last fight for our freedom. My students all had family members whom they couldn't leave. My own mother's legs were too poor for her to walk out and my father had said that he was too old to cross the high passes into Bhutan. As a monk, I wouldn't fight. So I felt that I had no other choice but to leave. I borrowed a horse, said farewell and set off."

Though Namro was only a few days from the border, the presence of Chinese troops forced Dr. Dhonden to hide for over a month before finally, in the company of eighty other refugees, he descended a steep snow-covered slope, trekked through a valley and crossed a glacial stream into the forests of Bhutan. With only a few texts, instruments and medicines in his possession, he then walked across Bhutan begging day to day. "After I was forced to flee my homeland, I was overwhelmed by a deep sense of renunciation," reflected Dr. Dhonden. "I saw life as essenceless, without real stability. I only wanted to practice religion." Arriving at Buxa, Yeshi Dhonden requested permission to remain with the monks there while the rest of his group was transferred to road work. The Tibetan government official in charge replied, "You have the right to practice religion and you are also young and fit to work on the roads. However, if the Kashag asks me, 'Has any doctor come out of Tibet?' and I've sent you elsewhere, what will I say? Therefore, you studied medicine at the government's expense, and now the time has come for you to help us."

Dr. Dhonden was sent to Dalhousie, where 3,000 refugees, including the elite monks of Lhasa's two Tantric colleges, Gyudto and Gyudme, were camped in squalid conditions. Tuberculosis, hepatitis and amoebic dysentery were rampant. Preparing what medicines he could from the few herbs available in Indian stores, he set up a clinic and went to work. "One day a sweeper in my clinic was bitten by a poisonous snake," he related. "Just as I was applying a Tibetan tourniquet, an Indian doctor arrived. He examined the bite and declared that unless his leg was amputated immediately the man would die in half an hour. I told him this was unnecessary; I had already given the man Tibetan medicine effective for poison. The doctor turned to the sweeper and said, 'You will die within minutes unless I operate, but this Tibetan'—indicating me—'thinks otherwise.' He asked him whose diagnosis he wished to accept. The sweeper had seen my work and so he replied mine. The doctor then compelled me to sign a paper releasing him from all responsibility in the case. There were many aspects to my treatment, but after ten days the sweeper could move about and in a month he was completely cured."

Despite the man's recovery, the episode proved to be the start of a serious conflict. Once a week Indian doctors came to inspect the refugees, in the course of which they dropped by Dr. Dhonden's clinic to demand that, as he was not certified in India, he discontinue practice. "During one of their visits I was examining a patient with skin disease," continued Dr. Dhonden. "The physicians saw this woman and together announced that she had chicken pox. They claimed that unless she was isolated an epidemic would sweep over all the refugees. I said bluntly that they were wrong. It was a minor heat disorder and no more. They departed, leaving medicine for her to take. I forbade her to. In a short while they came back and tried to remove her to an isolated house in the forest. I refused to let her go. They asked if I was willing to have an outbreak of chicken pox on my hands and I replied, 'The Tibetans are my own people. How could I ever harm them?' I then demanded that now *they* sign a paper, just as I had been made to, certifying that indeed this woman had chicken pox. They stalled and within a few days the woman was cured." Despite this minor victory, more battles ensued, until, in mid-1960, Yeshi Dhonden was unexpectedly summoned to Dharamsala. Word had reached the government-in-exile that a Mendzekhang-trained physician had escaped. Apprised of his existence, the Dalai Lama had called for Dr. Dhonden personally.

"I arrived in Dharamsala just before sunset," Dr. Dhonden remembered. "The hills were covered with tents. People were living in very poor conditions. They had refused to leave His Holiness and were going wherever he went." Directed to the kitchen area of the Secretariat compound at Mortimer Hall, Yeshi Dhonden sat and waited. He was finishing his tea when the Dalai Lama arrived. "Suddenly I heard His Holiness in the other room. 'Where is the doctor?' he said. I stood up, folding my hands in prayer, praying for his long life. I had a very strong mind of faith. But when he entered the room I began to weep. I had never wept upon meeting someone before. I must have been thinking of Tibet . . ."

The Dalai Lama questioned Dr. Dhonden on his escape and then requested him to treat those camped around Dharamsala. Working out of the Nursery at Conium House, Dr. Dhonden began seeing patients under the observation of Tibetan government officials. Having met with their approval, he was summoned to the Dalai Lama once more, this time in the capacity of examining physician. After curing the Dalai Lama of a skin disorder, he was asked to see Kyabjé Ling Rinpoché, the Dalai Lama's senior tutor and head of the Gelugpa sect, who was bedridden in a hospital in Calcutta suffering from a severe case of pericarditis, an inflammation and swelling around the heart. In little over a year Ling Rinpoché was cured and Dr. Dhonden was officially appointed to be the Dalai Lama's personal physician, a post normally filled by up to four doctors in Tibet. His enthusiasm for his practice now fully recovered, he set about the monumental task of preserving Tibetan medicine in exile.

Only two other doctors had escaped from Tibet, neither of whom could assist Dr. Dhonden in Dharamsala. Alone, he began to train ten students in the rudiments of his science, their progress hampered by an almost total lack of funds. Yeshi Dhonden could do little until, one day in 1963, his many run-ins with Indian doctors yielded an ironically positive result.

Responding to repeated complaints from local physicians that the Tibetan was "stealing" their patients, a senior minister in the Indian

Health Department arrived in Dharamsala to investigate. For a week he watched Dr. Dhonden diagnose patients by their pulse and urine, after which he carefully asked each individual his ailment. At one point, five officers from the nearby army cantonment came in to refill prescriptions. "When the minister saw them he exploded in a rage," recalled Dr. Dhonden. " 'We give you the best health care in India and now you've come here to eat shit from a Tibetan!' he yelled." The officers replied that in many cases they had been ill for fifteen years or more. Where Western medicine had failed, Tibetan medicine had succeeded. "Unlike other doctors," they said, "we don't have to tell Dr. Dhonden what's wrong. He tells us." The day before he departed for New Delhi, the minister came to Yeshi Dhonden's office. "You are doing very good work here," he said. "There is only one problem. You don't have enough students. I'm going to give you thirty thousand rupees a year and a twenty-bed hospital." In this manner, the Tibetan Medical Center was formally organized.

Dr. Dhonden assumed the roles of director and pharmacologist as well as chief examining physician. In 1965 he was joined by a second physician, who assisted in teaching the now seven-year curriculum, leading expeditions into the mountains behind Dharamsala to collect herbs and manufacturing 165 principal drugs. With 15 students graduating to join the 150 or so doctors practicing Tibetan medicine outside of Tibet and plans underway for a research wing, a museum and nine outpatient clinics in the settlements, Dr. Dhonden resigned from the Center in 1969. Opening a private practice in McLeod Ganj, he continued to see the Dalai Lama, taking his pulse each day just after sunrise, until in 1978 another physician was appointed to assist him. Dr. Dhonden was then freed to introduce Tibetan medicine to the West.

"THE INFORMATION REQUIRED before Tibetan medicines could be approved for use in the United States would take an army of lab technicians years to develop," commented Dr. Gerald Goldstein, speculating on the future of an exchange between Tibetan and Western doctors as Yeshi Dhonden's visit in Virginia drew to an end. "Each ingredient must be individually identified, purified from its crude state and then thoroughly tested. Who is going to pay for it?" "Research today is a cost-benefit situation," concurred Dr. Donald Baker. "How is a drug company going to collect all of these medicines in northern India and still make a profit at it?" "The impetus for the work, though, is clear," added Dr. Goldstein. "Over one third of our pharmacopoeia comes from plants and microorganisms, specifically some of our oldest and most effective cancer drugs. These are just the sort of materials Tibetans have acquired experience with over centuries of use. Personally, I think the drug companies are missing a bet. Some of these medicines are definitely going to be active."

In the East, the bet has not been missed. Whereas Peking destroyed every institution of the old Tibet soon after 1959, it preserved and later expanded Mendzekhang. Now called the Hospital of Tibetan Medicine, Mendzekhang's 127-member staff treats 700 to 800 patients a day. Though the doctors have been forced to curtail their unique knowledge of the mind's relation to the body (considered, as a basic component of Buddhist teachings, anathema), volumes of color photographs cataloguing medicinal plants have been compiled, while many of the most valuable herbs indigenous to the Himalayas have begun to be cultivated on high-altitude farms. Concurrently, Tibetan drugs are in widespread use throughout mainland China though they are referred to as Chinese in origin and not Tibetan.

"Tibetan and Western medicine begin from completely opposite standpoints," said Dr. Dhonden, summing up his view of the two sciences after visiting the United States. "To start with, a Western scientist looks through a microscope to examine the cause of a disease in terms of its molecular particles. Only then does he take into account the particular patient. Tibetan doctors begin with the patient. We consider his disposition in terms of wind, bile and phlegm. And then we approach the disease. The difference, I feel, makes for weakness and strength in both. We lack many of the symptomatic treatments modern physicians possess. On the other hand, it would be useful for Western doctors to understand the Tibetan presentation of the humors, their balance and imbalance in the human body. Without this, their medical system remains incomplete. It cannot establish a clear view of the correct causes and conditions governing all disease. If young Western doctors would come and train with us for a period of years—as well as relating their own system's analysis of disease—then, I feel, a true exchange could occur. So each of us it seems," he concluded, judiciously, "has something of value to learn from the other."

7

On Pilgrimage
with the Dalai Lama

NIGHT BLACKENS PATHANKOT. Headlights swerve across the buckled row of wood stalls lining one end of the main road. Inside, chilled keepers sit on platforms buried in unbought goods: old blankets, used rubber boots, discarded greatcoats from the nearby army base. Lighted by single bulbs dangling over their angular heads, they gaze balefully into the dark street. Even at night, its chaos refuses to subside. Tattered coolies, rearing up on bicycle rickshaws, press into the middle of the road in the trail of a bus, ignoring fierce horn blasts from the next, coming up behind. Dented, scarred Ambassadors, India's domestically manufactured car, jockey for position. From opposite directions they speed at one another down the center of the road, their drivers veering at the last instant only to avoid collision. The Tatas, towering diesel-powered trucks, festooned with somber portraits of blue- and red-faced deities illuminated by colored bulbs and framed with tinsel, supersede the bluffing. Refusing to slow for the town, they plummet through, horns blaring, spraying the road with fumes. In their wake hundreds of men, wrapped in shawls against the early-January cold, dash across the avenue. Obscured by the dark and even after a rain, the dust rises around their thin legs. As it clears, the scene behind appears. Scores of cubbyhole-sized repair shops specializing in one aspect of a vehicle—tires, radiators, fenders or batteries—have thrown their contents onto the open ground before their doors. While the older drivers of berthed trucks huddle about fires in trash cans, smoking leaf-wrapped *bidis*, gaunt young men clad in pajama-like pants, arms and faces black with grease, rush feverishly from part to part searching for any small item, of rubber, steel, black iron or wood, that might temporarily serve as a facsimile of a functioning thing. But the decay is irremediable. The very elements of this world, it seems, have devoured their vital force long ago.

Tibetan sweater sellers strike out from their few shared homes, through the town, to the old British-built train station. Passing the dry fountain in its muddy courtyard, they walk beneath the grand pillars of the portico into the main hall leading to the tracks, bounded left and right by ticket windows, now closed. Here they quietly form two facing rows, a broad aisle in between. The women wear ankle-length robes and rainbow-hued aprons, their black pigtails braided with ribbons; the men are in hiking boots, slacks and red or blue parkas. Bundles of incense are ignited. In a corner three nuns, their palms pressed together, recite prayer aloud. A man in a dark suit enters, followed by a troop of bearded Sikhs dressed in olive coats and blue red-finned turbans, bandoliered with cartridges and carrying massive, wooden-butted rifles—the Punjabi police. Mr. Dhawan, New Delhi's liaison officer to the Dalai Lama, proceeds slowly down the aisle. The crowd stiffens; there is a rustling of newspapers and in a dozen places bright bunches of pink, red and yellow plastic flowers materialize, making the hall suddenly jump to life.

A red light spins across the dark beyond the fountain. A jeep swoops up between two pillars, emitting a squad of police, who, flanking out, screen the station's entrance. It is followed by a maroon Mercedes-Benz which drives directly onto the marble floor of the hallway. Before the vehicle has stopped, its back doors are flung open, and Ngari Rinpoché, the Dalai Lama's younger brother, accompanied by a monk and a Tibetan bodyguard, leaps out. Now that he is in his early thirties, Ngari Rinpoché's great physical resemblance to the Dalai Lama conveys such authority that as he strides into the hall the Tibetans bow as one from the waist, audibly suck in their breath and distend their tongues in the traditional sign of greeting. The front door of the Mercedes opens and out steps the Dalai Lama, clad in burgundy robes and brown oxfords, a maroon monk's bag slung casually over his right shoulder. Bent slightly from the waist, palms clasped before his chest, he walks slowly down the aisle, his features composed, eyes lit with a warm humor, making contact with scores of expectant faces. Led by Mr. Dhawan, he turns left at the tracks, his retinue sweeping along behind, and heads for the "Retiring Room" to await the train. Ebullient from their brief glimpse of the "Wish-Fulfilling Gem," the crowd breaks and scatters down the platform after him, racing past a sign which optimistically reads: "Trains may either gain or lose time."

In half an hour, a black barrel-nosed steam engine, pulling a long rust-colored train, groans into the station from Jammu, the railhead two hours north of Pathankot. Called 33 Down, for its west-to-east direction down and across the breadth of northern India, the train contains a private saloon. Its exterior is worn and dusty like that of the other cars, the windows tightly shuttered by silver metal blinds; the interior, however, is equipped with a modern sitting-dining room and crisply made-up sleeping cabins, staffed by its own cook and servants who wait for their guests in a white-jacketed line, grinning nervously before pots of steaming water on the kitchen's iron stove. Crossing the short interval of platform, cleared by police of vendors and beggars, the Dalai Lama enters his car. It is already nine o'clock, and because he normally rises at five to meditate, he goes immediately to his room to say evening prayers and retire for the night. The nine-member entourage—four monks, two bodyguards, two officials of the Indian government and Ngari Rinpoché—choose cabins and sit for a late dinner. Within ten minutes the train pulls slowly out of Pathankot on its way across all of India, taking the party far to the east to Bihar, the first stop on the Dalai Lama's 1981 pilgrimage to the holiest sites of Buddhism.

For two days and nights, 33 Down traverses India. It is a local. It stops in every town, never running for more than an hour without break. As the cars turn south in a broad arc the first night, white clouds of steam and soot billow back from the locomotive across their flanks, shuttered against the northern cold. Inside, it is—for India—eerily silent. At the start of its trip the train is virtually empty. In second class there is room to spread out in the three-tiered cubicles sectioning the interior like human storage racks. The private compartments of first class are deserted. Jullundur and Ludhiana pass in jolting, chaotic pictures, scored by train whistles, couplings and porters' shouts. Between, the dark land stands cold and still. By dawn, having crossed the Jumna River on the way down to Delhi, both the Punjab and Haryana have been left behind; Saharanpur and then Moradabad are reached, well within the line of Uttar Pradesh; with 100 million inhabitants, this is India's most populous state and among the most crowded pieces of land on the planet. The train is no longer empty. Every car save the Dalai Lama's saloon is jammed. In second class there is no longer room to stand. Passengers hang off the uppermost bunks, clutching caged fans in the ceiling to keep their balance. Below, twenty-five people, packed in an area the size of a meat locker, shout, laugh, peel eggs, belch, play cards and chew betel nut, leering with bright red tongues and wet lips when they win a hand. Now the metal shutters have been pushed up as far as they will go, the cold of the mountains left behind, any breath of air welcomed to relieve the heat and sweat-filled atmosphere of the car. Even first class has not escaped the crowds. India's commuters, university students and businessmen, pour on to travel a half hour from one town to the next, up to twenty at a time boisterously filling compartments booked for six. The conductors are gone.

Rampur, Shahjahanpur, Sitapur, Lucknow, Rae Bareli, Jais, Amethi, Bela . . . The countryside is one. As the sun shoots up a hundred miles to the north over the distant Himalayas, touches its low winter noon midway in the sky and falls down to the right of the train, its flat light blandly pans through a hazy white sky. A maze of small dusty green rectangles, demarcated by two-foot-high gray mud walls, sit flush on an interminable plain, choking the level land: India's exhausted heart. Save for sudden wastes of sand or wide, dry riverbeds, every inch of earth is cultivated, the soil overworked and depleted. Few people, though, are visible in the fields. They come into sight at the brick factories bordering every town. Here the earth has been dug three or four feet down, exposing a brittle texture and a flinty, barren hue. In the midst of acres of stacked bricks stand twin funnel-shaped chimneys, the tallest points on the treeless landscape, resembling ruined pillars, their blackened spouts decapitated. Around the kilns at their base trudge the emaciated sari-clad bodies of women workers, flat bare feet and bony ankles wrapped in their greatest possessions: bulky, shackle-like bronze bracelets. The towns come on in choked pools of urine-soaked pea-green slime, their surfaces littered with paper, feces and trash, backed up against low walls scrawled over with political slogans and papered with torn lurid movie posters. Behind each, a chaos of cattle, traffic, compressed buildings and roads, spreading like broken veins, consumes the thin line of rail as it passes the outskirts and comes to a halt in a station. The full spectacle of society then appears, trooped out on the platforms. At one in the afternoon scores are asleep, wrapped in blankets side by side, their heads on their baggage. Before the engine halts, young vendors wash up against the cars bellowing in stentorian voices, *"Moongphali! Moongphali!"* ("Peanuts! Peanuts!"). Others hawk vegetable fritters, fruit, chapatis and milky tea in brown clay cups which, emptied, are thrown on the tracks and smashed. Muscular porters—sporting polished brass badges on red coats over their dhotis—hurl through the crowds, huge trunks balanced on their shoulders, the owners racing behind so as not to lose their luggage. The wealthy cut through the sea of poor making for first-class cars, where their names are posted on cyclostyled pages by the doors. As the reckless exchange between those embarking and those disembarking subsides, the broken bodies of beggars appear on the ground near the public fountains, where, twenty-four hours a day, a new group of risers are brushing, hacking, splashing and spitting, eager to feel fresh.

The second night. In the Dalai Lama's car, the quiet that has characterized the journey so far continues. The rear door locked, a bodyguard sits near the front monitoring the rare comings and goings at stations. Mr. Dhawan and Dawa Bhotia, Delhi's chief of security for the Dalai Lama, occupy the sitting room with Ngari Rinpoché, talking shop, smoking and reading newspapers. Lobsang Gawa and Paljor, the Dalai Lama's two personal attendants, who were chosen by him years before as young men from his private monastery, Namgyal Dratsang, occasionally pass some hours in the room joking with Ngari Rinpoché and the guards. The Dalai Lama himself leaves his cabin only to wash, taking his meals alone. He has spread a large orange and yellow cloth-bound scripture across the desk top beside his portable shortwave radio, tuned in the morning and evening for international news. Certain of Tibet's most sacred images, believed to be receptacles for divine protectors and always kept in the company of each Dalai Lama, are placed about the cabin.

Outside there is actual danger. Murdering "dacoit" bands, equipped with homemade "country" pistols, proliferate in the area. Unseen in the dark, the populous flats have given way to wild hills and gullies out of which the dacoits issue forth to hold up trains, hijack trucks and raid villages. Ironically, due to the great crowds, second-class passengers are safe. First class, with its private compartments and richer take, is the prime target. Here the passengers have locked their doors and refuse to open them without questioning all callers. At 4:00 a.m. Benares, the Holy City, is reached. Half the train exits; some have come to die by the burning ghats on the Ganges' shores, their long flames fueled for millennia by generations of the Hindu race. Beyond Benares the Ganges is crossed and the very heart of ancient India, Madhyadesa or "the Middle Country," spanning the Gangetic plain, is entered: the land of two kingdoms and nine republics forming the core of the Buddha's world. And then, by eight-thirty on the morning of the second day, the train finally reaches Gaya, six miles from Bodh Gaya in the state of Bihar, the site of the Buddha's enlightenment, the *axis mundi* of the Buddhist faith.

In the midst of a seemingly endless succession of stops, arrival comes as a surprise. There is a quiet around the Dalai Lama's saloon. The windows and doors remain locked. On the platform, the abbot of the Tibetan monastery at Bodh Gaya waits in a small group of monks. Their neat claret robes and bright yellow jerkins form a clean, tranquil pool of color in the stream of stained and torn figures swirling around. The front door of the saloon gingerly opens, and Ngari Rinpoché looks out. He pulls the door back and the monks are ushered in, bearing white silk scarves, to welcome the Dalai Lama. After a brief greeting in the dining room, the Dalai Lama briskly leads the party back out, not wishing to lose time.

There is something different in Gaya. It is apparent on the platform, in front of the station house, even before the town itself is reached. There are crowds, but their movement appears frail and somber. The frenetic pace has not slowed, yet its interior force has dissolved. The people abut one another more lightly, their appearance shrunken and strained. There is, as well, a less subtle sign of the change. As the Dalai Lama steps out of the saloon and walks toward a covered bridge spanning the tracks to the station house, he passes a small girl, no older than eight, alone on the platform. Unlike other beggars in other stations, she says nothing at all. She stands immobile in a torn gossamer rag, a glassy look in her dark eyes. The girl is severely starved. Her black matted hair is light red from protein deficiency. Her nose, jaw, shoulders, bare legs and arms are flat bone. The slight bulge of her lips forms the only fullness on her body. The quick movement of the large party passing by pulls her little head up, mouth drawn tight, forehead pinched at its center. Automatically her hands, holding a tin bowl, extend. Already past her, the Dalai Lama calls for Ngari Rinpoché and instructs him to return and give the child money. He drops behind, finds her and, bending down, speaks. The girl grabs the twenty-rupee note he has offered; twenty rupees—$1.66—eighty times the bunch of coins—twenty or thirty paise—normally given. Later Ngari Rinpoché himself is surprised—even appalled—over his recondite breach of the conduct governing the normal business done between beggars and donors.

The reason for such strictly regulated, small contributions is evident just outside the station. In the muddy plot before its entrance lie scores of crippled, dying people. Bihar, India's poorest state, is an area of unallayed suffering. It is dead winter now and the heat is still immense. At night the temperature drops down fast, killing hundreds who have only straw to cover themselves. In summer, thermometers regularly exceed 100 degrees, sunstroke killing hundreds again. Today it is overcast, stultifying. Earlier it has rained, and the station yard is soaked with puddles, the mud between them littered with red-stained leaves from the *paan* of betel-nut chewers, banana peels, orange rinds, *bidi* wrappers and the short green-tipped sticks used by the poor for brushing their teeth. Horse, dog and, in the corners by the walls, human feces sit amidst pools of urine, emitting a foul stench. Everything, fruit, paper and excrement, is coated with flies. Skeletal dogs, devoured by mange, their skin bearing only a patch or two of remaining fur, bolt about, rummaging through the grime. At the far end of the yard stand a row of horses harnessed to dusty black canvas-covered carriages, their thin spines and bloated bellies covered with sores. Between them and the station entrance an army of homeless beggars has come to camp. But they are not beggars in contrast to a markedly franchised population. They are the population itself, or so much of it that those who own homes—who have somewhere to go—look only slightly more purposeful as they move through the crowd. The worst have been literally broken in pieces. An old gray-bearded man, legless and crazed, pulls his cropped torso in circles near the building's walls, ranging from one piece of refuse to another, talking to each. About him wander those slightly better off: the blind, empty sockets exposed in their heads; young men, legs permanently wrapped around each other, swinging their wriggled bodies like buckets between the support of double crutches; middle-aged lepers, ears, noses and cheeks deeply pocked, filthy rags twisted around the stumps of missing fingers and toes; others with elephantiasis, dragging alien pillows of flesh, grown from their arms and legs, across the ground. These luckier ones, still ambulatory, move to the files of travelers going in and out and bet their morning meal, eyes frozen with ingrained anxiety. Among the travelers, not even those who carry bags and have the price of a train ticket wear shoes. They slip from the station trying to avoid the beggars while dodging the larger puddles of urine and trash.

The Dalai Lama and his retinue emerge from the building to a line of cars parked by the station entrance headed by a police jeep. Without waiting for the baggage, which will follow, they strike out of the yard at the deadly speed which, peppered with horn blasts, can alone clear the roads of people and animals.

With a population of 40,000, Gaya is a large town. But poverty has kept it gray and silent; unmechanized, buried in the past, buried in dust, its houses built from emollient mud and warped beams polished by the centuries into the dark likeness of glass. Its silent streets are powdered up to their enclosing porches with dust, each house tottering toward its neighbor across four yards of bleak, chalky road. Around this still web revolve thousands of bicycle rickshaws, spinning brief trails in the smooth ground, the myriad tingling of their bells melting into the walls on either side. Small fires have been made on the roofed-in porches; they deliver smoke to the buildings' upper reaches where the dust can't rise. In the haze, shrouded women emerge, trance-like, from low doorways, peer into the fires and stir a copper pot over the flame.

As the last eddy of rickshaws washes to either side, the column of cars is released from the gloom of Gaya and passes into a radiant green countryside. There is air, sky and light. Stalwart pipal and palm trees line the road. Children and farm animals animate the land. The bleak ghost city fades. Bodh Gaya appears in the distance and, with it, the mood dramatically alters.

A regnant note, resounding like a great ship's horn, rises from two ten-foot *thungchen* or Tibetan long horns, signaling, from the roof of the Japanese monastery on the outskirts of town, the Dalai Lama's approach. As the column speeds over an open plain, a second group of horns, at the ready before the Thai temple, takes up the call. Now the 180-foot-tall stone Temple marking the Bodhi Tree, under which the Buddha became enlightened, looms ahead. Around it a third clarion call—this one shrill and sour—is produced by hand-held silver *gyaling* or short horns played, beyond the Chinese monastery, from the roof of the Tibetan *Gonpa*, closest of all to the temple's block-wide base. The column slows under the overhanging branches of the trees at Bodh Gaya's edge. The sounds of drums and cymbals become audible among the horns, and then, on the left, the entrance to the Tibetan monastery appears, where 4,000 people, held back by police wielding bamboo staves, wait to greet the Dalai Lama.

"Our Warmest Welcome to H.H. the Dalai Lama" reads a banner draped across a gate, bearing on pink lotuses down its side the Eight Noble Ornaments of the Dharma. And as the Dalai Lama's car leads the others slowly through, thousands of hands fold in prayer, heads bow and eyes reverentially look up at the Precious Protector. His own hands joined in greeting, Tenzin Gyatso smiles with disarming informality from the back seat of his car. Incense billows from a chimney atop the monastery and a second gate is passed, crowned by the cardinal Buddhist emblem, two deer peacefully attending to a gold eight-spoked wheel in their midst, the wheel of the Dharma. Within the monastery's courtyard stands a crush of Tibetan and Western onlookers, many in the robes of the Tibetan monkhood. The Dalai Lama's car passes them and halts before the temple's white portico, where seventy monks holding silk victory banners, their 1,000-string crested hats resembling the helmets of the ancient Greeks, chant a liturgy. He emerges and is formally greeted by a group of high incarnates in their ceremonial robes. Among them stands the small figure of Thubten Tharpa Liushar, Tibet's last Foreign Minister and lay sponsor for the Dalai Lama's teachings, to be offered beneath the Bodhi Tree during the upcoming week. The drums, cymbals and chanting continue, while the Dalai Lama is shown to his rooms on the second floor. With his departure, the crowd, electrified, disperses to the sprawling tent city it has pitched behind the monastery's walls. Like Christmas or Easter in the West, the pilgrimage season, looked forward to by Tibetans as the most sacred and happy time in life, has opened.

The Dalai Lama takes a small meal of bread, jam and butter tea in his suite. He is joined by Kyabjé Ling Rinpoché, his senior tutor. Because he is the abbot of the Bodh Gaya monastery, Ling Rinpoché's quarters share the second floor with those of the Dalai Lama. Between them stands the monastery's main shrine room, in front of which small groups of lamas and lay people are already gathering. Welcomed in hushed tones by Ngari Rinpoché and the Dalai Lama's chief attendant, Lobsang Gawa, they wait to be ushered into his presence. Within half an hour of his arrival, Tenzin Gyatso has already begun a nonstop round of audiences, blessings, teachings and ordinations, which will fill without break the next seven days.

The monastery sits on the west side of Bodh Gaya, less than a hundred yards from the walled compound surrounding the Mahabodhi Temple and the Bodhi Tree. In an open field behind it, the Tibetan tent encampment stretches toward the horizon. A maze of sunken dirt pathways join the tents in an intricate weave, spilling in the rear onto a rocky flat used, out of necessity, as an open-air toilet. Ladakhis, Monpas and Sherpas, pilgrims from Kulu, Manali, Spiti, Lahul and Dolpo, Mustang, Sikkim and Bhutan compose the crowd, each group declaring its identity by appearance. The Bhutanese dress in orange, red and purple checkerboard robes; the ladies' hair is cropped short; the men sport knee socks. Women from the northwestern Himalayan valleys, clad in heavy poncho-like woolen garments, wear rings the full length of the earlobe. Wild, fierce-looking men from Dolpo—at 16,000 feet, the highest inhabited region on earth—dress in coarse black soot-stained *chubas* and tall felt boots, their daggers temporarily put away.

Evening. The Dalai Lama has retired for the night, and Ngari Rinpoché is off duty. After a quick meal in the monastery's dining room, he heads out into the dark. Passing the parked buses of Indian tourists, whose passengers, preparing to sleep on straw beds within, have strung their wash between the windows and nearby trees, he enters the main road and walks to the gate of the Mahabodhi Society, the international Buddhist organization in charge of maintaining the temple's precincts. There he is met by Bikku Gian Jagat, an Indian monk and chief caretaker of the temple grounds. Bikku Jagat has a most singular Brahmanical face—a long beaked nose, pointed ears with translucent tips, deep-sunken eyes and a slow, gelatinous voice. He wears the burnt-orange robes of a Hinayana monk over a yellow wool turtleneck sweater and a pumpkin-colored scarf, all elegantly arranged. His refined gestures and cultured bearing denote a worldly past; like all Indian monks, Buddhism having only recently been revived in its homeland, he has joined the Sangha late in life. Ngari Rinpoché, on the other hand, has given up the monkhood since his arrival in India and now wears gray slacks and a green army jacket, a legacy, though he denies it, of his days as a paratrooper in the Special Frontier Force.

"We will go to a very mystic place," says the Bikku with a wry, glinting smile. "I promise you will like it." Shutting the shoulder-high gate of his residence, he leads the way into the center of town. Much of the day's commotion has subsided. A shooting gallery with red and white balloons tied to its rear wall attracts the sole crowd: a few Indian boys and Tibetan sweater sellers, who, hoping that their pilgrimage will pay for itself, have opened shop along the pavement lining the temple's wall. Bikku Jagat walks past them and turns down a wide avenue leading to the front gate of the precincts. He nods to the ticket taker in his little house and ushers the way in, stopping for a moment at the top of three long flights of stairs. Before him the colossal edifice towers skyward. Begun by the great Buddhist king Ashoka in the third century B.C., two hundred years after the Buddha's death, it sits at the center of a giant square of land sunk fifty feet in the earth. In the gardens at its base grow majestic pipal trees, fringed by flowering bushes and interspersed with clusters of small stupas and shrines, feretories, that house the relics of Buddhist *arbats* or saints. Bounded by four lesser buildings joined by a wide terrace, the spire tapers upward, every inch of its exterior thickly carved in geometric patterns, culminating, like the flame of a monumental stone torch, in a twenty-five-foot-high round capstan.

"Just for one man to change one bulb costs fifty rupees," says Bikku Jagat, staring woefully at the four weak halogen lights illuminating the spire. "Nobody wants to climb up there. If they fall, that's it." Leading the way down the stairs, he tells of his efforts to restore the ancient shrine. "Until just a few years back everything here was very wild. Jungle grew all about. Four hundred huts stood around the tank in which the Buddha bathed. Cows grazed right up to the inner retaining wall. During the warm months you couldn't even come close," he concludes, covering his nose with his handkerchief to illustrate the point. "Quiet! Quiet, you boys!" he yells in Hindi at a group of teen-agers racing around the upper balcony of the temple. "No smoking," he admonishes another on the path. "They have good hearts," he says, turning to Ngari Rinpoché with a self-deprecating wink. "They just don't know how to behave."

In a low stone building before the entrance, Tibetans are performing prostrations. Descending onto well-worn boards, wearing knee pads and special gloves with wooden bottoms, they touch their hands in prayer to the crown of the head, forehead, throat and heart before stretching face down full length toward the shrine. The sound of their breathing, heavy from exertion, fills the night. At the monument itself, others are saying prayers, lighting candles and placing them with flowers and incense along the ledges to the left of the interior temple's door. Inside lies a hallowed image of the Buddha, said to be his actual likeness as approved by an old woman who had seen him. The statue sits on a golden throne under a midnight-blue canopy at the rear of three small rooms whose glossy orange walls, illuminated by hundreds of candles, glow serenely. Its half-closed eyes and composed expression exude tranquillity. "We believe the place in which a person attains a high level of spiritual development has been blessed by him," explained the Dalai Lama. "Just as an ordinary man or woman creates a certain atmosphere in a room in which they live, so have great beings in holy places. As you can draw conclusions about a person from the atmosphere in his room, so you can in Bodh Gaya about the Buddha himself. This is the basis for making pilgrimage: to draw some positive force from a blessed place, so that one's own merit—the store of good qualities within one's mind—will increase."

At day's end, three people, seated apart on rugs covering the floor, remain absorbed in meditation. In a corner beside the altar, a uniformed policeman, holding a rifle with a fixed bayonet, scrupulously eyes the devotees. On the occasion of his first visit to Bodh Gaya in 1956, the Dalai Lama offered a large butter lamp of pure gold to the temple. Normally kept in an underground vault in Gaya, it has made the journey to the temple for the week of pilgrimage, where its flame shines among all the others. Its presence, however, necessitates a platoon of ten guards camped out like a similar contingent at the Tibetan monastery, just beyond the shrine room.

Bikku Jagat leaves the temple and walks through the gardens. On their far side he halts by a large body of water sunk in a grassy basin, a tree at one end, a few red lotus growing by the shoreline. "Here," he says, widening his eyes with subdued glee, "our mystical place. The place Lord Buddha bathed after his enlightenment." There is no one about. The sky is shrouded. The still water looks flat and timeless, just as it might have two and a half millennia before. "The Buddha was a prince who had been kept in the palace, never seeing the world beyond," continues Bikku Jagat, "but on four occasions he stole out. The first time he saw a sick man, the next a dead man. Then he saw an old man. And then again, a recluse. And he simply thought, 'Is it the fate of man that he should be born, be sick and die, or is there anything greater than these flickering things?' These are the four signs which led him to ponder the world. They are not supernatural, just human and natural."

Born in the sixth century B.C., Siddhartha Gautama, as the Buddha was known before his enlightenment, began life as a prince of the small semi-monarchic Shakyan republic located 130 miles north of Benares at the foot of the Himalayas. He was raised in the capital city of Kapilavastu, a bustling center of politics and trade filled with merchants, bards and soldiers, the council hall of the Shakyan elders at its center, a twenty-seven-foot wall with towers enclosing the whole. Warned by an astrologer that his son would become either a world emperor or a Buddha, an "Awakened One," King Suddhodana sought to ensure the former by keeping the prince sequestered within the palace, removed from any influence but his own. In his twenty-ninth year, however, Siddhartha became so disturbed by his view of life on four forays into the city that, abandoning his wife, newborn son and kingdom-to-be, he fled Kapilavastu by night, shed his royal clothes, shaved his head and became a wandering mendicant. Traveling south, he studied with the most renowned philosophers of the time, the six great cities of Madhyadesa, like contemporary Greece, then in the midst of a great flowering of metaphysical thought. None, though, satisfied him. Reaching the village of Dungeshwari on the Naranjana River, some 225 miles southeast of his home, Siddhartha resolved to engage in unbroken meditation, mortifying the flesh, until he experienced direct realization of the ultimate nature of reality. For six years he practiced austerities without result. Then one day, while drinking from the river, he fell in, no longer able to hold himself up. Forced to discontinue his meditation, he journeyed with great effort two miles south to the outskirts of a village called Bakraur, where a young woman named Sujata gradually nursed him back to health. Once recovered, he forded the Naranjana in the full moon of May and, locating a large pipal tree a few hundred feet beyond the western bank, sat in meditation at its base until, at dawn the following day, he obtained enlightenment. The Buddha spent the next seven weeks alone in the environs of the tree, pondering how to explain the nature of his realization to others. He then walked a hundred miles west to Benares to begin the forty-five-year task of founding the first of the world's great pan-national faiths. With the Buddhist Sangha or clergy well established, patronized by the two greatest kings of Madhyadesa, he died at the age of eighty in the small town of Kushinagar, fifty miles from his birthplace.

"Now we must go this way," says Bikku Jagat, turning abruptly from the tank and walking back toward the temple. Between the silent masses of stone reliquaries and pink flowering bushes, a small light glows from candles lit at the base of the Bodhi Tree, the third living descendant of the original, rooted on the exact spot where the Buddha attained enlightenment. Bikku Jagat pauses briefly before it to say a prayer.

Monday morning, January 15. At nine o'clock the Dalai Lama leaves the Tibetan monastery. Thirty-five police clear the route through Bodh Gaya's single ramshackle street, an unspecified number of plainclothes security converging around the entourage like sullen, obtrusive dependents recognizable only by their misshapen Western jackets worn over white dhotis. Walking rapidly, the Dalai Lama enters the temple's grounds by a gate in the western wall. Here, he slows his pace, and with Bikku Jagat beside him, circumambulates the precincts along the widest and highest path, descending to pray in the shrine room. His offerings made, he follows the base by the shortest path, walking toward the Bodhi Tree. On the lawn beneath it, all 4,000 Tibetans have gathered. Compressed in tight, uneven ranks, monks and nuns to the front, the crowd rolls between the islands of reliquaries all the way back to the stone gate and its giant bell by which the Dalai Lama first entered. Beneath them, the ground is a patchwork of hundreds of small rugs and blankets. There are no aisles. Anyone who thinks he might leave has stayed at the edge. The rest are jammed knee to knee, making room only for a few young monks to hand out wallet-sized yellow booklets containing prayers written by the Dalai Lama, addressed to the protective deities of Tibet, for an improvement in conditions there.

The last monks, yellow robes flung quickly across their shoulders, find their places just as the Dalai Lama rounds the corner. The first to see him, they rise immediately, followed by the people behind. Palms together at his chest, back slightly bent, the Dalai Lama acknowledges the welcome with a smile. He stops before a resplendent six-foot throne, draped in yellow, red and gold brocade. Taking his shoes off and then prostrating, he mounts and seats himself on a small white pillow, placing his monk's bag on the table to his right. The foliage of the tree extends in a beautiful green canopy overhead. Squares of thin gold leaf along its four branching trunks, peeled by the weather, flutter so that much of the lower tree sparkles. Above them hundreds of multicolored flags and pennants have been rigged by pilgrims from all over the world and the tree appears as though dressed for a regatta.

The crowd's own prostrations done, the Dalai Lama begins to rapidly recite the Heart Sutra. Seated in the second row beside a scarf-draped microphone, the chant master picks up the prayer and is joined by the entire assembly. Two minutes later the lightning recitation concludes with three loud hand claps, performed to symbolically clear away obstructions to perceiving form and emptiness as one: the subject of the sutra and basis of Buddhist philosophy. Following further preliminaries, the Dalai Lama takes up his teaching, based on a popular text by Thogmey Zangpo, a famous fourteenth-century lama.

For five days, four hours each morning, Tenzin Gyatso describes the major practices on the path to enlightenment. His constant theme is that the essence of a Buddhist life lies in a person's own effort to purify the mind. By replacing its coarse, deluded states such as anger, attachment and ignorance with their opposites: patience, equanimity and wisdom, a lasting internal happiness can be achieved, independent of external conditions. His words are set against a backdrop shared by all the listeners, depicting the universe and man's role within it, from a rational humanistic view— the non-theistic Buddhist ethos so similar, despite its Eastern doctrine, to the secular thought of the modern world.

The Buddha described the cosmos as an infinite number of world systems forming, disintegrating and re-forming with neither beginning nor end. Within the worlds, he maintained, living beings undergo repeated birth, death and rebirth based on their innate misconception of reality. All creatures conceive things to exist independently, in and of themselves, he said, whereas, in truth, nothing is self-originated; phenomena arise in dependence on causes and conditions. This interdependence he called emptiness—specifically, the lack of an ultimate self. When the mind realizes that it is empty of such a substantial identity and exists merely in the manner of an illusion, freedom from the uncontrolled process of material incarnation, known as cyclic existence or *samsara*, is obtained. Such is the liberation of an *arhat* or saint. Once achieved, it is possible to expand consciousness to the omniscient state of Buddhahood, the simultaneous cognizance of all things throughout time and space together with their empty mode of being. Such wisdom is required for the purpose of leading other beings to liberation, the motivation underlying all Mahayana Buddhist practice. During the twenty eons for which our world system will endure, said the Buddha, a thousand universal or teaching Buddhas will appear to show the way to enlightenment. He described himself as the fourth. Between them, however, both high-level Bodhisattvas and Buddhas will continue to project emanation or form bodies. According to the Mahayanist interpretation, Sakyamuni Buddha himself was just such a projection. As the Dalai Lama explained, "We always look at Lord Buddha from two aspects. One as a normal, though exceptional human being, the other as an emanation body appearing simultaneously in a hundred million worlds of our galaxy to teach the Dharma. Of course, we don't directly know what type of person he was, but if you put the abstract theories aside and consider the essence of what he said, the whole teaching comes down to one point: love and kindness. This is his message. Not a single word promotes hatred or some kind of holy war. Such things are never mentioned. So, you see, I find it very good. Whether we can practice the teachings or not, that is the question."

The Dalai Lama's personal sense of the Buddha remained somewhat distant during his years in Tibet. On arriving in India, however, an affinity for the founder of his religion, akin to the feelings he had long held for Tibetan saints, began to grow. "During a discourse I recently delivered on the Wisdom of Emptiness Sutra," he recounted, "I became quite sure that when the Buddha was preaching this text I myself was one of the poor Indians listening on the fringes of the crowd. Although one of the lowest human beings in the society, yet I made some kind of connection with the Buddha during his time. It could be a baseless thought, and for a monk, you see, such a claim is very dangerous, but in the present moment, as I carry out some activity in serving Buddha's teaching, I feel there must be a cause. That is my reason."

The belief that past lives produce the present, just as the present does the future, lies at the heart of Buddhism as a practitioner's faith. "There are many logical proofs for rebirth," continued the Dalai Lama. "Fundamentally, though, we believe that a child's consciousness cannot come from his or her parents in the same way the body does. The mind is formless, mere illumination and knowing. Because of this, matter cannot act as its substantial cause. Only a previous moment of consciousness can serve as the first cause of a mind, in this case, that of a former life. Among some people I know, when a more subtle level of consciousness is produced in meditation, they are clearly able to remember seven hundred, eight hundred, a thousand years back." It is the karmic seeds, the residues of one's actions dwelling in the mind, that shape one life from another. As the Dalai Lama concluded, "One's actions in life are never wasted. In the future their karmic imprints will meet with the appropriate conditions and bear fruit. And in the present, you will never encounter the effects of actions you have not previously done yourself. For this reason, one's fate is entirely on one's own shoulders."

For the Tibetans, a stark proof of karma's inviolability appears by midweek. Word has spread of the pilgrims' presence, bringing hundreds of beggars into Bodh Gaya. Whoever walks from the monastery to the Mahabodhi Temple is accosted by up to twenty howling women and children clutching their clothes, moaning, "*Baba, Baba.*" ("Father, Father.") They appear to be suffering unendurable pain, as, so the first maxim of begging goes, the more pitiful the plea, the greater the chance of its success. In Bihar, begging is a vocation—specifically, a performing art. An incredible sequence of shrieks, groans and hysterical gestures, ending in maimed hands holding robes out for donations, whirls around the streets. During peak begging hours, while the pilgrims are coming and going from the teachings, it seems that Bodh Gaya is a battleground. If a pilgrim fails to heed his accosters, tugging escalates into hard pokes and louder shrieks, set up to alert more barefoot, bedraggled children and their shriveled mothers to descend in a reinforcing swarm and prevent escape. But the biggest mistake is to stop. Those who do, much less give money, are trampled by scores of beggars rushing from all directions. Their only hope lies in fighting their way free or, as most do, throwing money high into the air, so the beggars scatter to collect it.

By late in the week the situation changes. So many beggars have arrived that, ironically, most have been forced to give up the fight. Competition has become counterproductive. Instead, they have seated themselves down the long approach to the temple's entrance, backs to the compound wall, tin bowls before them. Even day care has been organized: groups of skeletal children are kept by single mothers at regular intervals. Here they sit and play with pebbles, pick lice from one another, laugh, fight and cry for succor when a crescendo of moans rolls down the line signaling the arrival of a potential donor. Content with this arrangement, the Tibetans come ready with small change and walk the full distance dropping a coin into as many bowls as possible. In this manner most manage to earn enough for a single meal of rice and dhal to share with their children, before sleeping the night, huddled together for warmth, in alleys on the outskirts of town. In 1943, the Great Bengal Famine, one of the worst of the century, killed three million people in Bihar and adjacent Bengal. Though chronic malnutrition is more the problem now, the potential for mass death from hunger alone seems ever-present.

As if to show one ray of hope, a demonstration marches through Bodh Gaya. Cutting into the midst of the human wreckage outside the temple, 200 Indian students and farmers angrily shake their fists behind snare drums and a phalanx of red flags, demanding more government aid for Bihar. "There is bound to be a revolution," says the Dalai Lama, commenting on the prevailing conditions, "but, at the same time, there will always be suffering. Inevitably beings will meet with the effects of unfavorable actions they have previously committed. Also, the very aggregates of a human mind and body have, as their actual nature, suffering. They serve as a basis for suffering, and as long as one has them one is susceptible to suffering. From a deep point of view, while we Tibetans don't have our independence and are living in someone else's country, we are subject to a certain type of suffering, but when we return to Tibet and gain our independence, then there will be other types of suffering. So, you see, this is just the way it is. You might think that I'm pessimistic, but I am not. This is the Buddhist realism. This is how, through Buddhist teaching and advice, we handle situations. These sorts of thoughts make one stronger, more active. It is not at all a case of losing one's strength of will when faced with the pervasive nature of suffering."

Tibet's cause is never far from the pilgrims' thought. Each day's teaching concludes with prayers for those under Chinese occupation, followed by a dedication of the merit gained to the speedy end of their suffering. Only by building up a store of collective merit or good karma through overcoming their own delusions, the Tibetans believe, can the situation resolve itself favorably. Thus, by midweek, a glut of devotion is underway. Each afternoon and evening thousands circumambulate the temple and tree, prostrating, reciting mantras, lighting candles and burning incense. Masses of offerings have been assembled at the Bodhi Tree's base: stacks of bread five feet high by four wide, baskets of bananas, apples and oranges, cookies, candies, money and flowers, bowls of saffron water and foot-high *tormas* or conical cakes, decorated with sculpted butter. The wires connecting the Dalai Lama's microphone to loudspeakers around the garden are draped with clusters of red, yellow and green cords, hung to absorb blessings and later to be worn around the neck. An endless stream of silhouettes sweeps along the highest path, outlined by the sky behind it; the short trail resembles a whirlpool, the great stone edifice churned into the heavens by the herd at its feet. In the prostration houses by the temple's entrance and tank, men and women, stripped to their undershirts exert themselves for hours, their effort interrupted only by one another's jokes. Children run, laughing and playing, between those seated in meditation on the lawns, and as the sun sets daily, the sanctuary is illuminated by thousands of tiny bright flames. Every inch of the temple's lower edge, the various small shrines and much of the three pathways are set aglow, a platform for butter lamps looking like a galaxy of light descended to earth. Clouds of incense billow through the treetops. A brilliant half moon floats just above the temple's pinnacle.

On one day, the entire Kangyur is read out loud—all 108 volumes of the Buddha's word. The monks have brought the monastery's massive clothbound edition on a wooden cart to a stone offering table beneath the Bodhi Tree. From here the yellow volumes are handed out to groups seated in circles on the grass. With a text open in the center of a circle, each person takes a page and begins to read out loud as rapidly as possible.

A wild cacophony erupts all over the precincts, but in a mere two hours every word the Buddha is known to have uttered is heard once more in the world.

Outside the temple, the sacred and mundane mix effortlessly. Sweater selling is brisk and business percolates in every corner of the tent city; an elephant is led through, its owner selling rides. The tea stalls are filled with avid conversation; scores help the monks to prepare noodle soup, cooked in giant outdoor cauldrons. Through it all, people's lips move in constant recitation of prayer. As is the Tibetan habit, between their own words or while listening to others, men and women continue to quietly recite mantras, spinning the beads of their rosaries, held nonchalantly from their right hands. The only tension comes on the day the Dalai Lama offers personal blessings in the main hall of the monastery. Though other occasions in Bodh Gaya and elsewhere have seen up to a hundred thousand so blessed, one at a time, the line still seems endless. Hundreds wait quietly holding white *katas*, dressed in their finest clothes, their expressions progressively more subdued until, ushered off the top of the stairs and into the monastery, where the Dalai Lama stands in front of a towering golden image of Maitreya, the Buddha-to-come, a look of awe mixed with panic overcomes them. Directed through a gamut of monks, their heads bow and backs bend ever lower. Then, suddenly, as they come before the radiant smile of the Dalai Lama himself, their apprehension at being in the presence of the living incarnation of the Bodhisattva of Infinite Compassion melts, replaced by childlike joy. The Dalai Lama, though, is not affected by the reverence shown him. Unhurriedly he holds people's hands, names their children, blows gently on the foreheads of the ill, blesses scriptures, containers of water and bunches of silk protection cords and frequently stops the line either to ask questions or to answer requests for personal advice. In an audience held for 200 Westerners he dispenses with Tibetan protocol altogether, sitting on a cushion among travelers from a dozen nations, answering their questions on Buddhism and insisting, at the end of the meeting, on shaking all of their hands and asking where they come from. The spread of Buddhism, as Bikku Jagat points out, has grown to the degree that, after the Tibetans, the largest groups arriving in Bodh Gaya are not Asian but Western. This year the Westerners are particularly enthusiastic because for the first time a two-day vow-taking will be translated into English under the Bodhi Tree itself. Daily, they have been meeting in the Ghandi Vihar, a vacant building on the edge of town provisioned, as a famine reserve, with heavy sacks of corn stamped: "Furnished by the People of the United States of America. Not to Be Sold or Exchanged." Most are in their late twenties and thirties, many having come to India in the migrations of the 1960s and stayed on, labeling themselves "Dharma freaks." A number are monks or nuns, among whom are some who have undergone the rigorous dialectical training of the monastic colleges, earning respect from Tibetans, who at first were skeptical of their conversion. "In the beginning Westerners were attracted to Eastern religions because it was like going on a mental vacation," commented the Dalai Lama. "Then, after some time, they became interested in studying more seriously, in delving deeper. In general, religion has no boundaries. If it helps people, that is sufficient, but in Buddhism, for any who practice, it is not enough just to have faith. You must examine with reason. The Buddha said, 'Monks and scholars should accept my word, not out of respect, but upon analyzing it as a goldsmith analyzes gold, by cutting, melting, scraping and rubbing it.' Only that which cannot be damaged by reasoning should be considered definitive. After ascertaining the truth, one should then have faith, but that isn't a blind faith leading you into a chasm."

At the end of the third day's talk the Dalai Lama wraps the pages of his text back in their red silk cover and says, speaking evenly into the microphone, "This morning I received word that my mother died. There's no need to feel sad. But if some of you have the time and no other engagements, perhaps you might recite some mantras for her beneath the Bodhi Tree this afternoon." The crowd is visibly affected. The Gyalyum Chenmo, or Great Mother, was a pillar of Tibetan society. One of the last major links to the Tibet of the past, she was particularly revered as the mother of three incarnate lamas. "When I heard that my mother had died," the Dalai Lama recounted later, "it was a real experience for me. A good chance. The idea of death and the length of a human lifespan struck me more. But I wasn't sad; I accepted it. I'd done a divination before I left Dharamsala which indicated that the end would be very soon, and I had visited her. When I saw my mother, I clearly told her, 'We all have to die; there's no place to hide. Not only you, everyone has to go that way.' You see, among religious-minded people one can talk openly about such things. With others, even though you know that he or she is about to die, still you must pretend they are healthy. So I told my mother, 'You are old. Sooner or later you have to die. At the last minute the most important thing is to have no attachment. Your only attachment should be to Chenrezi. Then there is no reason to worry.' She accepted my advice calmly and later I was informed that up until the very end she expressed concern for those around her, thanked them for caring for her and told Dr. Yeshi Dhonden that she was sorry to have given him so much trouble with her illness. So you see, these things are very nice; an expression of the Buddha's teaching.

In fact, one of the purposes of practicing Dharma is that, when the last moment comes, the person who disappears has prepared himself, and those close by also understand the laws of nature and are not worried. The opposite is usually the case. We don't even talk about death. We pretend that we are going to remain here forever and then when death occurs, we only cry, which cannot help a thing. Anyway, although I am supposed to be one of her prominent sons, I had no special dreams or signs," he concluded, laughing. "I recited some mantras, said some prayers, and nothing more. I am quite sure that she will take a good rebirth."

Benares station, the Tito Gate, January 19, 6:10 a.m. The Dalai Lama's saloon, disconnected from the Gaya train, slides into a private siding beyond the terminal. After breakfast Tenzin Gyatso walks down the narrow corridor to wash in the bathroom at the rear of the car. His fellow travelers are busy unpacking clothes to store in the saloon before commencing the next stage of pilgrimage.

Outside, three Ambassadors, their drivers polishing the hoods, wait beside the track. Samdong Rinpoché, the erudite principal of the Institute of Higher Buddhist Studies in nearby Sarnath, waits, *kata* in hand, to welcome the Dalai Lama. Around him stand the usual rifle-toting police, heads wrapped in scarves against the early-morning chill. Beyond, the pale yellow domes of the Benares station, one of the more dramatic legacies of the British Raj, rise in the gray light, the halls beneath filled at this hour with files of sleeping travelers, wrapped in blankets, against the walls. Between them meander white, slack-jawed, sloe-eyed Brahmin cows. Benares is the Holy City, and the sacred animals, better fed than people, wander about freely, defecating in sloppy wet piles on the marble floor. The acrid stench of their urine wreathes the station. Beside the Dalai Lama's car, a lone beggar scans the track picking half-consumed refuse cast from trains. The shrill whistle of an approaching steam engine stabs the silence.

The Dalai Lama exits the saloon. Greeting Samdong Rinpoché, he strides across the platform to the lead Ambassador, a squat dark gray sedan, its windows tinted brown, the rear one draped by pink curtains. Dawa Bhotia, chief of security, joins the driver. Comfortably adjusted, he is rammed to the middle of the seat by the abrupt entrance of a Tibetan bodyguard—an ex-trooper of the Special Frontier Force. Mr. Dhawan, Delhi's liaison officer, joins the Dalai Lama in the back. The two other Ambassadors, both cream-colored, fill quickly. A jeep full of police, rifles bristling from its open sides, pulls behind the Dalai Lama's car as the column heads for the station's gate.

The drive goes due north from Benares. Here, in the Gangetic plain, lies the very cradle of classical Indian civilization. Forests of banyan, coconut, ebony, date palm and acacia once canopied the land. Six rivers, flowing down from the Himalayas to join the Ganges, produced a zone of unmatched fertility, giving rise, in turn, to India's ancient city-states. As centers of commerce, arts, politics and philosophy, their urban milieus were the prime setting for the Buddha's teaching. Following his first discourse, delivered in the Deer Park at Sarnath, five miles outside of Benares, he engendered a revolution in thought. Crippling the Brahminical system of worship and prevailing over the theistic and non-theistic philosophical sects alike, he won the adherence of virtually all the region's chief powers to his new science of mind, crowning India's golden age. What remains in present-day Uttar Pradesh can hardly resemble its glorious antecedents.

Trees tell the whole story. Almost none are left. Not just on the flat, expressionless land, but even by the roadside. Here, as across all India, whitewashed tree trunks mark the highway. Yet, an hour out of the city, the law against harming them is flagrantly broken. Hacked, mutilated stumps appear to either side, fitfully attacked, swatches of their bark randomly stripped off, branches shredded and torn, chopped halfway down their length. Throughout, armies of road workers are camped in low, smoke-blackened tents. Every five miles a new colony appears, the road beside it ripped into long rocky stretches. In its midst sit women and children, breaking large pink and gray stones into smaller stones, and these into gravel, their piles often stretching four feet high up to a quarter of a mile in length. The men dig and carry dirt, creating a new roadbed. This is the same work that the Tibetans have done, though in the case of Indian laborers, born to a lifetime of such toil, it seems a far bleaker fate. Driving through the road work is tortuous. The cars proceed at no more than thirty miles an hour, swerving between boulders and ditches. Despite their tightly shut windows, a choking skein of dust coats the inside. Allergic to dust, the Dalai Lama holds his outer robe across his face for the entire journey. After two hours he suggests a rest stop for the drivers in a small village. All save himself get out to stretch, relieve themselves—as everyone in India does, by the side of the road—and order a quick cup of sweet tea from a ramshackle mud-and-straw stall. At a second stop an hour later, the Dalai Lama asks Mr. Dhawan to buy oranges and apples for the party. The column continues on, joined by a new police jeep, the escort changing at each district border. A dead cow is passed; a dog has been run over, its intestines spilled onto the road. By the bank of a stagnant river, a group of villagers sit silently before a rectangular pyre bearing a white-shrouded corpse being consumed in bright flames, a tall plume of smoke rising skyward. The marshy field behind them is strewn with a dozen more corpses, bound in muslin, waiting their turn.

After four hours the cars pass quickly through a nondescript town, take a right turn off the main road and drive past a large grove of tall, leafless trees, standing like burnt-out candles around a gentle knoll topped by a faded building; a sad, disheartening sight: the second stop on the pilgrimage, Kushinagar, scene of the Buddha's *parinirvana* or death.

A bright blue and orange Ashoka Travelers Lodge, its giant heart-shaped doorway looking like the entrance to a "tunnel of love," faces the grounds. Surprisingly clean and modern, it is surrounded by a neatly manicured lawn, dotted by palm trees. Beneath the entrance wait the manager and his aides, ties and jackets yanked tight, twitching with nerves. A platoon of red-turbaned police, bayonets fixed on their rifles, shuffle anxiously about. A bulbous officer, holster jauntily angled at his side, peaked cap glinting in the midday sun, swagger stick tapping the palm of his hand, barks out a command. As the Dalai Lama emerges from his car, rifles are jammed into the right shoulder, heels clicked, backs and eyes frozen. Led by the manager past the salute, the Dalai Lama is taken around the outside of the building, where, unprepared for an inspection, the rest of the shambling platoon seem to blush, gulp and shrivel inwards. Their fellows, freed from attention, do their best not to buckle, the rush of released tension visibly loosening their knees. The Dalai Lama is shown into the last room in a line opening on a shared veranda, and suddenly the excitement is over. It's just noon. For the first time since the pilgrimage began more than a week before, there is a free moment. A lone policeman is posted at permanent salute before the veranda; one of the Tibetan bodyguards pulls up a chair beneath the Dalai Lama's pastel-blue window frame. The entourage moves into adjacent quarters to unpack. The remaining police, their officer and a group of district officials who have arrived too late for the greeting, stand with the hotel staff, gawking at the Dalai Lama's door and the rather stern face of the bodyguard, plainly expressing that the show is over. But nothing, obviously, has happened in Kushinagar in a long while, and even if the honored guest is hidden from view, his very presence, merely yards away, is ample reason to stay and stare—as everyone does—for almost an hour more.

With the afternoon open ahead of them, Ngari Rinpoché, Dawa Bhotia and Mr. Dhawan pull up chairs in the warm sunlight before the porch. Towels and undershirts are placed close by to dry, following a quick washing. Newspapers are brought from the hotel lounge, among them a traveler's magazine, its cover featuring an article on Tibet. The photo depicts one of the handful of new white Toyota minibuses the Chinese have shipped to the country in their attempt, begun the previous year, to stimulate a tourist trade. This one, though, is stuck in the mud. Twenty-five ragged, poverty-stricken Tibetans, plainly recruited out of an adjacent field, are pushing it—a picture evidently not meant to be taken, much less used for a magazine cover. Ngari Rinpoché can't help but chuckle over the contradictions of the image, so symbolic, he feels, of his nation's fate. Silently he scans the article, the usual account of a Chinese show tour, conducted through a handful of recently refurbished monasteries in Lhasa. When he finishes reading he sits contemplatively and stares a hundred yards across the lawn and road to the grove of trees and the Parinirvana Temple in their midst.

The afternoon passes and, as the sun starts to set, a mist rises. It seeps from the moist earth, smudging the juncture of sky and land. Kushinagar, it seems, is grieving still. A burnt scent, conveyed in the smoke from nearby cooking fires, cloaks the grove where the Buddha died. The urgent, ascending wail of a lone bird contorts the silence. A waxing moon rises slowly over the temple and hangs there, its pallid light evanescent and mournful.

Three months prior to dying, the Buddha informed his disciples that his life's work was complete. At the close of the rainy-season retreat, he led them to Kushinagar, a small wattle-and-daub town in the jungle. There, lying on a couch between twin sal trees, he urged the order to ask any questions they yet had concerning his teaching. When none was forthcoming, he entered meditation and opened his eyes again in the third watch of the night only to deliver his final words: "I exhort you, brethren," he is reported to have said. "Decay is inherent in all component things. Work out your own salvation with diligence." Wrapped in new-spun cloth, the Buddha's corpse was cremated in an iron vessel on a pyre of fragrant wood decked with offerings by the people of Kushinagar. His remains were then divided among a group of eight kingdoms, republics and other claimants, each building, along with one for the vessel and another for the fire's embers, a commemorative stupa or cairn in their region.

The following morning the Dalai Lama wakes at five to meditate. After making offerings and prostrating to the image of the Buddha on the makeshift altar in his room, he sits on a cushion and assumes the prescribed position: legs crossed, eyes half-closed, tongue lightly resting behind the inside upper row of teeth. With one palm placed over the other in his lap, the tips of either thumb gently touching, he sets the Mahayana motive to obtain Buddhahood in order to benefit all beings. Like every Buddhist practitioner, he then contemplates the cardinal themes of his religion: the precious nature of a human life, impermanence, the inevitable unfolding of cause and effect, and voidness. As a tantric lama, however, his efforts soon turn to the advanced techniques that afford Tibetan Buddhism its reputation for possessing the world's most complex spiritual practices. By various procedures he endeavors to strip away the outer, more coarse levels of consciousness to expose the fundamental essence of mind: Clear Light. Once it is manifest, he focuses this most refined state of mind on emptiness, thereby beginning to eliminate the innate misconceptions of concrete existence, as well as their latencies or underlying traces, which together obscure omniscience. At the same time the Dalai Lama uses the energy of the Clear Light to generate a subtle body, capable of passing through matter unobstructed and multiplying itself infinitely to bring about benefit to beings throughout the cosmos. In this way he practices to attain both the mind and body of Buddha together, remaining absorbed in meditation for an hour and a half. Once finished, he dedicates the merit gained to the welfare of all sentient beings, prostrates once more and shortly, upon hearing a soft knock on the door, admits Lobsang Gawa, who bears his breakfast on a covered tray.

At nine o'clock the Dalai Lama visits the Parinirvana Temple. As he steps from his room, a squad of police present arms. This time Tenzin Gyatso slows his pace, gives the men a piercing look, walks in formal review down their length and at the end of the line actually salutes them. Entering his Ambassador, he is whisked across the street to where 200 Tibetans—also on pilgrimage—are lined up, *katas* in hand. Around them lie a maze of ruins: the ruddy brick walls of ancient monasteries and temples. Ahead, on the highest ground, stands the temple, a pale yellow oval building newly built for the 2,500th celebration of the Buddha's birth in 1956. At its door, the Dalai Lama takes off his shoes, dons his formal robe and, entering, prostrates three times on a red and gold cloth placed by an attendant on the marble floor. Six feet away, running the length of the room, lies a fifth-century statue depicting the Buddha at the moment of his death, reclining on his right side, head supported by the palm of one hand. It is believed to lie over the exact spot where he died. The Dalai Lama approaches and helps to drape a splendid fifteen-foot silk scarf in offering across the statue's upper shoulder and back. Circumambulating once, he returns to the front of the narrow room, touches his forehead in homage to the base of the statue and then, joined by the monks accompanying him, sits to recite the Heart Sutra and seven-limb *puja*, the two short but, for Tibetans, most popular Mahayana Buddhist prayers. The brief commemoration done, he leaves.

Outside, explosions rend the air, crows cawing frantically after each.

A celebration is in progress and the thunderous noise comes from fire-works. Three thousand Indian Buddhists have convened to unveil a statue of a Burmese monk who lived and recently died in Kushinagar. After a brief stop at the small Tibetan monastery staffed by a lone monk, south of the temple, the Dalai Lama is driven over to address them.

From its start, the gathering has been in a semi-delirious state. Far into the previous night the celebrants blasted Indian film music over a public-address system erected under a billowing red tent, suspended by a forest of old bamboo poles. The bodyguards turned uneasily in bed, their shoul-der holsters creaking. There was a good deal of rustling in the other rooms until finally, incredulous, Ngari Rinpoché strode through the "tunnel of love" and across the street to request silence. The organizers insisted they had only meant to express their joy at the Dalai Lama's presence, but early the next morning, irrepressibly, the commotion picked up again, with cherry bombs booming across the countryside and a flushed skinny man zealously exhorting the crowd, in the style of Indian political rallies, to cheer for the Dalai Lama. Thus, along with breakfast, *"Dalai Lama Khi Jai!"* and *"Buddha Bhagavan!"* ("Long live the Dalai Lama!" and "The Buddha is Victorious!") are pelted over the P.A. in crescendoing waves, continuing right through to the Dalai Lama's arrival hours later, the haran-guer still at his fearsome task, now hoarsely leading the frenzy while jumping about onstage, gesticulating wildly, his microphone jammed every few moments into an armpit to permit him the requisite round of applause topping each cheer. Like most Indian Buddhists, the people are members of the "scheduled classes" or "untouchables," millions of whom converted to Buddhism in the mid-fifties without any knowledge of the religion, simply to escape their caste designation.

As the Dalai Lama begins his speech, a troop of Indian monks dressed in a motley array of yellow, orange, tangerine and maroon robes, all wearing sunglasses, doze in the heat at the back of the stage. "Yellow Robbers—none of them study, they just live off the people," observed a disgruntled Western pilgrim earlier in the day. "Did you see those sleeping idiots?" he offers later, still disgusted by the often less than spiritual incen-tives for a religious vocation in India. "Not one of them knew the words to the prayer. Don't they even know monks look terrible in sunglasses?" he adds, flabbergasted. Meanwhile, during the Dalai Lama's speech, large portions of the crowd, like overexcited children at a party, boisterously exit the tent, their declaimer madly policing the aisles to force them back to their seats. When the Dalai Lama departs, the man hurtles to the stage to set off more cheers, which, however, never come. The crowd has found better sport. With the honored guest in their midst, they mob his party, not so much for blessings, as to be compressed with the object of their passions in the ultimate climax to their festival. After a great deal of trampling and commotion, the Dalai Lama finally arrives at his car and drives away, the mob scene behind oddly unchanged from the squabbling over the Buddha's remains reported to have occurred after his demise two and a half millennia before.

An hour and a half later, Tenzin Gyatso enters a large auditorium. A thousand professors and graduate students, members of the Nagarjuna Buddhist Society (one of the foremost Indian academic groups researching original Buddhist texts), convened at the University of Gorakhpur, give him a standing ovation. Speaking extemporaneously, the Dalai Lama reflects on the relation of scholarship to Buddhism, noting that despite India's fervid desire to import scientific knowledge from the West, it must not forfeit its ancient learning. It is not a religious seminary. It is a large university, yet virtually all of the introductory speeches refer to the Dalai Lama as the living manifestation of the Buddha, unselfconsciously joining intellect and faith. When the talk is over, the Dalai Lama receives a long line of well-wishers in an adjacent room; hundreds, though, ignore him completely. Compelled by a greater force, apparently, than reverence, they descend on the long tables of chipped teacups and plates adorned with free cakes and sandwiches. The professors, in fact, act as though they are half starved. After ten minutes of unabated gulping and chewing, the food and drink has vanished. Conditions in Gorakhpur—the city of almost 300,000 in which the next two nights will be spent—illustrate why.

Though no one is dying in the streets, clearly, very little food is available. The best restaurant in town caters to the Dalai Lama's entourage. On both days the menu is identical: cauliflower, rice, a bony meat dish and, for dessert, rice pudding, invariably coated with insecticide. The diet for those unable to eat such relatively resplendent fare is a lifelong pinwheel of rice, bread and *dhal* broken only by an occasional egg or fish caught from the flat soupy waters of a nearby river. Here is India's major problem, not the burgeoning famine of Bihar, but chronic malnutrition affecting hundreds of millions, shortening lives and abetting disease. Gorakhpur is not a happy place. In particular, it evinces the ever-increasing implosion of people that is consuming all India's cities. And with a spiraling population pollution is legion. A thirty-foot-thick canopy of pungent smoke, spewed from tens of thousands of cooking and coal fires, wraps the town, so dense that at night headlights penetrate no more than a dozen yards through the gloom. A continual citywide conflagration seems to be in progress. At its very center, not far from the train station, the party is boarded in two government guest houses. Their staff is bemused and venal both; alternately in awe of the guests and vicious to one another when work must be done. It is clear in the murderous grimace of the manager and the craven, half-fed slouch of his assistants what price a life of deprivation extracts from the human character; the impulse to put self before others is a constant prerequisite for survival. Their antagonistic inertia, too, is a form of endurance, so much so that, with the first guest house filled, Mr. Dhawan himself has to organize relocation for half the party to a second.

"Raghh! Damn bugs!" rips the night. A door bangs open and out of the second guest house, clad in his underwear and waving a pistol in the air, leaps Ngari Rinpoché. "Damn bugs! Eat all of me, you buggers!" he yells. Then, his small automatic jammed back into its holster, he runs into the building and reappears dragging a mattress. Throwing it on the dew-drenched lawn, he tears off his watch and scowls at the time: 4:00 a.m. There hasn't been a moment of sleep since going to bed at midnight. The sea of smog smothering Gorakhpur holds billions of mosquitoes, many malarial, but inside this guest house so many have collected, feeding on generations of Indian officials, that the air can barely be breathed. They swarm in clouds the size of basketballs, their buzzing irradiating the room. "Enjoy the concert tonight," said Dawa Bhotia, bidding Ngari Rinpoché good evening earlier, while carrying over his shoulder the mosquito net he had not forgotten to bring along. Without one, sleep is impossible. Now, out on the lawn, silhouetted by the limp moonlight trickling down like saliva onto the black earth, Ngari Rinpoché earns only ten minutes of peace before, having located a new prey, the outdoor hordes converge. Sleep then is entirely forsaken.

Regardless of the night, the coming day demands the utmost effort. For the first time in twenty-one years the Dalai Lama will enter the Kingdom of Nepal. Lhamo Tsering and the six guerrillas captured at Tinker Pass in 1974 are to be released in an amnesty on King Birendra's forthcoming birthday. And as a further gesture toward the Tibetans, the King has agreed to allow the Dalai Lama to pay a brief visit—despite its consequences in Peking—to Lumbini, the site of the Buddha's birth, seventeen miles inside the Nepalese border. For days most of Nepal's 15,000 Tibetan refugees have been traveling down from Katmandu, Pokhara and adjoining towns to welcome the Dalai Lama, who, according to a prearranged procedure will cross the border for an eight-hour stay with no checks, visas or other record.

Soon after sunrise a caravan of more than fifty Land-Rovers, Toyotas, Mercedes-Benzes and Cherokee Chiefs, all packed with Tibetans, lines up behind the stupa-crowned entrance gate to Nepal, dividing the border town of Saunali. In contrast to India, the scene is variously prosperous, the Tibetan refugees a visible cut above their Indian counterparts. Their wealth is well known throughout the diaspora—particularly that of the merchant chieftains of Katmandu, who deal, rather profanely, not just in jewelry and carpets but also in *thankas* and sacred images. Their affluence is displayed in their children's blue jeans and mod haircuts, in their own thick, well-tailored *chubas*, spotless fedoras and traditional turquoise and coral pendant earrings. The number of cars owned by Tibetans, collected here in one spot, probably approaches the total possessed by all the refugees in India. But it is Nepal, not the people, which makes such wealth possible. Balancing East and West by extracting roads from the Chinese, cement from India, hotels, tape cassettes, watches and the latest-model cars from Japan and Europe, the monarchy has brought in a wave of consumer items during the past decade and a half. Though the government itself has been accused of rampant corruption, wholesale suppression of the student-based democratic movement and duplicitous dealings with just about everyone else, its ability to spread a smooth veneer of goods over the centuries-old primitive life in its isolated mountain valleys appears to keep the country content. And unlike the unwieldy behemoth of India, the kingdom enjoys compact proportions, which have allowed a semblance, at least, of entry into the twentieth century to become an overnight reality. Even the intelligence service evinces the most up-to-date training. Its observers are everywhere, dressed—unlike their Indian counterparts—in elegant suits, equipped with miniature radios and cameras, recording every corner of the crowd. Nothing more important is happening in Nepal on this gray Wednesday morning than the Dalai Lama's non-visit. The Chinese ambassador has departed from Katmandu for Peking, fulfilling the requisite protest while claiming he is only going "for vacation," to mute the point. The Tibetans know, though, that Chinese spies are amply spread through their ranks. As a result, the event is strictly regimented. Behind the 200 waiting to welcome their leader at the border, 8,000 more are being marshaled by young men, dressed in beige bush hats and robes tagged with red and green ribbons, into a receiving line more than a quarter of a mile long before Lumbini's Tibetan monastery. In contrast, the Dalai Lama's three-car column, leaving Gorakhpur by eight o'clock for the two-hour drive north, seems woefully small—distinguished solely by the personal authority of its chief occupant.

The drive up is placid. Half an hour beyond Gorakhpur an unexpected lushness supplants the withered earth behind. The Himalayas stand fifty miles away. Bright fields of mustard, lentils and wheat grow abundantly. Unravaged trees reappear. Clumps of teak, each a perfect semicircular canopy, flat on the bottom, sprinkle the land like a story-book illustration, dark green groves of shiny mango rising between. The villages along the narrow one-lane road are sculptured from smooth brown mud, the porches, columns and walls of their homes all of a piece, thick pleats of thatch stuffing the roofs. Skin buckets distend from long poles ladling up and down in constant, tranquil movement in the nearby fields. The inhabitants show the same easy unity with their environment. They are tall, rich-skinned and fine-boned, with long elegant fingers, high cheekbones and clear deep eyes, their bearing instinctively noble.

It is not much past eight, but there is a traffic jam clogging the road —a pristinely silent one, of bullock carts and farmers. In it a vestige of India's ancient heartland is seen. Hundreds move to market in an orderly procession, all the carts triangular, mounted on two heavy-rimmed multi-spoked wheels, their beds piled twenty feet high with hay, lumber and produce. Each driver sits before the towering crest of his load, a switch in hand, his homespun robe spotlessly white. The animals are splendid. With long white faces, pink ears and scythe-shaped red-painted horns, some stand six feet at the shoulder, their sure, lolling motion and relaxed ambling gait matching the composure of their owners, who barely heed the honking passage of the cars.

After a brief reception under the border arch, the Dalai Lama's car drives at top speed over a modern bridge onto a smooth highway raised above a broad savanna. A cool breeze ripples down from the Himalayas, now only fifteen miles distant. For the third time in less than two hours the landscape undergoes a dramatic change; from waste to abundance and now to primordial expanse, stretching to the horizon like the East African plains, here at the foot of the highest mountains on earth. In half an hour a long grove of trees, surrounding a group of temples, appears on the right. In its center rise the tall maroon walls of a Tibetan monastery, a thousand tents pitched at their base. Before a yellow and red gate, wreathed in smoke from pine boughs burning in stone braziers on either side, the cars slow. Behind it the receiving line of 8,000 Tibetans has waited patiently in place now for five hours. The Dalai Lama's gray Ambassador moves gingerly under the gate and down the line. As it does, a wave of emotion overcomes the people. Heads bowed, hands in prayer holding incense and scarves, they gaze into the rear window, where the Dalai Lama can be seen, and almost everyone begins to cry. Old women and children, the young and middle-aged, rugged shepherds from Dolpo, former Khampa guerrillas from Mustang, tall and broad-shouldered, their wind-worn faces hardened by the long years of fruitless war—all break into wide grimaces and the tears pour freely down.

At the end of the line wait the monastery's sixty resident monks, playing *gyaling*, *thungchen*, drums and cymbals and carrying brocade victory banners. Escorted inside the temple, the Dalai Lama mounts to the second floor, where he is heard laughing heartily with the abbot. After a time, he returns outside and, followed by a large but carefully chosen coterie walks briskly toward the sacred tree under which the Buddha was born, 2,525 years before.

The tree grows out of a white brick island standing up, like a dolmen, thirty feet off the plain. Its luxuriant foliage sparkles in the late-morning sunlight; its root system spills exposed, like a wooden beard, down the entire eastern flank of the island. Bright red, green and blue prayer flags thread the branches, and the entire tree, top to bottom, stands entwined in extravagant umbilical-like vines, their abundance seeming more than coincidental. Unaware that the Dalai Lama is approaching, young boys climb through the branches to call one another from semi-concealed perches: below, three Tibetan women, each with a baby tied to her back, touch the trunk with their foreheads. The cool mountain breeze blows cleanly across the landscape. Nothing solemn or pontifical impedes the childlike ambiance of Lumbini, and despite its venerable array of roots, the tree under which the Buddha was born extends into the pastel sky in slender, supple and youthful lines.

The green water of a square brick tank is the Dalai Lama's first stop. By its side he enacts a simple ritual, pouring sanctified water from a silver vessel, then touching a drop of the tank's own contents to his forehead in blessing. Beside this water, then a lake, Queen Maya, the Buddha's mother, paused before giving birth. Reaching term, she had, according to Shakyan custom, set off from the capital city of Kapilavastu to give birth in her parents' house. The child's sublime nature was already known from portents and a remarkable dream of a six-tusked white elephant, the supreme symbol of royalty, entering the queen's right side at conception. Now, accompanied by miraculous signs and a host of *gandharvas* or angels, the birth took place by surprise in the open country, while the queen was still en route to her destination. Pausing at the lake in the center of the Lumbini Gardens east of the city, Queen Maya entered labor and, attended by her younger sister and maidservants, delivered standing up, holding the lower bough of a *palsa* tree. According to legend, the child emerged from her right side, took seven steps in each of the four principal directions, raised a finger and spoke, saying, "This is my final birth." Brought back to Kapilavastu, he was followed by a sage who, having been alerted by celestial messengers, arrived to identify the infant from the marks on his body as a fully enlightened Buddha. Seven days later, however, Queen

Maya died, the Buddhist records attributing her demise to a reward of rebirth in a heavenly realm on the completion of her exalted task.

"The very purpose of voluntarily reincarnating is to produce some good result for others," commented the Dalai Lama, reflecting on the Buddhist belief in the regular appearance of spiritually evolved beings in the world. "The reincarnation takes rebirth with choice, intentionally, deliberately, with the definite purpose of serving humanity through religious or other means. Now there are many levels of such beings. Among the highest are advanced Bodhisattvas and Buddhas who have the ability to project emanations. Among them there are also many degrees. For those of lower realization it is necessary for the central emanator to control each emanation separately. The emanations of higher beings can control themselves. The degree of spontaneity or acting without exertion defines the difference. I know of cases in which among one hundred emanations each one knows what the other one is doing while all have an individual sense of self or 'I,' though there is only one central emanator. But this is difficult to explain. Until one experiences it oneself," he concluded, laughing, "one might think that such talk was just senseless, something like science fiction, or shall I say religious fiction."

Led by a Nepalese archaeologist past a classical pillar built by King Ashoka in the third century B.C., the Dalai Lama offers a scarf and proceeds up two flights of stairs into the single dark room of a small shrine by the tree. Prostrating and making offerings, he chants prayers, accompanied by fifteen monks. In the close, hallowed quarters, lustrous and serene, the monks' mellifluous recitation filling the room, the pilgrimage briefly regains a personal moment. The Dalai Lama's thoughts naturally turn toward his mother. "Though originally there was another plan," he recounted, "somehow Lumbini became the last place I visited. When I was there, I felt this was auspicious. Because Lumbini is the place of Lord Buddha's birth, it represents the beginning of something. Now my mother has to take rebirth, so you see, that was nice."

After lunch the Dalai Lama is driven to an open field where, before a large tent enclosing a throne, the crowd is collected. At the conclusion of formalities, he begins his talk by beckoning all 8,000 to come as close to him as possible, which they do, bunching into a surprisingly intimate, tightly packed space at his feet. As though addressing his own family, the Dalai Lama speaks warmly for an hour and a half, on the necessity of living a good, moral and generous life day to day. Following his remarks he pauses and makes a pronouncement which astonishes his listeners: "The long night of our struggle is now coming to a close," he says pragmatically. "I am sure that we will see one another very soon again—in Lhasa."

Stunned, the audience musters a clattering, uncharacteristic round of applause—their happiness more deeply revealed in dozens of tear-streaked
faces as the implications of what they've heard begin to dawn.

The Tito Gate: 2:00 a.m. January 21. In his private car the Dalai Lama
has been asleep for many hours. Train 51 Up originating in Calcutta and
going all the way to Jammu, beyond Pathankot, will not arrive until four
in the morning. As the train pulls into Benares, the Dalai Lama's saloon
will be gently shunted from its siding and attached to the long line of
sienna cars trooped behind the black steam engine. In the meantime,
Samdong Rinpoché refuses either to leave or to nap. "His Holiness is in
my station," he announces. "Until he departs I must remain awake." He
and Ngari Rinpoché occupy a private retiring room beside the track.
While they recline on fully made beds, their conversation ranges breezily
from the world record for high-altitude parachute jumps, held by Tibetan
commandos in the Special Frontier Force, to a debate on doctrinal points
concerning the Buddha's life. When the conversation pales and the men
begin to get drowsy, Ngari Rinpoché manages to filch a silver-tipped
ebony baton from a police officer sleeping nearby. With his prize in hand,
he and Samdong Rinpoché abscond onto the dark platform to engage in
a balancing contest: the stick held on the upright end of the middle finger.
S. Rinpoché (endearingly referred to as such by his students) is a perfec-
tionist by nature. Swirling around the platform, his well-pressed maroon
robes gracefully distend like wings as he follows after the tottering stick.
Dawa Bhotia and Mr. Dhawan walk up, returned from a jaunt to the
movies in town, now that their duties are almost over. There is, as always,
a great deal of talk about whether or not the train will arrive and if so,
when. When it finally does, in the maw of the night, the baton is returned,
brief partings are exchanged and the two-day journey to the Punjab commences, the interminable stops reeling back now in reverse order: Bela,
Amethi, Jais, Rae Bareli, Lucknow, Sitapur, Shahjahanpur, Rampur, Ludhiana, Jullundur and finally, on a cold morning around nine, the dreary
but familiar site of the Pathankot platform.

The maroon Mercedes, newly polished, waits under the eaves of the
station's portico. Beside it stands Kunga, the Dalai Lama's chauffeur and
proprietor of the Kunga Café in McLeod Ganj, his face impassively drawn
after a sleepless night waiting for the train. A line of Willys Jeeps and
Ambassadors, their Tibetan drivers at the ready, receive the party. There
are no police in sight, however. Himachal Pradesh, it seems, is under the
weather and could not send an escort. The first snow of the year has fallen
the night before. In Pathankot it is only rain—dismal and mean—turning
the main road into a mud bath, cars and trucks slithering through the slop,

splattering the stalls, stitching its rim with showers of umber spray. The baleful proprietors cower against the back walls of their cubicles. Hidden behind their piles of blankets and coats, soothed by radios and glasses of lukewarm tea, they watch helplessly as each behemoth adds its ration of mire to their goods. None move to rearrange things and—despite the total dearth of customers—certainly not to close shop. Even though winter comes for two months each year, its cold, in the normally sweltering subcontinent, is oddly denied, treated as a temporary aberration for which an open stall with no front wall will do just as well as in any other season. Past this oblique refusal of reality, the Dalai Lama's column punches its way, charging the town, and the mile-long army base beyond, until, reaching the foothills, it crosses into Himachal Pradesh and enters the ancient labyrinth of river valleys, up which Alexander the Great himself is believed to have once passed, leading to the Kangra Valley and perched above it on the shoulders of the Dhauladar Range, Dharamsala.

There are no other cars on the road. Accordingly—with the Dalai Lama in his favored spot, the front seat—Kunga presses the accelerator to the floor whenever a straightaway opens in the forest between ravines. On one of them, a rear tire suddenly blows. The Mercedes skids to a halt, half off the road, followed by two Ambassadors filled with monks. Further back, the first jeep approaches at fifty miles an hour, its driver eager to keep up with the group, but, exhausted from his vigil at the train station, nodding at the wheel. Seeing the stopped cars at the final instant, he brakes too late and goes skidding into the rear end of the last Ambassador. Fortunately, no one is injured. At that moment a storm of hail and rain splashes down on the entourage, drenching Wangdrak, a tall Khampa in a green army jacket and heavy boots, frantically trying to change the Mercedes' tire. Under sleek trees, the cars wait, hammered with hail, their occupants lost in thought.

An hour later the majestic peaks behind Dharamsala appear in the distance, glistening with new-fallen snow. The storm gone, the day turns progressively bright, the air fresh and invigorating. Now both Lower Dharamsala and McLeod Ganj can be seen ahead, nestled on their respective ridge backs, white and pleasing. Though it is too small to make out, Kashmir Cottage, the home of the Dalai Lama's mother, stands halfway between the two. Scores of monks surround the house, having amassed at this moment sixty-two of an eventual hundred million mantras, but she is gone.

Pulling into Katwali Bazaar the snowstorm's toll is immediately visible. Even in Lower Dharamsala things are a mess. The road is so engorged that safe passage upward is impossible. Word is that a bus has gotten stuck on the long gradual route past the army cantonment and the Tibetan Children's Village. Even if it gets loose, there is no place for it to go in a foot and a half of snow. The decision is taken to attempt the back road, a thin track clinging to the mountain with a plunge down one side for hundreds of feet. This is the road most commonly used by pedestrians hiking between McLeod Ganj and Gangchen Kyishong, the Secretariat. At the end of Katwali Bazaar the column turns right and heads directly for the compound, where the Dalai Lama is driven to the Kashag building. Running inside through the cold, he is met by the Cabinet, assembled, according to protocol, to greet him. Here, though, he receives word of another delay. The back road as well is out of operation. Two jeeps have met head-on at the most dangerous curve. The descending one is stuck in the snow and starting to sideslip close to the edge. The second is unable to retreat down the hill for fear of doing the same. They remain frozen in a cockeyed embrace, blocking the last road to Theckchen Chöling. There is nothing to do now but walk up. While the Dalai Lama shares a cup of tea with his Cabinet ministers, an attendant is dispatched up the hill to the palace to fetch a pair of boots. Simultaneously, the heavy custom-built four-door salmon-colored jeep, given to the government-in-exile by the soldiers of the Special Frontier Force, is brought out from its berth. With it there is some hope of negotiating halfway up the road to the start of a rocky path through the woods. With the arrival of his boots the Dalai Lama departs, waving to a group of government workers and their families who have hurried over to see him. By a cluster of households belonging to the *gaddis* or hill folk, he steps from the jeep and sets off up the steep trail. Quickly, he picks his way from concealed rock to concealed rock beneath the smooth white surface. As he breaks the path for all those who follow, his red and ochre robes pass beneath a white cloak of pine boughs, his lone figure reappearing farther up, cast against the limpid sky at the summit of the hill, his pilgrimage complete.

8

The Wheel of Protection

DHARAMSALA FEBRUARY 14, 1981, 6:00 A.M. The Dalai Lama sits on his throne in the Central Cathedral. Outside, the night is black and still. A cold breeze blows down from Mun Peak. Two old women, up before dawn, circumambulate the temple. They cannot see within. The building's curtains have been tightly drawn, its front door locked, its side doors guarded by a watchful group of monks. Only a hint of the bright electric light inside appears around the border of each window.

This morning's proceedings are of the utmost secrecy. No outsider, Tibetan or otherwise, is permitted to view them. Except for the participants, few even know they are taking place. The principal monk has already engaged in extensive preparations. For two days the members of his monastery have recited prayers while he has labored to purify mind and body. His daily meditation practice has been conducted with special care. Fish, pork, garlic, onions and other impure foods have been eliminated from his diet. He has eaten from his own set of plates, kept separate from the others in the monastery. To complete his cleansing, blessed saffron water has been poured over the crown of his head and mantras recited.

On rising this morning, four attendants help the monk dress. His plain habit is put aside for an elaborate costume stored in two trunks. Ordinary pants are donned, followed by red brocade trousers, whose legs are six feet wide. It takes seven folds before the pads sewn into the garment are positioned at the knees. Fastened at the ankles, the trousers bulge a foot to each side. Matched by a red silk shirt placed over an undershirt, they are followed by two heavy robes loosely fastened with a belt and covered by a thick piece of brocade with an opening for the head. The monk's knee-high white leather boots are then tied on, toes curled up, wrathful eyes of crimson silk appliquéd on the ankles. So attired, he is helped into a jeep parked between his monastery and the Library of Tibetan Works and Archives in the Secretariat compound. In darkness, the jeep slowly winds its way over the back road, through McLeod Ganj and down the approach to the Central Cathedral. From here he is escorted up the building's front and into a small room in the rear, where preparations continue. A triangular jerkin fashioned of gold-leafed ringlets and styled in the manner of ancient Tibetan mail is put on, its points, front and back, ending at the waist. Next, a type of backpack is securely fastened about his middle. It supports four flags interspersed with three victory banners. The flags, made of doubled-up brocade, hang from flexible metal poles and run the full length of the monk's back; the banners, shaped like a roll of umbrellas, ascend from mid-thigh to above the head and are crowned with golden points. His sleeves are now bound with strips of red cloth; the left one, padded for archery, is stitched with three more scarlet eyes. Then a front piece of exquisite yellow, gold and red silk, its base exploding in hundreds of rainbow-hued threads, conceals all. At its center lies a golden mirror, the cardinal points dotted by clusters of turquoise around an amethyst, its polished silver core emblazoned with the Sanskrit mantra of a tantric deity. A three-foot-long silver sheath and sword are buckled on the left side, a golden quiver filled with arrows on the right; a golden thimble, used when drawing back a bowstring, is slipped over the right thumb. These are the accouterments of an epic Tibetan warrior, a hero from the days of Gesar of Ling, Tibet's great legendary king. But, despite the martial nature of the uniform, the monk is not going into combat. Rather, in a few minutes' time, as he sits beneath the bright lights of the cathedral, his consciousness will be cast aside in trance and replaced with that of Dorje Drakden—"the Renowned Immutable One"—chief spirit minister and bearer of counsel for the State Oracle of Tibet. More than a week ago the three days of the New Year's celebrations were concluded, and now, as it has for centuries, comes the first official trance of the year.

Inside the Cathedral's main hall, the Dalai Lama remains wrapped in silence. A giant statue of the Buddha rises behind his throne; images of Tibet's patron saints crowd the raised level at the head of the hall, where he sits. They are illuminated by large butter lamps, yet the chamber's darkness is far more radically dispelled by one hundred electric bulbs arranged, as offerings, in the shape of tiered cones on either side of the throne. Under their exacting glare, the varnished floorboards of the lower level give an almost antiseptic definition to the cathedral. But not entirely. Seven-foot spears, painted with scarlet eyes, are roped to the hall's front pillars. Behind them two files of young monks from Nechung Monastery bear musical instruments at the ready, while a table nearby supports dough offering or *tsog* and another holds a long bow and sword next to a banner-festooned helmet. The helmet, made of gold-coated iron, is almost three feet high. Five pearl-toothed ruby-eyed skulls adorn its facade beneath a crest of bear fur, surrounded by peacock feathers, and fronted by a flaming sword symbolizing penetrative insight into the ultimate nature of reality. The helmet's rear supports nine three-foot-long flags and banners stitched with silver bells. The top of the highest is crowned by a small group of golden bells and framed by aureoles of white cotton circling the three jewels of the Buddha, Dharma and Sangha, engraved in gold. Beside it lies a second helmet, belonging to the Gadong Oracle, who will also appear in trance this morning. The Dalai Lama's contemplative mood is matched by that of the ministers of his Cabinet, the Chairman and Vice-Chairman of the People's Deputies and their secretaries, all seated on low cushions to his left. A select group of abbots and lamas, their demeanor equally subdued, face them from across the way.

The ceremony begins. Two ten-foot *thungchen* or long horns produce a shattering blast. They are followed by the shrill notes of the *gyaling*, accompanied by cymbals, drums and the monks' recitation, invoking the oracular deity to descend into the *kuden* or "receiving body." A maroon curtain at the side of the temple parts. Three assistants appear, supporting the medium. He can barely walk. Altogether the eight layers of his clothing weigh more than one hundred pounds; the helmet, though only a third the weight of that used in Tibet, another thirty pounds. But it is not only his costume that makes it difficult for the Nechung *kuden* to move unassisted. He is already starting to enter the first levels of trance. A slight quivering rolls up and down his body. His breathing is short and loud. Between gaps in the music and prayers, its sound fills the room. As he walks forward, the *kuden*'s close-cropped head looks small and fragile above the costume's great bulk. His cheekbones jut out fiercely; his eyes are tucked in on the shelf of the skull and have a wild, startled look. The bushy left eyebrow points at an angle to the bridge of the nose, suggesting the crooked gaze of an Iroquois false-face mask. Like a false face, the cheeks also balloon above a large overbite, the lips protrude and the entire left side of the face has slipped a notch below the right, except where the mouth curls subtly up to produce a soft, quizzical smile. Soon a more severe distortion sets in. The skin draws tight on the skull, effacing the features. The whole countenance becomes clear and pure. The medium assumes a piercing, distant look. He is immersed in the visualization of himself as a tutelary deity standing at the center of a celestial mansion; without this meditation, he is unsuitable for possession.

Guided down the steps to the cathedral's main floor, the *kuden* sits on a brocade-covered camp stool placed over an imitation tiger skin in the middle of the room. An attendant bolsters him beneath either arm and the third man, holding the helmet, presses hard against his back to give further support. Legs wide apart, the Nechung *kuden* looks up to the Dalai Lama twenty feet away, whereupon his breathing quickens. The moment has come. The first prayer cycle concludes, the second commences, once more summoning the spirit minister Dorje Drakden to descend from the "inconceivable mansion" of the protective deity at the heart of "illimitable space" and enter the receiving body. The long horns' thunder shakes the temple's walls and the trance deepens profoundly. The *kuden* begins to be possessed. Abruptly, his head jerks back to the right and he commences to hyperventilate, at an immense rate. Each breath is ejected in a compressed hiss, like a radiator venting. The speed increases and he starts to gag violently. It is as if a long cord, running the length of his torso, is being tightly twisted, pushing breath and mind further out of the body with every bend. Suddenly both legs spring off the floor and begin to leap up and down. The medium's figure visibly expands, swelling two inches, so that the belts of the costume, purposely left loose before, now cut into the robes. The heartbeat is such that, in a separate movement all to itself, the mirror on his chest bounces.

Recognizing that the Choekyong or Protector of Religion has come, the attendant holding the helmet quickly places it on the medium's head. As he does, the medium's face turns bright red, his legs stick straight out and his head falls backwards. All three monks struggle to secure the helmet while the *umze* or chant leader brings the recitation to a quick stop. For a minute or two, only music is heard. When the trance concludes, the special slipknot used in tying on the helmet must be instantly released or the medium will die; it is a skill the attendants practice for days at a time, tying knots and releasing them around their own knees. But now the body itself is as though dead. Close up, the tiny golden bells atop the helmet can be heard tinkling; not from the shuddering of the head—they move even in the brief lapses when it is still—but from the presence of Dorje Drakden himself. The Protector is here, in the room, and as the attendants struggle to tie on the helmet, he shakes his borrowed legs and switches his head fiercely from side to side. Beneath the helmet's red silk brim the eyes open and close in staccato blinks, as if taking in an alien environment bits at a time, before briefly relapsing into their own thoughts. Minutes pass before the cords of the helmet can be secured. When they are, they are pulled so tight that if it were only the medium acting, he would be instantly choked. But as the helmet is finally fastened, the Protector shows himself to be in full possession. Leaping up, he swings a long sword in his right hand and begins to dance.

His movements are martial, wrathful, dignified. They are executed with supernormal precision. Where the *kuden* could not even walk for the constricting weight of the costume, Dorje Drakden can barely be contained by the body he is in. Bending straight down from the waist, he bows low, crossing both arms over his chest, then instantly springs back, the helmet's mass counting for nothing. Waving the heavy sword in the air, he first lifts his right leg and arm, the knee and elbow bent, and then his left. This is the basic step of the *cham* or ritual dance, interspersed with bows offered out of respect to the Dalai Lama. Spinning from side to side, he repeats the gestures with such alacrity that the attendants, hovering two feet away, appear to be in another dimension of time, their steps sluggish, their movements coarse in comparison to the frenetic agility before them. They remain where they are only to keep him inside the open space at the center of the room.

Three bows are completed within thirty seconds. Dorje Drakden throws the sword down and rushes up the steps to the Dalai Lama. Glancing over the seated members of the Tibetan government, he comes directly to the foot of the throne and, taking a scarf from an attendant, offers it. The Dalai Lama swiftly accepts it while the three assistants rush to place the *mendel tensum*, the traditional offering of the Buddha's body, speech and mind, into his hands. The ritual cord placed over his shoulder, the Protector clasps the reliquary, scripture and image of the Buddha one at a time and offers them upwards to the Dalai Lama, who, touching them with only slightly less speed to his forehead, passes them back down to a monk on his left. In the interval, the two make direct eye contact. In that brief moment, Dorje Drakden looks up with a gentle, caring gaze, his pupils brilliantly dilated. A polished silver cup on a long silver stand, containing dark black tea, is given to him. He raises it to the Dalai Lama, who takes a small sip. In communion, he then drinks himself and steps to the right side of the throne, so that the Dalai Lama can lean over to whisper in his ear. This is the first, most secret question asked. It is quickly answered by Dorje Drakden, who then moves away to offer scarves to the main images. Rushing into the cramped space behind the throne, he hurls one twelve feet into the air, directly onto the Buddha's begging bowl. The force and aim are astonishing, given the obvious difficulty of accurately projecting a scarf so far without its coming unraveled. The offering is repeated to the other images, and then, at the same scurrying pace, he returns to the camp stool at the center of the temple's floor.

While he continues to drink tea in short sips, Cabinet ministers, the Chairman and the Vice-Chairman of the People's Deputies descend to him. The immense physical upheaval of entering the small human frame has stabilized. Now the hissing breath comes in precise, neatly calibrated spasms. As the officials file by offering scarves, Dorje Drakden takes red protection cords from an attendant and knots, blesses and places them around the neck of each man. They assemble in a group on his left, and Venerable Tara, the Dalai Lama's chief private secretary, reads from a two-foot-long scroll. It is the official petition, composed in verse, requesting the Protector to reveal specific aspects of the Dalai Lama's, the Tibetan people's and the government's future. It contains no more than three questions. On this occasion the questions and the ensuing answers are public, heard by all. At other times, however, greater secrecy is required and the questions are written on small pieces of paper, which the Protector pushes under his helmet. When he is ready to respond he throws them to the floor without reading them. Now, before the answers are given, a further *cham* is performed.

The officials return to their seats. Again Dorje Drakden takes a sword in hand and dances, flags and white cotton-topped banners fluttering in the air behind him. Helmeted, bracketed by the bristling array of wing-like pennants, standing jauntily in the white upturned boots, his golden gown and polished shield sparkling, he displays the proud character of a mythic hero, an ancient warrior chieftain of the Tibetan highlands. As the second *cham* draws to an end, he twirls to his left, sword circling over his head, and, arriving at the table holding the conical dough offerings, lops off the top of the tallest one in a swift blow. Then, flinging the weapon to the ground, he strides forth once more to offer counsel.

Three secretaries, one holding a clipboard and red ball-point pen, are waiting to the left of the throne. The Protector is offered tea, but this time he pushes the cup away and begins to speak. His voice is startling. Each word is crisply enunciated, yet in an ethereal, halting, hollow tone suggesting immense age and distance. Because of its high, wavering pitch, it has been thought that Dorje Drakden is female, but the timbre is that of a spirit. As he speaks, his eyes appear to blaze, split open with a riveting sharpness reflected in the taut skin of the face. Though it is composed overall, the secretaries can see his entire body seething with energy, vibrating like an electrified filament, which, it is said, has merely to touch an object unawares to shatter it. Yet Dorje Drakden takes hold of the Dalai Lama's hand with the most refined and intimate gesture. Shifting his face to look up, he speaks humbly, with endearment, out of comradeship whose origins reach far beyond the present. As the words are pronounced, the Dalai Lama assists, repeating them slowly back, followed in chorus by the secretaries. In this manner the message is received word by word, spelled out like a telegram. It is by no means easy. The Protector works hard, straining to pronounce exactly, pulling the meandering plastic mouth, prone to gaping open, into the design of each word, looking up to the Dalai Lama afterwards to ascertain that it has been correctly understood. The transmission is undertaken in an informal spirit of warmth, distinct from the rest of the ceremony. The message itself is delivered in a lilting metered verse. Each line is prefaced by a high, wailing "eh" sound which trails off into the short stops of the following words. This year the New Year's message commences with a two-verse poem honoring the Dalai Lama as "Holder of the Lotus," the emanation on earth of Chenrezi, the Lord who looks with compassion in a thousand directions:

Surrounding destitute beings who are without a protector
Are a thousand benevolent eyes
Acting to guard all suffering creatures.
To the One with Lotus in Hand I pay homage.

A great compassionate treasure is the Lord of Migrators in the Land of Snows
With compassionate activities that fully encompass all directions,
Whose kind, skillful methods are like those of a mother for her only son,
This compassionate care is a vast excellent gathering.
I am well pleased.

The prophetic answers to the questions follow, given in the order in which they were asked.

The long horns emit a resounding boom. The canvas stool is brought forward by attendants, and Dorje Drakden sits, still gyrating from side to side, before the Dalai Lama's throne. As the maroon curtain parts again, he glances toward the doorway. The medium of the Gadong Oracle enters, supported by attendants. He is starting to undergo trance. The spirit possessing him, known as Shinjachen or Wooden Bird, sometimes called Black Vulture Hat, is also a minister, like Dorje Drakden, of one of the main protective deities of Tibet, Pehar Gyalpo, the ultimate source of the oracular pronouncement. Unlike the Nechung mediums, however, those of the Gadong monastery are not monks. The mediumship is passed in a lay lineage from father to son. The present medium is a man in his mid-thirties employed as a secretary in the Dalai Lama's private office. He has served as *kuden* for little more than a year and is still finding it difficult, the process of clearing the psychic channels or *tsa* by which the Protector will enter him, extremely painful. In addition, Shinjachen is a more abrasive, manifestly wrathful spirit. Because of these factors, the two spirits have been summoned together, so that, using special methods, Dorje Drakden can assist in breaking in the new medium.

As the Gadong *kuden* enters the hall, his breathing sounds dense and heavy. Unlike the Nechung *kuden*'s proficient acceptance of the deepening levels of trance, his chest heaves thickly, erratically. He is dressed in full-length gold robes, and his long black hair contrasts with the cropped head of the monk *kuden*, though just like the latter, as he sits on a second canvas seat five feet inside the door, his breathing abruptly accelerates and grows rougher. Shinjachen appears to take possession all at once. With each inhalation the medium starts to scream in sharp pain; his eyes bulge, his body shudders wildly. Attendants strain to place his helmet on and rush him forward to offer the *mendel tensum* to the Dalai Lama. In a few chaotic instants, the offering is made, after which the Dalai Lama struggles to place a green blessing scarf between the *kuden*'s helmet and neck. But the trance is too violent; the choking and convulsions have increased dangerously. The Dalai Lama delivers a curt command; the *kuden*'s helmet is immediately loosened and in the next moment he collapses, the trance suddenly dispelled. Unconscious and totally rigid, the Gadong medium is lifted into the air. Dorje Drakden leaps off his seat and, grabbing handfuls of yellow barley grain from a monk, showers them across the medium's prone form. And then, as the lifeless frame of the Gadong *kuden* reaches the door, Dorje Drakden himself vanishes; the monk's body stretches out stiffly and is caught before it crashes to the floor by his attendants, who carry it out. The session is finished.

There is silence. In the recovery room, the two mediums lie on adjacent low beds wrapped in golden brocade blankets and orange silk covers. The Gadong *kuden* continues to shudder and breathe spasmodically. The Nechung *kuden* lies perfectly still, his face placid. The aides have loosened his costume and are massaging his body. In time, he briefly opens his eyes: he is at peace. He closes his eyes and rests. Now the Gadong *kuden*, his trance less deep and lengthy, has fully emerged, and sits up in bed, his head in his hands, leaning forward, breathing evenly.

After changing their costumes, the two *kudens* and their staffs walk to the front door of the cathedral, enter and prostrate three times before the Dalai Lama. Dressed in plain maroon robes, the Nechung *kuden* seems to have been only slightly jarred—his hands do not quite match up in prayer as he prostrates—yet, as always, he has no memory of the event. The

Gadong *kuden*, dressed in a handsome green khaki *chuba* and red sash, looks like a perfectly normal Tibetan layman. He follows the Nechung medium up to the Dalai Lama, where all receive protection cords and scarves and then return to seat themselves, looking freshly decorated, in two rows, a *kuden* at the head of each. The Dalai Lama continues to look down in silence. Tea is served, and the gathering of twenty drink from their bowls, each man staring at the floor by his feet. Draining his cup, the Dalai Lama leaves his throne, ties on his brown oxfords in the anteroom and, as the Indian guards snap their rifles to attention, exits the building to return to his residence. Outside, the precincts of the Central Cathedral are as empty as they were forty minutes before. A blanched gray light is filling the sky. The night has passed; it is Saturday. Within the cathedral the bright yellow barley seeds thrown by Dorje Drakden are collected, one by one, from the floor, to be kept and treasured as blessings of the Protector.

FOR 1,300 YEARS TIBET'S CHIEF ORACLE has been consulted by the nation's leaders on virtually every key decision of state. Although on sacred occasions the oracle would appear before up to 80,000 people in Lhasa, the inner workings of his monastery, the nature of the possession and, in particular, the experiences of those most closely involved have been kept strictly secret. As part of Tibet's entry to the world, however, the Dalai Lama agreed to have some details of Nechung Monastery and the story of its most important resident, the *kuden*, revealed.

On January 5, 1930, Lobsang Jigme, twelfth medium of Tibet's State Oracle was born to a family of middle-class shopkeepers in Lhasa. His father died when he was still young, leading his mother to give her only child to the monkhood. The family had cousins in both the Je College of Sera Monastery, Tibet's second-largest cloister, and the small but eminent monastery, called Namgyal Dratsang, belonging to the Dalai Lama and housed in the Potala. To decide which to approach, his mother sought a *mo* or divination from a renowned lama, named Demo Rinpoché. On the basis of his prognostication, Demo Rinpoché stated that the child should be sent to neither monastery. Rather, the lama related, he had "very important work" to do at Nechung Monastery and, hence, should go there. He added that the boy must be treated carefully and always kept "clean"—meaning that things should be done with decorum in his presence. On receiving this advice, Lobsang Jigme's mother thought that perhaps her son was an incarnate lama who had, as yet, to be recognized. His sensitive, introspective nature seemed a further indication of his special nature. Securing a place at Nechung monastery, she sent him from home at the age of seven, and the young boy took up life as a *getsul*, or novice monk.

Nechung Dorje Drayangling—The Immutable Island of Melodious Sound—as Nechung Monastery was formally called, lay four miles west of Lhasa, in a large grove of juniper and fruit trees just below Drepung Monastery. Since the seventeenth century, its 115 monks had been supported by the Tibetan government who held them responsible for keeping intact a daily link with Tibet's main spirit Protector, Pehar Gyalpo. Believed to inhabit the spirit world invisible to humans, Pehar Gyalpo and his principal emissary to Tibet, Dorje Drakden, were contacted through eight hours of ritual conducted in four sessions a day, beginning at six in the morning and ending at ten-thirty at night. To learn the invocations, Lobsang Jigme was required to memorize five hundred pages of tantric liturgy—far less than the hundreds of books memorized by some scholars training for the Doctor of Divinity degree, but, due to the premium put on its correct incantation in ritual, a demanding task. In conjunction with recitation, he was instructed in the monastery's unique style of chanting, the playing of religious instruments, the fashioning of elaborately sculptured offerings and *cham* or religious dance. Most complex were the intricate visualizations which each monk had to generate during prayers. It was by virtue of their own powers of meditation as well as the visualized offerings of blood, meat and alcohol that the Protector, it was believed, was actually summoned, imagination being the link to a higher, more refined level of reality. Lobsang Jigme soon learned that advanced practitioners whose psychic channels had been opened by years of meditation, would see Dorje Drakden, garbed in the robes of a stately monk, during daily prayers. The rest, however, received their only glimpses of the Renowned Immutable One during the five official trances held each month.

Though private trances often occurred at the request of the Dalai Lama, on the second day of each lunar month, without fail, Drepung's abbots would arrive soon after sunrise for their monthly audience with the Protector. While the medium underwent trance before the two-story-high statute of Hayagriva, a ferocious, multi-armed, multi-headed tutelary deity, poised at the rear of the monastery's hall, the monks would seek advice on a wide range of issues affecting Drepung's vast estates. During the next week, four government departments—Cabinet, Office of the Lord Chamberlain, and two offices of the Treasury—would submit formal requests to the monastery for their own sessions with the Protector. Meticulous records of each prophecy delivered at these meetings were kept by Nechung Monastery's secretary, who recorded predictions on nine two-foot-long black, red-rimmed boards, oiled and dusted with limestone powder. Using an inkless bamboo pen, he wrote in the shorthand necessary to keep up with the oracle's often rapid speech. At the conclusion of each trance, Lobsang Jigme watched as the tablets were taken to the temple's eastern wing, where they were copied for the records of the department in attendance, as well as for his Monastery's own archives. The latter were kept in large, wood-framed books, wrapped in brocade and stored in tall, brilliantly decorated yellow cupboards. Beside them lay scrolls of golden silk upon which Nechung Monastery's regulations had been personally composed by the Fifth Dalai Lama. Elsewhere heavy steel swords were displayed, tied in knots and given as a blessing by Dorje Drakden. The monastery's true spiritual riches, though, consisted of a number of sacred vessels through which the Protector, without the use of a medium, was believed to communicate directly. These hallowed objects had been preserved since the dawn of Buddhism in Tibet.

From his fellow monks Lobsang Jigme soon heard tales of the oracle's miraculous abilities. Throughout Tibet's history, he was told, the Choekyong had intervened to protect those following the path of religion from harm. In recent years, he had manifested the week-long vision in the sacred lake of Lhamoi Lhatso that had revealed the birthplace of the Thirteenth Dalai Lama. When the young ruler had reached his majority and was about to assume temporal power, the Protector had exposed an assassination attempt on his life by directly challenging its mastermind, the Regent, during a trance. At the end of his reign, the oracle had bid the Dalai Lama farewell by facing him as he walked away at the conclusion of a public trance held in the Norbulingka—an act performed only at final parting, which, though puzzling at the time, became clear four months later when Tibet's ruler died unexpectedly. All these accounts showed Lobsang Jigme how intimate the connection was between his monastery and the government of Tibet. None, however, illustrated the establishment's vital role as clearly as the ceremonies undertaken during Tibetan New Year's, the first of which brought the entire world of spirit protectors into direct contact with the affairs of men.

As a state institution, Nechung Monastery stood at the apex of a nationwide system comprised of thousands of mediums and their respective spirits. The network, through which the human and spirit worlds were connected, was reenfranchised annually, in the so-called Lhatrel or God Tax. Once a year Tibet's 120 district governors collected offerings from the mediums in their region on behalf of their spirits. Forwarded to Nechung Monastery, they were given, on the third day of the New Year, in a colossal *tsog* or offering ritual, to Pehar Gyalpo. After the rite, Nechung's monks moved to the center of Lhasa for the oracle's appearance in Tibet's most spectacular celebration, the three-week-long Monlam Chenmo or Great Prayer Festival. At this time, over 20,000 monks, joined by thousands of pilgrims from all across the country, crowded into the capital. The Nechung medium was required to undergo trance on at least ten separate occasions. In the most dramatic event, following days of parades, athletic meets and religious convocations, he marched in a regal procession south of the city to a field below the Potala, where, wielding his bow, sword and trident before a bonfire, he ritually dispersed the negative spirits of the old year.

As Lobsang Jigme grew older, his principal teacher gradually related to him the account of how Tibet's spiritual hierarchy had come to be, imparting through it the deeper significance of his role as a Nechung monk.

Thirteen centuries before, Tibet had been an uncivilized land, its people and indigenous spirits alike, savage and unruly. When Shantirakshita, the first Buddhist missionary to cross the Himalayas, had attempted to preach the Dharma in Lhasa, he was, despite eleven years of royal patronage, finally driven off by Tibet's native deities, whose wrathful nature was not inclined to the pacific tenets of the new faith. In his wake the great Indian saint and tantric master Padmasambhava was invited to Tibet. Glutting the populace with miracles, he vanquished the recalcitrant spirits and pledged them to henceforth protect Buddhism. As each spirit was subdued he placed him in a hierarchy according to his powers until all were accounted for save the five most arrogant. These he defeated in a series of supernatural battles, whereafter one came before him to offer fealty for all, in the form of an eight-year-old novice monk wearing a golden hat and holding a crystal rosary. Taking his *dorje* or ritual thunderbolt, Padmasambhava branded the child on the crown of the head, anointed the tip of his tongue with nectar and named him and his brother spirits Pehar Gyalpo—the Five Ferocious Kings. He then made Pehar Gyalpo head of the entire hierarchy of protective spirits. With all opposition to the Dharma overcome, Padmasambhava helped build Samye, Tibet's first monastery, and placed in the sacred vessels through which Pehar Gyalpo could be contacted, the *den* or material bases of the spirits. As the kings were too mighty to concern themselves directly with this world, however, two of their ministers took on the task: Dorje Drakden, minister of the Western King of Speech, Sung Gyi Gyalpo, and Shinjachen, minister of the Southern King of Superior Qualities, Yonden Gyalpo. Two more potent spirits were appointed to assist them: Tsangpa, appearing through the medium of Lamo Monastery, north of Lhasa, and the seven Tsemars or Blazing Brothers of Samye Monastery itself. As Lobsang Jigme learned, all of these spirits were exempted from the God Tax because of their preeminence. At the same time, their mediums were frequently used to check the secret prophecies given by the Nechung Oracle, thereby ascertaining whether or not the original transmission had been correctly received. Beneath them, in turn, came thirty generals whose task was to marshal the remainder of the lesser spirits.

Once Padmasambhava had completed his work, Tibet's hierarchy of guardian spirits took its place in a universal order, symbolically described as the Wheel of Protection. In it, Bodhisattyas and Buddhas were believed to manifest, not just peaceful, but also wrathful forms for the specific purpose of guiding unruly beings who could not be influenced other than by force. The Wheel operated throughout the cosmos, much like an angelic host, each group responsible for promoting the path of virtue in its local zone.

With the aid of the protective spirits, the task of spreading religion in Tibet moved apace. The founding of Lobsang Jigme's own monastery had marked an important stage in its development. In the last decades of the twelfth century Dorje Drakden himself had prompted a renowned lama to build the small shrine of Nechung, dedicated to Pehar Gyalpo, in the open country west of Lhasa. As a result, the protector's main base had been extended from Samye to the vicinity of Tibet's capital. Two hundred years later, in 1414, Dorje Drakden helped to create Drepung, where the Dalai Lamas eventually ascended as abbots. When the Fifth Dalai Lama gained temporal power in 1642, he instituted Pehar Gyalpo as Protector of the new central government. To house his medium he built Nechung Monastery around the original shrine. Thereafter, a number of the sacred vessels were moved from Samye and the monastery was instituted as the official home of the state oracle of Tibet.

Lobsang Jigme's indoctrination as a Nechung monk would have progressed normally if it were not for the sudden onslaught of a strange illness around the time of his tenth birthday. In the middle of the night, he would quickly rise, don his robes and proceed, sleepwalking, out of his room. During the next year he began to show signs of irrationality during the day as well. One moment he would be conversing with the other young monks; the next, he would look into space and speak in a disjointed manner. When the fit passed, he claimed no recollection of it. But at the same time his ravings seemed to impart a logic of their own. Often he described animals—eagles, elephants and monkeys in particular. On one occasion, he told of a huge throne being built by five people. In the future, he concluded, he would sit on that throne.

As no external cause for Lobsang Jigme's illness could be found, the doctors of Mendzekhang and Chokpori were unable to cure it. Their diagnosis, though, was clear. As opposed to mental illness, this was a case of spirit possession. The physicians suggested that Lobsang Jigme make a pilgrimage to Sharbumpa stupa in Phenbo, north of Lhasa. The stupa contained the relics of a great lama named Geshé Sharbum, and was famous for alleviating possession. Given a fifteen-day furlough to undertake his cure, Lobsang Jigme was warned by his superiors that Nechung Monastery's rules were strictly enforced; return on the appointed date was mandatory. Because of this, his stay at Sharbumpa was rigorous. To complete the number of prayers required for deriving curative benefit, he had to spend the entire day, breaking only for meals, walking around the stupa. With considerable effort, he completed the full course on time, but he experienced no relief; his affliction returned with him to the monastery. Two years later, at the age of twelve, Lobsang Jigme once more went on pilgrimage—this time to a stupa east of Ganden Monastery. Again he performed the prescribed number of circumambulations, and again there was no result.

By the age of fourteen, Lobsang Jigme's madness had increased to the point where he could no longer attend Nechung Monastery's daily rites. Frequently confined to bed, he lay numb and unresponsive between fits. At such times friends brought him meals, but he took no notice of them. Sleepwalking ruled his nights; during the day he experienced seizures and hallucinations and he often ran a high fever. Despite his troubles, though, he managed to complete his memorization and passed his exams.

One day Lobsang Jigme was taken on a short stroll around the monastic complex by his closest companion, a young monk named Kesang. Reaching a familiar tree in front of the monastery where they normally practiced playing short horns, the two young men decided to rest. They lay down on the grass and looking into the sky, began to doze off. Suddenly, Lobsang Jigme leapt up screaming. Burying his head in Kesang's lap, he pleaded to be covered with his *sen* or outer robe. Kesang asked what had happened, but at first Lobsang Jigme couldn't speak. Finally, he begged his friend to take him away from the tree, adding that he never wanted to see it again. Kesang shepherded his charge to the rear of Nechung Monastery, where their dormitories were. Once there, Lobsang Jigme told him what had occurred. He had been gazing into the top branches of the tree when two scorpions the size of yaks had appeared in the sky above. Their pincers were interlocked, and they seemed to be playing with one another. Then, without warning, they disengaged and one of them fell directly onto him. At that moment, he had screamed and buried his head in Kesang's lap.

Soon thereafter Lobsang Jigme began dreaming of scorpions coming into his mouth. Dogs appeared, scorpions in their mouths as well. His ravings now became so intense that once more the monastery granted a brief leave of absence. Initially, he went to his mother's house in Lhasa. There, he lay in bed all day, staring blankly over adjacent rooftops. As he watched he saw elephant faces appear at the window, followed by those of monkeys. His mother and the others in the household didn't know how to care for him. The fits had become so bad, in fact, that they wanted him to move on: his presence was disrupting the family business.

With Lobsang Jigme having reached a desperate state, his mother sought advice from Kyabjé Motroké Rinpoché, a great lama of the Go-mang College of Drepung Monastery. She asked him if a certain technique, known as *tsagak*, should be applied to her son to block his psychic channels, thereby stopping the unwanted possessions. Motroké Rinpoché performed a divination and announced that under no circumstances should the procedure be followed. If it was, he said, the young man would die. He then assured her that contrary to all appearance, the seizures were a positive sign. Lobsang Jigme had "the seed for accomplishment," he said, and in time everyone would know what this meant. No longer able to stay at home, the young monk left in the company of Kesang's uncle and rode thirty miles east to Ganden Monastery, where he arrived in September of 1944.

Built across a 14,000-foot-high crescent-shaped ridge surrounded by a sea of peaks, Ganden was among the most beautiful monasteries in Tibet. Its scores of buildings and shrines, framed on all sides by spectacular vistas, dazzled pilgrims from across Central Asia who came to worship at the golden tomb of Je Tsongkhapa, founder of the Gelugpa sect, housed in a maroon temple in its midst. Here, Lobsang Jigme hoped to stay unnoticed in the quarters of Samling Rinpoché, an incarnate lama in his late thirties who during the annual Monlam celebrations had frequently rented a room in his mother's house.

Despite Ganden's refreshing views, Lobsang Jigme's condition worsened after only a week. He now sensed that something very much like the trances he had often witnessed was occurring to him. Unlike the hallucinatory fits of the past five years, an episode would begin with a numbing, vibratory sensation pervading his body. His breath would shorten and begin to catch, uncontrollably, but then, thankfully, the symptoms would recede. In a few days' time, the new sensations no longer disappeared. He now started to experience genuine trance on a daily basis. Light days brought only one trance; more often, though, he would undergo as many as two trances in the morning and three in the afternoon. Moreover, the trances soon became violent: the moment they struck he would shout and thrash wildly about with tremendous force. On their conclusion after ten minutes or so, he experienced intense pain but would have no memory of what had taken place. As Lobsang Jigme and his companions soon found out, he was at this time being forcibly prepared through lesser spirits for possession by a higher force. The process, known as *tsalam jangpa* or "clearing the channels," was being undertaken in progressive stages of intensity. At the start, relatively weak spirits took possession, the trances being proportionately light. In the second stage, however, the seven Tse-mars or Blazing Brothers of Samye took him turn by turn, one after another. As the Tsemars were among the most powerful spirits, the trances became violent and Lobsang Jigme experienced tremendous sickness and pain in their aftermath.

As if Lobsang Jigme's troubles were not bad enough, further difficulties now befell him. The uproar coming from Samling Rinpoché's rooms provoked Ganden's authorities to inform those caring for him that the young monk from Nechung was no longer welcome. Despite the boy's condition, they insisted he return to his own monastery. Three times he attempted to leave, but each time he reached the gate of Ganden a particu-larly severe fit overtook him; choking and writhing about for a few se-conds, he would fall unconscious onto the ground, whereupon Samling Rinpoché and Kesang's uncle, who were accompanying him, had to carry the youth back to the hostel. But it was not only Lobsang Jigme who experienced such suffering. With the worsening of his illness a message had been sent to the young man's mother. Distraught, she again decided to contact high lamas for help. Setting out for Ganden, she hoped to obtain their advice and then take her son back home. She made it as far as the Kyichu River on Lhasa's southern limits. There, just before setting foot in the coracle to cross to the far shore, she herself suffered an attack. Collapsing on the bank, her right arm, right leg and stomach gripped by intense pain, she had to be carried home on a stretcher. Every effort to alter the young monk's situation now seemed forcibly blocked. The reason for all this appeared shortly thereafter.

In the course of one of Lobsang Jigme's heavier trances, the spirit in possession gave the following message, heard by Samling Rinpoché and all those close by: "On the fourth day of the sixth month, as the sun rises above Wongpo Ri Mountain, the Choekyong Dorje Drakden will take possession." The news of Tibet's chief protector entering an unknown monk's body was almost unbelievable, yet the fourth was the following day and Wongpo Ri, the highest mountain in the area, was plainly visible through the window in Lobsang Jigme's room. Samling Rinpoché and Lobsang Jigme's teacher, who had come to Ganden, made a point of being by the young man's side early the next morning. Entering the room, they found that he had been up before dawn reciting prayers. Already, he felt poorly. Then, as a faint light from the window began to replace the tranquil glow of butter lamps within, both men noticed a ball of yellow and red string, normally used to tie incense bundles, lying on the floor. For days they had been burning incense and reciting prayers whenever Lobsang Jigme went into trance; it seemed to be the only thing that helped. On seeing the string on the floor, Lobsang Jigme's teacher leaned over from his seat to pick it up, wanting to keep the room clean. As he took the string in hand, it suddenly turned into a live scorpion. Starting, he flung it to the floor and at that instant, Lobsang Jigme, who had been sitting quietly on his bed, leapt up in trance, his face and body attenuated. Simultaneously, the sun's first rays struck the bare rock summit of Wongpo Ri. A short while later, Lobsang Jigme collapsed, the trance ending as abruptly as it had begun. After laying him on the bed, the two men looked for the scorpion. Though it was a small monk's cell, they could find neither it nor the ball of string.

Following this incident, Samling Rinpoché began to piece together the facts. He concluded that, indeed, Lobsang Jigme was being taken into the employ of Tibet's main protector. Three factors supported the conclusion. To begin with, it had been specifically announced who the possessing entity would be. Though the message could have been misinformation from a malignant spirit, the intensity of the trance indicated the presence of an extremely powerful being. Second, the appearance of the scorpion was a familiar sign of Dorje Drakden. But the third factor was considered most significant. At that time, the current medium of the Nechung Oracle, a middle-aged monk named Lobsang Namgyal, had suffered a stroke and was thought to be close to death. It seemed clear that Dorje Drakden was preparing his successor.

The truth came a few weeks later. After prayers and breakfast one morning toward the end of July, Samling Rinpoché, Lobsang Jigme and his teacher decided to take a devotional walk through Ganden's many shrines. At the heart of the monastery stood the temple containing Tsongkhapa's tomb—one of the holiest sites in Tibet. The tomb lay within a chapel, the walls of which were lined with silver reliquaries containing the remains of successive Ganden Tipas who, as "holders of Tsongkhapa's Throne," had governed the Gelugpa sect for five and a half centuries. At their center was pitched a Mongolian yurt given as an offering after Tsongkhapa's death by Sunde, Emperor of China. Tsongkhapa's tomb lay at the rear of the yurt, behind a three-foot-high golden statue of the saint. The small party arrived at the chapel and entered the yurt at ten o'clock, well after morning prayers before the tomb had been concluded. Lobsang Jigme had been at ease throughout the devotional walk, and neither of his companions were paying close attention to him. As they passed the red-lacquered walnut pillars supporting the yurt, though, and began to prostrate before the image, the young man was struck by an extremely potent seizure. His companions tried to restrain Lobsang Jigme but were immediately thrown to the floor. From there they looked on in amazement as the young man's body, now fully possessed, performed the unique honorific dance of Dorje Drakden before the tomb of Tsongkhapa. When the trance ended five minutes later, the boy collapsed and the two men quickly dragged his prone figure to a side chapel in the corner of the room.

For half an hour after regaining consciousness, Lobsang Jigme was too nauseated to move; his head, shoulders and chest all ached intensely. His last memory had been standing before the golden tomb and beginning to pray. Then he had begun to feel as if thousands of insects were crawling over him. In the midst of the tingling vibration a stronger, more painful sensation appeared, as if his "funny bone" were being pressed throughout his body. His breathing began to accelerate, his head started to pound, his heart heaved in his chest, he felt congested, as if he had run too fast up a steep hill, and abruptly the room started to recede from his vision. The sound of the monks praying beside him grew fainter and then all combined to overwhelm him, and he blacked out. Though he realized the sensations must have occurred in a few moments, they seemed to take an unbearably long time. While walking back to their quarters, Samling Rinpoché told Lobsang Jigme what had happened afterwards. They all agreed that the event had to be kept strictly secret; an unknown adolescent monk could hardly claim, on the basis of one or two experiences witnessed by a few friends, to have been chosen as the new "receiving body" for the state oracle of Tibet.

Dorje Drakden's possessions, nonetheless, continued. Confining himself to his room for fear of being possessed in public, Lobsang Jigme felt himself entering a new stage, becoming stronger and stronger, "like a horse," as he described it, "filling with hot blood." At the beginning and end of each trance, he experienced severe pain. Though the trances themselves lasted only for two to five minutes, he would invariably shout in agony at the top of his voice—something which the authorities of Ganden, despite the peculiarities of the case, could not permit. Forced finally to leave Ganden, the young monk could return neither to his own monastery nor to his mother's house. His illness had made him an outcast. Through friends, he eventually found a family in Lamo, east of Ganden, who agreed to take him in. Able to depart without interference, he stayed in Lamo for a further month and a half, where he suffered, as before, not just from the newly developed trances but also from the ceaseless round of hallucinations, fits and sleepwalking that had consumed his life for six years.

At this time, Lobsang Jigme's mother received a message from Nechung Monastery. Though regretting his illness, the note nevertheless demanded his immediate return on penalty of being struck from the monastery's rolls. The other monks were complaining of Lobsang Jigme's long absence, the letter said; despite the severity of his condition there could be no exceptions to the rules. His mother replied that her son had been sick for so long, with no cure in sight, that even if his name were to be struck, it couldn't be helped; he was not yet able to return. The monastic officials then softened their stance and tried to effect a compromise. Through his mother they informed Lobsang Jigme that for the time being his name would not be eliminated from the roster; still, he would have to return soon. Convinced that his days as a Nechung monk were over and with no place to turn for help, Lobsang Jigme decided to retire to a cave and live in isolation from the world. He was just turning sixteen.

Aware of the young man's plans, Samling Rinpoché came to his aid. He offered to lead him through a three-month meditation retreat at Legpai Lodru, the cave of a great hermit, above Sera Monastery, hoping that by reciting mantras and conducting purification rites some of the negative influences affecting the youth could be dispelled. Accompanied by Kesang's uncle, they went to the cave and commenced the retreat. At the start, Lobsang Jigme was in such a depressed state over the impasse his illness had brought him to that he could barely follow Samling Rinpoché's instructions. Though he managed to fulfill the daily quotas of recitation, there was still no discernible change in his condition. Then, one morning in the middle of the retreat, he woke feeling well for the first time in years. The next day, he felt well again—and the next. Remarkably, all signs of the illness had left at once. A messenger now arrived bearing the startling information that Lobsang Namgyal, the Nechung *kuden*, had died. The day of the medium's death had been the very day on which Lobsang Jigme's illness disappeared. Furthermore, the messenger informed Lobsang Jigme, he had been dispatched by the abbot of Nechung Monastery, Nechung Rinpoché, to summon him back. None other than Taktra Rinpoché, then Regent of Tibet, had ordered him to present himself at the

Norbulingka. With a single message, it seemed, Lobsang Jigme's fate had completely reversed itself.

As all those associated with Lobsang Jigme would soon learn, the Regent had consulted Shinjachen, through the Gadong medium, shortly after the Nechung *kuden*'s death. Asking where a new medium for Dorje Drakden could be found, he had been told that the candidate was a monk from Nechung Monastery itself. The oracle went on to say that the prospective *kuden* was still very young—a child of fifteen, born in the Year of the Iron Horse; his name, Lobsang Jigme.

The news was greeted with a mixture of amazement and relief by Nechung Monastery's superiors. Ironically, among the eleven mediums who spanned the three hundred years of the monastery's existence, no *kuden* had risen from the ranks of its own monks; all had been chosen from elsewhere. To confirm the message, the Regent undertook a series of extremely sensitive tests. They involved placing Lobsang Jigme's name, along with those of six other candidates—all chosen for their reputations as mediums—inside precisely weighted balls of barley paste. The balls were then put in a precious vessel and brought before three of the holiest images in the land. Questions posed by the highest authorities were believed to be answered by the respective Bodhisattvas through the displacement of one of the balls. Though the vessel was rotated to produce a gentle momentum, there was an unmistakable pattern by which a single ball would be ejected. Out of the seven balls placed in the vessel by the Taktra Regent, the one with Lobsang Jigme's name on it came out on all three occasions. Nechung Rinpoché was then requested to have the young man brought immediately to the Regent.

Lobsang Jigme descended from his retreat a day after the messenger's visit. Arriving in Lhasa, he was met by Nechung Rinpoché and a delegation from the monastery, in whose company he rode two miles west to the summer palace. Leaving their mounts by the great stone lions flanking its front gate, the party was received in the gardens beyond and led down a narrow lane running between tall, shady trees, their leaves turned red and gold in the late autumn, to the Shabten Lhakhang, the temple in which the Regent received visitors. Directed into an ornate receiving room Lobsang Jigme nervously took a long white scarf and walked forward. It was the last thing he remembered. As he came before the Regent's high throne and offered the scarf, Dorje Drakden instantaneously took possession, greeting Taktra Rinpoché through the new *kuden* in a direct demonstration of his validity. The trance lasted for five minutes, during which time Dorje Drakden spoke to the Regent in private. At its conclusion, Lobsang Jigme collapsed and was returned to Nechung Monastery. There, he was

Dr. Yeshi Dhonden,
personal physician
to the Dalai Lama.

Lobsang Jigme, the Medium
of the State Oracle of
Tibet, in repose.

*Tibet's State Oracle in the first public trance
conducted in exile, Mundgod, India, March 1983.*

Monks returning from work in their fields, Mundgod, India.

Monks leaving Drepung Monastery in Mundgod, India, enroute to a religious ceremony.

Members of the Tibetan Youth Congress practicing maneuvers with wooden rifles.

Tibetan road workers in northern India.

Night view of the Mahabodhi
Temple at Bodh Gaya, India, site
of the Buddha's enlightenment.

Monks of the Gelugpa
sect in debate.

His Holiness the Dalai Lama
greeting 100,000 people
at a Kalachakra initiation
offered in Bodh Gaya, India.

housed in separate quarters while being subjected to a series of tests to determine if indisputably it was truly Dorje Drakden taking possession and not another strong, but lesser spirit.

The need to thoroughly test the authenticity of the Nechung *kuden* had, for centuries, been a critical concern of the Tibetan government. As the most delicate policies of state, both domestic and foreign, were involved with the oracle, the possibility of a leak, either from a malignant spirit taking possession (and subsequently relating information via another medium) or from the medium himself retaining some trace memory of the trance, was ever-present. So, too, was the danger of a garbled or mistaken transmission. To protect against the latter, the level of the medium's trance was closely observed, a complete possession, inducing unconsciousness, being the ideal state. Such a possession could occur only if the 72,000 psychic channels upon which, according to tantric theory, consciousness is mounted in the human body were clear of all obstructions. In such a case trance would be undergone swiftly, continuing without fluctuations or other irregularities. Though Lobsang Jigme's trances revealed him to be a very pure "vessel," the next task, that of checking whether or not it was in fact Dorje Drakden who possessed him, required, following preliminary observations, three levels of tests.

Initially, four signs of Dorje Drakden's immense power were sought: swelling of the medium's body up to two inches, effortless support of the heavy costume, ringing of the golden bells on the helmet's top and shuddering of the mirror on the chest from the increased heartbeat. The character of the possessing spirit was then observed. Dorje Drakden's *cham* was particular to him, as was the fact that his fierce, prideful attitude gave way to humility only if the Dalai Lama, his picture or an article of his clothing was present. Otherwise the spirit minister demanded complete subjugation from all those in attendance. With these factors present, three categories of tests, known as outer, inner and secret, were undertaken. In the outer test, the medium was presented during trance with sealed boxes and requested to name their contents. This exam was considered easy, as the majority of spirits were believed to possess a minor form of clairvoyance. It was followed by the inner test, in which the possessing spirit was requested to quote verbatim prophecies given by the Protector on specific dates in the past. With hundreds of prophecies on file, all imparted in Dorje Drakden's poetic, often cryptic style, this test was virtually impossible to pass if the Protector himself was not present. The two tests comprising the secret category, however, were believed definitive. Prior to the trance the *kuden*'s breath was checked to make sure that it had no odor. During trance it was examined again. If Dorje Drakden was in possession, the breath would invariably have a strong scent, similar to that of alcohol but described as actually being that of nectar. At the moment Padmasambhava had converted the Five Kings, in the form of the eight-year-old novice, to the Dharma, he had anointed the child's tongue with a few drops of nectar. Its odor was maintained by the spirit as a sign that his vows were being upheld. While exacting allegiance, Padmasambhava had also placed the blazing tip of his *dorje* on the head of the kneeling child. As the trance ends and the thickly padded helmet is quickly removed before the *kuden* chokes, Dorje Drakden's possession is revealed in the well-defined imprint of a *dorje*, clearly visible for a matter of minutes, on the crown of the medium's head.

Successfully passing all of the tests, Lobsang Jigme was publicly proclaimed, early in 1945, to be the new medium of Tibet's State Oracle. On the day of his investiture he took part in an elaborate ritual at Nechung Monastery after which the abbot conducted him to the *kuden*'s personal residence, a large well-appointed building within the monastic complex. Here, cared for by a carefully chosen staff, he spent most of his time engaged in the practice of deity yoga, pursuing meditation techniques which enabled him to enter trance with consistently less discomfort. Collecting the ample salary given to all Nechung *kudens* by the government, was treated with the utmost respect, on a par with that accorded to high lamas. Most rewarding of all, for the first time since the age of ten, Lobsang Jigme continued to enjoy good health.

The position of Nechung *kuden*, however, was neither easy nor even necessarily desirable. It held the potential of a high as well as an ignominious fate. Many *kudens* had suffered the later; only a few had achieved the former. The very first *kuden*, appointed at the monastery's founding in the seventeenth century, had been executed when, through possession by lesser spirits, secret government information had been revealed to the public. Though no such drastic measure had occurred since, two of the three *kudens* preceding Lobsang Jigme had been disgraced, fired from their posts, after their meditation practice had deteriorated to the point of interfering with the coherence of their trances. Shakya Yarpel, though, the renowned *kuden* prior to them, had been so beloved by the Thirteenth Dalai Lama for the clarity of his possessions that he had been accorded honors above even those granted the Prime Minister and Cabinet, actually being conveyed when he traveled in a *pep jam*, the gold palanquin normally reserved solely for Dalai Lamas and Regents. Aware of the difficulty of the post, Lobsang Namgyal, Lobsang Jigme's predecessor, had run away on being singled out during a trance of the Gadong Oracle as the new Nechung *kuden*. Nonetheless, unable to prevent his destiny, he had been possessed by Dorje Drakden and, until his death (attributed by some to the immense strain placed on his heart by possession), accepted the role.

Lobsang Jigme's favorable response to the post was augmented by a sense of personal affinity with Dorje Drakden himself. For the first three years following his recognition, on the night preceding a scheduled trance, the same odd event would inevitably occur. Past midnight, a loud banging would be heard in Lobsang Jigme's room, waking both him and his attendants from sleep. Unable to find a source for the commotion, the aides would turn to the *kuden*, who by then would be staring at the door and laughing. After some time, he agreed to relate what others heard but only he saw. Scores of small monks, no more than two feet tall, would appear in a jovial mood, and rushing altogether through the doorway, collide with one another and fall to the floor. Those who reached his bed brazenly stared at him and then burst into infectious laughter. It was clear, Lobsang Jigme felt, that these visits were being paid as a welcome of sorts to the new *kuden* by the followers of Dorje Drakden, due to enter him in trance in a few hours' time.

On only two occasions a year did Lobsang Jigme experience serious discomfort in his occupation. At these times, two of the Five Kings, the superiors of Dorje Drakden and Shinjachen, would come with the ministers and very briefly take possession of the Nechung and Gadong mediums. In the case of the Nechung *kuden*, Trinley Gyalpo, the Northern King of Action, would follow Dorje Drakden into the medium's body. This happened on the second day of the first month and again on the twenty-fifth day of the third month. Initially, Dorje Drakden took possession. Then, within "the stomach," as it was metaphorically phrased, of the Renowned Immutable One, Trinley Gyalpo would manifest himself. Without the intervening energy of Dorje Drakden to modulate the current of White Pehar, as Trinley Gyalpo was often called, the medium would immediately die. So much was made clear during the single minute—and sometimes only a few seconds—of possession. At the moment of entry, the medium's body, already swollen from Dorje Drakden, would become rigid, arms and legs outstretched, blood gushing from his nostrils. Those present would quickly offer a scarf in honor of Pehar Gyalpo, after which the Northern King would depart. Dorje Drakden remained in possession while the blood stopped flowing and the body was restored, and then he too would leave.

Following his appointment, Lobsang Jigme's duties became increasingly crucial to Tibet. The Dalai Lama was ten years old when the new medium took over and, to begin with, things went smoothly. As the Dalai Lama himself recalled, the relationship with Dorje Drakden, his personal protector, was on a most intimate footing. "In one respect the responsibility of the Dalai Lama and that of Nechung are almost of an equal status but in different fields," he reflected. "My task is peaceful; his is forceful. From another aspect, though, the Dalai Lama is like a commander and Nechung similar to a lieutenant or subordinate. So the Dalai Lama never bows down to Nechung, but Nechung bows to the Dalai Lama. In any case, as a friend to a friend, Nechung is very close to the Dalai Lama. When I was very small, it was touching. Nechung liked me a lot and he would take care of me. Suppose I was not dressed properly when the trance took place. Once the trance had begun, Nechung would literally arrange my shirt, fix my robe and so on. Then later, during my childhood, the relationship between the Cabinet and the oracle deteriorated. During every trance when Nechung was asked about the welfare of the Dalai Lama, he used to respond enthusiastically with a positive statement, but when he commented on the government's policies and concerns, he always gave a big 'if' and was sarcastic."

During the late 1940s, prior to the Dalai Lama's majority, corruption in the Regency's administration was such that Tibet's protector overtly opposed the government. On one particularly dramatic occasion, the Cabinet, aware of its precarious position with Dorje Drakden, requested Shinjachen, in the person of the Gadong medium, to intercede with him on their behalf concerning a specific point. Shinjachen complied, but the moment he had completed making the request for the Cabinet, Dorje Drakden struck him hard and both trances instantly ended. The Dalai Lama continued: "You see, dealing with Nechung is not easy. It needs time and patience. He is very rigid, almost like a great man of the old society. He is not talkative, he's reserved. Very much reserved. He does not bother with minor things. He takes a tremendous interest only in the bigger issues."

Regardless of the country's own internal decline, Dorje Drakden did not neglect to warn of the external threat from China. The Dalai Lama vividly recollected the first such indication, which occurred in 1945. "On that occasion," he related, "when Nechung was questioned concerning the welfare of Tibet, he didn't say a thing. Instead, he faced eastward and began shaking his head up and down. It was quite frightening, because for an ordinary person the helmet would have broken his neck. At least fifteen times he did this—very violently—and then the trance went off." In 1945, no one in Tibet imagined that Chinese aggression, driven off more than three decades earlier, would soon reconstitute itself. In 1948—two years before the invasion—Dorje Drakden directly warned that in the Year of the Iron Tiger—1950—Tibet would face extreme danger. He instructed that a specific *shabten* or religious activity be undertaken, one component of which was the construction of a large chorten at a designated spot. Such acts could not eliminate the threat of conquest, but it was believed, as part of the Protector's efforts, that they would deter the invasion for a good number of years, during which time the situation might improve on its own, so that when the onslaught did come, it would do so with considerably less destructive force. However, in the self-seeking climate of the time, this and other advice was ignored. As the invasion approached, Dorje Drakden repeatedly alluded to the need for the Dalai Lama to take temporal power. Finally, in November 1950, following Lhasa's first word of the attack, Shinjachen insisted that Tenzin Gyatso take control. Confused and defeated, the government had to agree.

In 1951, Lobsang Jigme inexplicably fell ill once more. This time, he contracted arthritis, due, perhaps, to physical stress from repeated possessions. Soon all of his major joints were so inflamed that he could no longer walk and had to be supported by two helpers. The doctors at the medical colleges could not effect a cure. Again, he lived in daily pain—save for those occasions when he underwent trance. In the meantime, Dorje Drakden continued to use him, giving the vital instruction that the Dalai Lama go to India in 1956 to forge the first contacts with Nehru and the Indian government, on which, subsequently, the Tibetan refugees' survival was to depend. Then, in 1958, a year before the Dalai Lama's flight, the Choekyong prophesied: "In this great river where there is no ford, I, Spirit, have the method to place a wooden boat." His meaning was clear; the Dalai Lama would have to flee, guided by him through the impassable "river" of Chinese troops.

In the early hours of March 20, 1959, Lobsang Jigme woke, with the rest of the city, to the sounds of the Chinese bombardment. Two miles east of Lhasa, Sera Monastery was attacked, but four miles west, Drepung remained unmolested. As the evening of the twentieth approached, Nechung Monastery was hit by stray bullets from fighting near the PLA's Nordulingka camp, little over a mile away. Concerned for the *kuden*'s safety, those in charge suggested that he move up the hill to Drepung, where he would not be so isolated. While the monks were in prayer, Lobsang Jigme and one companion went before the statue of Hayagriva in the main assembly hall. It had been this wrathful form that Padmasambhava adapted to subdue Pehar Gyalpo. Hence, the deity was employed by all Nechung *kudens* to invoke the Protector by visualizing themselves as such, within a celestial mansion, just before possession. Placing two balls of barley paste in a sacred vessel, one with a message to go to Drepung, the other to stay at Nechung, they watched as, in the midst of the appropriate ritual, the note with Drepung written on it came out. That night, in darkness, the Nechung *kuden* made his way, assisted by attendants, up the hillside. What was normally a half-hour walk took almost three times as long, since the PLA periodically shot bright flares over the mountainside, forcing the party to hide behind large boulders. The journey was successful, though, and the next morning Lobsang Jigme awoke to find Drepung in a feverish pitch of activity. Rifles, mortars and ammunition had been delivered, as they were to all the major monasteries around Lhasa, from the Potala arsenal. It was assumed that Chinese tanks would arrive to shell the cloister at any moment. Cut off from Lhasa by artillery and small-arms fire throughout the valley, the abbots of Drepung requested that Lobsang Jigme go into trance, permitting them to consult Dorje Drakden on the best course to follow. The trance was conducted, and in their request the abbots noted that because Sera had already been shelled they now feared Drepung would be as well. Dorje Drakden replied that if the Chinese were unprovoked, they would not fire a single cannon shot at the monastery. Whatever course they followed, he indicated, within three days all the fighting would be over. (Both statements were accurate: the morning of March 23 dawned with the revolt suppressed and Drepung unharmed.)

Before the end of the trance, the senior attendant of the Nechung *kuden* stepped forward to ask Dorje Drakden what should be done for the medium himself. Dorje Drakden replied that after Lobsang Jigme recovered from possession, he should leave Drepung immediately and begin walking south. He was to follow the same route the Dalai Lama had taken. The Protector guaranteed that nothing untoward would happen, and then, wrapping blessed barley grains in a white scarf which he gave to the attendants, he instructed them to burn a single grain whenever difficulty was encountered. Whatever thoughts occurred to them at the moment, he said, they should immediately act on.

When Lobsang Jigme regained consciousness, he looked up from the bed on which he had been placed and saw the small group of monks weeping over him. He inquired if shells had fallen on Drepung and if so whether or not any of them had been hurt. They replied in the negative. "Then why are you all crying?" he asked. After conveying Dorje Drakden's message, the senior attendant said, "This is the Choekyong's advice, but how can we follow it? You are a sick man. During the celebration of the Buddha Jayanti in 1956 you went by car through India and even under those conditions suffered tremendously. Now we have to walk and ride for weeks. How can we possibly cope with this problem?" As Lobsang Jigme had no answer for them, one and all lapsed into silence, pondering Dorje Drakden's other statement: the stunning news of the Dalai Lama's flight from the Norbulingka—unknown to Tibetans and Chinese alike until the following week.

Lobsang Jigme's own escape began the same day. In extreme pain, he spent two months walking from Drepung, through the heart of the fighting in Lhoka, to India. On numerous occasions he just missed capture by the PLA, who were consistently delayed by a series of unexpected events. After arriving safely in the NEFA and being processed through Missamari, he went to see the Dalai Lama in his temporary quarters at Birla House in Mussoorie. Thereafter, he took up his duties once more as a medium, alongside the Gadong *kuden,* also in exile.

Six out of Nechung Monastery's 115 monks managed to escape Tibet. In 1962, Nechung Rinpoché, the monastery's abbot, fled, bringing with him the most precious vessel of the Protector, originally stored at Samye, thirteen centuries before. A few years later Dr. Yeshi Dhonden succeeded in curing Lobsang Jigme of his incapacitating arthritis and by 1983, with Nechung Monastery's two most important figures actively at work, dozens of young monks had been ordained and a new monastery built across from the Library of Tibetan Works and Archives in Gangchen Kyishong. Here, once more, the daily invocations of Dorje Drakden proceeded with a full complement of monks—much of the refugees' progress being attributed by them to the ongoing guidance of their Protector over a quarter century of exile.

I V

9

Tibet Enslaved

1959–1965

The following order is hereby proclaimed.

Most of the *kalons* of the Tibet local government and the upper-strata reactionary clique colluded with imperialism, assembled rebellious bandits, carried out rebellion, ravaged the people, put the Dalai Lama under duress, tore up the Seventeen-Point Agreement on Measures for the Peaceful Liberation of Tibet and, on the night of March 19, directed the Tibetan local army and rebellious elements to launch a general offensive against the People's Liberation Army garrison in Lhasa. Such acts which betray the motherland and disrupt unification are not allowed by law. In order to safeguard the unification of the country and national unity, the decision is that from this day the Tibet local government is dissolved.

—*Order of the State Council of the Chinese*
People's Republic, March 28, 1959

PEKING MOVED QUICKLY following the Lhasa uprising. Martial law was ordered on March 20, just prior to the shelling of the Norbulingka. On March 23, the day after the revolt was crushed, the Military Control Committee of Lhasa was established, followed by others throughout Tibet, save in Shigatse, which, under the jurisdiction of the Panchen Lama, had remained peaceful. Five days later, on March 28, the Tibetan government was dissolved and Tibet was no longer an occupied if self-governing land but a conquered territory.

In Lhasa corpses littered the streets. Almost 10,000 people had died in three days of fighting. By the PLA's own account, 4,000 "rebel troops" had been captured along with 8,000 small arms—Smith & Wesson .38s, Colt .45s, Sten guns, Enfields and Mausers—81 light and heavy machine guns, 27 mortars, 6 pieces of artillery and 10,000,000 rounds of ammunition. Nevertheless, to ensure its control the PLA imposed a 7:00 p.m. curfew, confiscated every conceivable weapon, down to kitchen knives four inches long, and then arrested virtually every adult male in the city, filling dozens of large houses and temples to capacity. Lhasa's two jails, Ngyentseshar in the city proper and Shopa Lhekung just below the Potala, were emptied of their jubilant inmates, their cells refilled by the capital's citizens. The Ramoché Cathedral, still in flames from the bombardment, served as the initial collection point for hundreds of monks and was soon joined by the Central Cathedral, which received close to 1,000 monks from 28 monasteries around the city. Outside Lhasa, 8,000 prisoners were detained in the Norbulingka, and the three great monasteries of Sera, Drepung and Ganden, all encircled by Chinese troops, saw those who had remained of their 20,000 members locked in assembly halls under heavy guard.

Disposal of corpses was a particularly difficult problem. While the wounded were left to die, thousands of cadavers were collected in piles and burned for three days beneath the willow trees of the summer palace. Because fuel was so scarce in Tibet, cremation was temporarily suspended and communal graves dug. The stench from decomposition, however, compelled the Chinese to disinter the corpses and burn them as well. Meanwhile, with stacks of captured weapons covering the Norbulingka's charred grounds, specially detailed troops began requisitioning its priceless art treasures for shipment to China.

With the Dalai Lama gone, Peking turned to the Panchen Lama to bolster its image of Tibetan collaboration. Whatever his personal views on the situation, the twenty-two-year-old incarnation signed a telegram on March 29, addressed to Mao Zedong and Zhou Enlai, supporting their decision to dissolve the Tibetan government. On the afternoon of April 5, he arrived in Lhasa under heavy military escort, to take up his duties as the newly appointed Acting Chairman of PCART. To maintain a semblance of normality, Lhasans were briefly permitted to greet the Panchen Lama by burning pine boughs and offering prostrations, as flanked by Chinese generals, a bouquet of flowers in hand, he entered his new residence at Shuktri Lingka, below the Potala. The following night he was given a banquet by the military, and on the seventh he entered the city to pray at the Tsuglakhang and Ramoché. On April 8, 20,000 troops of the PLA's Lhasa command marched south to combat the guerrillas in Lhoka. Four abreast, bayonets fixed, they wound in an awesome line down the banks of the Kyichu River, following a route parallel to that the Dalai Lama had taken three weeks before. The next day the Panchen Lama walked on the stage of PCART's auditorium to thunderous applause from Chinese and Tibetan cadres. In the first plenary session of the "new" organization, eighteen past members were replaced as "traitorous elements," six new departments added—beginning with a new Public Security Department—and General Dan Guansan and eight others appointed to its standing committee. With PCART reformed, most of Tibet's high officials flew from Damshung Airport, north of Lhasa, to attend the first meeting of the Second National People's Congress in Peking, the very event to which the Tibetan people had feared the Dalai Lama would be kidnapped.

While they were gone, PCART was not idle. In its new form, it was controlled by two groups: the Tibet Work Committee of the Chinese Communist Party and the Tibet Area Military Command. The three generals who ruled Tibet headed both: General Zhang Jinwu, First Secretary of the Tibet Work Committee, General Zhang Guohua, commander of the PLA and Vice-Chairman of PCART, and General Dan Guansan, Political Commissar. Their jurisdiction applied only to inner Tibet— ranging from Ngari in the west to Chamdo in the east, Nagchuka in the north and the Himalayas in the south. The bulk of Kham and all of Amdo —two thirds of Tibet—was thus severed from the nation. Incorporated into eleven Tibetan autonomous districts and two autonomous counties appended to Sichuan, Yunnan, and Gansu, as well as into an entire province, Chinghai (previously Amdo), these areas ceased to exist as part of the Tibetan nation. Henceforth Chinese statistics reported a population of 1.3 to 1.8 million for Tibet, making the country seem small and insignificant.

As PCART divided it up, the new Tibet consisted of seven districts, seventy-two counties and one municipality, Lhasa. Controlling the population, through the "strengthened" administration, was China's paramount concern. To that end, the first of a seemingly limitless set of policies which would govern Tibet for the next quarter century was instituted—the "Three Cleanlinesses"—cleanliness of "reactionaries, arms and hidden enemies of the people." Enacted by committees called "Offices to Suppress the Uprising" (not disbanded until 1962), the "Three Cleanlinesses" saw either the *dzong* (fortress) or the largest monastery in each locale converted into a makeshift prison filled with men between the ages of fifteen and fifty. In Gyantse, Tibet's fourth-largest city, first the post office was used and then the Gyantse Monastery, in which 400 monks and laymen were bound and manacled, among them the temple's medium, who, dressed in his ceremonial robes, was tortured while being challenged to undertake a trance to free himself. In Shigatse, the nation's second-largest city, the town granary became an ad hoc prison, its 700 inmates forced to construct the high detaining walls which converted the building to its new use. All unauthorized movement was banned, and work committees were created to marshal the population. Lhasa was divided into three quarters—south, east and north—between which passage for those given bad class designations was so strictly supervised that family members living little more than a mile apart often had no knowledge of one another's condition for up to twenty years. Thereafter the city broke into 3 zone committees, 12 neighborhood committees and about 240 block committees staffed by one collaborator for every ten people. Thus construed, control filtered down to the smallest group. By April 15 the rudiments of organization were sufficiently in place to mount a demonstration of 20,000 women, children and monks—all those not imprisoned—on the open grounds at the base of the Potala. Carrying huge red banners and triangular pennants bearing Marxist slogans written in Mandarin, these Lhasans "demanded," as China's periodicals reported, that the rebellion "be put down," while "enthusiastically greeting" an announcement of "new plans" for their future. The plans were just then being drawn up in Peking. Though Mao Zedong had promised in 1957 to delay "Democratic Reforms," Peking now viewed the uprising as cause for abrogation of all its pledges to Tibet, including the original Seventeen-Point Agreement. China's goal, though, remained the same: to incorporate Tibet into its political framework as the last of five autonomous regions. Before unification could be attained, a major transformation in Tibetan society had to be implemented. In 1956 Tibet had been classed on the third level of the Marxist scale—as a "feudal" society, above "primitive" and "slave." The reforms of a "democratic revolution"— switching the economy from private to state ownership and destroying the "exploitive" class structure which had run it—were designed to catapult the country past the bourgeois capitalist stage directly to socialism. From there a "socialist revolution"—implemented primarily through communization—would achieve the absolute goal of a purely Communist society.

Such had been the formula for China as well. How to enact the plan, though, was a subject of fierce debate within the Party itself. For years two "lines" or camps had vied for the ascendancy of their respective doctrines: the right or moderate line, advocating an evolutionary approach, led by Liu Shaoqi, China's president, and Deng Xiaoping, the Party General Secretary, and the left or radical line, demanding quantum leaps forward, led by Mao Zedong. In framing China's "minority policy," the moderates desired a "knitting together" of nationalities with their "elder Han brother"; the radicals held that nationalism was ultimately a product of bourgeois mentality and hence had to be eradicated by forceful means. The result for China's fifty-four minority peoples was correspondingly mild or harsh depending on who was in power. In 1959, following the economic disaster of Mao's Great Leap Forward, the moderates once more stood at the helm, as they had for most of the PRC's first decade. Therefore, the degree of Democratic Reforms recommended for Tibet by the Second National People's Congress was, from the Party's standpoint, rather benign.

Returning to Lhasa late in June, the Panchen Lama and Chinese generals took twenty days to outline two stages of reforms. The first was dubbed the "Three Antis and Two Reductions." The second was land reform. Both were to be completed by 1961. The Three Antis (the first of which subsumed the initial Three Cleanlinesses of March) were anti-rebellion, anti-unpaid labor and anti-slavery; the Two Reductions were of rent and interest. The *wulag* or tax which peasants paid estate owners in labor, in return for land, was abolished. Also eliminated was the position of household worker or *nangzen*, which the Chinese termed slavery.

The Two Reductions directly dismantled the estate owners' holdings. Under a sub-policy called "the crop to the tillers," the property of the three major estate owners—government, monasteries and nobility—who were deemed to have taken part in the rebellion was given outright, along with their crops, to those who worked on the land. In the case of estates said not to have taken part in the rebellion, a full 80 percent of the crop was apportioned to the workers and 20 percent to the owners. This effectively disenfranchised every vested interested in the society above the lowest grades. The second reduction, that of interest, applied mainly to debts. All debts owed by tenant farmers to landlords through 1958 were canceled outright, and the interest rate on those incurred in 1959 was reduced to 1 percent a month. At meetings convened from every segment of the populace great bonfires were lit, into which the records of loans—and generally all the other documents of the large farms, mercantile concerns and monasteries—were thrown. While PLA contingents stood by, Tibetans were forced to circle the flames, applaud and shout slogans condemning the "dark order of the past"—a rather novel form of the traditional New Year's celebration in which the smoke from pyres of juniper and incense would be sent skyward accompanied by prayers for the good luck of all.

The foundation upon which the reforms rested was class division. However, class division under the Communists was far more strictly defined than it had been in the old society. People with 50 percent of their income remaining after expenditures were dubbed manorial lords; those with 45 percent, agents of the manorial lords; those with 35 percent, rich farmers or nomads; those with 25 percent, middle-class farmers or nomads; and those with no income set aside at all, poor farmers or nomads. A final class, called *logchoepas* or reactionaries, could include people from any of the above groups; in particular, at this time, it applied to all who had participated in the revolt. According to Chinese statistics, only 5 percent of Tibet's population, those in the reactionary category, were officially considered "enemies of the people" to be openly attacked and excluded from any benefits of the new order. In reality, those designated as land-lords, their agents, and rich farmers or nomads, as well as their children and relatives, were henceforth ostracized, leaving only middle-class and poor farmers or nomads with an acceptable class affiliation. In Tibet's case —unlike China's—the majority of the people, though tied to the land and beholden to their respective estates for taxes, were living above the poverty line; the "masses" of the poor, as defined by the Communists, constituted, in fact, a minority. This contradiction was not lost on the Tibetans, no matter how abstruse the novel vocabulary defining their lives appeared at first. The reality of class division was further brought home in the second stage of the Democratic Reforms, the attempted reassignment of wealth from the upper to the lower classes.

In Lhasa, as elsewhere, the committees called "Offices to Suppress the Uprising" carried out the redistribution. PLA squads systematically visited the houses of all "rebels" held in prison. Their families were either evicted or, in the case of those who had no relatives to stay with, permitted to remain with the livestock in their buildings' first-floor stables. All of their possessions were then inventoried, with anything of value being placed in the empty quarters. Finally, the front doors of the building were sealed with long paper strips covered with black Chinese characters exhorting the populace to put down the revolt. A few days after the initial sealing, the soldiers returned with a truck to requisition the owners' property. Every-thing was taken: furniture, rugs, kitchen utensils and even such stores of food as remained. Possessions were divided into several categories: the most valuable objects, such as jewelry, gold and silver, offering bowls and precious images, were marked to be sent to China, packaged and sealed with wax; good furniture and rugs were designated for the use of leading Han civil and military personnel in Tibet; items such as watches and expensive clothing were set aside for the Commerce Department of PCART to be sold individually to Chinese office workers. Following distribution loudspeakers summoned the poor to assemble at neighbor-hood committee offices to receive the wealth of those who had once exploited them. They found a haphazard array of broken chairs and tables, empty boxes, worn-out garments and an occasional teapot.

In the countryside the division progressed along similar lines, save that the wealth divvied up was labeled that "of production and of livelihood." The wealth of production was supposed to include all livestock—yaks, dzos, mules, sheep, horses—Tibetan currency (despite its being banned) and farming tools. But most of the livestock—as well as other valuable possessions—were taken by the Chinese. This left the same old clothes, furniture and clay and aluminum utensils that the city poor had received. Meanwhile, the real plunder began to depart in truck convoys for China, seized from the true treasuries of Tibet, the monasteries, and from the Dalai Lama's personal storehouse in the Potala. There was so much of it that the process continued all the way to the middle of the Cultural Revolution. While the antique markets of Hong Kong and Tokyo were flooded with priceless Tibetan artifacts, in China gold and silver images, the accumulated art and wealth of a millennium, were melted down into bullion.

The cornerstone of the second phase of the Democratic Reforms was land reform. An average of 3.5 mus of land (about half an acre) was designated to be given to all members of the lower class and even to the "serf owners from whom it was taken." By the autumn of 1959 it was already underway in areas adjacent to Lhasa. Once land belonging to those associated with the revolt had been appropriated, a policy of "buying out" was announced for that of the "three Big Serf Owners," who, not having aided the rebels, had nonetheless "passed the barrier." This meant, as Ngabo Ngawang Jigme, the former Cabinet minister and now a leading collaborator, summed up in one of his speeches, that "those serf owners and their agents who opposed imperialism, love the country, and accept democratic reform are protected. . . . political arrangements have been made for their benefit and their livelihood is being taken care of according to their actual conditions." The "conditions" referred to the fact that all landowners who had succeeded in turning an annual profit of 45 percent or more, after having lost 80 percent of their assets in the initial reforms, were now to lose the rest. Lands and goods belonging to them were appraised at 10 percent of their actual market value and then taken in return for a receipt guaranteeing eventual payment. Once more the PLA conducted a massive inventory of this segment of the population's possessions. Where it didn't go, individuals were required to itemize their property at the local work committee whereafter it was confiscated.

The land reform materialized in full during November 1960 in the form of 200,000 deeds, written mainly in Chinese, and sporting a portrait of Chairman Mao flanked by red flags. These were distributed in grand ceremonies to the peasant class and those below—beggars and mendicants, often old or crippled, who knew nothing of farming and had no desire to pursue it. As Ngabo Ngawang Jigme said, summarizing the achievements of the Democratic Reforms at the National People's Congress in Peking a few months earlier: "The class consciousness of the broad masses of peasants and herdsmen has been greatly elevated; they say, 'The sun of the Kashag [the Cabinet] shone only on three big manorial lords and their landlord henchmen, but the sun of the Communist Party and Chairman Mao shines on us—the poor people.' They warmly sing praises: 'Chairman Mao is the father of the various nationalities of our motherland and is closer to us than our own parents.' They say, 'Reactionary elements of the upper strata spoke the same language as we did, but their hearts were different from ours; the Han cadres speak a language different from ours, but their hearts are the same as ours.' "

Class struggle was the crucible in which the order of the future was to be forged. Its fuel, the fire which burned away the old and gave birth to the new, was *thamzing* or struggle session. Through it the "broad masses" would emancipate themselves by making their own people's revolution. In practice, this meant setting workers against employers, peasants against landlords, monks against abbots, students against teachers, and children against parents. Those who held positions of authority in society were automatically seen to possess them, not on the basis of merit, but through having usurped their place, with the support of others of like kind, for the sole purpose of oppressing the people. Despite admonishments from the United Front Work Department and the Nationalities Affairs Commission in Peking to respect minorities and to nurture unity between the many peoples of China, the reality in Tibet was unremittingly racist; Chinese occupation troops were unable to relinquish their millennia-old view of the Tibetans as barbarians. As Communists, they marshaled ideology in support of this prejudice, depicting the government as "dark, feudal and cruel," the monks as "red robbers" or "insects" sucking the blood of the people. But the "people" themselves were physically repugnant to the average Chinese in Tibet: dirty, dark, smelling of yak butter and altogether barbarously free in their behavior, they were poor material from which to fashion willfully self-regimented proletarian masses. All of this served to nourish the dedication with which *thamzing* was carried out, while to Tibetans *thamzing* was made all the more repugnant by the condescension of the Han, who prefaced every round of punishment and bloodshed with the prim assertion that what was to follow lay solely in the victim's best interest.

By the end of July 1959 *thamzing* was well underway in Lhasa. It occurred periodically within the framework of the daily "political education" meeting, held by every block committee for the hundred to two hundred people under its jurisdiction. In their more quiescent form, these meetings, conducted in abandoned monasteries and in the courtyards of large houses, served as mere platforms for propaganda designed to heighten class consciousness. A common question at the start was: "What is oppression and deception?" The correct reply: "The old society."

Much of the reeducation in 1959 focused on the Dalai Lama. As they maintained to the world, the Chinese in Tibet announced to Tibetans that the Dalai Lama had been kidnapped by reactionaries. Due to the utter lack of external news, various wild rumors abounded. In some renditions, he was said to have hidden in a forest for ten days, whereafter he was captured by the PLA and freed from his abductors. In Shigatse it was announced that though the Dalai Lama had indeed been kidnapped and taken to "Pandit Nehru's country," India could not feed him or his party, as its people were already dying of famine by the millions. Nehru was said to have given the Tibetan leader a job on board a ship but he could not earn enough to support himself. As a result, the Chinese consulate in Calcutta had fed him for twenty-one days, then flown him to Peking, where he now lived with Mao Zedong and the Panchen Lama, "sharing the same meals with them and enjoying equal status." It was just then being arranged for the Dalai Lama to remain in Peking while Mao himself would come to Tibet to take his place. Finally, the populace was assured that any thought of escape to India was futile, as those who had fled were not only starving but were soon to be transported back to Tibet by Nehru himself.

Thamzing, while equally fanciful, was a carefully orchestrated undertaking, much like a collective Passion play. *Thamzing* proper took place with the people seated on the ground before a tribunal of Chinese officials ensconced behind a table. An opening speech was made by the ranking Chinese. In it the people were informed that *thamzing* was not a matter of one or two meetings, but would continue until a full confession, followed by repentance, had been obtained—until the accused himself, "with the help of his revolutionary brothers," had cleansed his mind of reactionary thoughts. Furthermore, it was designed to teach the "serfs" to stand up, unafraid of their masters, and expose past injustices. On this dramatic note—with the official gesturing angrily and yelling, "Bring that bad person in!"—the prisoner would be led to the head of the crowd, and made to bend over from the waist, hands on knees, eyes to the ground. A list of crimes was then read from the charge sheets, the official saying at the conclusion: "These are the crimes committed by this person. It is now for the people to help him admit his evil ways and decide the punishment he should receive." At this signal the first accuser, invariably an "activist" in

Chinese employ, would spring up, race forward, and denounce the "exploiter," by yelling such epithets as "Kill the stinking dog! Skin him alive! Your mother's corpse! Your father's heart! Confess your crimes!" After recounting the supposed suffering he had been subjected to, the witness would beat the victim, rebels often being thrashed by their guards with the butt end of a rifle. In these cases, it would frequently be the task of those at the meeting to execute the victim, not, however, before suggestions were elicited as to the best means. Burying alive, wrapping the accused in a blanket and setting it on fire, suspending him from a tree and lighting a bonfire beneath, hanging, beheading, disemboweling, scalding, crucifixion, quartering, stoning to death by the whole group, small children being forced to shoot their parents—all these methods were suggested (by collaborators) and subsequently employed, as reported in case after case to the International Commission of Jurists. In the first year alone after the revolt's suppression, thousands of Tibetans died as a result of *thamzing*, while many more were permanently maimed, losing, in part, their teeth, hearing or eyesight.

Following this basic pattern, *thamzing* was conducted throughout Tibet in one of three forms: small, medium and large. Small *thamzings* were often spontaneous, occurring during regular reeducation meetings when someone gave the wrong answer to a question—and thus exposed himself as having an "old," "green" or "unripe" mind. Medium-size *thamzings* involved one person being "struggled" for weeks at a time in large neighborhood or multi-village meetings. Large *thamzings* were a step below formal public executions. In Lhasa, the first of them began on July 26, 1959, nine days after the Democratic Reforms were announced. Lhalu Tsewang Dorje, the Cabinet minister who had organized the defense of Kham before relinquishing it to Ngabo just prior to the invasion, had been captured during the uprising and was accused of being one of its chief perpetrators—which, of course, he was. Interrogated and beaten in the maximum-security prison located inside Silingpu, the PLA's headquarters, he was chosen as a prime example of past corruption and paraded through Lhasa receiving multiple beatings in front of huge crowds, before eventually being thrown back in jail, to be kept alive for future propaganda campaigns. Less important figures, though, came off worse, such as a sixty-year-old nun named Gyanisha Anila, who was marched through the Barkhor on October 21 while the PLA ordered onlookers to strike her. When none did, local "activists" were recruited and paid to attack her on the spot, after which, according to witnesses, she died ten days later from the injuries sustained. Tantric monks from the Ramoché were forced at gunpoint to break lifelong vows of celibacy by publicly having intercourse with nuns before the entrance to the Central Cathedral.

By October 1959, the population was cowed. Not only had "struggle session" produced a profound fear of the Chinese; it had also, as intended, created an atmosphere of mutual distrust among Tibetans. Old friends could no longer confide in one another; parents ceased speaking frankly before their own children. In the monasteries, an even more difficult atmosphere prevailed.

It was on the clergy, the most cohesive and hence threatening group in Tibetan society, that the Chinese vented their full wrath. Monasteries were ransacked, cartoons scrawled on their walls by the PLA. One of the most popular, called "the two-faced lama," parodied the multi-limbed style of Buddhist deities by rendering a monk with two faces and six arms; one face and three arms were gentle, the hands in prayer and giving blessings, the other—meant to be the real one—lurid, its hands abusing and molesting helpless supplicants. In Drepung, where about 2,800 of the almost 10,000 monks remained, a museum of past horrors was hastily created, with four rooms set aside for the exhibit. The first displayed captured weapons, surrounding an effigy of the Nechung *kuden* in trance, who, as a nearby inscription related, was telling the people to revolt, thereby leading them to defeat. Next, an "economic exploitation" room represented Drepung as a great machine for systematically robbing the common man. The presentation recounted how, over its numerous estates, Drepung extracted a series of outlandish taxes—on dogs, cats, chickens, donkeys, flowerpots, cigarettes and snuff. A quarter of Drepung's income was purported to come from usury. On display was a warped board, allegedly used for measuring grain taxes, illustrating how the monks cheated the people. When debts could not be paid, it was claimed, the monastery had the right to "enslave" the creditor for twenty-five years. Drepung was also held to routinely deal in opium. Monks who toured the monastic properties to collect taxes were accused of raping indiscriminately wherever they went; those who would not submit to their voracious sexual appetites were said to be flogged, exiled or tortured to death. A brisk traffic in young boys was supposedly constant. Simply put, as one monk related to a Western author permitted to visit Lhasa soon after the revolt, "The monastery is a hell in the universe that you cannot escape from."

The degree to which the Chinese believed their own propaganda was made evident in *thamzings* such as those at Sera. Ignorance of various aspects of religious practice yielded unlimited opportunities for punishment, as with the *lama gyudpas* or tantric monks most of whom, having mastered esoteric chanting techniques, wherein three notes or a chord was intoned at once, were given *thamzing* on the ground that they possessed "bourgeois voices." While lamas and scholars were singled out for struggle sessions, the Chinese succeeded, only after extreme intimidation, in assembling a small group of "activist" monks to enact *thamzing*. Their victims, rather than being "struggled" against one at a time over a long period, were brought forth at a rate of ten a day into the assembly hall—otherwise kept in total darkness—and then bound and taken from the monastery by the truckload. Concurrently, the thousands of remaining monks were compelled to sign statements attesting to atrocities committed against them by Sera's administrators. By late autumn, seven months after the revolt's suppression, the Chinese decided what to do with the majority. A group of 150 of the "most dangerous" were sent to Drapchi Barracks, now a prison. The rest, along with prisoners from the Norbulingka and other locations around the Lhasan Valley, were confined in the first slave-labor camp in Tibet proper—Nachen Thang, a few miles east of the city on the shores of the Kyichu River.

Nachen Thang was the site of a large hydroelectric plant. It had been under construction—with seven brigades of paid Tibetan male and female labor—for some time, and was said by the Chinese to be fondly referred to by Tibetans as "the Pearl of the Lhasa River." After the revolt, there was no longer any need to pay workers. By the end of May 1959, less important prisoners started to arrive at Nachen Thang, bringing its work force up to 3,700, guarded by 500 troops. By the end of December, the number had grown to 8,000. The prisoners were kept in ten compounds ringed in by barbed wire on three sides, with the Kyichu at their rear. They lived in tents, divided into groups of a hundred, and hauled rocks and earth for the construction of dam sites, support ditches, tunnels and service buildings. In the evening, each group's daily output would be announced and those who fell short of the quota subjected to *thamzing* and additional labor. The plant's first generator was officially opened in April 1960, its second in October 1962. Refugees reported that hundreds died from starvation and exhaustion during their construction, famine being prevalent through all of China at this time. A monk from Drepung Monastery who managed to escape to India in 1961 maintained that in Drapchi, where manual labor was not a factor, 1,400 of the 1,700 prisoners perished from starvation between November 1960 and June 1961.

Three of the principal labor camps created after Nachen Thang were Golmo, far north in the Tsaidam Basin; Tsala Karpo, in the *changthang* or northern plains, where borax was mined; and Kongpo, in the forests of southeastern Tibet. Kongpo, primarily engaged in deforestation, was the easiest camp—the climate mild, the work not excessive. Golmo and Tsala Karpo, however, were death camps from the start.

Golmo, taken over in 1964 by the Public Security Bureau for Tibet, had already been in service as a prison camp for Chinese and Tibetans from Amdo. It represented one of China's most important mass-labor enterprises—a railroad linking Tibet and the far northwest with the mainland. Much of the Communists' success in absorbing Xinjiang had depended on the railroad connecting it to Langzhou. Tibet's own railroad was viewed as the key to defending China's southwestern frontier against India, as well as to stabilizing the country and eventually exploiting its natural resources. The landscape though, 10,000 feet above sea level at the heart of Asia, was cold and arid, with gale-force winds blowing up to seventy days of the year, vast stretches without water, and six months of full winter. At the eastern end of the region was the immense Kokonor or Blue Lake, favorite camping spot of Mongol tribes for centuries and considered by Tibetans as the northern boundary of Amdo.

Hundreds of prisoners from the Norbulingka were transported in convoys 600 miles northeast to Golmo in September and October 1959. Within two years, they were joined by thousands more. Though it was in the Communists' interests to keep them alive, they apparently lacked the ability to do so. Worked twelve hours a day on starvation rations, with no medical treatment and insufficient clothing against the cold, huge numbers died in the first few years alone.

At the same time, in Tsala Karpo, a dry lake bed at the heart of the *changthang* northwest of Lhasa, other prisoners were set to work digging for borax. Here, as in the Golmo region, water had to be trucked in daily; the ground was so barren there weren't even stones for cooking fires—iron tripods were used to support the pots—and the climate was scarcely tolerable. Prisoners shoveled borax, found in white, red, blue and yellow lumps, out of the lake bed. Sometimes deposits were a yard down; at other times holes the height of a house had to be opened. The original 500 Chinese guards informed the prisoners that a truckful of borax was more precious than one of silver dollars; accordingly, they worked hundreds to death, by forcing labor from dawn to sunset daily and providing only the worst grade of barley flour mixed with sawdust as rations. On Sundays, contingents were sent on a six-hour trek to a grassy region where sticks could often be found. Each group was to gather seven and a half pounds of firewood before returning at dusk. These trips afforded the sole opportunity for escape. With a small supply of food, some borrowed clothes and the assistance of nomads, it was possible to reach southwestern Tibet and, from there, Nepal. After a rash of escapes, the Chinese temporarily relaxed their policies, suspended *thamzing* and the indoctrination meetings in which it was conducted, held each night till midnight. When this had no result, though, the meetings were resumed, and a stricter watch was kept on the wood-collecting trips. There was, however, an added risk to the security of Tsala Karpo, that of the organized guerrilla forces under Chushi Gangdruk, still—a full year after March 1959—fighting the Chinese deep in the interior.

Hundreds of guerrilla bands remained active in Tibet long after the suppression of the Lhasa revolt. While the number of major battles decreased as the guerrillas were isolated from the villages they used for support, ambushes of PLA convoys continued intermittently. Besides Lhoka, the main theater of combat lay in a zone above Lhasa where southern Amdo, northwestern Kham and the *changthang* met. Here, large groups, cut off from escape routes through Central Tibet, fought major battles for a full three years following the revolt. The Goloks, a nomadic warrior tribe from Amdo numbering over 100,000, were particularly stubborn. Their name meant "Backwards Heads," or rebel—which they had always been, mainly against the central government in Lhasa. They had fought fiercely from as early as 1952, waging guerrilla campaigns in which large numbers of Chinese had died. By the time the revolt erupted in Central Tibet, they still had not been crushed. Though both they and the other "wild men" of Tibet, the Khampas, were hampered by limited supplies, catching them, in the rugged and trackless countryside, was not so simple. Once a guerrilla band was located, the Chinese, equipped with machine guns, mortars and field artillery, would attack its camp in the middle of the night, or at dawn, and the massacres that resulted were characteristic of the fighting all across Tibet, just as the stand at the Norbulingka had been. But despite the Tibetans' massive losses, combat continued. In December 1964, almost five years after the uprising's official suppression, General Zhang Guohua noted publicly that "the feudal lords have not been eliminated; they are resentful of their defeat and attempt to regain power by all means." Almost a year later, he again referred to internal turmoil by stating: "The people can thoroughly smash the reactionary administration of the feudal lords only by carrying out resolute struggle, especially armed struggle."

Covert resistance as well hampered China's assimilation of Tibet. Peking claimed that both the Democratic Reforms and the "rechecking" of those reforms (a euphemism for a second wave of mass arrests) had in the main been completed by the end of 1961, but they had not. On April 2, 1961, Radio Lhasa assured Tibetans that they would remain at the stage of "democratic revolution" for a further five years before socialization began in earnest. Completing the Democratic Reforms—as well as all the other policies on which the rudiments of civil administration depended—was relegated to a non-military bureaucracy comprised of Tibetan and Han cadres alike. As the hierarchy came into place, reforms could often be carried out only at gunpoint, with PLA support. Yet the army was primarily engaged initially in destroying the remaining groups of freedom fighters and later in the 1962 border war with India. Furthermore, the universal social leveling sought by the reforms was only the first of two steps necessary before the Tibet Autonomous Region could be inaugurated. While the population was reduced to a classless state, it also had to be organized in collectives. This first stage in socialization—beginning around Lhasa with the Mutual Aid Teams (MATs) in mid-1959—was crucial to stabilizing the region. Without it, higher degrees of collectivization—including centralized control and increased production for the state —could not be achieved. It was a time-consuming task, matched only by that of creating the veneer of self-government, a cardinal component of Chinese policy pursued to demonstrate that Tibet had attained political emancipation. But though general elections were officially discussed by PCART in August 1961, the actual Election Committee could not be installed until a year later, the rules for the election were not passed for another several months, and once they were enacted it took more than two and a half years to carry them out, the longest election period of any region in the People's Republic.

Meanwhile, as the *People's Daily* and the New China News Agency heralded the "new socialist paradise on the Roof of the World," Lhasa found itself glossed over with new names to create in illusion what could not as yet be produced in reality. The city's thoroughfares became Great Leap Forward Street, Liberation Street, Victory Street, Happy Street. In reality, the more than three hundred shops that surrounded the Central Cathedral in the Barkhor were now all closed. The marketplace was empty and even the best-kept buildings showed signs of the decay—peeling mortar, chronically leaking roofs, and rotting woodwork—which would, within a few years, reduce the Tibetan quarter of Lhasa to a slum. Just outside town, Chokpori Hill, where the medical college had been razed during the fighting in March 1959, sprouted radio antennas and artillery emplacements as it grew into an important military installation and ammunition dump linked by underground tunnel to the Yuthok Bridge more than a mile distant. At the Panchen Lama's insistence, those portions of the Tsuglakhang, Ramoché, Potala and Norbulingka that had been damaged in the 1959 shelling had their facades repaired, while according to Chinese needs, many of their interiors were put to a new use as granaries, meeting halls and military barracks guarded by detachments of PLA. With most monks imprisoned in labor camps or returned to the countryside, the "three seats" of Drepung, Sera and Ganden maintained only skeleton crews of aged caretakers. The Tsuglakhang remained open until 1966, and on Wednesdays—considered an auspicious day—Lhasans rose before dawn to offer incense and prayers at the Central Cathedral and at Bhumpari Hill across the river. Prayer flags were still made and displayed but except for these small reminders of the old life, the daily routine of the capital's citizens was unremitting labor. Building the "new town," the administrative center for the new rule, was the order of the day. To this end, the whole city was marshaled into labor gangs. For lifting rocks and dirt, women and able-bodied men—many of whom were released from prison a few months following the uprising—were paid between 1.2 and 1.7 yuan daily, or roughly 60 to 85 cents. People with "bad" class designations received a maximum of 40 cents a day. But more often, work was denied them and their children. "In short," as the Panchen Lama stated in his report to the Standing Committee of the National People's Congress in December 1960, "a wonderful situation prevails in Tibet today. Prosperous scenes of labor and production are found in every corner of the vast countryside and the towns. This is the main trend of our work in Tibet."

"Prosperous scenes" did indeed exist in the countryside, though the Tibetans were hardly the beneficiaries. In the first years after the revolt, agricultural production increased dramatically—the result of the Mutual Aid Teams, the embryonic form of collectivization from which fullfledged communes would be built. The teams themselves were of two kinds, seasonal and permanent, with the latter gradually supplanting the former. Seasonal teams were generally comprised of from seven to ten families who shared for a season the work of sowing, cultivation and harvesting on one another's land and then disbanded. Permanent teams pooled labor and land, but held property, tools and draft animals in common as well. The seasonal teams were in many ways typical of perennial village farming methods in Tibet, and thus represented no implicit threat to traditional Tibetan society. But again, in no case were "class enemies" permitted to join. They were generally issued the worst bit of land in the neighborhood, occasionally given a single draft animal for plowing and told to till it on their own.

In the summer of 1959, 4,741 MAT teams were reported to have been formed in four secure regions. By the next summer, more than 15,000 had been founded; by 1964, there were 22,000 for farmers and 4,000 for nomads. Besides leaving "no arable land idle," the teams embarked on massive irrigation projects, built dams and reservoirs, collected human and animal waste as fertilizer and planted a second and even third crop where only one had been sown before. Bumper harvests were reaped. That of 1959 showed a 10 to 20 percent increase over the previous year. A further 15 to 20 percent increase was set as the production target for 1960. By 1961, cultivated land had expanded by 22.5 percent. By 1964, grain output was claimed to be 45 percent above that prior to the Democratic Reforms, and the number of livestock had increased by 36 percent. The Tibetan people's reaction to these miraculous increases in producton was described as one of pure ecstasy, the "million serfs who stood up" now "celebrating with songs and dances" their "enthusiasm for production" being "unprecedentedly high." But in reality, in every corner of Tibet, save perhaps Ngari in the far west—still beyond stringent Chinese influence—Tibetans were starving to death by the thousands.

The source of the famine lay not in Tibet but in China. Harvests had been poor, and the Great Leap Forward had led to a schism with the Soviet Union, which had cut off its shipments of grain. As a result, 1959 was the first of the three "lean years" in which millions all across China perished from hunger. To feed them, Tibet's crop was no sooner harvested than it was taken from the Tibetans and either consumed by the PLA or shipped to the mother country. This was the most immediate and pressing purpose of Tibet's socialization: to create a bread basket for the starving People's Republic.

Given the situation in China, the compulsory formation of MATs in Tibet was tantamount to the creation of forced-labor gangs. Ration cards were distributed to one and all—on which were recorded vital statistics for the Public Security Bureau, such as the number of people in each household, their age, sex and relation—and the monthly grain ration was set at 22 pounds per person. This represented a decrease by two thirds in the average Tibetan's diet. With travel almost completely banned, the population in the countryside hoarded wild vegetables; those in the cities—deprived now of the free markets on which they had subsisted—were even worse off, receiving as little as 18 pounds of grain per month. Horror stories abounded. People ate cats, dogs, and insects. Parents fed dying children their own blood mixed with hot water and *tsampa*. Other children were forced to leave home to beg on the roads and old people went off to die alone in the hills. Thousands of Tibetans took to eating the refuse thrown by the Chinese to the pigs each Han compound kept, while those around PLA outposts daily pieced apart manure from the soldiers' horses, looking for undigested grain. Even for Tibetan cadres, normally better fed than the population at large, meat and butter were unavailable, salt and black tea being the sole supplement to barley grain.

The famine lasted through 1963. By then tens of thousands had died from starvation all across Tibet. When it lifted, it did so only to the extent that the meanest conditions necessary for survival could be maintained. Until the next severe famine—which struck in 1968 and lasted through 1973 —every available commodity was scrupulously rationed. In Lhasa, one of the worst-hit areas in Central Tibet, each family was issued a single candle per month, 250 grams of tea and 10.8 grams of sugar. Phari, one of Tibet's most prosperous towns—a center for trade with India, Sikkim and Bhutan —remained, owing to its delicate position close to the border, at the opposite end of the scale. Here, a man classified as a "strong worker" could draw as much as 30 pounds of barley a month; weak workers drew 26 pounds; old and infirm, 20 pounds; children from eleven to seventeen years old, 15 pounds; children under six, 5 pounds. When they were available, butter, oil, sugar, tea, gasoline, five packs of cigarettes a month, up to six boxes of matches and 10.5 meters of cloth rounded out the list of goods available to these most prosperous Tibetans. Even in Phari though, the dearth of goods reduced the norm by two thirds, resulting in numerous cases of starvation. Each day scores of families could be seen going from house to house with *tsamba* bags, either borrowing or repaying grain. Soon this flow of empty-handed people took on a melancholy name, "the tide of emptiness." Conscripted into labor gangs, in this case without pay, the people of Phari vented their sufferings in songs, one of which concerned a water mill constructed to grind grain for the Chinese:

> *It is not very long since the water mill was built,*
> *But tell us the reason why we have to dust our tsamba bags so soon.*
> *It is not very long since the people were liberated,*
> *But tell us the reason why we have to tighten our belts.*
> *This water mill, built through our hardship and suffering,*
> *Will serve as a throne for the Dalai Lama when he returns,*
> *But if Mao comes, it will be his grave.*

But no matter how bad things were in the countryside, conditions in Tibet's prisons were far worse. Here, hidden from the outside world, lived a race apart—including at one time or another one out of every ten adult Tibetans.

IN THE WINTER of 1959, Dr. Tenzin Choedrak, one of the Dalai Lama's four personal physicians, lived in Yabshi House, the residence of Tibet's first family. Having served as the Dalai Lama's physician for three years, he had become a close friend of the young ruler's family, almost half of whom remained in Tibet. The atmosphere at Yabshi House, though, was burdened by anxiety over the growing revolt. In its midst Dr. Choedrak remained undecided on what role he should play—unsure whether the Chinese would help Tibet and then leave, as they said, or whether the congenial facets of their occupation were a facade designed to conceal some unspecified but inevitably harsher form of domination. Finally, when Khampa refugees poured into U-Tsang with stories of atrocities and forced collectivization, he resolved to support the revolt. During the March 10 demonstrations, he met with colleagues from Mendzekhang and representatives of all the major religious institutions in the Norbulingka. There he put his name to a document (later valuable to the Chinese in making arrests) which, declaring Tibet independent, swore its signatories to fight for freedom.

Late on the night of March 19, 1959, Tenzin Choedrak woke to the sound of artillery as the PLA bombardment of Lhasa began. Yabshi House was less than a quarter of a mile away from the Potala and directly in line with incoming rounds from Drib, a village on the far side of the Kyichu. Donning a layman's *chuba* and pants, he retreated from his room near the front gate to the main house, where no one knew that the Dalai Lama himself had already fled.

On the afternoon of March 22, the day Lhasa capitulated, Chinese troops arrived at the compound. Without warning they fired a field gun, destroying the gate that led to the main house and called for those within to surrender. Four of the sixteen people in the house decided to walk out to meet them. As they stepped through the front door, they were killed by machine-gun fire—having neglected to raise their hands. Soldiers armed with machine guns then stormed the building. While some guarded the remaining Tibetans, the rest ran through the house, shooting at each storage trunk, closet, cupboard and bed, throwing grenades into the toilets and finally emerging to riddle the outhouses with bullets. Families who rented apartments in the Yabshi compound, thirty people in all, were brought to the main house and locked in a windowless room without light on the first floor. The following morning they were permitted to relieve themselves, and were then locked in once more. That evening, a Chinese officer informed the group through a translator that they had been selected for "studies," an expression all believed to be a euphemism for execution. With two soldiers before and behind, they were marched through the compound's demolished gate and down the empty road leading to the edge of the city. Here they were deposited in a small room in Tsarong House, the private home of one of Tibet's great popular leaders, Wangchuk

Gyalpo Tsarong, which had been requisitioned by the PLA as a collection point for prisoners. Dr. Choedrak stayed there for two days, incarcerated with other prisoners in the room once lived in by Heinrich Harrer. During this time, he received no food or water. More than once he heard bursts of machine-gun fire mowing down those who tried to escape. As his second night began, his group was summoned and marched in a new detail to PLA headquarters. There, he was brought to a maximum-security prison, originally built by the Chinese to hold their own people: two stockades surmounted by barbed wire, the outer corners of which were capped with guard towers manned by sentries. Each quad housed 350 prisoners, in 12 30-man cells facing the central courtyard; the northeast quad contained additional isolation cells.

Relieved of their watches and jewelry, the Tibetans were manacled—some merely in handcuffs, others, like Dr. Choedrak, in foot-and-a-half-long leg irons. The irons were so cumbersome that Dr. Choedrak had to untie the cloth laces of his boots and loop them around the bar, lifting it each time he took a step.

Unprepared for the inundation of prisoners following the revolt, the PLA took six days to classify Dr. Choedrak's group (with subsequent detainees this classification was performed immediately). Members of the upper classes—lamas, physicians, government workers and traders—were kept in the maximum security prison, the others were sent to the Norbulingka. Those who remained soon realized they had been singled out as prize prisoners, the core of the alleged "reactionary clique." Once informed that the "local government" had been dissolved, they were told that, as its chief "running dogs," criminal charges would be preferred against them. It was then announced that the first duty of every prisoner was to "study" so as to acknowledge his crimes. The initial question asked was: "Who fed you?" The correct answer: "The people—whom I exploited." To reveal his "crimes," each prisoner was compelled to dictate an autobiography from the age of eight—a process that lasted a month. Thereafter, seven months of study, self-criticism and *thamzing* followed —their goal to elicit a confession of crimes and a sincere adoption of Communist ideology.

In essence, the procedures mirrored those imposed on the population at large. In prison, however, they were conducted with far greater rigor. Dr. Choedrak's case was, moreover, exacerbated by two incidents. One morning while washing his face in the prison lavatory, he found himself next to a fellow physician from Mendzekhang. Though guards stood all around, he seized the chance to relate a piece of news he had just heard.

It was May, and the Dalai Lama's arrival in Mussoorie had been reported in a Chinese newspaper seen by some prisoners. "There's no need to worry now," Tenzin Choedrak whispered to the doctor. "Gyalwa Rinpoché—the Precious King—is safe in India. Soon the truth will come out." Under the pressure of *thamzing*, the man reported the comment to the Chinese. Meanwhile, as struggle sessions got underway in his own cell, Dr. Choedrak proceeded to make an even more serious mistake. Three of the five friends with whom he had exchanged anti-Chinese sentiments in the past were in the prison. Observing how the smallest incident was elevated into a crime, he wrote to warn the men to avoid mentioning their conversations. Though he delivered the notes undetected all three were later caught and under pressure identified Dr. Choedrak as the writer. Following this discovery he was immediately put on trial, accused of being an accomplice of Gyalo Thondup, who, according to the Chinese, had masterminded the revolt, on the behest of Taiwan.

The trial began early in June. An officer, accompanied by two adjutants carrying pistols, entered Tenzin Choedrak's cell, leaving a sentry armed with an assault rifle just outside the door. The officer motioned his assistants to one side and ordered Dr. Choedrak to sit in the middle of the room, surrounded by his fellow prisoners.

The few episodes of *thamzing* already witnessed by Tenzin Choedrak had been gruesome. They included an interrogation device peculiar to the Communists, which was worse than that used by the Kuomintang during its occupation of eastern Kham. The Nationalists had merely tied a prisoner's hands behind his back and then to a rope around his neck. The new technique was considerably more complex. The rope was first laid across the front of the prisoner's chest and then spiraled down each arm. The wrists were then tied together and pulled backwards over the man's head. Next the rope-ends were drawn under either armpit, threaded through the loop on the chest and pulled abruptly down. Immediately the shoulders turned in their sockets, wrenching the prisoner in a grisly contortion without, though, strangling him. The pain from this torture was so great that a man would invariably lose control of his bowels and bladder.

Dr. Choedrak's trial began with questioning. He was asked about his life in Choday Gonpa, the monastery he had lived in before attending medical school. He replied matter-of-factly that he had studied religion. "What were your thoughts though? You must have had bourgeois tendencies?" the officer asked. Not comprehending precisely what a "bourgeois tendency" was, Dr. Choedrak was unable to respond. As the questioning progressed, however, his silence turned into willful intransigence. The

Chinese, he realized, had singled him out for a specific purpose: to defame the Dalai Lama's character. To avoid *thamzing*, the officer informed him, he would have to detail every element of the "Dalai's plots"—the comings and goings at Yabshi House, what foreigners Gyalo Thondup was in contact with and the exact nature of their discussions. Furthermore, he continued, though the Dalai Lama posed as a religious man, it would have been apparent to Dr. Choedrak, of all people, that, in reality, he was a thief and a murderer who also had affairs with women—in particular, his own eldest sister, Tsering Dolma. Expected to verify the accusations, Tenzin Choedrak continually replied that, as medical officer to the Tibetan leader, he saw the Dalai Lama only briefly each day at dawn to read his pulse. "To denounce His Holiness with these lies was unthinkable," the doctor explained. "For us Tibetans he is like our parents, our very own heart. Who could say such things?"

Nonetheless three prisoners in Dr. Choedrak's group chose—after receiving *thamzing*—to support the Chinese. Becoming "activists," they turned on the others and were rewarded by removal from the cell. If found to be lenient during subsequent struggle sessions, they were pointedly asked: "Are you breathing from the same mouth as this man? Are you wearing the same pants?": questions sufficient to keep them in the forefront of the attacks. Thus, Dr. Choedrak knew his time for *thamzing* had come when, after a few more days of interrogation, the PLA commander singled out the activists one morning for praise: "You have been doing very well, it's commendable." he said. "But today we must get to the bottom of this reactionary nest. You should question Tenzin Choedrak very closely. You must find the truth." Shortly after the day's questioning began, the officer stared at the activists, whereupon one stood up and said, "If you continue to lie like this, it will only lead in one direction, the dark way. So for your own sake, you'd better tell us everything you know." As he spoke the others grabbed Dr. Choedrak, and tied his arms across a long board in a variation of the method that had previously been used. Trailing the rope off either end they pulled Tenzin Choedrak's arms tight while his questioner demanded in a shrieking tone that he denounce the Dalai Lama for having committed incest with his sister. When Dr. Choedrak refused, the man took off one of his shoes and started beating him across the face. This was the signal for the other cellmates to join in—which, under the careful scrutiny of the guards, they did—pulling the doctor's hair and ears, spitting in his face and pummeling his head. The pain in his arms was so great that Dr. Choedrak began to scream but only when his legs gave way and he collapsed did the officer call a halt. After a short rest, the beating began again, repeating the pattern throughout the morning. Finally, completely numb, his face and body bleeding, swollen and covered with black welts, Tenzin Choedrak heard the officer conclude the session. It had lasted four hours. Once he was untied, placed back in handcuffs and leg irons, the Chinese officer spoke directly to Dr. Choedrak. "If you reveal the truth and admit what the Dalai Lama has done, your future will be bright. This need never happen again. You will be released," he said. "Now remember what your friends have asked you today and think it over well." With that, Dr. Choedrak was removed from the cell and taken to the prison's northeast quad where he was thrown into isolation.

When he recovered, Dr. Choedrak found himself in a dark room, four by eight feet, with a small, barred window, high in one wall, and a six-inch-square hole for receiving food. On the mud floor lay a straw mat, a discarded PLA overcoat and a bucket for relieving himself. He had been in prison for two and a half months. He was to spend the next four in isolation—the remainder of the summer of 1959. Throughout, an inviolable routine governed his existence. In the morning, kitchen workers opened the hatch by the door and as best he could, in irons and cuffs, he got to his feet, stuck his bowl out and received a small steamed bun together with some rice and a vegetable. After eating, he was required to sit on the mat and think over his crimes for the entire day. He could not lie down or rest, as periodically, the door of the food portal would snap back and the eyes of a Chinese guard appear, making sure that he was visibly pondering. His only relief was a brief glimpse of sky and breath of air on the evening walk to the toilet. In reality, Dr. Choedrak's thoughts were confused and depressed. After the pain of the beating wore off, he fell into a stupor, staring for hours at a time at the stone walls, convinced that he would soon be executed. He imagined the rows upon rows of people on either side of him, all locked in the dark, waiting to die. At night his dreams were a chaotic mix of memories: his childhood, medical studies and practice blended with scenes from his arrest, prison life and the beating. When he woke, he found his only hope in wishing for death. Suicide, though, even if he had devised a method, was ruled out. A monk from Namgyal Monastery had killed himself by jumping into the Kyichu River when the prisoners had been taken out to bathe. But this was an exception. Like most Tibetans Dr. Choedrak dreaded the results of suicide even more than present suffering, no matter how great it became. As he said, "With so many life forms in this world and so few people, it is extremely hard to be born as a human being. So if you destroy this precious human life, we believe it is very sinful. It is like having a sack of gold and without utilizing it, just throwing it into the river. According to Buddhist teachings, if you do commit suicide, you will have no hope of being reborn in a human existence for at least five hundred lives."

On the last day of each week, two guards would enter Dr. Choedrak's cell, yell for him to stand up and then escort him at rifle point to a bell-shaped tent pitched in the center of the prison courtyard. Inside, an officer from the Public Security Bureau sat behind a bare table with a Tibetan interpreter on one side. Pushed onto a mat on the ground, Dr. Choedrak was subjected to interrogation: "Have you decided to tell the truth?" the questioning always began. When Tenzin Choedrak responded that he had told the truth all along, the officer would lose his temper, shout, "What have you been thinking about for these six days?" and, taking his pistol from its holster, bang it on the table. After a few sessions he threatened Dr. Choedrak with "consequences" for his obstinacy. At the end of a month's time they came.

Halfway through July, Dr. Choedrak was subjected to a second session of *thamzing*. Removed one morning from isolation, marched to the southern quad and placed in the center of his old cellmates as before, he was asked by the officer in charge: "Have you recognized reality yet? Do you now have a confession to make?" Despite his fear, Dr. Choedrak refused to comply and, tied to the board once more, was beaten. Struck repeatedly across the face with heavy boots, his vision soon blurred, not so much from blood but from damage to his eyes. By the time he was dragged back to his cell a few hours later, Tenzin Choedrak realized that the retina of his left eye had been detached and the eyeball itself knocked to the upper left side of its socket, so that it could no longer focus straight ahead. During the next few days, he discovered that the entire upper row of his teeth had come loose. At first he was able to push the teeth back in place but within a month all of them, one by one, had fallen out, leaving bruised holes in his still swollen and bloody gums. Although the immediate pain wore off, Dr. Choedrak's shattered mouth and eye remained as a permanent legacy of his second *thamzing*. Nevertheless, a third, substantially worse beating occurred the next month.

In August, after repeatedly "failing" his weekly interrogation, Dr. Choedrak was again returned to his old cell. The same incredulous questions ensued, followed by the board and a virtual storm of beatings ordered by the enraged officer. As his arms were pulled from their sockets, his head and face becoming swollen from repeated blows, Dr. Choedrak gradually lost all sense of pain. He seemed to float in a dull daze; his single sensation that of an intense dryness in the mouth. The dryness increased, and then suddenly he blacked out. He regained consciousness, still imagining blows. In reality he was lying on the floor of the isolation cell; a bucket of cold water had just been thrown over his face. When the guards saw that Dr. Choedrak had revived, they yanked him to his feet, handcuffed him and then let him collapse on the mat.

Dr. Choedrak's next impression was of a group of men entering his cell. One of them, clearly a Chinese physician, examined him. Months later, back with his original cellmates, Dr. Choedrak heard what had occurred. Following his collapse, a PLA doctor had been sent for, there being, in fact, a premium on Tenzin Choedrak's life. After his examination the doctor pronounced Dr. Choedrak on the verge of death and refused to take responsibility for the case. The news was relayed to the prison camp commander who dispatched a senior officer to the cell group. In the presence of the officer in charge, the aide warned that if Tenzin Choedrak died, the prisoners themselves would be held accountable and punished: "Why did you beat this man?" he asked. "It is not the policy of the Chinese Communist Party to beat prisoners. You are meant only to study, not to harm yourselves. Now you will discuss why you have done this, and who is to blame." Soon afterwards, *thamzing* ceased—not, however, due to a new policy of leniency, but simply because the initial process of determining who were the most dangerous reactionaries was complete.

On October 15, 1959, the prison's seven hundred inmates were drawn up in long files surrounded by Chinese troops, in the southern quad. Seated at a small table before them, the camp commander spoke, "Among you there is a very stubborn group who persist in telling lies and refuse to recognize the truth," he said. "We have decided to send them for further study in China. Conditions are far better there than here. Food is more plentiful, and their needs will be amply provided for." The results of seven months of interrogation were then read out: 4 prisoners were to be released and 21 would be sent to work at the hydroelectric plant at Nachen Thang. The 76 men bound for China were to leave within two weeks. The prisoners, however, were not told who had been selected for the last contingent until three days before their departure. At that time, on the morning of October 29, Dr. Choedrak was informed that he had been picked. Because neither charge nor sentence had been given him, he didn't actually believe he was going to China. Instead, he assumed that the selected prisoners were to be taken somewhere nearby and, under one pretense or another, executed, their separation having been for this purpose only.

The next day Tenzin Choedrak's handcuffs and leg irons were removed and, along with the seventy-five other men, he was driven to the Norbulingka. Quartered there for two nights and a day, Dr. Choedrak gradually made the acquaintance of his new prison mates—all of whom had held high positions in Tibetan society and government. The men were of one mind: even if China was, in fact, their destination, singled out as they were, there could be little doubt that their remaining time was limited. Their fear increased when, on the morning of their departure, they were permitted to bid farewell to their relatives. As dawn broke the prisoners were brought near a wall, from where two or three at a time were called to a window for a strictly allotted few minutes with their families. Despite Chinese threats to cancel the meeting if a single Tibetan showed emotion, everyone wept. The guards then ordered those who had yet to go forward to console their relatives. They were fortunate. They were going to the motherland itself—to receive education. On the far side of the wall the families—all of whom had brought food, clothing and blankets—were assured that their relatives would be living under the best possible conditions in China. Nonetheless, the prisoners were permitted to accept the gifts.

When Dr. Choedrak's name was called, he walked to the window and saw his elder brother Topgyal. In tears and unable to speak, Topgyal took Tenzin Choedrak's hands in his. Dr. Choedrak then said, "Now it's best that you forget about me forever. You must go back home and take good care of yourself." Topgyal offered him *tsamba*, a woolen sleeping rug, two blankets, some clothes, a food bowl and a washbasin. He bent over and unlaced his tall Tibetan boots, but Tenzin Choedrak refused to take them, insisting, "You'll need to walk in these boots. I won't."

Their farewells completed, the prisoners were directed into two roofless troop trucks, a soldier mounted on the corners of each. A truck bearing a machine gun aimed at the Tibetans led; another, carrying ten soldiers and a second machine gun, took up the rear. With no room to sit, the thirty-eight prisoners in each truck stood shoulder to shoulder and stared in silence as the engines started and they were driven off, their wives throwing dust and crying after them the traditional phrase for dispelling sorrow, "Let all of Tibet's suffering be gone with you! And now be done!"

Dr. Choedrak and his companions were indeed en route to China. November 1 had been earmarked for a massive transfer of prisoners from the capital; numerous convoys had already set out ahead of them and as they passed Drepung, the road behind filled with six more trucks, transporting three hundred young monks from the monastery, all thirteen and fourteen years old. Grown to ten trucks and over four hundred people, the convoy headed north for Damshung, and its first major stop, Nagchuka. For the entire journey, the prisoners, forced to stand, were whipped by the late-autumn wind as they repeatedly crossed 15,000-foot passes. Nighttime provided little respite. Jammed into the largest quarters available in whichever village they stopped in—often, for convenience' sake, a single room—half the men had to sit on one another's laps for lack of space. Every night was punctuated by loud yells as arms or legs were trampled. Those who had to relieve themselves could do so only in their bowls, which they then had to hold so that nothing would spill. Irritability was heightened by the drastically reduced rations, now down only to a cup of boiled water and six steamed flour dumplings a day.

On the eleventh day, the column halted on the north shore of Lake Kokonor. Herded into boxcars on a railroad, the prisoners rode east, toward Langzhou, the capital of Gansu province. Though few had seen a train before, they were too exhausted to care. Together, they sat in silence bunched against the cold, watching the light dance between the slats of the car's walls. After one day they arrived at Langzhou, and the two groups were separated. While the young monks remained on board to continue farther into China, Dr. Choedrak's group was placed in trucks and driven north once more. Though Langzhou had been the jumping-off point for the Great Silk Road for centuries, the surrounding countryside was empty, perennially ignored by the Chinese and populated only by the Hui, Moslem people, now a minority themselves. On the city's northern edge, the silt-filled Yellow River ran west to east. Beyond lay Mongolia, its alien nature attested to by the ruins of the Great Wall and the edge of the Gobi Desert.

It was toward an outcrop of the Gobi, the Tengger Desert, that the prisoners were driven. A giant tract of flat rocky debris, the Tengger served as a springboard for windstorms and fierce winter gales which rifled the featureless land between it and the Wall. This forlorn expanse was traditionally spoken of as having "three too-many's"—too much wind, sand and rock—and "three too-few's"—too little rain, grass and soil. It had always been an area of transit—Mongols passing through, north to south and back on pilgrimage to Tibet, traders moving east or west on the Silk Road. The Communists, however, had found a new, seemingly ideal use for the region—as a vast zone for prisons.

The number of prison camps dotting the barren landscape of northern Gansu and Amdo (renamed Chinghai by the Chinese) was known only to those in Peking. Nevertheless, the general estimate was that these two provinces contained a vast sea of prison camps housing up to 10 million inmates, a "black hole," as a 1979 *Time* magazine article dubbed it, "from which little information ever reached the outside world or even the rest of China."

Owing to its 300,000 square miles of inaccessible terrain, Chinghai had been designated, soon after 1949, as the future site of most of China's prisons. In the early fifties, small camps, holding a few hundred prisoners, had begun as tent compounds surrounded by barbed wire—sometimes electrified. As their first task, the inmates had constructed their own prison walls out of brick or mud. By the middle of the decade, these had given way to colonies of prisons—fortress-like compounds lining dirt roads for miles at a stretch. Containing from 1,000 to 10,000 inmates each, the archipelagos provided the backbone of the system. The strip north of Langzhou, for which Dr. Choedrak's group was destined, was considered the worst. It was followed in severity by four zones, two north and one south of Chinghai's capital, Xining, the fourth, four hundred miles due west, on the way to Xinjiang. Prisons and labor camps, though interspersed with nomad flocks, distinguished the entire countryside.

At sunset, the Tibetans passed through a ragged village of packed-mud houses, by a few stunted trees. Five miles beyond, they caught their first sight of Jiuzhen Prison. Four fortress-like stockades, set a sizable distance from one another, constituted the camp. Approaching one, the trucks passed staff quarters and a group of outbuildings behind which the prison's twenty-foot-high five-foot-thick brick walls stretched a half-mile long by 1,000 feet wide. Two guard towers rose on either side of the red flag raised over the gate in the eastern wall; one was positioned at the center of the western wall. Within stood seven cellblocks, housing 1,700 prisoners, in either fourteen- or twenty-seven-man rooms, built in files down the central yard. The kitchen ran along the western wall; the toilets were in a block in the southwest corner. A single notice board hung to the left of the gate. In the main, the prisoners were Chinese and Hui of high social standing: ex-officers of the Moslem warlord Ma Bufeng's army, as well as doctors, professors, judges, civil servants and other members of the intelligentsia now marked as reactionary. It was clear there was no hope for escape: the area was far too barren and remote to live alone in for more than a few days.

Inside the yard, the men were processed by four Tibetan and Chinese officials who had accompanied them, working together with the Jiuzhen authorities. Each was given a hat, a pair of gloves, a padded cotton blanket and either a black or a navy blue prison suit, the pants of which, held up by a string tie, were so baggy that they were soon nicknamed "clumsy pants." Their parcels were individually searched and almost everything—including bedding, eating utensils and extra clothing—was taken. Then they were led to their quarters: three of the large twenty-seven-man cells located by the toilets on the south side of the prison behind an internal wall that closed them off from the main courtyard. The cells were identical.

The front door of each cell was bordered by windows, their panes blocked by sheets of newspaper, but with enough clear space for guards to look through. A small foyer stood before a central aisle bisecting two mud platforms which ran the length of the room. The platforms were two feet off the floor and covered with straw to sleep on. They were the prison version of *kangs*, the traditional bed of northwestern China under which a fire was kindled in winter to keep sleepers warm. As there was no fuel for the prisoners, though, there was no heat. Huddled together the first night, the Tibetans discovered that there was barely enough space for thirteen or fourteen people on each *kang*. Fights broke out, until finally, a few days after their arrival, the men scratched demarcation lines into the brick wall above each person's head. The divisions revealed that there was no more than a foot and a half of width space available for a single sleeper.

Two other Tibetans were already in the camp. After being placed in with the group it was then learned from them that they were the sole survivors of three hundred monks from Labrang Tashikhiel, Amdo's second-largest monastery, imprisoned three years before, in 1956. The rest had died from starvation. Two months later, when the first propaganda play was staged before the kitchens in the main yard, those from Central Tibet immediately noticed that the maroon curtain used for a backdrop had been fabricated from the robes of monks. Subsequently, during a work assignment in a storage room, one of their number came across the distinctive boots of Tibetan clerics, the soles worn off by hard labor and only the leather tops remaining, saved for a future use.

The day following their arrival the men were acquainted with Jiuzhen's rules. Communication, save for practical necessities, was forbidden. "This is a maximum-security camp for those who have committed the worst crimes," the guards informed them. "No spreading of reactionary rumors will be tolerated." On the basis of recommendations by the officials who had accompanied them, a "progressive" leader was appointed from each group of ten to fifteen prisoners. Although the leader lived side by side with his cellmates he was exempt from *thamzing*. In return, he was required to report the most minute occurrence down to potentially significant looks exchanged between their prisoners. Accordingly, from the first days of their new life in Jiuzhen, a second invisible prison held the men, a virtual moratorium on all human contact. The only statements made were for the informer's benefit and were stock phrases such as: "The new Communist leadership is so much better than the exploiters of the past." Or: "The conditions here are truly excellent, we are really enjoying it."

Each day, before dawn, the prisoners were mustered. Once in line before their cells, they were led in a rousing propaganda song, the first verse of which began: "Moscow has announced revolution so the imperialists are shivering with fear." They were then marched to work in the fields, returned briefly for lunch and, after the day's labor, required to sing again before dinner, which was served, as were all meals, in the cells by the kitchen staff. Following dinner, political "study session" lasted until ten o'clock, after which they slept. Every ten days each prisoner was subjected to a private interrogation session. In addition, prisoners were randomly taken to a small room in the staff quarters outside of Jiuzhen's walls where, for an entire day, four interrogators would question the man in turn, trying to wear him down by probing for "crimes" in the smallest details of his past life. Otherwise not a moment was spent away from the group, which was marched to and from the toilet as well as the worksite by armed guards.

It was the middle of the "three lean years," and Jiuzhen's produce was not for the prisoners' own consumption but that of the staff and the army units in the region. Guarded by the PLA, who shot on sight any man crossing his field's perimeter, each prisoner, equipped only with a shovel, had to break enough barren ground daily, including irrigation ditches, to be suitable for cultivating thirty pounds of wheat. The soil was turned a foot deep, covering an area of roughly 4,000 square feet. The task was so daunting that, even with clear soil, a strong man could barely manage to complete it. More often, the earth was hard and stony. In this case, after they had removed the larger rocks, the prisoners were ordered to fetch sand and clay from a nearby area in pairs; a long bamboo pole from which two baskets were hung suspended between them. The new earth was then mixed in with the old. Speed was of the essence. A point system rewarded those who completed their quota. Those who did not were punished. On returning from collecting sand, the inmate received a blue or a white slip of paper. Tabulated at day's end, the slips determined the number of baskets he had carried. The next day a red flag would be placed beside the field of the best team, whereas all those groups who had failed to approach its level were given increased labor time and a longer nightly meeting. Stretchers were always on hand for the frequent cases of collapse. If a field was close to the pickup point for sand, sixty trips could be made in a day, running both ways; if far, no more than twenty-five.

Reeducation proper took place at the nightly study meeting. The subjects generally fell under the heading of either China's domestic or foreign affairs. The most frequent topics dealt with the dictum that increasing production through hard labor was the key to social harmony and how, in the past, imperialist nations such as the United States, Great Britain and Japan had oppressed China. The prisoners were required to express individual opinions on the subject at hand. In the beginning, though, some of the men had yet to learn the correct terminology. Labeled "stone heads," they repeatedly suffered *thamzing* until soon, most knew what to say. The first man would begin: "Tibet was a feudal state run by reactionary serf owners and running dogs of the imperialists. Then, after Comrade Mao Zedong liberated the motherland, we struggled against the earth, fought against the sky and cultivated everything, so that now our people are living in peace, happiness and prosperity." The second man would improvise: "The imperialist and reactionary cliques worked hand in glove to exploit the masses. But now they have been overcome. This is because the Chinese Communists are the vanguard of all Communists. This is because Mao Zedong is the leader of the whole world. Right now he is the only one worthy of even being called a leader!"

With the arrival of summer, arid desert heat replaced the dry cold. Prisoners were issued baggy, gauze-like cotton uniforms. On the morning of May 1, 1960, six months after the Tibetans' arrival, the kitchen staff came to their cells bearing the usual basket of dumplings and a bucket of greens. The dumplings, though, were the size of an egg. When the prisoners asked why they were so small, they were told that rations had been cut from sixteen and a half to eight and a half pounds a month. Henceforth, three dumplings a day were given and they were no longer even made from wheat. To save yet more grain Jiuzhen's authorities had instituted the mixing of indigestible roots and barks with the food. Three types were most easily identified. The first was rotten bark taken from trees in an area of low-lying hills far from the camps. After it was powdered and mixed with the dough, the dumplings were tinged red; they left a heavy, painful feeling in the stomach. If ingested over too long a time the bark produced bleeding sores inside the stomach and intestines. After eating them for even a few days many of the men found blood in their stools. Chaff was also mixed in and, in the autumn, a further additive which destroyed the semblance of a bun altogether. This consisted of waste material from soybeans. With the kernel of the bean removed to make tofu for the staff, its remaining skin was steamed to form a sort of porridge mixed with flour. The gruel was so loose, though, that the steamer itself had to be brought to each cell, where two spoonfuls per man were dispensed. Over the winter, meals had included the exterior layers of cabbage and other leafy greens, their interiors already taken by the guards. Now a native plant with flat green leaves topped by a yellow flower was used. Collected by periodic details, the plant was boiled in water and one ladle's worth for each man given out. Altogether, a single meal comprised little more than a mouthful of food.

Hunger governed the prisoners' every thought. Order broke down. The strong bullied the weak over who had received a larger ladle of greens. Even when the Chinese took to skimming off each spoonful with a chopstick to make sure all the portions were of uniform size, the men's anguish about potentially unequal allotments focused itself as an obsession over the size of their bowls. There had never been a standard issue of containers. Thus, each man used what he had been permitted to retain from his relatives' gifts or, failing that, from containers he had somehow managed to pick up from guards. The assortment was varied. Dr. Choedrak had brought a mug as well as a washbasin. As the mug proved too small to eat from, he secretly procured a pair of scissors from a brigade of ex-prisoners, kept on as laborers, who lived outside Jiuzhen's walls. With these, he cut down the high sides of the basin so that it fit fully over his face and could easily be licked clean. Most were not so fortunate. Some had cups, others tin cans, the rest metal ashtrays—given out by the Chinese. Those worst off possessed only pieces of wood in which crude indentations were carved. Eventually, the men devised a system for randomly exchanging containers after the meals were portioned out and just before they ate. In this way, some measure of peace was restored, though as the next month unfolded it mattered little.

With the beginning of summer, the first symptom of starvation appeared: extreme enervation. While walking, their knees frequently buckled, and a number of the men found themselves unable to stand once they had fallen. Even if they managed to sit, their legs would not carry them until after a few hours of rest. By July one and all resembled living skeletons. Ribs, hips and shin bones protruded, their chests were concave, their eyes bulged, their teeth were loose. Gradually their eyebrows and hair, once shiny and black, turned russet, then beige and then it fell out, the hair coming loose from the skin with just a slight pull. Each morning, those who could rise placed both hands against the wall and inched up, carefully balancing their heads in an effort not to fall. Once erect, they would edge dizzily through the straw down the back of the *kang* toward the cell door. From there they would go to the toilets by supporting themselves against the window ledges and walls of the buildings en route. From now on no one could walk securely, much less run for baskets of sand. Leg joints felt locked in place; feet were dragged along, too heavy to lift. When the men returned to the prison at night, they lowered their bodies gingerly onto the platform, this time only one hand against the wall, the other used to steady the head; tilted to the side, its weight was sufficient to bring one crashing down, unable to check the fall.

The first man to die was a lama from Nagchuka. He had fainted many times in the fields, and was repeatedly carried by stretcher to the hospital room, where he was permitted to rest for a few days at a time. One day in September he could no longer lift himself from the sleeping platform. The prison guards arrived and demanded to know why he was not out working. He replied, "How can I work when I can't lift my legs or my head?" Then he added sarcastically, "Now I finally understand the policy of the Chinese Communist Party. It's very good. I'm a person who can't move and might live for just a day or two more—that's all—but I'm asked to go to work. This is truly a policy for the people." After this, he was taken to the hospital, where, as he had predicted, he died two days later.

This first death, which Dr. Choedrak and the others had expected almost daily for a year and a half, was notable only in that it had taken so long to occur. It was greeted indifferently; no mental breakdowns had occurred since arriving at Jiuzhen, no expression of fear or depression, and none appeared now. Save for continued quarreling over food, starvation had stunned all other feelings into abeyance. The Tibetans now recognized, though, that they would not be executed or tortured to death; they were to die through forced labor, so that the authorities—by their own standards at least—could appear blameless.

Within just a few days, the next man died—a government official named Rongda Jamyang, whose sister later married an American and moved to the United States. From then on, an average of two to three prisoners died every week with the longest interval between deaths lasting no more than a fortnight. The process was always the same. Those who succumbed without complications, from starvation alone, would simply lie immobile on the *kang*. Their breath became softer and more shallow until, at the last moment, bubbles of saliva slipped over their lips and they died. In some cases, a man would linger for months before passing away. The elder of the two monks from Tashikhiel, who had survived the demise of his 298 fellows, ultimately perished in this manner. For two months he remained prone, sustained by spoonfuls of gruel and water given by his fellow prisoners. After each feeding he regained some strength, looked around and even spoke briefly before relapsing into a semi-conscious state, saliva continually seeping from his mouth. For others, death would come after only a few days of lingering, as with another early victim, the ex-abbot of Gembung Lhakhang temple in Lhasa. Those who had died during the night were removed by the hospital staff, stripped of any useful possessions and placed in a pile in front of the toilets. Before dawn, the corpses were taken out of the camp by a three-man burial detail. The graveyard was a field not far from the prison walls. Its markers were made of hand-sized stones picked at random by the detail, who then wrote the prisoner's name in red enamel paint before placing the stone over the grave. The earth was so hard—frozen in winer, dry and tensile in summer—that only a shallow hole could be dug, into which, without ceremony, the naked body was thrown. Dr. Choedrak saw Chinese families wandering through this field, searching to retrieve the bones of a deceased relative. Some had come to visit from as far away as Peking or Shanghai, only to be informed of their family member's death on arrival. Lent a shovel, they were told to find the remains and take them away if they wished—a gruesome and heartbreaking ordeal, due to the sometimes incompletely decayed cadavers unearthed.

For the prisoners, a death occasionally provided an increase in rations —for a single day at least. If they were lucky, the loss could be hidden from the guards and the deceased's ration obtained. Dr. Choedrak himself benefited from this. Waking one morning, he noticed that the man lying next to him was unusually still. He nudged him, listened closely and realized that he was dead. By then, the prisoner on the fellow's far side had realized the same thing. By mutual consent, they managed to partially cover the dead man's head with his blanket, telling those around—and the Chinese, when they arrived—that he was too sick to move. By this, they obtained an extra portion of food, which they discreetly shared between themselves after the kitchen staff departed.

As the death rate increased the Tibetans began to consume their own clothes. Leather ropes, used to tie the bundles brought from Tibet, were cut into daily portions with stones and shovels. Each piece was slowly chewed during work, in the hope that some strength could thereby be gained. Small leather bags were put to the same use. Dr. Choedrak owned a fur-lined jacket, which had proved invaluable through the first winter, but in the course of the following summer he was compelled to eat it. He began with the fur. As winter came again, he managed to secure a small quantity of brush with which to make a fire under the *kang*. Piece by piece, he roasted the rest of his coat. Walking to and from the fields, prisoners picked as many plants—dandelions were a favorite—as they could eat, scavenged leaves from the few trees in the area, hunted for frogs and insects and dug for worms. One worm was particularly sought after as a source of grease, there being no fat of any kind in the diet. White, with a yellow head, the inmates nicknamed it "Mapa," after the best, most tasty form of *tsamba* mixed with butter.

A more constant source of food was the refuse discarded by Chinese guards. Crowds of prisoners would gather around bones or fruit rinds thrown by the roadside. Those lucky enough to have arrived first masticated their finds for hours to make them last. The results of this scavenging, though, could be perilous. One day Dr. Choedrak was assigned—in company with a low-level government official named Lobsang Thonden —to work on a garbage pile outside the prison walls. It was in a large area where the camp's waste was mixed in with human excrement before being taken to the fields as fertilizer. Together, the two men shoveled the feces into trunk-sized baskets, which were then carried off by their cellmates. As he shoveled, Lobsang Thonden came upon a small baby pig—pigs were kept by the staff—dead and almost completely decomposed. When the guards were not looking Lobsang retrieved it and whispered to Dr. Choedrak, "We should eat this. It might help us." Wiping the excrement from it, he pulled the pig apart to see if there was any edible flesh to be had. A portion about the length of an index finger remained, still red, between the shoulder blades. He then decided to take it back to the prison to eat more palatably with the evening's greens. Dr. Choedrak admonished his companion to consume the meat immediately. On one count, Tenzin Choedrak pointed out, he was so weak that it would be of instant benefit; on the other, if it was discovered during the check at the prison gate, there might be trouble. Lobsang Thonden ignored the advice. Instead, he placed the meat in his back pocket, where, as Dr. Choedrak had warned, it was found a few hours later at the evening check. The Tibetan's small piece of meat infuriated the prison guards. That night he was threatened and abused; the next day work was delayed and a public *thamzing* involving the entire camp was convened in the prison yard. Lobsang Thonden was brought forward and tied by the special method used to twist the shoulders in their sockets. The camp commander shouted indignantly: "Taking such unclean food is a grave insult to the Chinese Communist Party and to the nation itself. Eating anything that can be found is a direct attempt to abuse the government. The conditions and rations here are very good. Such an insult cannot be ignored. It must be corrected by *thamzing*." "Activist" prisoners jumped up to beat and "struggle" Lobsang Thonden in the usual manner, repeating the charges against him. Soon, however, he collapsed. Afterwards, he could no longer walk or care for himself and was taken to the hospital. There, for the one and a half inch of flesh, he died four days later.

Despite such harsh reprisals, the prisoners had nothing to lose and were little dissuaded. On one occasion a group of Chinese inmates attacked the kitchen staff—all of whom were fed to the point of being portly—as they were leaving the kitchen carrying baskets of dumplings. Grabbing all they could, the men ate as they ran away; yet by that night each had been identified and punished. Unprovoked cruelty was common as well. While Dr. Choedrak was in the toilet one day, a Chinese prisoner came in to relieve himself. The man was so weak that when he squatted down, he fell on the floor, foaming from his mouth, unable to move. A guard entered. He began kicking the prisoner, berating him for lying in the toilet until, in a minute's time, he died on the spot. Taunting was a favored means of abuse. Dr. Choedrak witnessed a Chinese inmate being dragged helplessly to the fields, the guards reproaching him for being "too lazy to work." After moving about listlessly for a few minutes, he simply collapsed and died. On another occasion Chinese inmates were discovered eating a donkey's head which they had retrieved from the same pile of feces and garbage that Lobsang Thonden's pig had been in. Handcuffed and severely beaten, they were brought in front of 900 prisoners for *thamzing*. The prison staff railed at them, "You Kuomintang officials have badly abused the poor people under you, and now you're even abusing the Communist Party by eating a donkey's head. This is why you're dying, because you don't know how to look after yourselves." Twice Dr. Choedrak himself received *thamzing* for "insulting behavior" concerning food. In one instance he was caught eating cabbage leaves from the manure pile. The other involved his training as a physician. With the traditional Tibetan doctor's vast knowledge of plants, he quietly advised prisoners what to eat and what not to eat in the fields, despite the risk of such unapproved communication. Discovered, he was brought to trial once more on the grounds that his actions were premeditated provocation of the authorities, who maintained throughout that the entire camp was receiving "ample sustenance."

Dr. Choedrak's advice, though, was badly needed. Prisoners ate anything they came across. Some items were not so dangerous. One cellmate managed to find the knee joint of a small sheep. There was no meat on the bone, but for an entire month he kept it hidden under his bedding, taking it out each night for a few precious gnawings. On New Year's Day, to demonstrate magnanimity, a single mule was boiled for the entire prison. A friend of Dr. Choedrak, a steward for a noble family in Tibet, noticed that the water the animal was cooked in had been thrown by a staff member onto a refuse pile not far from the kitchen. Though not the toilet proper, this was a place where prisoners also went to relieve themselves, and the whole area was covered with pools of urine. Regardless, Dr. Choedrak's friend ran to the mound with his mug and collected all the surface dirt he could, in the hope that some of the boiled water could be strained out of it. He showed Dr. Choedrak the soaked mud and asked if he thought this would benefit him. Like every prisoner, the steward had been suffering from an inability to sleep, difficulty with his vision and a constant loud rushing noise in the ear—all caused, according to Tibetan medicine, by the rising of "lung" or wind, which was produced by starvation. Dr. Choedrak agreed that if he could succeed in getting some of the soup water separated from the mud and urine, it would help to repress the "lung." The man did so and actually felt better for a short while. But other cases were not so salutary. People were dying in the most horrible manner from abrupt dysfunctions in their digestive tracts. A prisoner named Gyaltsen Dagpa, whom Tenzin Choedrak was unable to assist, perished when his intestines burst. For weeks he had been indiscriminately picking and eating whatever wild grass he could find. Soon he had a bad case of diarrhea and after a few days a viscous, jelly-like substance emerged with his stools. Then, only water was ejected. At this point, whenever the man ate or drank he would scream from the excruciating pain. Soon the pain became constant, and he could no longer consume either liquids or solids. For two days he lay on the *kang* clutching his stomach, screaming, and then he died. Dr. Choedrak deduced that the interior lining of the man's intestine had been scraped away by the roughage, accounting for the viscous substance. Once worn through, the intestine then burst—at which stage, when the man drank water, it passed into his abdomen, causing intense pain. At the very end, when nothing at all emerged, the internal wound had disrupted the digestive tract entirely and become fatal. Another man, named Teykhang Chopel, succumbed when his sphincter cracked apart due to the hard indigestible objects lodged in his intestine.

Though he knew what not to eat, Dr. Choedrak could not endure such conditions long. As the anniversary of the Tibetan's first year at Jiuzhen arrived, he too collapsed and was taken to the hospital—a place visited at one time or another by all the prisoners. It was here, during an intermittent stay lasting three months, that he gained a view of camp life outside the isolation of his own group's daily existence. The hospital itself—no more than a barren room—existed as such in name only. There was virtually no medical equipment or supplies except for a few ointments for applying to wounds and some Chinese herbs said to help digestion. On occasion, when a patient was in the most dire condition, a shot of glucose would be administered or a mug of carrot juice given. The main function of the hospital staff was to dispose of the dead, many of whom had perished on its premises. Staff members were mostly prisoners who had received the jobs as a reward for being "progressive." It was, in fact, a substantial dividend. Not only did the assignment replace grueling field labor; it also provided a veritable cornucopia of extra food, the staff routinely disguising deaths and thus continuing to receive the dead men's rations.

The hospital was run by three so-called doctors, all prisoners, but only one of whom was actually a physician. There was little he could do. The other two were the only women in Jiuzhen. Both were rather remarkable. They belonged to the work brigade of semi-released prisoners who lived beyond the camp's walls. They too had once served terms within the prison, but, via a policy applied throughout the Chinese penal system, they were not released following completion of their sentences. Instead, their status was merely upgraded to that of "permanent laborer" and freedom forever postponed. Such laborers no longer received food, but had to toil, as did the population at large, for "work points," which enabled them to purchase rationed grain. In Jiuzhen, the 800 to 900 additional people so classified were mainly allotted the light labor of planting fields the prisoners had already broken.

Of the two women doctors, one was compassionate and selfless, the other driven and businesslike. The kind woman was a Christian, and fearlessly so: she openly wore a cross around her neck even after receiving repeated *thamzing.* An energetic and skilled worker, the guards had come to depend on her despite her attempts to thwart their practice of forcing patients back to field work. Her care was the sole sign of humanity in the prison. In one case witnessed by Dr. Choedrak, a Chinese inmate, bedridden for months, developed severe bedsores over his entire body. Once infected, the sores filled with maggots. Each morning the woman arrived from outside the prison walls and sat by his side to pick the maggots from the sores one at a time. Going to the kitchen, she obtained ashes from the stoves which she carefully strained so that only a fine powder remained. Spreading this on a large cloth, she placed it beneath the man. Whereupon great numbers of maggots fell off. The patient eventually died, but until the end, she continued to relieve him in this way.

The second woman, named Wangchen, was, with the male physician, at the hub of a thriving black market. At night carrot juice was brought to the hospital by the kitchen staff—one carrot's worth for each patient who had been put on a list by the doctors. Coming into the room, the staff would announce, "Carrot juice is ready," at which point, Dr. Choedrak noticed, the same three Tibetans always received portions though they were far from the worst cases. At the time, he could only guess the reasons. Suspicious themselves, the authorities called in the doctors and the patients concerned, and soon had it out that the latter had bribed the former with such articles as shoes and even a German fountain pen brought from Lhasa. But long before this news was made public, Tenzin Choedrak himself was deeply involved in this new avenue for survival.

Wangchen's activities went far beyond small bribes taken from those under her care. The bulk of her business involved serving as go-between for transactions amongst the prisoners and the labor brigade. Whatever goods were dealt, she always took a large commission in kind. While the prisoners procured bits of clothing to trade, the laborers had worked out a technique for obtaining extra dumplings. To discourage theft of the grain given out for planting, Jiuzhen's guards coated it with poison before distribution to the laborers. Despite this precaution, because they were never searched, the laborers stole handfuls at a time, which they later washed. This they cooked for their own fare, reserving the dumplings they received from the prison kitchen, on the basis of their work points, to trade through Wangchen. Dr. Choedrak offered Wangchen an old *chuba*, the wool of which had been rubbed off. In exchange he received thirty dumplings: unfortunately, the kind tinged red from rotten bark. Of these, Wangchen took five as commission, and he obtained the rest two or three at a time over a month. But whatever the black market offered, it was still far less than that required for subsistance. Hence, the prisoners continued to eat whatever they could. One day Dr. Choedrak saw a Chinese inmate holding a long red worm in his cup. Through a fellow Tibetan who spoke Chinese he asked where he had found it. The man replied that he had defecated the worm in his stool. Careful not to be caught by the guards, he had picked it out, washed it and brought it back from the toilet to eat —which he did that day mixed in with his other food.

The hospital also served as an additional place for interrogation. Shortly after a Tibetan was admitted, he would be visited by the security cadres, whose ongoing task was to question the prisoners. Their purpose was dual. While it was clear that the authorities considered a man's borderline state to be fertile ground for extracting a confession—hunger accomplishing what struggle sessions and beatings had, as yet, failed to achieve —interrogations also discouraged inmates from entering the hospital and thus kept them at work filling the labor quotas.

At the beginning of 1961, Tenzin Choedrak was released from the hospital and resumed work. His recovery was due not only to rest but also to his own form of cure. He had noticed one symptom shared by all those who died: severe diarrhea. In most, a thin watery stool was constantly emitted; to absorb this flow, a rag had to be kept in the pants. In Tibetan medical theory, Dr. Choedrak knew, the digestive power or heat of the stomach is the key to health, the level of digestive heat determining not only metabolism but, through it, the harmonic function of the three humors. In Jiuzhen, however, this heat had been subjected to a twofold attack: from the severe cold and the consumption of coarse, indigestible material with no grease or fat. To increase his digestive heat, Dr. Choedrak

quietly practiced, for half an hour each night, an advanced form of meditation—called Tum-mo Bar Zar, literally meaning "Rising and Falling
Heat." After his cellmates had gone to sleep, Dr. Choedrak visualized
purifying energy—in the form of white light—suffusing him, drawn in
with each inhalation to a point just below his navel. Picturing a triangular
flame the size of a rose thorn, he imagined it extending up the central
channel of his body, through the tantric energy centers at the navel,
stomach, heart, throat and crown of his head where, burning away the
layers of mental impurity, it released a fountain of clear, nectar-filled light
which returned, blissfully, down his body. He would then conceive all of
the sufferings experienced in prison to be washed away, replaced by the
ineffable joy embodied in the light. "In the beginning, one just imagines
all this," he recalled. "But after five or six months there was an unmistakable improvement, a slight rise in body heat. I was very weak, but I never
had any more diarrhea or other digestive problems. Also, despite all the
suffering we experienced, the meditation gave me more courage. I had no
more fear, I just accepted my fate."

Dr. Choedrak returned to work at the worst possible time. The death
toll had soared since early autumn. There was now more room on the kang
—one could turn in one's sleep—but lacking a fire, the prisoners still had
to huddle together. The winter weather made work almost impossible.
Their hands and feet wrapped in whatever scraps of cloth they could find,
the men trudged to the fields under guard, where, in a frozen wasteland,
they were expected to break the same amount of ground as they had in
summer. The sores on their hands never seemed to heal, making it agoniz-
ing even to hold a shovel. Paradoxically though, the weather provided an
occasional respite in the form of the so-called Mongolian wind. Rushing
down from the Tengger Desert, the wind collected the gobi or rocky sand
beneath it into a whirl of stone and dust which, resembling a needle from
a distance, struck down from the sky, scouring the land. The first warning
of its onslaught came from the village of Jiuzhen, five miles away. Over
the intervening fields the prisoners heard the town's loudspeakers faintly
call for the inhabitants to take cover, at which time their own guards would
send up a cry to retreat to the ditches they had dug for refuge around the
work site. Here the prisoners could rest for up to three hours, battered
from above by pebbles and debris, but otherwise undisturbed, until the
all-clear command was given and work resumed.

By the spring of 1961, forty of the original seventy-six Tibetans had
died. The worst, though, was still to come. Even beyond the camp, no
place in the countryside could hope to break loose from the tide of starvation. The prison itself was now sought out as a source of hope by the

people of Jiuzhen village. The first sign that the local population was suffering as well came with the admittance of two new prisoners, both Chinese, from the town. One, a little man with a slightly hunched back, was so hungry that he had killed and eaten an eight-year-old boy. Although cannibalism was unknown within the prison walls, the prisoners had, on occasion, joked about it. Now the surviving Tibetans nicknamed the man "the Vulture"—after the vultures who were given corpses to eat in Tibet. The second arrival, an eighteen-year-old boy, had killed his own mother for nine pounds of flour which she had refused to part with.

More direct evidence of life in the village of Jiuzhen was witnessed by the prisoners later that summer while laboring in the fields. Looking up from his work one day, Dr. Choedrak saw a large group of children, carrying small bamboo baskets, heading toward one of the fields. They were of all ages and all uniformly destitute—barefoot, emaciated and naked save for ragged shirts. Dr. Choedrak did not notice them again until some time later, when he heard a nearby officer detailing a detachment of guards to round up the children and bring them to the prison. At the end of the day, passing the field where the children had been, the Tibetans saw that the beans planted for that year's crop had all been dug up. Later they heard that when prison guards asked the children which adults had sent them to steal the beans, they replied that none had; they were so hungry they had come on their own. Unwilling to arrest them, the authorities sent the group home. The guards, however, remained extremely sensitive about this clear evidence of famine. Their ire was such that one prisoner, overheard referring to the children as "human birds," received *thamzing* for this single comment.

A second incident, soon after, could not be denied. Dr. Choedrak's group was now working on a field some distance from the prison. To get to it, they had to use the main road. As in many places in China, the road was lined on either side with trees. Beneath one of these, the inmates, on their way to work one day, came across a young mother in her late teens. She was plainly starving, her face and body badly swollen. Clinging in tears to her was a child of six and another four years old. The group leader stopped the procession and asked if she would like some vegetable to eat. The woman replied, "There's no point in living any longer under such a government as this. I'd rather die. I don't want this vegetable you're offering me." The prisoners left her and went on. The next day, they passed again and saw the family still hanging listlessly about the road. On the third morning, the prisoners found them lying across one another, still at the foot of the trees, all dead.

Finally, the starvation in town was brought home to the prison itself.

It began with an act Dr. Choedrak himself participated in. On the way to the toilets one afternoon, Dr. Choedrak and a companion named Champa Thondup encountered a young Chinese girl who had managed to slip into the prison. She was extremely thin, but swollen, her hair light brown and matted. On seeing them, she begged for something to eat. They managed to get her a small portion of vegetables and water and then watched as she started to consume them. The moment she ate, however, fluid poured from her nostrils and she began to cry out in pain—a common symptom of extreme famine. Hearing the commotion, the staff took her to the kitchen, where they gave the girl one egg-sized bun and then sent her back to the village. The result of their charity became apparent the next day. As the prisoners passed through the gate on their way to work, they witnessed a mass assault on the prison walls by scores of men and women from Jiuzhen demanding food. A full-scale melee ensued until, beaten back with rifle butts by the guards, the townspeople retreated across the fields.

Despite the breakdown of conditions within their domain and the chaos without, the Chinese prison officials never deviated from their policies. With hundreds of prisoners already dead, executions—a constant feature of the camp—continued to be carried out. Charges were never specified. The names of those to be shot would simply appear on small posters periodically glued to the prison walls, beside such observations as "stubborn" or "suffers from old brains." When the executions had been carried out—they were not, as in other prisons, held publicly—a red check would appear next to the names of the executed, and the poster would be left up for some time as a warning. Then in the nightly meeting the officers would repeat a well-worn observation: "If one reactionary is destroyed, that is one satisfaction. If two are destroyed, that is two satisfactions. If all the reactionaries are destroyed, then you are fully satisfied."

Propaganda plays, performed on three holidays a year, also continued. One play depicted the defeat of the Japanese occupation of China, another celebrated the virtues of hard labor, the third—always received with the greatest interest—portrayed the evils of capitalism. With a translator for the Tibetans standing beside them, the action would begin on the high platform framed by the backdrop of the dead monks' robes. A figure representing Uncle Sam emerged. Wearing a beige suit and black top hat, he sported a long red nose, sharp birdlike claws and a tail, hung from which was a sign in Chinese characters identifying him and noting that he was "a nuclear power." Holding his hands before his chest like a cat about to pounce, Uncle Sam went about exploiting Africans, played by prisoners in blackface. After suffering much brutal oppression, the Africans, with the help of the Chinese people, ultimately overcame their oppressor in a glorious revolt and subjected him to the all too familiar *thamzing*.

The third year of the Tibetans' stay at Jiuzhen brought sudden, unexpected relief to all the prisoners in the PRC's northwestern gulag. According to one survivor who spent twenty-one years in five separate camps, roughly 70,000 Tibetans were imprisoned north of Langzhou, 35,000 of whom perished from starvation in 1959–61. The death rate throughout Qinghai and Gansu was so high during the early sixties that prisoners had to be continually shifted around in order to keep the prisons functioning as labor camps. One system located ten hours west of Xining and called Vebou housed 30,000 inmates in thirty camps, the larger ones holding 9,000 men, the smaller, 7,000, 5,000 and 1,000. Ten percent of the inmates were Tibetans and members of other minority groups, the rest Chinese. By the time the famine lifted there, Chinese officials sent from the mainland to take a census reported that 14,000 had died. Another prison, named Bhun-cha tsa Shen-shu, contained six camps within a three-mile stretch, housing 12,000 men, more than half of whom also died. In Jiuzhen, twenty-one Tibetans were still alive, enough to fill only one of three cells the group had originally occupied. Early in the year, the four security officers who had accompanied them returned from their main office in Lhasa. With fifty-five dossiers closed, and the remaining ones as complete as could reasonably be expected, it was determined that nothing more was to be had from the Tibetans. Interrogation stopped, the "reeducation" classes lost their zealous fervor and the number of *thamzing* declined dramatically. The survivors were transferred to three adjoining rooms in a corner of the prison. A front door opened on a small entranceway, to the right and left of which were cells designed to accommodate ten men. At night the door was left unlocked, making it possible to go to the toilet unattended; this minor relaxation, in turn, afforded the first opportunity since the men's arrival for unobserved contact. As the interpersonal barriers melted, so did mutual suspicion, and in consoling one another over the loss of their comrades, the prisoners began once more to speak hopefully about the Dalai Lama and the thousands of Tibetans they knew had escaped with him to India.

The new leniency was soon complemented by an increase in rations. As China's famine eased, sixteen and a half pounds of grain a month—borderline rations under normal conditions, but a feast for the inmates—were issued. New Year's Day 1962 featured a meal of pork soup, with actual bits of pork in each prisoner's portion—their first taste of fat in two and a half years. The new cells, as well, afforded unexpected benefits. Permitted to keep some of the wheat chaff and small kindling from the autumn harvest, the men made fires at night beneath their sleeping platforms. Sometimes they were lucky enough to corner a rat on the floor, which they cooked and ate. Rats also ran in the hollow space between the wooden beams of the ceiling and the old newspapers which covered them. Open hunting for them soon got underway. Each night, the rats scurried over the papers, while the men waited below, armed with long sticks, following the sound of their feet. With good aim and a fierce upward thrust, it was possible to stun a rat long enough to capture and kill it. As infrequent as these meals were, they nonetheless provided meat.

With the worst of the famine over, the death rate quickly dropped. In two years Jiuzhen had lost over 1,000 prisoners—more than half its population. Most of the Chinese survivors were now transferred to prisons in other areas of Qinghai and Xinjiang, where their labor could be of more use to the state. As they embarked, the remaining Tibetans gained access to a far greater supply of food.

The newly empty cells throughout the camp were used by the kitchen staff to store cabbages, turnips and carrots. Aware of this, the remaining prisoners began to make nocturnal raids. One night a man named Thubten Tsundu shook Dr. Choedrak's feet and whispered, "Now's our chance to steal some cabbages." The two men snuck from their cell with a pillowcase and pair of pants, its legs tied. Breaking into a nearby storeroom, they waited for a Chinese prisoner to pass on his way to and from the toilet, filled their bags with cabbages and hurried back to their cell, where they hid the load under their bedding. On their return from work the following day, a prison guard singled out Dr. Choedrak. "Tell me yourself what you have done," he said threateningly. Knowing that execution was the punishment for stealing, Dr. Choedrak replied that he had done nothing. The guard then ordered him inside, where Tenzin Choedrak saw that not only his bedding but all the bedding in the cell had been turned upside down. The cabbages that he and Thubten Tsundu had stolen were surrounded by a vast quantity of other cabbages, carrots and turnips. Everyone was stealing, it turned out—making punishment impossible. In the new plenitude, any item at all could buy at least a few extra dumplings on the black market, resulting, ironically, in a rather odd form of crime wave. During the day, those who had been detailed—with Chinese approval—to guard their mates' cells often took the opportunity to raid neighboring rooms. Even the patients in the hospital would drag themselves out of bed in the hope of finding something to bargain with. After dark, prisoners slipped from their cells and broke into others. There were fights, ambushes were laid by one cell against another and even group forays occurred. To steal grain directly from the prison store, Tibetans concealed handfuls in their socks and shoes, fashioned pouches in their undershirts and made long, narrow bags which, hanging inside their pants tied back to front between their legs, could be discreetly filled while bending over to sow seed.

By the autumn of 1962, only 300 inmates remained in Jiuzhen. A rumor began to spread that some men had arrived from Lhasa. On September 28, the announcement was officially made: "Now you have been well educated," a Chinese official said to the twenty-one Tibetan survivors lined up before him. "So we have decided to let you return to your home. And look," he continued, holding up a rubberized oxygen pillow of the kind used by the Chinese in Tibet, "we have gone to great effort on your account and spent a good deal of money. We've bought five such bags at twenty yuan each so that you will not die on the high passes on the road. You will be given a holiday until your departure. Now wash yourselves and clean up," he advised. "But don't damage your bedding. Don't tear it or burn it. It has to stay here."

For the entire week excitement and doubt gripped the prisoners until, the night before their announced departure, an officer arrived with new suits for them to wear, sewn together from the clothing of prisoners who had died. The cotton padding had been redistributed smoothly, then covered over with a fresh piece of rough linen. Jiuzhen's authorities, it seemed, cared a good deal about the Tibetans' appearance now that they were to be released into the custody of other guards.

At eight o'clock in the morning of October 5, 1962, a canvas-covered army truck was driven into the prison yard. Carrying small bundles, the Tibetans marched to the truck, where the weakest were helped up by the stronger. As they left, the prison staff bade them farewell: "Now that you're finally going home," they called out, waving vigorously, "look after your health and take good care of yourselves." Incredulous, the Tibetans replied through their translator, "Thank you so much. And we promise to do as you say." Then, as the engine started, they cursed under their breath, and with that, waving and cursing, they were driven through the gate, on their way out of China.

FIFTEEN DAYS AFTER Dr. Choedrak's release from Jiuzhen Prison, the 1962 Sino-Indian border war broke out. For China it represented the greatest dividend to date from the years of effort expended in Tibet. Following 1959 the PLA had hurried to consolidate its position for an eventual strike on India, a move Peking viewed as essential to its drive to assert military and thereby political dominance over Central Asia. Accomplished exclusively with forced Tibetan labor, a network of roads was created linking the PLA's three forward headquarters in Chamdo, Shigatse and Rudok, in the Himalayan border regions. Once the roads were in place, observation posts, airfields, bases and supply dumps all had to be carefully built at night and with the utmost secrecy. As readiness for the attack was stepped up, thousands of Tibetans from southern and western Tibet were conscripted to supplement local workers by carrying supplies. Simultaneously, those left behind were told in nightly meetings that India had occupied the very best regions in Tibet making it the PLA's sacred duty to regain them for the people. Reinforcements of men and ammunition now arrived from China, and with them came a further drain on the Tibetan economy, the greater portion of the harvest being diverted to feed the newly arrived troops. But the most ruthless aspect of the war occurred for Tibetans after the fighting started. Blood donations became compulsory and though 3,000 or so Indian prisoners were captured, it was soon obvious from the extent of the blood drive that the Chinese themselves had not been immune from losses. In as many areas as it could be mounted, the policy required Tibetans between the ages of fifteen and thirty-five to give one and a half times the amount of blood normally taken. Chief donors were those labeled as "class enemies"; the Chinese themselves were exempted. At the start, it had been claimed that all who voluntarily came forward would receive twenty-five yuan (or roughly $12.50), a half pound of butter and a full pound of meat. When no Tibetans volunteered, however, large numbers were forcibly subjected to blood donations. As a result, many already on the verge of death from starvation perished. Only token Tibetan cadres received the promised gifts. Both human and animal blood was stored in Lhasa at a newly built blood bank at Dohdun, northeast of the Potala, to which many of the more serious Chinese casualties were eventually transported from the front.

While blood extraction was one of the grimmer campaigns of the early 1960s, sterilization and the forced marriage of Tibetan women to Chinese soldiers were considered by many to be even more threatening. As the "leading elements of the masses," Tibetan cadres were the first to be sterilized, at the Lhasa Municipal People's Hospital, constructed in 1952 as a "research and training center for medical science and medical cadres of minorities nationalities." To sterilize as many people as possible, novice Chinese still in medical training routinely operated on Tibetan patients. Many cadres, both male and female, who underwent the operations emerged paralyzed below the waist or having lost control of their bladder.

A number, admitted to the hospital for unrelated conditions, discovered that during surgery they had also been sterilized. Witnessing such results, Tibetans henceforth resisted sterilization. But while this method of population control was gradually phased out, the considerably more widespread practice of inducing Tibetan women to marry Chinese soldiers was launched. (Tibetan men were strictly barred from marrying Chinese women.) In the early 1960s almost all of China's occupation troops continued to be those soldiers who had arrived with the original invasion force in 1950. Young men at the time, they had been granted no leave in over a decade and were now approaching middle age without families. It was convenient to bolster the troops' morale by encouraging them to marry Tibetan women, but it was also an obvious boon to Peking's overall policy of assimilation, as any offspring would be raised as Chinese. Broad inducements—including cooking utensils, extra food and clothing rations—were offered to all Sino-Tibetan couples, and under the desperate circumstances, quite a few such marriages occurred. In secret many Tibetans condemned those who had collaborated in what appeared to be a blatant attempt to dilute the race. Publicly, though, the stigma went the other way. A common Chinese expression, often said on hearing of the birth of a Tibetan child, was: "The crows in the sky are all black. There are no white ones," meaning that only Chinese babies would be "white" crows, or good signs.

Following the 1962 war the Indian-Tibetan border, together with its support zones, remained on constant alert. In Mustang, Chushi Gangdruk had regrouped and accelerated the pace of its attacks. The PLA, faced with a hostile, if temporarily cowed, Indian army, was deeply concerned about the guerrillas. In addition, despite the tightly sealed border, hundreds of Tibetans continued to escape during the summer months bringing with them tales of suffering under the Chinese. In July of 1964 PCART formulated a policy, announced in large posters hung in Tibet's major towns, to cope with the problem: Tibetans who returned from India, and those guerrillas who gave themselves up, were to be richly rewarded; cash prizes specified for each type of weapon as well as the number of extra people brought in. Radio Lhasa continually broadcast pleas delivered by the families of those who had escaped, begging them to return to the "socialist paradise." Agents filtered through the Tibetan communities in Kalimpong, Darjeeling and Nepal, wooing the destitute refugees with promises of prosperity at home. A few did return. The most prominent of these was Dorje Phagmo, Tibet's highest female *tulku*, or incarnate lama, who was immediately conscripted into the "upper strata" United Front. But there were not many others. Meanwhile, concerned families in Tibet were informed that they were responsible for inducing their relatives to return and would be punished unless they succeeded. A newly coined Chinese proverb was often quoted to bring the point home: "The lama might escape, but his monastery cannot."

Four more policies covering the years 1962–1964 led up to the founding of the Tibet Autonomous Region. The first, "Rechecking the Democratic Reforms," began as early as 1960 and continued for years throughout the countryside. "Rechecking" amounted to ascertaining whether or not all reactionaries and "class enemies" had indeed been ferreted out in the reforms themselves. The natural corollary was the creation of a separate prison and labor camp system for Tibet, comprised of four levels, under the jurisdiction of the Public Security Bureau in Lhasa. So many reactionaries were found that quotas were established though, according to Tibetan sources, never carried out, limiting the number of arrests to no more than 5 percent of the local population. Concerned about Tibetans fleeing abroad, a second policy, commonly known as "Go Easy," was adopted. This included a ninety-six-point program issued in 1962–63 for all of Tibet, ten points of which applied especially to the sensitive border area, where greater personal freedom, tax exemption and higher rations were all instituted. In 1963–64 came the third and fourth policies, entitled the "Three Big Educations" and the "Four Cleanlinesses." The first Big Education was "Class-Consciousness Education." The middle class was now divided into "upper" and "lower" middle class. Being placed in the "upper" category was tantamount to receiving a bad class designation. It brought *thamzing* and frequently imprisonment. Concurrently, the "lower" middle class and the poor were given "thought classification"—all those having old or reactionary thoughts receiving the same treatment as class enemies. As a result, every strata of Tibetan society was found to be rife with *logchoepas*, or reactionaries—there being scarcely any group left intact save the Chinese and their collaborators, to represent the "broad masses serving as the revolutionary vanguard." The second Big Education was called "Socialist Transformation Education." In theory, this meant "destroying selfishness to establish unselfishness." It was aimed at breaking down the last resistance to MATs and increased collectivization. The third one, "Scientific Technical Education," was a propaganda drive designed to introduce communes. It consisted of creating a few prototype showpiece communes supplied with modern equipment, fertilizer, seeds and tools. The final campaign, the Four Cleanlinesses—of Thought, History, Politics and Economics—set forth the party line on correct interpretations of Tibet's history—arguing, for instance, that Tibet had always been an integral part of China.

Tibetan cadres were responsible for implementing this turbulent stream of policies on the grass-roots level. During the early to mid-sixties, the number of the best-trained workers stood between 6,000 and 10,000; by the end of the eighties, approximately 80,000 Tibetans were working for the Chinese, 30,000 having been trained in China itself. These were the cream of the crop—Tibetan children who had often voluntarily left their homes in the mid-fifties, lured by the modern world in its Chinese manifestation, eager to see a land where "no one had to walk" and the roads "shone like mirrors." Brought into the burgeoning network of China's Nationalities Institutes, they were trained as a fifth column to eventually replace the "upper strata" indigenous leaders who had to be used for the time being. On them, China placed its greatest hope.

Throughout the 1950s, the Peking Institute of National Minorities, located on the western side of the city led sixteen other academies attended by Tibetans, most of which were located in western China. Constructed on an ancient graveyard, its monolithic dormitories, auditorium and class buildings, brightly fringed with flower gardens, pine and willow trees, offered a curriculum which, though including science, mathematics and, in the early days, painting and music, concentrated largely on learning Chinese language and Marxist ideology. Local folk songs and dances were encouraged. Caucasian students from Xinjiang were permitted to wear their native garb, and on special occasions Tibetan students, too, were provided with new *chubas*. Social life at the Institute was active and varied, punctuated by frequent field trips around Peking, visits to the planetarium, the zoo and the Forbidden City; on Saturday evenings, films were shown, and a wide variety of novel sports were offered, including soccer, basketball and track and field. So, for a while, these young Tibetans found pride in their roles and looked forward to their eventual return home as leaders under the new order in Tibet.

Following the reversal in 1957 of the liberal Hundred Flowers Movement—in which Mao had encouraged intellectuals to openly criticize the Party—the CCP itself destroyed its own best hope for a successful minorities policy. The "anti-rightist" campaign which ensued saw every vestige of liberality at the Peking Institute crushed. With the radical left line in ascendancy, the first wave of *thamzing* fell on the students. The principal of the Institute, Phi Shadong, was singled out as a "capitalist-roader"; posters were hung in the dining halls, classrooms and dormitories denouncing the liberal methods of his "petty-bourgeois administration" and accusing its adherents, in a new and frighteningly vehement tone, of being "pigs fed by the people," having "human bodies but a snake's head" and being "divorced from the masses." Excursions, dancing and the practice of religion were forbidden. To create a proletarian lifestyle, monthly stipends were cut by three quarters, new clothes were no longer issued, food was strictly rationed and the students were forced by "activist" cadres of the Communist Youth League to criticize themselves for everything from wearing pointed shoes and pants that fit too tightly to having gone to movies or plays in the past. As the repression worsened, whatever sympathies young Tibetans had for Communism were destroyed, and replaced by their antithesis: underground organizations. Using sports teams and the bands as their cover, groups such as the "Ear" and "Nose" Society hung posters denouncing the administration with its own Marxist terminology. In other minority schools as well, similar groups took shape—sometimes not even in secret—as in the case of the Gansu Nationalities Institute, where fifty-two Chinese and eighteen Tibetans died in open clashes during the early sixties. In Peking, though, members of the underground were soon uncovered and subjected to a bloody round of *thamzing* held in the Institute's dining hall. As the Great Leap Forward got underway in 1958, fleshed out by a campaign to oppose "local nationalism" among the minority students, an estimated 60 percent of the Tibetans at the Institute were given *thamzing*—a number of them dying at the hands of their friends in the process.

In the middle of the night of March 20, 1959, the 1,000 Tibetan students studying at the Peking Institute of National Minorities were awakened by Chinese instructors and made to assemble in their classrooms. There they heard for the first time of the revolt in Lhasa. Ordered to write letters home dissuading their families and friends from taking part in the rebellion, they were shortly divided into three groups according to readiness. By the middle of May the first two hundred were returned to Tibet as the vanguard of a hasty effort to create a new bureaucracy. During the summer of 1959 almost 3,500 Tibetans were transferred home from nationalities institutes in China. Before leaving they were issued new boiler suits, hats, canvas shoes and blankets—items of great value under prevailing conditions. They returned to their country, after many years' absence, wearing the emblems of the ruling elite.

In reality, the majority of China's new workers were virulently anti-Han. Thus, while required to rely on Tibetans to administer the country, China was in fact putting in place those who would soon lead Tibet's burgeoning underground. Well versed in both Marxist ideology and Chinese administrative procedure, the cadres learned to carry out orders while seeking promotion to higher office from which they could more effectively undermine policy. Over the next twenty-five years, those trained in China joined two other cadre groups working in Tibet. The first was comprised entirely of wholehearted collaborators—local "activists" of poor background selected during the implementation of the Democratic Reforms and subsequent policies. By 1965 there were 20,000 of them. Due to their genuine allegiance, they received choice positions in factories, schools, the army and government offices. They were, however, despised by the Tibetan people, and derisively labeled "Lions with a Dog's Bite." The second type of home-grown cadre represented the opposite of the first. Loosely selected, they were trained in two- to six-month crash courses beginning in the early sixties. Their studies consisted almost exclusively of the revolutionary ideology they were to implement. Many had been forcefully taken from their villages, and their open hatred for the Chinese often landed them in prison. But it was the elite, China-trained group that continued to cause the greatest trouble. Employed as teachers, nurses, reporters for Radio Lhasa and the *Tibet Daily*, they remained a constant problem for the Chinese, who, in spite of their suspicions, remained dependent on them. By 1962, almost 3,000 of the new cadres had to be dismissed as unreliable. Nonetheless, by 1965 there were between 30,000 and 40,000 Tibetans employed by the Chinese in administration. But none of them, from the highest collaborators to the lowest activists, had a say in governing Tibet: each reported directly to a Chinese party member from whom he or she took orders. After six years in the making, as shaky as the system was, it did manage to function as a feasible bureaucracy. Based on it and on the so-called election process—whereby its members were automatically placed in "office" at various administrative levels—the Tibet Autonomous Region approached its long-awaited inauguration. Only one obstacle remained—"a big rock on the road to socialism," as both Generals Dan Guansan and Zhang Jinwu described him—an impediment, ironically enough, at the very pinnacle of the dummy Tibetan infrastructure, the supreme collaborator himself: the Panchen Lama.

Despite the veneer of the Panchen Lama's unquestioned complicity with China, signs of trouble had appeared as early as 1958. At that time, even though it was rumored that the Panchen Lama's father had supplied arms and horses to Chushi Gangdruk, no reprisal was forthcoming. Two years later, however, at the end of December 1960, while the Panchen Lama was in Peking delivering a "Report on Work in Tibet in the Past Year," the PLA surrounded his monastery—Tashilhunpo, in Shigatse, the only one to have escaped the Democratic Reforms—and seized all of its 4,000 monks. Accused of complicity in the revolt, some were among ten

Tibetans publicly executed three months later, on March 21. From fear of a similar or worse fate, others—including a few of the monastery's most respected scholars and incarnate lamas—committed suicide. The remaining monks were then deported to Golmo and Tsala Karpo for forced labor.

The destruction of Tashilhunpo had a profound effect on the Panchen Lama. His collaboration appeared to falter even further in the second week of July 1960, when the Panchen Kanpo Lija Committee in PCART was disbanded. The committee had controlled the civil administration of Shigatse, thereby securing some degree of self-rule for the city unavailable elsewhere. Though few facts emerged to explain why these moves were taken, it was known among Tibetan cadres that following 1959 the Panchen Lama became increasingly recalcitrant toward the Chinese generals who were running Tibet. Besides demanding the restoration of all religious monuments damaged during the fighting in Lhasa (he personally financed the refurbishing of frescoes in the Potala and the Norbulingka), he arranged for the removal of images in the Potala to the Tsuglakhang, where they stood a better chance of protection by Tibetans. Moreover, his support of religion was not limited to the preservation of sacred objects. From his new residence at Shuktri Lingka, the Panchen Lama continued to receive pilgrims and offer discourses. During his sermons—which were attended by thousands—he never failed to mention that the Dalai Lama was Tibet's true leader. He repeatedly stated that the development of Tibet must be led by Tibetans, as the Chinese were only there to help—a comment which was particularly galling, as it was taken from Mao himself and thus unassailable.

At the close of 1961, the Panchen Lama openly defied China. Late in September he and his entourage were invited to Peking to attend the 12th National Day Celebration. In Tibet, thousands were dying from starvation. Lhasa and Shigatse were dead cities, without stores, goods or commerce. Monasteries were gutted. Work gangs covered the countryside, prisoners and free alike toiling over dirt roads lined by dull green PLA convoys carting the harvest and religious wealth of Tibet to the People's Republic. With nothing left to lose, Lhasans abandoned their labor and converged on the Panchen Lama as he made his way out of Lhasa, petitioning him to plead with China for food and medical care. Their appeals galvanized him to act. Once in Peking he delivered a 70,000-character memorandum to Mao Zedong describing conditions in Tibet, included in which were demands for more grain for farmers, care for the aged and infirm, a genuine acceptance of religious freedom and a cessation of mass arrests. Mao assured the Panchen Lama that the proposals would be heeded. To demonstrate good intent, pamphlets were printed and distributed throughout Tibet announcing that Mao had personally acceded to the Panchen Lama's requests and that improvements were forthcoming.

When the Panchen Lama returned to Tibet early in 1962, he found the situation unchanged. General Zhang Jinwu informed him that what had been said in Peking and what was done in Tibet were entirely different matters. Not only were the demands not to be carried out, said General Zhang; as the ranking party member in Tibet, he had a request of his own to make of the Panchen Lama. It had been decided, he related, that, in light of the Dalai Lama's appeals to the United Nations and re-forming of the Tibetan government abroad, the assertion that he had been abducted by reactionaries was finally to be abandoned. The Panchen Lama himself was to publicly condemn Tibet's exiled ruler, after which the word "Acting" would be dropped from his own title, he would become Chairman of PCART, and would move into the Potala as the head of the country. The Panchen Lama refused outright, stating that an attempt to take the Dalai Lama's place would only infuriate Tibetans and thus undermine the very purpose of the act. Immediately thereafter, the Panchen Lama was denied permission to speak in public and was henceforth seen only among large groups at official events. To further signal the change in his status, the remaining crew of caretaker monks at Tashilhunpo was accused of five crimes—including keeping a portrait of the Dalai Lama—and subjected to *thamzing* before the people of Shigatse.

Two years later, in 1964, the Panchen Lama made a brief, but substantial reappearance. As a result of his acts he now enjoyed extensive support among the Tibetan people, and General Zhang Guohua was forced, before inaugurating the Tibet Autonomous Region, to clarify his position. Accordingly, the Panchen Lama was offered a final chance to rectify his obdurate stance. Once more he was to denounce the Dalai Lama, this time during a celebration of the Great Prayer Festival or Monlam Chenmo, traditionally lasting three weeks, permitted now for a single day for this express purpose.

The gathering occurred in March and was attended by more than 10,000 people. From a high throne overlooking Lhasa's main square on the south side of the Central Cathedral, the Panchen Lama once more advocated, as he had in the past, freedom of religion and the need for Tibet to be developed by its own people. Then, at the moment he had been expected to denounce the Dalai Lama as a reactionary, he paused and looked for a long while over the crowd. After audibly sighing, he stated: "His Holiness the Dalai Lama was abducted from his country to a foreign land. During this period it is in every Tibetan's interest that His Holiness should come to no harm. For if the Dalai Lama comes to no harm, then the Tibetan people's stock of good fortune is not exhausted. Today, while we are gathered here, I must pronounce my firm belief that Tibet will soon regain her independence and that his Holiness the Dalai Lama will return to the Golden Throne. Long Live His Holiness the Dalai Lama!"

Stung by the magnitude of this display of defiance, almost five years to the day after the March revolt, the Chinese placed the Panchen Lama under house arrest. Generals Zhang Guohua and Zhang Jinwu flew to Peking to consult directly with Mao and Zhou Enlai. They returned in July to initiate a campaign called "Thoroughly Smash the Panchen Reactionary Clique." In its first stages, the drive assembled evidence of the Panchen Lama's "crimes against the people." Bulky dossiers were compiled from witnesses who testified to a broad range of crimes. When the files were completed, three hundred Tibetan cadres—including the ranking members of the patriotic upper strata such as Ngabo Ngawang Jigme and Dorje Phagmo were assembled in Lhasa. Before reaching the capital, they were told that they had been brought together to denounce certain "leading reactionaries" who had recently been discovered plotting against the motherland. Their chief was the "big rock on the road to socialism," the Panchen Lama, who, the collaborators were subsequently told by General Zhang Guohua, had organized a secret guerrilla army to fight China. The cadres were enjoined to remove the rock from the road.

The Panchen Lama's trial, convened in August 1964 in the auditorium of a new PCART building (the old one having been burned to the ground by saboteurs), lasted seventeen days. Generals Zhang Guohua and Zhang Jinwu sat at the center of a table on the stage, with the Panchen Lama between them. Zhang Guohua opened the proceedings with a long speech in which he alluded to the Panchen Lama's wrongdoing and listed the traitorous activities of the as yet unspecified "reactionary clique." He concluded by saying, "If you squeeze a snake its insides will come out" —the signal for beginning a prearranged skit of *thamzing*. Phakpala Gelek Namgyal, a member of the patriotic upper strata from Chamdo, having long nursed a personal grudge against the Panchen Lama, was the first to openly denounce him. "Big mistakes have been made," he said. "And the responsibility for this lies on the Panchen. Because of this, I therefore criticize the Panchen, Chairman of the PCART." "These are serious charges against the Panchen," said General Zhang Guohua, standing up on cue. "It is necessary to expose these faults at this meeting." Thereupon the meeting broke into subcommittees, each headed by a prepared cadre who, during the group's deliberations, "discovered" crimes committed by the "big rock."

On the third day, the proceedings turned violent. Repeating his metaphor of the snake, General Zhang Guohua observed, "If you squeeze a snake its intestines come out. But to kill a snake it is necessary to crush its head. If we squeeze the Panchen by *thamzing*, many hidden reactionaries and enemies of the state will be forced into the open. If we kill the Panchen, the whole reactionary clique will collapse like a house whose foundations have been destroyed." Cadres sprang from their seats and began to slap, punch and kick the Panchen Lama, who was pulled from his chair and brought to the center of the stage. The spectacle of seeing one of Tibet's highest lamas beaten by his own people deeply disturbed the majority of delegates. No matter how often they were urged, they could not bring themselves to join in. Having anticipated this, a select group of sympathizers cited ten major crimes as evidence against the Panchen Lama and conducted more beatings to induce a confession to each crime. The list included murder, cohabitation with his brother's wife, participation in orgies and stealing images from monasteries. The most serious charges, however, were those which claimed that the Panchen Lama had raised a guerrilla army trained in the use of machine guns and augmented by a force of twenty cavalrymen. The basis upon which the charge was made centered on a school in Shigatse, originally established by the Chinese themselves, to train cadres for the Panchen Kanpo Lija. In 1959 it had been converted to an industrial training school where carpentry, auto mechanics and blacksmithing were taught. Now it was described as an "underground factory" in which students manufactured arms and ammunition to be used in a future uprising. For evidence, two foreign cars, fitted with extra gas tanks (a not uncommon aid to driving in Tibet), were exhibited to the delegates as proof that, at the very least, the Panchen Lama was planning to escape (once more less than convincing, as there were large convoys and periodic checkpoints on all roads). As for the cavalry: years before, the Panchen Lama had received twenty Mongolian ponies as a gift. He was fond of the horses, and in his spare time often helped his grooms to exercise them. It was with this cavalry that he was to have attacked the motherland.

The Panchen Lama denied every charge brought against him. He repeatedly stated that though he might have erred in his work at PCART, he had received Zhang Guohua's approval for every decision—an observation which further incensed the general. In the meantime, the Panchen Lama's aged tutor, Ngulchu Tulku, attempted to take the blame for the "crimes" by stating that he had personally taught his charge from an early age that "Communists were devils." The Panchen Lama pointedly dismissed these remarks during the trial. Nevertheless, both his tutor and his steward were subsequently taken to Golmo, where they died.

With the conclusion of *thamzing*, General Zhang asked for suggestions regarding punishment. Execution, deportation and imprisonment were all proposed, but in reality the sentence had been determined long before. Eulogizing the magnanimity of the Communist Party in the face of the Panchen Lama's dire provocations, the general informed the delegates that he would not be executed. After the trial, the Panchen Lama, his parents and the remaining members of his entourage were chained, thrown in closed trucks and driven out of Lhasa under heavy guard—their destination unknown. The next word came from Peking on December 17—four months later—during the 151st Plenary Session of the State Council. Here, for the first time, the Dalai Lama was publicly denounced as a traitor to the People's Republic, stripped of his title as Chairman of PCART and accused of having "staged the traitorous armed counterrevolution of 1959, set up an unlawful government abroad, proclaimed an illegal constitution, supported the Indian reactionaries in their intrusion into our country, organized and trained the remnant bandits and alienated himself from the motherland." Four days later, Zhou Enlai informed the First Session of the Third National People's Congress that the Panchen Lama likewise had fallen from grace, having "led the reactionaries against the people, against our country and against socialism in a well-planned manner." In retribution, he also was deprived of his title in PCART, but, as an indication that he might again be of use at some future date, his name was left on the roster as a common member. Following Zhou's speech and a brief mention a few months later, nothing more was heard of the Panchen Lama, then twenty-seven years old. He simply disappeared.

One year after the Panchen Lama's trial, elections from the county level up—the rules for which had been announced in March 1963—were finally completed in Tibet. Three hundred and one delegates were chosen in an electoral process that, according to Chinese periodicals, was conducted much like a festival. Tibetans had flocked to polling places beating drums and gongs, dressed in their finest clothes, adorned with flowers and scarves; cripples, maimed by the old feudal lords, hobbled on crutches to cast their ballots "in high excitement." As the New China News Agency reported in August 1965, candidates were nominated "after lively discussions by the electorate who chose those they believed would act as real representatives of the poor peasants and herdsmen in this first free expression of the voice of the Tibetan people."

In reality, free elections simply did not exist. At the grass-roots level, villages were broken into small discussion groups, each one led by an "activist" from the subdistrict office. Presented with a prepared list of acceptable candidates from the lower middle class or "non-reactionary" poor, villagers had only to discuss the merits of their prospective candidates. Anyone nominating someone else was severely criticized. The cadre then made a speech announcing the Party's choices. The groups could not disband until each one had unanimously voted for the favored candidate —a result guaranteed by the fact that the ballots were marked in full view of the chairing cadre.

General Zhang Guohua was elected. So was Ngabo Ngawang Jigme, chosen by the Party to fill the Panchen Lama's place as chief figurehead of Tibetan self-rule. A year earlier, Ngabo had assumed the title of PCART's Acting Chairman, having risen from Secretary-General to Vice-Chairman following the revolt. His merit now lay not so much in his title, as in the fact that he represented the sole surviving link to the old government of Tibet. As such, he was indispensable. Ensconced in a modern home with Western furniture on the northeastern side of Lhasa, surrounded by a large flower garden and staffed by two servants, he took nominal charge, as its elected chairman, of the newly founded Tibet Autonomous Region's leading body—The People's Council—three quarters of which was Tibetan, the rest either Chinese or members of other "minority groups" in Tibet. Simultaneously the name of the central committee of Tibet's CCP was changed from Work Committee to Party Committee, indicating that the highest organ of the Communist Party in Tibet was now fully operational with General Zhang Guohua as First Secretary.

On September 1, 1965, the first session of the First People's Council of the Tibet Autonomous Region convened in Lhasa. *China Reconstructs* recorded the entrance of the elected delegates: "With the bright red ribbons identifying them as people's deputies fluttering on their breasts, they walked into the meeting hall with heads held high, representatives of their emancipated people. During the nine-day session, with tears of emotion in their eyes and smiles of triumph on their faces, they spoke of their past misery and present happiness and expressed the deep love of Tibet's million emancipated serfs and slaves for the Chinese Communist Party and Chairman Mao." On the closing day, 30,000 Lhasans, including a Vice-Premier and 76 delegates from 27 other provinces, municipalities and autonomous regions were flown in for the ceremonies, assembled in the city's newly built "stadium"—an open field surrounded by banners and flags to celebrate the inauguration of the Tibet Autonomous Region. For internal and external consumption alike the event marked a propaganda threshold. For those who had been in Tibet since 1950, it represented the culmination of a decade and a half of work. Moreover, it had come a decade to the month after the last autonomous region, Xinjiang, had been formed, a fact which could not but have reminded the Chinese in Tibet of the immense amount of difficulty they had experienced in carrying out the Party's work on "the Roof of the World." Unknown to them, however, a period even more difficult than that of the past six years waited just ahead. For eleven months off lay the most tumultous upheaval in China since the Civil War itself—the start of the Great Proletarian Cultural Revolution.

The Long Night

1966–1977

Under the new situation of the Great Proletarian Cultural Revolution, and amidst the sound of the war drum for repudiating the bourgeois reactionary line, the Lhasa Revolutionary Rebel General Headquarters is born!

What is this Rebel Headquarters of ours doing? It is to hold high the great red banner of Mao Zedong's thought, and to rebel by applying Mao Zedong's thought. We will rebel against the handful of persons in authority in the Party taking the capitalist road. We will rebel against persons stubbornly persisting in the bourgeois reactionary line! We will rebel against all the monsters and freaks! We will rebel against the bourgeois Royalists! We, a group of lawless revolutionary rebels, will wield the iron sweepers and swing the mighty cudgels to sweep the old world into a mess and bash people into complete confusion. We fear no gales and storms, nor flying sand and moving rocks. . . . To rebel, to rebel and to rebel through to the end in order to create a brightly red new world of the proletariat!

—*Inaugural Declaration of the Lhasa Revolutionary Rebel General Headquarters, December 22, 1966*

BY THE LAST WEEK of December 1966, Red Guards in Lhasa stood poised to seize power from Tibet's CCP Central Committee. Four months before, the Great Proletarian Cultural Revolution had officially been proclaimed. Far more than a "cultural" revolution, as its name implied, the policy signaled the most severe outbreak to date of the decades-old power struggle between the left and the right dividing the allegiance of Chinese Communists across both personal and ideological lines. Despite the debacle of the Great Leap Forward, the left's first attempt to push China toward pure Communism by radical means, Mao Zedong had continued to call for class warfare as the best method for leveling Chinese society to a homogeneous, proletarian whole. For much of the early sixties, Liu Shaoqi, China's President, had led a renewal of the moderate line. By the autumn of 1965, however, Mao, undaunted by his earlier failure, had set the left back on par with the right. Having done so, he determined to wipe out once and for all the conservative opposition. With the army's support under Lin Biao he succeeded by June 1966 in purging his opponents from the powerful Peking Party Committee; in August, at the 11th Plenum of the CCP Central Committee he announced the Cultural Revolution. Every organ of the Party and the government bureaucracy throughout China was ordered to subject itself to upheaval, summarized by the slogan "to bombard the headquarters," a euphemism for eliminating the right. While the ideology of the Great Leap had emphasized increasing production, the left line now stressed violent "cleansing" of China's "rotten core," which was held accountable for the country's slow political and economic progress.

Liu Shaoqi and Deng Xiaoping were targeted—at first privately and later publicly—as the main "capitalist-roaders," and a Cultural Revolution Group was established in Peking to oversee the nationwide purge. Members of the army, Maoist cadres and representatives of mass organizations, a synonym for the newly created Red Guards, were called on to join together, seize power from their local Party organizations and establish Revolutionary Committees whose task it would be to perform the duties of both Party and government until the two could be separated once more, with the left firmly in control. The "three-in-one" groups were bequeathed an eight-point program by which to implement the radical policies held in abeyance till now: the destruction of "Four Olds" and the creation of "Four News." The "Four Olds" were old ideology, culture, habits and customs; the "Four News," their inverse, Mao's new ideology, proletarian culture, Communist habits and customs. China's vast number of disaffected youth seized the opportunity to rebel against the status quo, and were encouraged to do so by Mao's wife, Jiang Jing, who oversaw Red Guard activities. Licensed to travel anywhere in China to "exchange revolutionary experience," they were given free rein overnight to vent their frustrations channeled by Mao against his enemies.

Of all regions in the People's Republic, minorities areas proved the most vulnerable to the new directives. Compared to the mainland, they had maintained the "Four Olds" in fulsome dimensions; the very fact that their people possessed separate languages, much less culture, was regarded as reactionary. Chinese administrators in autonomous regions, districts and counties were singled out as responsible for having failed to obliterate vestiges of "decadent" societies under their tutelage. The much-vaunted United Front policy of working with the minorities' "patriotic upper strata" was cast aside; the people everywhere were urged to generate new activists, directly from their own ranks, to wage this, China's second revolution.

On August 25, 1966, the Cultural Revolution began in Tibet. Following a rally held to celebrate its inauguration by the 11th Plenum, the Central Cathedral was invaded by Red Guards. Hundreds of priceless frescoes and images, dating to the time of Songtsen Gampo, the temple's founder and Tibet's 33rd king, were defaced or destroyed. Its two court-yards were filled for five days with mobs burning scriptures. The destruction was particularly devastating as the Tsuglakhang had, under the Panchen Lama's direction, become a warehouse for countless invaluable artifacts brought from neighboring monasteries. With the height of the rampage past, Tibet's holiest shrine, equivalent, for its people, to the Vatican, was dubbed Guest House #5, its yards used to keep pigs, and its catacombs of old government offices, storage rooms and chapels taken over as headquarters for the most radical of the burgeoning Red Guard groups. Within the next few days the Norbulingka was opened to an orgy of destruction, following which the entire city, given over to the Red Guards, was again renamed. Street plaques were smashed to the ground and replaced with new revolutionary titles such as Foster the New Street and Great Leap Forward Path. As the first week of September got underway, 40,000 prints of Chairman Mao's portrait were distributed in Lhasa, draped with red ribbons and placed over every gate and in every home, office and factory in the capital. Giant red posters on the Potala and elsewhere heralded the Cultural Revolution; others, supporting the North Vietnamese, condemned U.S. imperialism or offered quotes from China's Great Helmsman, Mao.

As early as July, a small number of revolutionary youth had arrived in Lhasa to instigate a Red Guard movement in the TAR. Progressing slowly at first, by mid-September their work had produced enough Red Guard groups in the city to mount the first open attack on the establishment. Their initial handbill called for "burning the capitalist-roaders in authority in the Party." In practice, such an undertaking gave rise to a complex power struggle, just then being reduplicated throughout China. Because the Central Committee of the CCP had itself issued orders to commence the Cultural Revolution, those in authority at every level of the bureaucracy were paradoxically compelled to attack themselves. Failing to carry out a facsimile, at least, of the Central Committee's dictum would immediately mark them for genuine destruction by "the masses." However, almost all were marked to begin with, the assumption being that whoever held office was—until proven innocent by the people themselves—guilty of revisionism. Accordingly, General Zhang Guohua and Comrade Wang Jimei, Secretary of the Secretariat of the region's CCP Committee and a Deputy Political Commissar of the PLA, quickly organized Lhasa's own Cultural Revolution Group to oversee the work of rebellion and hopefully deflect its "spearhead" away from themselves. In the beginning, they emphasized "study" and "discussion" over violent "exposure," discouraged—until it appeared counter to the trend of the times—the hanging of big-character posters and, most importantly, dispatched observation teams of loyal cadres into every office and factory in Lhasa in an attempt to check any spontaneous organization of Red Guards. Their efforts were successful through the end of October, despite Lin Biao's clarion call, announced from the rostrum of Tienanmen Square, to wage a "mass campaign of repudiating the bourgeois reactionary line." But as more and more Red Guard groups organized and pressed their sanctioned attacks, the establishment's attempt to save itself began to falter. By mid-November, four Red Guard groups, bolstered by more than a thousand Red Guards from beyond the region, began to gain the upper hand by demanding, directly from the broadcasting studios of Radio Lhasa, an open repudiation of those in power. They accused both Zhang Guohua and Wang Jimei—who headed Tibet's Cultural Revolution Group—of suppressing the revolution while pretending to support it. The two tried to profess their innocence but continued to come under increasing pressure over the next month. Finally, on December 22, the first coalition of Revolutionary Rebels—representing fifty Red Guard groups—announced its inception and prepared to "seize power."

The affiliation could hardly help but instill terror in the hearts of Tibet's middle-aged Communist bureaucrats. Like Revolutionary Rebels all over the country, Tibet's Red Guards were mainly in their late adolescence and early twenties. Having matured under one dogmatic campaign after another, their thinking was governed by absolutes which now, abetted by their age and the regime's failure to incorporate them into the mainstream of the Party, justified attacking the power structure. The language of their inaugural proclamation summarized their philosophy:

To rebel! To rebel! We are a group of Revolutionary Rebels combined through our own free will under the banner of Mao Zedong's thought. . . . This organization of ours has no cumbersome rules and regulations. All can join us so long as they are Revolutionary Rebels who share our viewpoints. . . . We will persist in the struggle by reasoning, not by violence. However, when we do rebel, we will certainly not measure our steps and act with feminine tenderness, and will certainly not be so gentle, and so temperate, kind, courteous, restrained and magnanimous.

Among the dozens of groups signing the document, a huge variety of officers in Lhasa's civil administration were represented, among whom were a bevy of Red Rebel combat squads such as the "Prairie Spark Combat Contingent," the "Fiery Fire Combat Group" and the "Municipal Trade Headquarters Dog Hunting Corps." "To make revolution is innocent, and to rebel is justified!" they opined. "Long live the Revolutionary Rebel spirit of the proletariat, and a long life, and a long, long life to Chairman Mao, our supreme commander and the most reddest red sun in our hearts!"

On the evening of January 10, the Revolutionary Rebels staged their first assault by seizing power in Lhasa's north zone at the *Tibet Daily*, the official paper of the TAR, read by all the Chinese colonists. They had been inspired by the momentous seizure of two newspapers in Shanghai a day earlier, which, in its challenge to the city's municipal Party committee, had received prompt public support from Chairman Mao himself. The following night, twenty cadres of the Public Security Bureau formed a Red Guard group of their own at the reception center of the Lhasa Cultural Palace, a pillared hall in the city's new Chinese suburbs. Here they received approval from a regional CCP secretary for a big-character poster denouncing the takeover of the paper. Sanctioned to "encircle"—for *thamzing*—all Revolutionary Rebels, they were told to label them counterrevolutionary, a particularly charged term in Tibet's case. In a deceptive show of support for the takeover, Tibet's CCP Central Committee arrested two leading cadres of the paper while at the same time stating that under no circumstances would it relinquish its power, as the rebels had demanded. Again behind the scenes, party officials successfully induced much of the paper's staff to go on an undeclared "no show" strike. None of their efforts worked. Three days after the takeover of the paper, a hundred or so Revolutionary Rebel groups staged a mass "oath-taking rally" pledged to "smashing the new counterattack"—a far more provocative and potentially explosive gathering than the establishment's rally two weeks before, at which 20,000 Tibetans were convened to sing Mao's quotations. And as the Red News Rebel Corps, in charge now of the *Tibet Daily*, tauntingly editorialized in its January 22 edition: "You squires, wield all your weapons, including the 'nuclear device,' nothing extraordinary, only so and so. Judging from your crimes of suppressing our Revolutionary Rebels, don't we know who should wear this 'all-powerful' dunce's cap of 'counterrevolution'? Be vigilant, revolutionary comrades! Diehards persisting in the bourgeois reactionary line are again inciting the hoodwinked comrades to go on strike."

They were doing a lot more than that. Within a few weeks those in power brought out the PLA itself to forcibly suppress the rebels throughout the city. Subsequently known as the "February adverse current," this bloody reprisal—the first in a series of violent clashes over the next two years—was paralleled all across China, as Mao directed the army to intervene, hoping that it would restore order while accelerating, through its role in the three-in-one formula, the creation of Revolutionary Committees. Instead, the majority of garrisons, often under the command of the very men who were being threatened, forcibly suppressed Red Guard groups. Prior to the suppression or "white terror," as it was called by Red Guards, the rebels' efforts in Tibet were so effective that Zhang Guohua himself had been forced to flee on January 21, securing from friendly superiors in Peking a transfer to Sichuan, where he eventually reemerged as head of the Revolutionary Committee. Before his flight, Zhang had lost almost everything. The rebels openly accused him of an assortment of crimes, dubbing him the "Overlord of Tibet" and maintaining that since his arrival at the head of the invasion troops in 1950, he had worked to set himself up as the "Emperor" of an "independent kingdom" on "the Roof of the World."

While Zhang fled for his life, the emboldened rebels formed a new umbrella organization, the "Attacking Local Overlords Liaison Committee." In a storm of leaflets dropped over Lhasa on January 25, they proclaimed that they had seized power from the Central Committee of the Tibet Autonomous Region itself: "Beneath the sky all is ours. The country is ours. The masses are ours." Eleven top members of the Committee were paraded from beating to beating through the streets, while more leaflets, detailing their reactionary crimes, were distributed.

Having displaced those in civil authority, the rebels turned their attention to the army, without whose support they could not secure control of the city. An attempt was made to engineer a coup in the PLA command. The coup, though, was swiftly put down, and the army stabilized in time for its massive attack on the rebels, whose seizure of power had come so close to victory. Before his departure General Zhang had personally helped lay plans for the "adverse current" subsequently carried out by Ren Rong, Deputy Commissar of the Tibet Military Region and Zhang's close subordinate, supported by three new divisions loyal to Lin Biao—one sent all the way from Peking. On March 3, the *Tibet Daily*, back in the hands of the authorities, reported that the army had directly taken over everything from the functioning of the Public Security Bureau to the radio station and banks. With the PLA in control of Lhasa, martial rule was established. It was backed by the "Great Alliance," a new coalition of Red Guard groups formed by the establishment to counter the Revolutionary Rebels and their now banned Attacking Local Overlords Liaison Committee.

The Great Alliance, like its counterparts across China, faced the inexorable dilemma of having to prove itself more Maoist than its opponents, by outdoing them in attacking the very order it represented. To skirt the problem entirely, it attempted to recast the equation of struggle by launching an assault on the rebels, who, it claimed, as functionaries of foreign imperialists, were attempting to destabilize the region under the guise of the Cultural Revolution. The *Whirlwind Emergency Battling Newspaper* was created, and on March 10, the eighth anniversary of the Tibetan uprising, it delivered a scathing attack on the rebels, by identifying them with the Tibetan freedom fighters: "At the present critical moment when the proletariat is engaged in a decisive battle against the bourgeoisie, all the monsters and freaks have also come out of hiding. Under their camouflage they have sneaked into the revolutionary ranks." This has entirely revealed that it is an out-and-out topsy-turvy big hodgepodge and a stinking cesspit." So saying, the Great Alliance stood firm, backed, temporarily, by the army, whose standing orders, despite the various factional affiliations of its troops and offices, were to keep Tibet stable. Apparently, they had triumphed.

But in April more than 8,000 new Red Guards began arriving from China. Sanctioned by the Cultural Revolution Group in Peking, which, on April 6, ordered the PLA to cease "repressing" the left, they were part of a nationwide counterassault by Party radicals against the "adverse current" of bureaucrats attempting to save their posts and their lives. By April 16, Red Guards in Tibet had mounted a 20,000-person mass rally supporting the rebels and denouncing the Great Alliance. They were buoyed in their "counterattack" by the success of a rebel seizure of power, publicly supported by Peking two months earlier at the Kongpo Nyitri textile mill, the most developed industrial complex in the TAR, located near the Tsangpo River at the juncture of Kham and Central Tibet.

With the capital against it, the Great Alliance lost control. On June 8, the *Red Rebel News* announced the Revolutionary Rebels' official reemergence on the scene: "With red banners fluttering, the morale of the troops is high, ten thousand horses are galloping amidst urgent calls for fighting. Amidst calls for fighting, the Lhasa Revolutionary Rebel General Headquarters has been formally reinstated." It wasn't long before the "calls" were answered in the form of street battles all over Lhasa, raging from house to house, stronghold to stronghold, between rebel and Great Alliance groups. The rebels' strength was such that the Great Alliance found itself compelled to sacrifice one of its chief leaders, Deputy Commissar Wang Jimei, pretending to have exposed him and thus, as always, attempting to claim the true revolutionary zeal. (Wang, who had been the original PLA commander of Chamdo following the invasion, was later reported to have committed suicide in a prison in China.) Things got so out of hand —despite incidents on July 9 and 14 in which Great Alliance gangs successfully encircled and trounced large groups of rebels—that by the end of July even Ren Rong and his adjutant, Yin Fatang, found it preferable to be in Chengdu, Sichuan, with their erstwhile boss, General Zhang Guohua, rather than remain in their own army headquarters in Tibet. While Zhang eagerly professed allegiance to representatives of the rebels who came after them, back in Lhasa, their supporters had a full-scale war on their hands, street fights giving way to frontal assaults on strategically critical locations.

In September, the PLA, supported by a five-point directive from Peking ordering both factions to "join ranks" and cease "armed struggle," reasserted its position. But while heavier arms such as machine guns and mortars were confiscated, the fighting did not cease. Dismantling large portions of the Tsuglakhang's roof, Revolutionary Rebels fashioned knives, spears, axes and clubs to supplement the pistols and other light arms they had retained—and with these they continued to attack the Great Alliance. Moreover, the fighting now spread from Lhasa to Shigatse, Gyantse, Nagchuka and elsewhere, groups on both sides having established rival headquarters in touch with those in the capital—from where all attacks were carefully coordinated. While these clashes included raids on military convoys they were, during the autumn of 1967, primarily confined to assaults on factional strongholds. Prominent buildings in Lhasa such as the cement factory and the transport center sometimes were taken and retaken; prisoners on both sides, with one of their ears cut off to mark them, were forced to join their captors. As the autumn progressed and the two factions rearmed with heavier weapons, Lhasa's rebel groups managed to secure control of the city's four hospitals, thereby preventing wounded Alliance members from receiving treatment. To enlist support from the

Tibetans themselves, the rebels released all of the chief Tibetan collaborators, whom they had apprehended and publicly tortured the previous
January in their bid at a seizure of power. No sooner was Tibet's "patriotic
upper strata" released, however, than the Great Alliance rearrested them,
beat them brutally as "counterrevolutionaries" and reimprisoned them.

January 1968 saw the greatest outbreak of fighting to date. Hundreds
died in Lhasa alone, where, with the city's electricity cut off, the rebels,
now headquartered in Yabshi House, forced the Great Alliance, based in
the TAR building in front of the Potala, to flee to the Chinese sections in
the outskirts. By the end of the month all transportation, construction and
communication in Tibet had come to a halt as disarray in the army, free
of trouble itself since February 1967, broke out. Entire units were reported
to have joined one faction or the other, bringing with them automatic rifles
and grenades. The weapons, in turn, were responsible for pushing casualty
figures far beyond what they had been. Furthermore, as it was no longer
possible adequately to define the army's allegiance, a clear distinction
between pro-Maoists and pro-Liuists was problematical in any sector of the
Chinese community in Tibet. Thus the "topsy-turvy big hodgepodge," as
the Great Alliance had labeled the Revolutionary Rebels, could now safely
be said to be all-pervasive. Chen Mingyi, the officer in charge of all occupation troops, desperately tried to keep border posts stable but could do little
more. Concurrently, the large, heavily guarded grain warehouse at Cha-
rong, east of Drapchi prison, was cut off from Lhasa and the most devastating result of the disruptions occurred as Tibet's delicate system of food
distribution abruptly fell apart. By the end of January, subsistence conditions—which had prevailed since the easing of the famine in 1963—gave
way; once more, starvation reappeared. This time, it was not to depart for
a full five years—until 1973—with isolated regions thereafter continuing to
experience famine until 1980.

On September 5, 1968, two years after the Cultural Revolution's inception, a Cultural Revolution Committee was finally formed in Tibet. Along
with Xinjiang—announced on the same day—Tibet was the last of China's
twenty-nine provinces and municipalities to be officially brought under
the control of Peking, though both factions, despite being disarmed, once
more continued fighting. The Committee represented a bargain of sorts,
worked out in China's capital between radicals and those in the army
responsible for maintaining order. Zeng Yongya, a Deputy Commander
of the Tibet Military Region closely aligned with Lin Biao was made
Chairman, thereby satisfying the left, while Ren Rong, mistrusted by
ardent Maoists for his part in the February 1967 "adverse current," took
a high but subordinate position as first Vice-Chairman. Chen Mingyi, who

had ruled briefly as Zhang Guohua's successor received an even lower post and was clearly out of power. With a flock of new Tibetan collaborators instated, among whom only Ngabo's name was familiar, the job began of instituting subregional committees at lower administrative levels. Elsewhere in the PRC Red Guard, clashes had come to a halt following a directive from Mao, issued in July of 1968, empowering the army to disband the various groups by dispersing their members to the countryside. In Tibet, however, it took to the Ninth Party Congress, held in April 1969, before even six of the necessary seventy-seven district, municipality and county level Revolutionary Committees could be established, attesting to the region's continued instability. In December, almost a year and a half after the fighting in the TAR had been officially quelled with the formation of Revolutionary Committees, Radio Lhasa was still referring to "bourgeois factionalism," making it clear just how deeply rooted Tibet's civil strife had become.

For all of its fury, the political contest of the Cultural Revolution in Tibet was limited, in the main, to the Chinese themselves. The bulk of the suffering it produced was endured by the Tibetan people. While a few thousand Chinese died or were arrested and tortured, Tibetan casualties —including fatalities and those imprisoned—ran into the tens of thousands, with millions experiencing extreme abuse. Worse, for the legacy of subsequent generations, Tibetan culture suffered what would have been— were it not for the refugees in India—nothing less than a fatal blow. Everything Tibetan was destroyed; everything Chinese and Communist adopted. The practice of religion was officially outlawed. Folk festivals and fairs were banned, traditional dances and songs, incense burning and all Tibetan art forms and customs prohibited. A large outdoor exhibit was erected at Tromsikhang, near the Barkhor in Lhasa, in which all forbidden religious and ornamental items were displayed under a banner ordering their immediate remission to work committees and the "Offices to Suppress the Uprising," which had been reinstituted for the duration of the upheaval. All over Tibet people with bad class designations, who had not as yet been imprisoned, were dragged into the street and paraded in paper dunce caps—beaten and spat upon as they passed, tags listing their crimes pinned to their naked chest—in processions led by Red Guards beating drums, cymbals and gongs. Lashed to heavy religious statues lamas were bent double while ex-aristocrats and merchants had large empty vessels, once used for storing grain, roped to their backs. Loudspeakers, which had previously broadcast for only three to six hours daily, now emitted a nonstop stream of propaganda songs and paeans to Mao, their shrill whine permeating the streets and penetrating to within every household.

Between parades Red Guard factions vied for preeminence in the work of demolishing every vestige of Tibetan culture. The few remaining prayer flags were ripped down and replaced with red banners. The religious landscape of Tibet—lines of *chortens* gracing valleys and ridges, piles of *mani* stones before towns and mantras fashioned across hillsides out of whitewashed rocks were demolished and replaced by colossal slogans of Mao. The distinctive black borders framing Tibetan windows, as well as the bands of bright color decorating the interiors of most rooms, were chiseled out or painted over. In Kham and Amdo, the second floors of homes were decreed to be "bourgeois excesses"; their inhabitants were forced to raze them and live in the damp, windowless stables on the first floor. Long plaits of hair worn by both men and women were labeled "the dirty black tails of serfdom" and, if not cut by the individual, were slashed off by roving gangs of Red Guards. Others had their heads half shaved, to mark them as backward. By March 1967, tens of thousands of copies of Mao's Little Red Book—issued with a red purse, inscribed with the slogan "Long Live Chairman Mao"—were given out. Tibetans were required to memorize passages from the book. They were tested both in nightly meetings and on the street—randomly waylaid by Red Guards who demanded flawless recitation on pain of violence. Boiler suits had to be worn, bracelets, earrings and rings discarded; even the traditional Tibetan greeting—equivalent to shaking hands—of sticking out one's tongue, while sucking in the breath, was forbidden. Private pets were exterminated by Red Guards moving from home to home, where they forced the inhabitants to hang portraits of Mao in every room and wrote slogans on the walls. Tibetan youths—members of the Communist Youth League and schoolchildren—were also marshaled into pet and insect extermination campaigns in an effort to counter the Tibetans' abhorrence of taking life. Tibetan writing and even the language itself were targeted for destruction, replaced by a bizarre, mainly Chinese patois called "the Tibetan-Chinese Friendship language"—the grammar and vocabulary of which were incomprehensible to most Tibetans. Great numbers of Tibetans—particularly cadres and others employed directly by the Chinese—were forced to change their names to Chinese equivalents, each with one syllable of Mao's name included. When parents resisted naming their offspring for Mao, the children were officially called by either their date of or weight at birth—so that, as far as Chinese administrators were concerned, many of Tibet's upcoming generation were literally no more than numbers. As a new expression describing the dementia that had gripped the Chinese stated, "First they make us laugh, and then they make us cry."

As preposterous as the fanaticism of the Cultural Revolution seemed to most Tibetans, they had reason to fear it far more than the Democratic Reforms and their attendant campaigns of class cleansing. During these there had been a strict adherence to authority in the administration of various punishments; the Cultural Revolution was pure mob violence. The early parades through Lhasa soon gave way to branding with hot irons, executions and impromptu *thamzing* on the street—so much so that for years Tibetans feared to leave their homes, venturing out only to and from work and even then refusing to acknowledge friends, as it was the duty of watchers on every corner to report suspicious behavior. Then, as early as August 1966, gang rapes began. The female children of four hundred Tibetan families engaged in lumbering at Po Tramo were marched naked in public by Red Guards, submitted to *thamzing* and then raped. Appeals were made to the authorities in Lhasa, but they refused to intervene out of fear for their positions. In the winter of 1966–67, Revolutionary Rebels traveled to Nagchuka, north of Lhasa. Here they subjected vast numbers of nomads, gathered at the town during the cold months, to similar atrocities. Women were stripped, bound and made to stand on frozen lakes under guard. A man and his daughter, Karma Sherab and Tsering Tsomo, were compelled to copulate in public. Throughout Lhoka similar wanton acts took place, as classed Tibetans were left tied in gunnysacks for days at a time. At the Ngyang-chu River (a tributary of the Tsangpo) outside Gyantse, families, including the women and children of classed men, were made to stand in freezing water for five hours, wearing dunce caps, heavy stones strapped to their legs. More rapes and public beatings occurred in Shigatse. A wave of suicides swept over the country as many Tibetans, sometimes in family groups, chose to kill themselves by leaping from cliffs or drowning rather than die at the hands of Chinese gangs. In Lhasa, suicide attempts became so common that PLA guards patrolled the shores of the Kyichu River night and day.

As the fighting between the Red Guard factions intensified, so did the atrocities—committed not only by civilian bands, but by the PLA as well. Rapes and beatings turned into executions in which victims were forced to dig their own graves before being shot. The bloodletting re-created the worst of the crimes that followed the suppression of the 1959 revolt. According to a new influx of refugees escaping, in the confusion, to India, Tibetans were routinely mutilated, their ears, tongues, noses, fingers and arms cut off, genitals and eyes burned. Boiling water was poured on victims hung by the thumbs to extract information they were thought to possess concerning rival factions. Crucifixion was also employed: on June 9, 1968, the bodies of two men were dumped in the street in front of Ngyentseshar—the old Lhasan jail—riddled with nail marks, not just through the hands, but hammered into the head and the major joints of the torso. As late as 1970 a group of ex-monks near the Nepal border were required to stand on pedestals in public and read Mao's Little Red Book aloud for three consecutive days. Those who refused were shot on the spot by the PLA. Their corpses were dragged through the streets, where the people were forced to spit and throw dust on them. Two who would not were also summarily executed. Finally the bodies were prominently displayed beneath signs proclaiming their lot to be the natural end of all reactionaries.

The fate of the Tibetan people was duplicated in the country's 6,254 monasteries. But while so much Red Guard behavior was uncontrolled, the destruction of the monasteries was the result of a carefully planned campaign inaugurated prior to the Cultural Revolution. Beginning in 1959, it had been the ongoing task of the Cultural Articles Preservation Commission to catalogue, according to specified grades of value, every item in every monastery in Tibet for eventual shipment to China. Metallurgy teams were sent from Peking. Nevertheless, it was a massive task, and the work had progressed slowly. The large monasteries around Lhasa, Shigatse, Gyantse and the main cities of Kham and Amdo alone contained so much that few in the countryside had been thoroughly examined prior to 1966. By September 1967, however, a year after the first Revolutionary Rebel group had formed in Lhasa, widespread destruction began in earnest. Older Red Guards supervised the operation equipped with booklets in which each article's designation, either to be saved or destroyed, was noted. Images of gold, silver and bronze, expensive brocades and ancient *thankas* were packed and sealed. Intricately carved pillars and beams were dismantled for use in the construction of Chinese compounds. Then, under red flags—with drums, trumpets and cymbals providing a fanfare —local Tibetans were forced to demolish each monastery. Giant bonfires were lit to burn thousands of scriptures, while those not incinerated were desecrated—used as wrapping in Chinese shops, as toilet paper or as padding in shoes. The wooden blocks in which they were bound were made into floorboards, chairs and handles for farm tools. Clay images were ground to dust, thrown into the street for people to walk on and mixed with fertilizer. Others were remade into bricks for the specific purpose of building public lavatories. *Mani* stones, once among the most common expressions of prayer, were turned into pavement. Frescoes were defaced, the eyes of their images gouged out in a manner reminiscent of the twelfth-century Moslem destruction of Buddhist monasteries in India. Bronze and gold pinnacles crowning every temple's roof were pulled down and— along with other metals—resmelted.

When the pillaging was done, dynamite was placed in the gutted buildings and their walls blown up. Field artillery was also used, so that within a three-year period the entire landscape of Tibet stood scarred by ruins resembling bombed cities. Because the buildings' walls were so thick, virtually none, not even Ganden—slated for total obliteration as the Gelugpa sect's most sacred monastery—could be completely razed, but stood as ghostly ever-present reminders of what had been. The destruction of Tibet's monasteries came as a collective shock that all but the youngest Tibetans found incomprehensible. Whatever personal tragedy Tibetans had experienced paled in the face of what now seemed to be the end of civilization as they knew it.

An essential corollary to the attack on Tibetan culture took the form of a reinvigorated propaganda campaign vilifying the old Tibet. The chief scapegoats were the Dalai and Panchen Lamas. In December 1968, Radio Peking delivered its most scathing attack yet on the Dalai Lama, portraying him as a "political corpse, bandit and traitor." In Tibet itself he was condemned as a "red-handed butcher who subsisted on people's flesh with a red mark on his hand to prove it." It was alleged that whenever the Dalai Lama recited scripture, a human heart, liver or arm was sacrificed. He was said to be too frightened to return home, lest these facts be proved to the Tibetan people, who would then take retribution for his having lived on their "flesh and blood." The stock questions of the nightly meeting were now: "Tell us who masterminded the revolt?" The answer: "The Dalai Lama." The next question: "What type of life did he lead?" Answer: "He was a pleasure-loving lama who loved women, gold and silver and sold our country to imperialists."

China's ultimate portrait of the old Tibet was constructed, toward the close of the Cultural Revolution, in the Tibetan Revolutionary Museum, situated in the village of Shöl below the Potala. It was a mandatory stop for all foreign visitors allowed into Lhasa in carefully screened groups, from the mid-seventies on. In the museum's first room documents were displayed purporting to prove that Tibet had been an inalienable part of China since the thirteenth century. These were followed by what a reporter for the Washington *Post*, accompanying George Bush (then U.S. liaison to China), on a three-day visit in 1977, termed a "revolting depiction of the alleged atrocities of the old regime." The exhibit featured hands, arms and legs severed as punishment for minor crimes, the skins of two children said to have been flayed alive during a religious ceremony and an assortment of whips, knives and manacles used by the "feudal lords" to torture their "slaves." "Pushing aside the black curtains at the exhibition room door, one enters the living hell which was old Tibet," recounted

China Reconstructs in a 1976 piece regaling the museum's dramatically lit dioramas of 106 figures. Orchestrated by tape-recorded music and explanations, the dioramas were arranged in four groups entitled: The Feudal Manor—Hell on Earth; The Lamasery—Wicked Den for Devouring Serfs; The Kashag—Reactionary Local Government; and the Serf's Struggle for Liberation. The scenes included a "serf" forced to carry his "master" up a steep cliff in a snowstorm, "hatred flashing from his eyes"; a boy bartered by a feudal lord for a donkey; a leering monk standing over a debtor about to be dragged to death by a horse; another monk, enclosing a screaming child in a box as a sacrifice; and a woman, said to have led a people's uprising, tied to a stake and sentenced to have her heart gouged out. In the final scene the "slaves" rise up and slaughter their masters, and a dying girl, scrawling a red star in her own blood on a boulder, expresses "her longing for the serfs' delivery, Chairman Mao and the Communist Party."

The chaos and destruction of the Cultural Revolution lasted for three years. Its political aftermath lasted another seven—until the death of Mao Zedong in 1976. In Tibet's case, though, there was a more durable legacy —communes. Central Tibet was the sole region in China to have thus far avoided communization, a fact Maoists viewed as the most flagrant example of the local party's "revisionist" policies. No matter how pressing other duties were, all Red Guards considered it their sacred task to communize Tibet. But it was not so easy, as their predecessors could have testified.

The drive to communize had actually begun as early as 1962. At that time, communes were introduced on an experimental basis around Lhasa, Shigatse and Lhoka. They were not developed, however, owing to the shaky state of the Democratic Reforms, the same difficulties which delayed the founding of the TAR. Tibetans viewed communes as nothing less than mass imprisonment: the ultimate means of social control in which the modicum of freedom they had maintained—including ownership of land, farm tools, animals and the few possessions remaining to them—would be lost to a final leveling of society by the state. Their fears stemmed from the awareness of the effects of enforced collectivization in Kham and Amdo both before and after 1959. Though production goals had risen annually, harvests had been systematically appropriated and famine was now endemic in the once bountiful east. The people of Kham—in the main women and children after years of fighting—were said to be yoked to plows like beasts of burden, toiling year round to meet state quotas.

As with the Democratic Reforms, the desire for communes had to appear as if it emanated from the people. Hence, Tibetans were compelled to sign documents requesting communes, whereupon the Tang or CCP promised to "grant" them. In addition to its propaganda value, this technique had long been recognized by Chinese cadres as a valuable tool for forestalling criticism of daily work. Complaints were easily dismissed with the simple observation that the people themselves had requested that the policy be implemented—so how, then, could they now claim to oppose it? In Central Tibet's case, the stage in socialization following Mutual Aid Teams, cooperatives, was bypassed altogether. Where others had walked, the Tibetans were thus to "leap" to communes—and they needed the Party's help to do so.

The Chinese began by galvanizing the "leading element" of people's activists. Meetings were called in 1964 at which it was promised that, if communes were successfully established, they would be allowed to govern them, holding the ranks of *turing* and *dbutang*—chairman and overseer— a promotion over their usual position of *tsoutang* or group leader. Their methods were to be twofold. On the harsh side, commune formation would constitute the key topic for three to four months at the nightly meeting; whoever opposed it would be made an example of by *thamzing* and imprisonment. The *burtsun chenpos* or "diligent ones" carried this out so eagerly that—acquainted now with the requisite behavior for survival —people all over Tibet, as refugees recounted, were soon saying, "Even if the communes cannot be established today, please set them up tomorrow!" On the soft side, the Chinese promised that communes were none other than "the Golden Bridge to the Socialist Paradise." A few model communes, amply supplied with yaks, sheep, horses, pigs, carts, tools and fertilizer—all of which were promised to every burgeoning commune— were established to serve as inspiring examples. Immediately following the inauguration of the TAR in 1965, some 130 communes had been formed. Then, with the advent of the Cultural Revolution, the "soft sell" was abandoned and communization was implemented across the country. By the summer of 1970, more than one thousand communes had been set up; by December 1975, the drive had been completed in 93 percent of the TAR's 71 *chou*, or districts—some 1,925 communes having been established.

Getting people to relinquish their possessions—the first stage in communization—proved the greatest obstacle. A compensation rate was set— far below the actual worth of the given item: 150 yuan or roughly $75 was to be paid for the best horse; 70 yuan or $35 for a yak (the usual value being $250); $15 for a donkey and plow; $2.50 for a hammer; $4.00 for a long knife; $3.00 for a shovel and saddle; $2.00 for a rope. In most cases reimbursement was to be made over a three- to five-year period. Tibetans, however, never received the promised money. Payment would begin, the Chinese said, only when the commune produced a surplus—a stipulation which made a mockery of the entire premise of "compensation," as the Tibetans' own labor was to "pay back" what they had given to begin with. Thus, the state expended nothing at all on communes—its propaganda claiming, all the while, vast contributions of materials and seeds. To add insult to the injury, each person over sixteen years of age had immediately to contribute up to 11 yuan toward his commune's starting capital. As no one had this money, the Chinese were compelled to lend it—bringing the entire nation into their debt and thereby justifying a regular raising of taxes through interest at each harvest. Short of bringing in the PLA, it was difficult to get Tibetans to voluntarily impose such devastating conditions on themselves. Eventually, though, the army was dispatched to many regions, mass arrests were carried out, and to those who remained intransigent it was soon made clear that while survival inside the commune structure might be distasteful, existence outside meant certain doom—the communes having confiscated all water sources and the best land in each area. Only a few classed families, purposely not permitted to join, henceforth remained beyond the fringe of the new society.

An average commune comprised from 100 to 200 families, or 1,000 people. It was organized in production teams (but not, due to the low population, in brigades as in the rest of China) usually encompassing a single village, with a bank and general store shared by up to seven communes in the local subdistrict. As the 1970s progressed, the limited facilities, including health care and primary schools, were spread even thinner, as communes were conglomerated into groups of four while still being treated as a single unit. The communes were run by a staff of officers under a leader who issued work orders based on demands received from the local party office. In the administration of certain communes there were as many as fifty different ranks. These positions were held exclusively by Tibetans, who were required to carry out their duties over and above their daily burden of farm labor. Under them, the Tibetan people's remaining freedoms were lost. Movement beyond one's house and field, not just the surrounding area, was forbidden. Even trips to collect firewood required prior permission. To take a day's leave for illness or to tend to a sick relative, often necessitated signatures from as many as twelve officials.

The day began with the dirgelike, monochromatic notes of China's favorite anthem, "The East Is Red," played from loudspeakers on Peking time—two hours before sunrise in Tibet. After roll call in one's production team, work commenced at 5:00 a.m. Labor then continued until 8:00 or 10:00 at night, depending on the season, followed by the two- to three-hour political meeting that ended about midnight. Though many people took one Sunday every fortnight off from work, there were only seven sanctioned holidays a year—three days for Communist celebrations, three for Chinese New Year's and one for Western New Year's. Mothers with new babies were granted the special dispensation of a half hour in the morning and another in the evening for breast feeding. Though the old, the infirm and children below school age were officially exempt from labor, without work points they received no grain ration. Thus every man, woman and child in Tibet from the age of six or seven to that of eighty or more was compelled, if physically able, to work. Exhaustion was so common and the rules so strictly enforced that frequently the corpses of those who died went unburied for days at a time. As Tibetans commented, in a new expression, on their lot: "In Tibet there are only three things left to see. In the morning you see the stars, during the day the locks on the houses and at night, returning from work, the moon."

In addition to farming, miles of canals were dug, dams, roads and water tanks built. Breaking new land became an obsession with the communes —as was, by the early seventies, planting winter wheat. The Chinese preferred wheat to barley, so 80 percent of the arable land was sown with it. When the shoots were five inches high, local officials took inventory of the expected crop, and the harvest was scrupulously checked against their figures to make sure there was no pilfering. Acreage, though, was not allowed to lie fallow on alternate years, a practice which, in Tibet's fragile environment, leached the soil and resulted in massive crop failures. This abuse of the land, not rectified until the end of the 1970s, accounted for ongoing pockets of famine throughout the country.

Tibet's nomads, many of whom had delayed for long periods of time in Mutual Aid Teams, were by no means excluded from communization. Their possessions and herds were collectivized and a strict breeding requirement with 90 percent of a given herd's mature females having to reproduce annually—was enforced. Accidental casualties of up to 2 percent of the animals were permitted; any beyond had to be turned over to the authorities with a full explanation—whereafter, if the herder was found responsible, he was punished. The staple nomad diet of meat, cheese and butter was replaced, in the main, by state-issued barley. In Central Tibet, meat was appropriated for the PLA; in Amdo and Kham, it was shipped, along with hides, directly to China.

Within a year of their founding the economic oppression of the communes drastically altered life in Tibet once again. An intricate system of work points and taxation combined to reduce the population to below subsistence level, with grain rations running out, unless further apportioned by individuals—from now until the late seventies—on average, three to four months before year's end. The work-point system had been originated in Dazhai, China's leading commune (whose astronomical production figures, it was later revealed, had all been falsified), and represented the ultimate in collectivization. In Tibet, the people were rewarded with *karmas* or stars, recorded in a small booklet called a *kardeb*. Every three days, group leaders took their charges' books and noted how many stars they had earned; at two-week intervals the numbers were totaled. In a day, the best worker earned eight toten stars, the worst earned five and children earned four. Though varying in worth when translated into currency, the average *karma* was valued at around 1 motse or 5 cents. Thus, the maximum earned by top-ranked Tibetan cadres was 50 cents a day, $14 a month, $168 a year. The general per capita income, taking into account both dependents and the average wage earned, fell in the vicinity of $60 a year, making Tibet at this time the poorest nation on Earth, below even Bhutan, whose people earned $10 more each, annually. However, with all goods obtained by rationing only, monetary value was secondary. Where work points or stars mattered was at the end of the year. At this time, a full twelve months' labor was assessed and translated into grain rations. Not, though, prior to taxation.

Before work points were tallied and the grain ration for each production team determined, up to eight different kinds of taxes were levied on the harvest: these included 6 percent State Grain (called either Loving the Nation Tax or Voluntary Tax—as Tibetans were supposed to give it voluntarily out of their love for the party), Seed Grain, Fodder Grain, Famine Prevention Grain, War Preparation Grain, Grain for Commune Expenses and two categories of so-called Surplus Grain, the last of which, though not strictly a tax, would be "voluntarily" sold to the state at incredibly low prices—1 *khel* (or 28 pounds) generally going for a little more than 3 yuan, or $1.50—the price of three packs of cigarettes. In addition, the money was then placed in commune banks, to which individuals had no access. After all of these taxes were subtracted, workers, depending on their performance, would be awarded rations for the year. Under this system each person's normal annual intake of grain amounted to 8 to 12 *khels*, or 224 to 336 pounds, for most far less than a pound a day. Meat, vegetables, butter, milk, yogurt and tea, all previously staples, continued to be absent from the diet. Families with aged or infant dependents suffered the most. Their food, insufficient for two adults, often had to be shared among five people. A new beggar or "loitering" class was thus created. And while the commune would extend an initial loan to some of these unfortunates, it would never do so twice. As there was no means of paying back the loan, people continued to beg, and the party announced that it was not its responsibility but that of the "better off" members of the community to support them. Produced by the system itself, the new class became a millstone overnight, increasing in weight as children were born and more families fell into debt. Tibetans now said among themselves, "Liberation is like having a wet leather cap put on one's head. The quicker it dries, the tighter it gets, until it kills you."

The truth of the aphorism turned increasingly clear under a new wave of famine which, despite increased cultivation, was the sole result Tibetans experienced from the communes. To add to the Cultural Revolution's disruptions, a slew of natural disasters befell Tibet—the worst drought in a hundred years, the heaviest snowfall in fifty and, in 1972, severe earthquakes. All produced widespread crop failures. Where small pockets of famine had occurred in the lull between 1963 and 1968, the Chinese had occasionally agreed to loan grain from state stores. In 1969, however, in the midst of a nationwide war preparation campaign, they ceased doing this, and retained all reserve stocks for the PLA alone. Furthermore, when harvests were poor the Chinese refused to reduce taxes, creating a devastating drop in the already subsistence-level rations. Even when hundreds of starving people poured into Gyantse and Shigatse in 1972, grain rations having descended from 7 to 5 and then an incredible 4 khels or 112 pounds a year—thereby running out after only four or five months—nothing was forthcoming from the well-stocked army granaries. Unwilling to arrest the demonstrators—because they would have to be fed—the PLA dispersed them back to the countryside. Here, they subsisted by foraging for wild herbs, roots, mushrooms, scorpion plants in particular and a plant called *chung*, used in the past for making green dye. Previously such foraging had been the only means of survival for many old people who could neither work nor receive support from their families. Now almost the entire population of Tibet took, often with fatal results, to living off the land, returning, as they had in the early sixties, to picking undigested grain from the manure of PLA horses, stealing discarded food thrown by the Chinese to their pigs and chickens and digging for worms. The plight of the city dwellers, though, remained even worse than that of the country folk. From early in 1968, both Shigatse and Lhasa ceased to receive supplies. Stores remained empty—devoid even of matches, kerosene, candles and cigarettes, much less sugar and tea. For years nightly meetings were held by the light of a single candle or two—a boon, ironically, for Tibetans, who no longer had to strain to stay awake for fear of being caught inattentive. When the chaos of the Cultural Revolution began to ease, commodities returned to Tibet; yet through the end of the famine in 1973, they remained in such short supply that only cadres and Chinese settlers had consistent access to them. For Tibetans a box of matches a month was considered a luxury. A tin of cooking oil cost more than the average laborer earned in two months. The four yards of cloth issued a year, insufficient in itself to make even a single new *chuba,* was in many cases forgone, people's clothes now becoming so reworked that the original material could no longer be seen for the patches. As Tibetans were barred from such necessities as soap, mud was used instead. Chinese, however, were rationed a single cake of bathing soap every three months, and half a cake for washing clothes every two months. There were so many instances of looting and robbery that those who were caught had to be released after making a simple confession.

Tens of thousands of Tibetans died during the 1968–73 famine. According to survivors, the famine brought the total number of Tibetans who had perished as a direct result of the Chinese invasion close to the million mark, reducing the nation's population by one seventh. Just prior to it, the Chinese had introduced a dish called the *dug-gnal drenso thugpa* or "remembering sufferings soup." This was a thin gruel of *tsamba* and water, without salt, which people were made to drink in order to recall the supposedly horrid conditions under which they had suffered before liberation. Younger Tibetans incredulously asked their elders, "Was it really that bad in the old society?" The adults carefully replied, "Yes, the masses subsisted only on this gruel, while the aristocrats regaled themselves at banquets." Unfortunately for Chinese propagandists, the distorted image of the past paled in comparison with the realities of the present.

Communes and their attendant starvation were both intimately related to a third phenomenon, commencing late in 1968 and lasting into the second half of the seventies: war preparation. On October 1, 1968, Lin Biao and Zhou Enlai issued a new call for massive war preparedness. Just as the 1962 border war with India had been employed to galvanize China following the "three lean years," once more an external threat was used to stem the tide of internal disorder. It was complemented by the Hsia Fang movement, also inaugurated in the autumn of 1968, in which as many as 30 million Red Guards were forcibly sent to the countryside. There was a special note to the war drive, however, which accounted for both its great duration and its intensity. With heavy concentrations of Indian Jawans perched on Tibet's borders, a divided Korea to the northeast, relations with the Soviet Union about to erupt in the volatile border clashes of 1969 and the Vietnam War at its peak, the People's Republic was encircled by hostile forces. Belief in the inevitability of a third world war capped China's fears, party theorists now holding that a nuclear holocaust was due at any moment. Under the threat of imminent destruction, almost anything could be demanded of the population. For the next seven years Tibetans were warned that the moment had finally come when India would attack. Accordingly, while the population starved, military grain stockpiles—which the PLA boasted were sufficient for decades (a not altogether fanciful notion in Tibet's high altitude)—grew immense. Communes were the very engine of the war machine; nonetheless, war preparedness entailed far more than farm work.

By 1969 three categories through which all Tibetans were to assist the PLA had been created. The first, entailing conscription directly into the army, was reserved for young Tibetan men possessing the best class designation—that of poor farmer, between the ages of seventeen and twenty-five. Recruited for up to five years, they were given two months of basic training, whereafter, mixed with different recruits, they were organized into four- or five-man units appended to every 100 Chinese soldiers, one Tibetan generally to each PLA squad. Their job was to translate to the local population as well as coordinate support in the event of war. They were forbidden either to associate with other Tibetans or to discuss defense matters among themselves. Officially, they were not even supposed to know the strength of their own company. Each was given a notebook in which to periodically record his misdeeds, further enforcing security. Compelled to volunteer by 450 subdistrict offices, as many as 30,000 men in the TAR alone were initially conscripted; the numbers in Kham and Amdo unknown.

The second category, called *yulmag* in Tibetan, was a people's militia. It had been introduced on a small scale during the 1962 war, mainly in the border regions. In 1969, it was again organized in border zones, though now on an all-inclusive district, subdistrict, commune and production team basis. Two types of recruits, both between the ages of fifteen and thirty-eight, comprised the militia. The more important were *burtsun chenpos*, or activists, two of whom were assigned to every militia unit. Trained separately, they were enjoined to seek out spies, counterrevolutionaries and those trying to escape to India. One was equipped with an automatic weapon (such as a Sten gun), the other with its ammunition. Together they guarded strategic points including bridges, grain warehouses and dams. The majority of militia, who composed the other group, were not armed. They practiced with either wooden guns or long staves, though by the mid-seventies some three-member teams carried weapons: one man held the rifle, another the bullets, the last accounted for each round expended. Not to lose time in the fields, training was held in place of night meetings. An average commune produced one brigade of militia. While some brigades were trained in guerrilla warfare, most were given rudimentary marching drill and were counted on to function mainly as a police force when war called the PLA and elite militia away.

The third category was called the War Preparation Army. As part of it, Tibetans thirty-five to forty-five were to accompany the PLA to the front as laborers and transport workers. Those aged forty-five to fifty-five were assigned as medical assistants; besides carrying bandages and other supplies, their job was to remove the wounded and bury the dead. The oldest and least useful Tibetans, those fifty-five to sixty-five, were called "Support the Army." Unarmed, they were to attack ahead of the regular troops in human waves, absorbing the enemy's fire. In all the border areas, yaks and horses were organized into transport teams.

While the Tibetans in western, southern and southeastern Tibet were engaged in training, their brethren in the big cities had an equally tiring drama to act out. Like cities in China proper, Lhasa, Shigatse, Gyantse, Chamdo, Jyekundo, Dartsedo and all other major towns were hardened against aerial assault. Parallel walls were constructed in the strongest room of each home; parallel trenches and air-raid shelters were dug—by Tibetans—lining main thoroughfares. In Lhasa, civil defense exercises were carried out day and night, a siren atop Chokpori Hill signaling their start and finish. Even hospitals were evacuated as PLA antiaircraft batteries and civilian fire squads took control of the city for an hour or two. Underground headquarters for all of the TAR's major departments were tunneled into the hills around the valley, plans drawn up for relocation at a moment's notice. It was rumored among Tibetan cadres that important documents had already been transported out of the city to the secret locations.

War preparation provided a check not just on Red Guard violence but on revolts by the Tibetans themselves. The Cultural Revolution had offered a natural opportunity for a renewal of attack against the Chinese. Young Tibetan men began by joining the Revolutionary Rebels, who, in exchange for their enlistment, promised higher grain rations and even—remarkably—freedom of religious practice. Under their auspices, Tibetans donned the Red Guard's universally worn red armband, "encircled" hated Chinese cadres, ambushed convoys and whenever they could provoked clashes between rival factions. Freed from labor for the first time in their lives, youths spent long hours avidly fashioning staves, spears and axes for pitched battles with the Great Alliance. Their elders, Tibetan cadres working in the employ of the Chinese, denounced their superiors, walked off their jobs and threatened anyone who sought to prevent them with the dreaded accusation of being "pro-Liuist." Insubordination, though, was a comparatively mild form of resistance. By the end of 1968 a number of popular revolts had swept the country, catalyzed by the withdrawal of Chinese troops to the capital, with only isolated garrisons, their communications cut, left in the countryside.

One incident in particular galvanized Tibetans into revolt. On the morning of June 7, 1968, a group of teen-agers became embroiled with a PLA unit in the courtyard of Yuthok House in Lhasa. Two Chinese were killed. Frightened, the youngsters fled to the hallowed interior of the Jokhang, the Central Cathedral's inner sanctum, where they were soon surrounded by three hundred military police. The PLA commander informed them that, unless they returned weapons and ammunition stolen in the fight, he would open fire within five minutes. The youths insisted that they had taken no weapons; moreover, they claimed that they all came from poor and middle-class backgrounds. With no further word they held up their copies of Mao's Little Red Book and began to chant a Communist slogan, hoping to defuse the confrontation: "The army and people are one; beneath the sky none can separate them." When the time elapsed, the PLA fired directly into the crowd, killing twelve and wounding forty-nine, many of whom were bayoneted and beaten with rifle butts following the fusillade. The Chinese commanders then denied those wounded medical attention until a team of Tibetan doctors from Mendzekhang arrived to take them away. In the interim, the large crowds gathered outside heard the survivors within singing a well-known underground song:

> "Do not mourn, people of Tibet,
> Independence will surely be ours.
> Remember our sun,
> Remember His Holiness."

Word spread quickly of the massacre in Tibet's holiest shrine. Popular resentment was brought to such a pitch that Chinese authorities, to dampen the crisis, announced that there would be an investigation (which was never, in fact, conducted). But the city's will to resist could not be diminished. Anti-Chinese acts proliferated, and a full year later, in June 1969, mass disobedience occurred when the entire population openly defied the ban on religion by celebrating Saka Dawa—the anniversary of Buddha's birth, enlightenment and death. The following month office workers in the capital walked off their jobs, ostensibly to celebrate World Solidarity Day. Erecting tents in Lhasa's old *lingkas* or picnic grounds by the Kyichu River, they opened their Little Red Books on the ground, as though studying, and proceeded to play dice and mah-jong for an entire week. Outside Lhasa, in Lhoka, resistance took a less playful turn. There,

3,000 young Tibetans attacked the PLA, killing 200. Two months later, 200 more troops were killed in Tsethang; similar uprisings were reported to have occurred in five areas of western Tibet as early as 1967. By the summer of 1970—long after Red Guard fighting had subsided, communes had been imposed and war preparation begun—a major revolt broke out across southwestern Tibet, in which more than 1,000 Chinese soldiers died, by the account of a local PLA commander. A spate of mass executions followed—the victims usually members of underground groups—often scheduled to coincide with public holidays. Undaunted, the inhabitants of Kham's original eighteen districts began openly attacking Chinese under the Tibetan flag. By 1972, fighting had yet to be put down, with the largest revolt of all affecting some sixty of the seventy-one districts in the TAR and reportedly claiming the lives of 12,000 Tibetans.

Despite both the formation of a Revolutionary Committee in the autumn of 1968 and an end to Red Guard fighting in 1969, Peking felt that Tibet required a massive purge to regain stability. It began early in 1970. Officially designated as simply another "class-cleansing campaign," the purge was directed, unlike the Democratic Reforms and their rechecking, not just at the upper strata, but at all segments of society. "Traitors, conspirators, saboteurs, arsonists and anarchist elements"—everyone from ultra-leftists to those remnant anti-Maoists who had somehow escaped the Cultural Revolution were subjected to "weeding out." In April 1970, tens of thousands of Tibetan cadres who had proved their untrustworthiness during the upheaval were culled from the bureaucracy. Simultaneously, the records of every Tibetan in the TAR, meticulously kept by each branch of the Public Security Bureau, were reviewed. Afterwards, thousands were arrested in surprise nighttime raids, taken to prisons and submitted to interrogations. In each area, groups of ten to twenty were singled out as examples to receive one of three fates; *thamzing*, imprisonment or public execution. The photos of those to be executed were posted around each district, the requisite red X marked across their body or face, their crimes of "anti-party and anti-people activities" listed beneath. The executions themselves took place on large public meeting grounds where the victim, a wire pulled tight around his or her neck by a Chinese guard (to keep them from yelling a last word of defiance) would receive a bullet to the back of the head. Immediately thereafter, their family members, assembled at the head of the crowd, would be made to applaud, thank the Party for its "kindness" in eliminating the "bad element" from among them and then bury the still warm and bloody corpse, unceremoniously and without covering, in an impromptu grave. In this manner, almost four years after the Cultural Revolution had plunged Tibet back into the turmoil it had just begun to leave behind, Chinese officials hoped once more to regain control over the population.

AT MIDNIGHT on October 18, 1962, Dr. Tenzin Choedrak's truck drove in sight of the Potala. The twenty-one survivors of the group who had left Tibet three years before had been taxed to the utmost by their return trip from China. Only the strongest could balance themselves against the shifting movement of the vehicle as it plied the mountains and valleys on the Xining-Lhasa route. With each turn, the others were helplessly thrown about, despite their efforts to press against one another for stability. As the Thangbu Pass, five hours from Nagchuka, was crossed, all required drafts from the oxygen pillows to breathe; even so, a number fainted. From then on, the thin air and cold dulled the men's anticipation of returning home. It was briefly revived only at journey's end as the somber mass of the Potala, its windows blank and featureless, came into view silhouetted against the mountains behind.

Taking the northern road, the truck skirted Lhasa, and passed ten minutes later through a gate in the twenty-foot-wall surrounding Drapchi, Tibet's foremost prison. Originally headquarters for the Drapchi Regiment of the Tibetan army, the compound's barracks had, by September 1959, received 3,000 prisoners, the majority of whom were monks from Sera and Drepung monasteries. Ordered to build their own cells, the men had begun by constructing a windowless maximum-security block, capable of housing 200 high lamas and officials, behind an interior wall. An outer courtyard and cellblocks bounded by exterior walls came next, followed by a hospital, for the use of Chinese personnel in Lhasa. Thereafter Drapchi began serving as the region's chief clearinghouse for prisoners arrested during the Democratic Reforms. Once their cases were decided, most were dispatched to the TAR's growing string of labor camps, which eventually held upwards of 100,000 people. Drapchi's permanent inmate population was kept, according to one ex-inmate, at 1,700, which despite frequent deaths, was replenished by a monthly addition of between ten to fifty new prisoners.

At Drapchi the real meaning of "reeducation" was brought home to Tenzin Choedrak. Unlike the other five prisons in and around Lhasa, which, well into the eighties, held 7,000 to 8,000 political prisoners— almost a fifth of the city's Tibetan population—Drapchi did not emphasize forced labor. Indoctrination was its specialty. Permitted to leave their cells only for trips to the toilet, Dr. Choedrak and his companions were to spend every waking hour in study—an assault on the spirit, which, in its own way, proved more destabilizing than the physical hardships of the past. It was now that mental breakdowns, depression and suicidal behavior appeared—previously held in abeyance by the body's suffering, but unavoidable when the mind alone had to bear the brunt of hardship. Eight rules, required to be memorized on the prisoner's arrival, served as the basis of "reeducation." Inmates were not permitted to discuss their backgrounds, the reasons for their incarceration or any topics other than those being taught. Instead, faults were to be confessed daily; to which end, it was every man's duty to inform on his neighbor. On the other hand, the prisoner had to regularly extol the Tang or CCP, citing examples from his personal experience to demonstrate how much he had benefited from the Party's guiding light. Finally, no complaining about rations was permitted, all orders were to be obeyed without appeal, no destruction of property, laughing, singing or loud talking was allowed, and a clean appearance was to be maintained at all times.

Dr. Choedrak was placed in a fourteen-man cell on the east side of the prison's outer courtyard. Only sixteen by twelve feet, it was so small that when the men slept head to head in two rows, their feet hit the walls, forcing them to bend their knees. The diet at Drapchi consisted mainly of *tsampa* gruel and boiled greens with hot water. Fifteen days after their arrival, however, Dr. Choedrak's group were given their first taste of butter tea in years, which they continued to receive once every other day. Over the next two weeks, relatives were allowed to visit, bringing gifts of meat, roasted beans and barley. Dr. Choedrak's brother Topgyal came, bearing with him the head of a yak—all he could obtain. The gifts, though, were a mixed blessing. As the prisoners devoured the new food, divided carefully into daily portions, they experienced excruciating stomach pain followed by diarrhea. Long before the day's three toilet runs began, the small wooden box kept in the cell as a night toilet would overflow, feces and urine spreading onto the floor. The foul odor made the already claustrophobic conditions unbearable. During this period, the first signs of flesh began to appear around Dr. Choedrak's emaciated torso. Miraculously, it seemed, hair and eyebrows returned, giving him and his comrades a more human look. Still, they remained creatures of such fragility that, with their senses reviving, the slightest stimulation brought sharp pain. When the kitchen staff, almost two dozen yards away, began boiling tea and cooking food, the odor produced devastating hunger pangs. Hunger itself, which long ago had disappeared beneath a haze of enervation, now returned with such force that no matter how much they ate, the men continually felt famished. Between a ravenous appetite and its resulting diarrhea, the return to life was made, and the legacy of Jiuzhen slowly faded.

Led by a group leader chosen amongst themselves, "reeducation" got underway. Supplied with a current issue of the *Tibet Daily*, which served as a starting point for discussion, the leader was required to take copious notes of the proceedings. *Thamzing* also continued, the less intelligent men still falling victim, unable to shade their answers with the required nuances. Then, for reasons never explained to them, it was announced by the Chinese that Dr. Choedrak's group required more severe punishment. In the autumn of 1963, a year after their arrival in Drapchi, the men were transferred into the maximum-security block. The walls of their new cell, just as small as the old, contained only a few holes, each the size of two bricks, to let in light and air. Belts and bootlaces were confiscated by the guards to prevent suicide. As the Tibetans later learned, prisoners throughout the camp were hanging themselves from planks beneath the smoke hole in each cell's roof. Few could cope with the confinement, inactivity and continual prying into the core of their thoughts.

One day Dr. Choedrak and his cellmates heard shouts followed by gunfire in the yard outside their room. Brought out on a toilet break sometime later, they saw the bullet-torn body of ∑ peasant farmer from Phenbo, left in the dirt where it had fallen. The man had been confined in the cell behind theirs and on being taken to the toilet had run amok. In a later incident Dr. Choedrak heard a prisoner outside his cell defiantly shout, "I don't want Marxism, I want religion!" After returning to his cell, the man was overcome by rage and tying a piece of cloth to a twig from a broomstick—all he could find—started yelling at the top of his voice, "Tibet is independent!" Taken away, he was never seen again. Dr. Choedrak himself remained extremely depressed through this third stage of his confinement.

In May 1965, a guard came to Tenzin Choedrak's cell and told him to pack his few belongings. Once more without explanation, he was moved. This time a jeep waited in the prison's outer yard. Dr. Choedrak was driven northeast up the Lhasan Valley. Here, built into a canyon between two spurs of a mountain, stood the prison of Sangyip. Two compounds, Sangyip proper and its slightly less severe branch, Yidutu, lay at the front of the gap inside three walls crowned by periodic guard towers, the rear wall being formed by the cliff itself. The prison's third and least severe branch, Utitu, lay surrounded by its own wall five hundred feet south of the canyon near a compound for the Chinese staff, also separately enclosed. It had been six years since Dr. Choedrak's imprisonment. He had yet to be formally charged with a specific crime, brought to trial or even given a sentence. Deposited in a maximum-security cell for thirteen men, bisected by a concrete path, on either side of which sand was scattered for

Dr. Tenzin Choedrak, chief physician to the Dalai Lama.

Gendun Thargay in New York.

Tempa Tsering in Dharamsala.

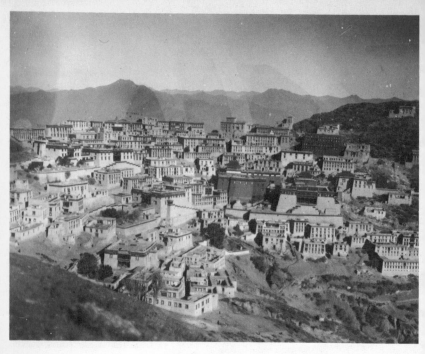

Ganden Monastery, the
third largest monastery
in the world, early 1920s.

The ruins of Ganden Monastery today.

*Yambulakhang
in the late 1940s;
Tibet's first palace,
built in 127 B.C.*

Yambulakhang today.

A monastery being used as a machine shop.

Buddhist temple converted to a granary.

A commune school room in Central Tibet.

*Tibetans surround the
bus carrying the first
delegation in Lhasa.*

*Lhasans storm the Central
Cathedral to greet the first
delegation sent to Tibet
by the Dalai Lama,
September 1979.*

*Tibetans run to greet
the second delegation
below the ruins of Dayab
Monastery in Kham.*

*A twenty-five-foot-tall
pile of destroyed statues,
photographed by the
second delegation in a
palace of the Norbulingka.*

The Panchen Lama with
members of the second
delegation in Peking, May 1980.

Lobsang Samten, the
Dalai Lama's brother, blessing
crowds at Labrang Tashikhiel,
the first delegation's
initial stop in Tibet.

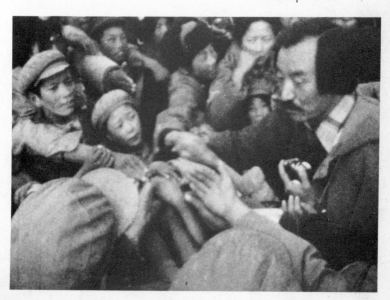

*Crowds seeking blessings
from Pema Gyalpo,
the Dalai Lama's sister
and leader of
the third delegation.*

*The ruins of Dungkhar
Monastery visited
by members of the
third delegation.*

sleeping, he once more took up the endless task of placement "reeducation."

With his removal from the dungeon of Drapchi and among new men, Dr. Choedrak's perspective began to shift. He now found that somehow the worst of prison life had been overcome. From his first series of *thamzing* in the maximum-security prison at Silingpu, Lhasa's PLA headquarters, when he had lost his teeth and suffered damage to his eye, through subsequent ordeals in Jiuzhen and Drapchi, he had learned to enact a pretense of "self-improvement" while remaining inwardly beyond the reach of indoctrination. Above all, faith in religion had preserved his equanimity. Each night he continued his Tum-mo exercises, augmented, since his last year in China, by silent recitation of mantras. Now, in Sangyip, he took a major risk. Tying 108 knots into a piece of string, he fashioned a rosary with which to say prayers. Before going to sleep, he recited four to five hundred mantras: half those of Avalokiteshvara, the Bodhisattva of Infinite Compassion, the other half of Manjusri, the Bodhisattva of Infinite Wisdom. The same idea, in fact, had occurred to a number of inmates, all of whom, as they grew to trust the new man, revealed their practices to him. Whereas Dr. Choedrak managed to recite three million mantras in Sangyip, he knew others who recited almost double that number.

One morning a little more than a year after Tenzin Choedrak's arrival in Sangyip, the men placed their mugs, as usual, outside the cell window to receive tea. When the kitchen workers came by, however, they learnt that its rationing had been discontinued. Drinking butter tea was henceforth labeled a habit of the "old, rotten system, indulged in only by reactionaries." From now on, only "proletarian" boiled water would be served. Vegetable gruel was discontinued as well, so that the entire diet now consisted of small portions of *tsampa* given three times a day. When a few weeks later copies of Mao's Little Red Book were handed out, the prisoners surmised that great changes were occurring beyond the prison walls. For the next ten years, the book's contents were to be the principal topic of study, the Cultural Revolution having penetrated the prison as well. But though the return to conditions of near famine was distressful, the political shift which accompanied them came, ironically, as a blessing. The book, it turned out, provided a perfect vehicle for further recitation of prayers. By saying a mantra for every letter in a line and calculating the number of mantras at day's end, the entire cell was infused with a new spirit of hope. No matter how often they looked in, the unwary guards beheld all thirteen men poring over their books, apparently deeply engrossed. Even the slight movement of the lips—enough to have earned many prisoners *thamzing* in the past—now appeared to be a sign of concentration on Mao's aphorisms.

In 1972, Dr. Choedrak finally received his sentence, based on a penal code adopted four years earlier. The code specified four categories of prisoners who would never be released: those from border regions; major "reactionaries," such as guerrillas and members of the underground; prisoners without families; and the worst group—to which Tenzin Choedrak belonged—upper-class intelligentsia associated with the former Tibetan government. Along with the other grades of prisoners, they received one of six types of sentences, ranging in length from twelve to thirty years. Some were eligible for review, others not. There were also death sentences, delayed for one to two years, after which they could be commuted to life imprisonment if the culprit was deemed sufficiently reformed. Dr. Choedrak was given a seventeen-year sentence, thirteen years of which he had already served. He could not, though, look forward to release in four years' time. Even if no new charges were placed against him, at best his status would be upgraded to that of a *lemirukha*, or "free laborer." As in Jiuzhen, such workers lived in unguarded cellblocks outside the prison, from which they reported to work on their own recognizance. Once every two weeks, in groups of three, they were permitted to visit their families in Lhasa. Receiving work points like the rest of the population, they purchased their rations and were given nothing by the prison. Because of this institution, inmates had little hope of ever becoming free. The need for labor brigades was made evident each year in the annual winter accounting. At this time, Sangyip's profit—how many hundreds of thousands of yuan each work section had brought in—was posted. This figure determined the production targets for the coming year. Without the army of "free laborers," topping the previous year's work would have been impossible. Thus the prison depended on a steady, if not increasing, population of workers. On the other hand, the moment either a prisoner or a laborer became too ill or old to work, he was discharged and told to return home. Dr. Choedrak witnessed numerous examples of aged prison mates who, though they requested not to be sent home, where there was no one to support them, were turned down and forcibly evicted, left to beg or die on their own.

Following sentencing, Dr. Choedrak was transferred from Sangyip to Yidutu, the milder branch located next to it. Here his decade of inactive confinement finally came to an end. His "reeducation" deemed complete, he was assigned to hard labor in the prison's quarry, a job, along with brickmaking, reserved for Tibetans. While Chinese prisoners repaired automobile parts or held other factory jobs, he now had to chisel ninety twelve-by-eight-inch stone blocks a day from boulders blasted out of the mountainside behind the camp. Working with five other inmates, he could barely perform his share of labor, his muscles having atrophied from lack of use. While two men hammered boulders to produce smaller rocks, the remaining four hurriedly fashioned blocks from these, having to fill their own quotas as well as those of the first two. It was dangerous work. The prisoners were often struck in the eyes and face by flying chips of rock. Wedges and sledgehammers were used and the man holding the wedge was frequently hit, due to the accelerated pace of the labor. A blackboard, hung under a tin canopy on one of the prison walls, kept the daily tally of each group. And as with all work in Chinese prisons, anyone falling below his assigned number was subjected to struggle session to improve his performance.

As Tenzin Choedrak adjusted to his new life, the fresh air and exercise combined to gradually improve his health. In the following year, he experienced a relative sense of contentment, above and beyond the mere detachment he had already learned to cultivate. Then one day he was summoned away from his work. Brought into the presence of a Chinese prison physician named Dr. Li, Dr. Choedrak listened in astonishment as the man spoke to him in a pleasant, even ingratiating tone. The doctor explained that he had discovered Tenzin Choedrak's name among Sangyip's records and had thought it advisable to consult him about an ailment he had been suffering from for many years. He then asked Dr. Choedrak to diagnose his case. The request was particularly surprising because, though Mendzekhang had remained open after 1959, Tibetan medicine had never been given credence by the Chinese. Dr. Choedrak read the physician's pulse. His hands were rough, the skin so thick and bruised that it was difficult to make a clear diagnosis. Nonetheless, he detected—correctly—a liver ailment. Impressed, the doctor explained that his illness was severe enough to have warranted two trips to the mainland. He had tried both Western and traditional Chinese medicine, but both had failed. Dr. Choedrak prescribed Tibetan medicines, and predicted that a cure would not be difficult to effect. Soon after he obtained the pills from Mendzekhang, the physician became well and with his recovery came a remarkable improvement for Dr. Choedrak as well. Holding a high rank in the Public Security Bureau, the doctor took it upon himself to discuss Tenzin Choedrak's case with its chief officers at their headquarters in Lhasa. There he pointed out that Dr. Choedrak's skills might be of value to the state, which had just announced a brief liberalization called "the Four Freedoms," designed to rehabilitate "local culture." Three security officers, all suffering from chronic ailments, went to Yidutu, where Dr. Choedrak was called upon to diagnose and treat them. All were cured. As a result, Dr. Choe-drak was removed from his cell and, to his utter disbelief, sent to work as a doctor in Sangyip's hospital. Then, in 1976, having served his full seventeen-year sentence, he was transferred outside the walls to Utitu, the mildest of Sangyip's prisons. Here he lived as a "free laborer," although he was officially still considered an "enemy of the people," his identity papers marked by a "black hat."

Dr. Choedrak's sudden elevation in life seemed to him like an ascent from hell. He was excited by the chance to practice medicine once more, but he knew that, on a moment's notice, from either a stray remark or the whim of a disgruntled bureaucrat, he could be hurled below again. The improved circumstances themselves provided a constant reminder of his vulnerability.

A Chinese woman physician named Dr. Liu, whom he described as "very rough, very crude, very bad," had been sent to Tibet for a three-year tour of duty and was among the four doctors at Sangyip's hospital, where Tenzin Choedrak and another physician were to practice Tibetan medi-cine. With the Party's blessings, the female physician made it her business to discredit the Tibetan doctors and their practice, hoping to prove that Tibet's culture held nothing of value. In the summer she insisted that the Tibetan doctors receive their patients in a corner of the hospital porch. While the Chinese physicians occupied heated offices during the winter, the Tibetans were relegated to an unheated storage room, empty save for their one table and a few chairs.

Dr. Choedrak received 28 yuan or $14 a month as salary and only 500 yuan, or $250, with which to purchase the year's medicines from Mendze-khang. Patients who visited him were afterwards summoned to the woman physician—whether they wished to be or not. Asking for his diagnosis, she then offered her own, whereupon she would bring the patient back to Dr. Choedrak and then to prison officials to denounce his methods. In the meantime, the battle became so heated that the authorities intervened to conduct a systematic survey of the conflicting diagnoses. After months of investigation, they reached a consensus which bestowed an unexpected blessing this time upon both Tenzin Choedrak and Tibetan medicine itself. In a public pronouncement, Chinese officials stated that although Tibetan medicine's worth had long been doubted by the government, its value was now clear. Mendzekhang, it was decided, was worthy of state funding. Furthermore, under its auspices, a large-scale search for medical texts not destroyed during the Cultural Revolution was to be initiated. Plans for a modern building were drawn up, and a research project in Tibetan medi-cine, based at Drepung Monastery and headed by Dr. Choedrak, was begun. Dr. Choedrak himself was given the public title "Master Teacher of Tibetan Doctors." His salary was raised to 53 and then 63 yuan. Moreover, by 1979, his persistence won the right for all Tibetan doctors to issue, on their own authority, work release permits to their patients. Though still based in Utitu, Dr. Choedrak felt that he had crossed a threshold in life. While the Chinese gave no sign that his designation as a class enemy was to be removed, their recognition of his skills was now beyond doubt. A modicum of freedom, at least, was finally his.

AFTER TWELVE YEARS of Chinese rule, Tibet seemed broken: a poverty-ridden police state in which the land, people and even their captors all suffered from a pervasive loss of will. To the Chinese in Tibet, it was plain that the Cultural Revolution had failed. Rather than acting as a magic path to pure Communism, it had destroyed much of the six-year effort to create the TAR. The shining trophy of a socialist paradise seemed further off than ever. To recoup their losses, party planners looked to the 1970s as a period of entrenchment. Tibet would no longer serve as a forge for the creation of the new man; it would simply be required to produce grain and support the army. These now were the unglamorous goals of occupation, and as with all new policies, their implementation began with a reworking of the existing party structure, one tied to similar changes in China proper.

In the summer of 1971, the fourth shift in Communist rule took place in Tibet. This time it was the result of a struggle between Mao Zedong and his designated successor, China's Minister of Defense, Lin Biao. In an attempt to undercut the power base of the very man he had raised, Mao replaced the military chiefs of the three most important of China's five autonomous regions: Tibet, Mongolia and Xinjiang. The majority of those involved belonged to Lin Biao's Fourth Field Army. In Tibet, Zeng Yong-ya was transferred to the Shenyang Military Region. Ren Rong, who had waited in the wings among thirteen vice-chairmen of the Revolutionary Committee, regained the leading role he had briefly exercised in the 1967 "February adverse current." Though Ren Rong himself was a Fourth Field Army man, his conservative reputation gained him the spot. To restrict his power, however, another loyal Maoist and ex-leader in Tibet, Chen Mingyi, reappeared for a short while as the commander of the Tibet Military Region. Ren Rong was designated Chairman of the Revolutionary Committee, as well as First Secretary of the TAR's Party Committee when, in August 1971, five years after the Cultural Revolution had begun, a Communist Party structure was reinstated in Tibet, one of the last to be formed in China. As they had in 1959–65, the Chinese once more had to build a regional Communist Party apparatus to govern Tibet. Four subregional committees were established in 1972. Of 66 seats in the Lhasa Municipality Committee only two were held by Tibetans at the level of secretary; among the 293 office bearers in remaining committees, only 6 were Tibetan. Besides the virtually uneducated people's activists, the only Tibetan of repute in the country's administration was Sangay Yeshi, better known by his Chinese name, Tien Bao. Appointed as a secretary of the new regional CCP committee as well as second political commissar of the Tibet Military Command, he eventually succeeded Ren Rong himself in August 1979 as the head of the TAR's government, if not of its party. His ascendancy was meant finally to convince the world that Tibetans indeed ruled their own affairs. In reality, although he was born in eastern Tibet, he had been a Communist since joining the Long March at the age of eighteen. His wife was Chinese, and he did not even speak Tibetan.

On May 8, 1972, Radio Lhasa announced that a "grand picnic" of Communist youth had been held in the Norbulingka, now called People's Park. Singing, dancing and games had taken place, signaling a liberalization policy which was intended to assure Tibetan cooperation with the new administration. Two months later, "Four Freedoms," unheard of since 1959, were officially proclaimed: the freedom to worship, to buy and sell privately, to lend and borrow with interest and to hire laborers or servants. The ban on wearing *chubas* was lifted, upper-strata collaborators, such as Phakpala Gelek Namgyal, were rehabilitated from the disgrace of the Cultural Revolution and a program to repair the much damaged Tsuglakhang and a few other temples got underway. By the end of the year, a more familiar campaign was being conducted at nightly meetings, entitled "one struggle and three antis." The struggle was against "counter-revolutionaries"; the three antis excised the very freedoms the liberalization had encouraged, now titled "bourgeois extravagance, capitalistic profit motive and economic waste."

The year 1974 opened in Tibet with a renewed attack on the Dalai Lama and the Panchen Lama. While Lin Biao was being vilified in China (following his attempted coup and assassination), a high official arrived in Lhasa shortly after Tibetan New Year's to address key party members at PLA headquarters. He stated that two dangers still confronted Chinese rule in Tibet: externally, the Dalai Lama in exile, backed by India, and internally, the Tibetan people's continued admiration of the Panchen Lama for defying Peking. "Jackals of the same lair," the two Lamas were to be freshly denounced at meetings, traveling dramas and exhibits displaying items such as a rosary of 108 cranial bones, purportedly made from "victims" sacrificed to the Dalai Lama, as well as grenades and machine guns collected by the Panchen Lama for his attempted uprising. The campaign continued into 1975, supplemented by a new effort to woo Tibetan refugees home. Broadcasts on Radio Lhasa, sometimes played sixty times or more, were particularly painful for those relatives who heard them. In a typical case, on June 5, 1976, a Mrs. Youdon of Chamdo read a letter to her brother Jampa in exile. "My dear brother Jampa," it began.

> I am your younger sister, Youdon. We have been separated from each other for eighteen years. You might still remember me as the girl who was fond of singing and dancing. Of all our sisters, I was the one you loved most. We are leading a happy life with good living standards. The whole city has come up with huge buildings, hospitals, general stores, schools, banks, post offices, restaurants and cinema theaters. . . . In the evening when the bulbs are lighted, long and sweet melodies are played over the loudspeakers. . . . Brother, you used to be very fond of tongue. I still remember your sending me to buy tongues for you. With the coming of many food industries, many food articles, including tongue, are on sale in the market. If you would like to taste all these once again, you must come back. . . . Oh, how glad we shall be if you come back to share all our happiness! As our proverb goes, as they grow older birds miss their nests and men their native country. . . . Brother, believe me, if you want to leave darkness and come to light, then please return and join us. Your family relations, the Communist Party of China and the People's Government would welcome you and respect you.

Replying to the broadcast in an open letter published in the *Tibetan Review,* Jampa described his almost trance-like experience on hearing her voice again and remembering the faces of his father and other relatives. He expressed outrage, however, at her being forced to read such a message, a sentiment apparently shared by other exiles, as by 1975—after fifteen years of attempts to lure the refugees back—Radio Lhasa had announced the return of only a handful of Tibetans from abroad.

In 1975, the six-part class division of Tibetan society was revised in yet another attempt to stabilize the country. For four months the nightly meetings, renamed "special meeting on social reforms," pursued individual interrogation, conducted by special committees, into every Tibetan's past, from the age of eight. Once compiled, the accounts were read to the meeting for "criticism and evaluation." Following this, the people were required to classify themselves—a momentous decision, as a poor class designation affected every aspect of life. Anxiety ran high among all, parents in particular worried about the class category given to their children. Eventually eight classes were defined, the two new ones being "those who work hard but not in the country," that is, city dwellers, and "those who roam around," prostitutes and pickpockets. "I've never been a prostitute or thief in my life," young people, classed by their parents' acts, joked among themselves. "But now that I'm officially in the prostitute class, I consider it my duty to go out and be one."

September 1975 marked the tenth anniversary of the founding of the Tibet Autonomous Region. Given Tibet's continued instability, it was perhaps no accident that Hua Guofeng, then Minister of Public Security for all China, led the delegation from Peking. For the first time in seven years, Ngabo Ngawang Jigme returned to Tibet. Having flown in just ahead of the delegation, he greeted them for the cameras on their September 6 arrival at the newly built Gonkar Airport south of Lhasa. Three days later 50,000 people assembled on the Lhasa sports ground to hear speeches praising the ten years of the TAR's existence while condemning the "Dalai cliques' counterrevolutionary aim of restoring feudalism." According to Tien Bao, there were indeed many triumphs to extol. Although the region was still rife with "class enemies," it was alleged that 90 percent of its communes had, from their inception, experienced consecutive years of increased production. In the past decade, grain production had grown by almost 50 percent, livestock by 25 percent. Tibet, it was claimed, had become self-sufficient in 1974—an assertion disputed by a 1979 CIA report as well as refugee accounts. Despite the cultivation of some 46,000 hectares of winter wheat, Tibetans were amply aware that there were still large pockets of famine in the countryside. Nevertheless, the reality of the nation's poverty had little bearing on the need to show progress in the aftermath of the TAR's anniversary. As Ngabo Ngawang Jigme commented for a 1976 interview in *China Reconstructs*, "I am over sixty now, and I have never seen the Tibetan people so happy, in such high spirits, so firm in their determination. . . . Even our enemies have to admit it. It's a rare thing in the world for a people to move from an extremely backward feudal serf society to an advanced socialist one in only a quarter of a century, as it has in Tibet."

The Chinese had, though, experienced some success during the second decade of their rule in Tibet. It lay exclusively in the economic and military spheres. Economically, Peking's exploitation of the plateau concentrated on forestry and animal husbandry—both of which increased during the seventies. Entire mountainsides in Kham and the low-lying districts of Poyul, Dakpo and Kongpo were denuded, sending what seemed to be an unlimited supply of timber down the great rivers running into Sichuan and Yunnan. Only when devastating floods swept over the mainland in 1981 and 1982 did China realize how foolhardy the wholesale deforestation had been. The slaughter of livestock for hides and meat in Amdo proceeded at an equal pace, though more soberly planned. Expeditions to search for geothermal, mineral and oil wealth were mounted by the Chinese Academy of Sciences, which, from 1973 on, dispatched over four hundred specialists to Tibet. Coal and borax, already being mined, were joined by iron, copper, chromium, lithium, tungsten, lead, gold, silver, oil and salt—all, despite their amounting to some 40 percent of China's verified mineral reserves, taken in minor quantities, due to the difficulty of shipment from remote deposits. By 1980, roughly two hundred factories, double the number of the mid-sixties, were said to be in operation. Small-scale enterprises staffed primarily by Chinese immigrants, they produced sugar, fertilizer, matches, toothpaste, soap, ink, biscuits, blankets, flashlight batteries and agricultural tools. Though hydroelectric stations and road-maintenance crews, stationed every five miles or so, existed across much of the TAR, the Tibetan quarters of large towns received electricity late at night only, after Chinese sections no longer drew heavily on the current; and save for select Tibetan cadres, the newly installed bus system remained exclusively for the use of Han civil and military personnel. Next to Lhasa, with its large cement plant (completed in 1964) and motor repair workshops, Kongpo Nyitri remained the sole industrial area. As with Tibet's other factories, both its employment opportunities and its products were solely for the use of Chinese settlers, who, for the first time, began arriving in significant numbers.

In 1952 Mao Zedong had stated that 10 million Chinese would eventually settle in Tibet. Before the influx could begin the country had to be stabilized. Until 1966, Tibet was governed by the PLA and a limited number of cadres and technicians. Early Red Guard arrivals brought the first large groups of Chinese civilians to "the Roof of the World," and these were augmented by the Hsia Fang movement in 1968. On May 16, 1975, Radio Lhasa began announcing the systematic arrival of Chinese settlers. Seven years later, according to the PRC's 1982 census, their numbers had grown to 96,000. Nonetheless, Tibetan cadres estimated that, including dependents, there were as many as 600,000 in Central Tibet alone—one third of the region's population. Whatever the precise figure, they were still below Mao's original hopes.

The most visible effect of Chinese immigration appeared in the "new towns"; cement and corrugated-roofed compounds combining offices and residences that literally surrounded every Tibetan city. From 1970 on, Lhasa's new town expanded the old city by up to eight square miles, ninety-one new roads bringing the development beyond Sera in the east and Drepung in the west. Though built exclusively by Tibetan labor, only those Tibetan cadres closely associated with the Chinese were permitted access to the new neighborhoods. Here they witnessed a lifestyle far superior to their own. Brought in through the "back door" by pulling strings, the families of officials in Tibet received, in a matter of days, jobs sought after for years by Tibetan workers. With all business, from store receipts to government reports, conducted in Chinese, the newcomers found themselves socially as well as physically insulated. While Tibetans received medical treatment either from "barefoot doctors," trained for six months in first aid, or, in the case of severe illness, by gaining admittance to Chinese hospitals through bribery, Han settlers received free medical care and medicines. Their children attended special schools, while Tibetan schools were virtually nonexistent. Closed during spring and autumn so that the children could help with field work, those few students who could attend—their parents not requiring the extra work points earned from their labor—were often marshaled during the rest of the year to undertake road repair, cut grass, collect manure and exterminate birds and insects. The only topics studied were the Chinese language, Marxist doctrine and mathematics. But the crucial difference in the living standards of the immigrants was their greater access to rations. Even when supplies were scarce, the Chinese received thirty to thirty-five pounds of rice and flour per month, twice as much as the Tibetans. Furthermore, they had priority in the purchase of all consumer goods, the best item a high-ranking Tibetan cadre could hope to buy being a "Red Flag" transistor radio manufactured in Hupei especially for the Tibetans. To make a three- to four-year tour of duty more acceptable to Chinese technicians, winter leaves were routinely granted, the mainland community in Lhasa visibly depleting at autumn's end, every plane and bus serving the region arriving empty and departing full.

A side effect of Chinese immigration was the decimation of Tibet's heretofore strictly protected wildlife. In mass slaughters—reminiscent of the nineteenth-century buffalo hunts in the American West—PLA machine-gunners exterminated, for both food and sport, vast herds of wild ass or *kiang*. At the same time, Chinese settlers, who were always armed when they traveled in the countryside, hunted to the brink of extinction numerous rare species—including snow leopards, Himalayan monkeys, gazelles, and *drongs* or wild yaks. When a group of over sixty Western scientists from seventeen nations was finally allowed to tour the region, in May 1980, they saw no large mammals and very few birds. Not even the once endless flocks of bar-headed geese and Brahmani ducks remained.

China's one unqualified success in Tibet lay with its military. Building roads capable of bearing seven-ton loads had been the army's major task during the fifties and the first half of the sixties. By 1965, 90 percent of the districts in the TAR were linked; by the early seventies, almost all were joined. Two roads of great strategic value led southward out of Tibet, one to Nepal, the other to Pakistan. Numerous bridges—all-important in Tibet's many river valleys—complemented the road network.

Its road building completed, the PLA concentrated on transforming Tibet into an impregnable fortress. While the original three provinces were divided among four of the PRC's eleven military zones, each of the TAR's seventy-one districts saw the construction of many minor bases and a single major base. They in turn took orders from six regional headquarters, each commanding a 40,000-man division. Lhasa remained the general headquarters for the 500,000 troops in the autonomous region alone, roughly half of whom were deployed on the Himalayan border. Fourteen major airfields, augmented by twenty airstrips, were built exclusively for the military, with only one, Gonkar Airport, south of Lhasa, used for civilians.

The Himalayan front was most critical. Nicknamed "Mao's Underground Great Wall" by Tibetan refugees, it comprised scores of secret bases, subterranean troop positions and supply depots joined by tunnels, stretching 932 miles all the way across Tibet. At their core lay the all-important Chumbi Valley. Following the 1962 war at least 40,000 troops —one *bri*—occupied the valley, each village receiving its complement of soldiers, with major installations planned for about twenty of the towns. East of the Chumbi Valley, China's line of bases faced the NEFA, their rear command located in Chamdo. Westward they stretched 638 miles to Rudok, with the command center for the whole Himalayan front based at Shigatse.

A key unit lay on the northern slope of Mount Everest, near the district headquarters of Dhingri. Early in 1967, a high-ranking team of military officers escorted six scientists to the mountains. After their departure eight days later, a twenty-square-mile zone was sealed off, even Tibetan road workers in the area being replaced by Chinese soldiers. In company with twenty-six PLA officers, half the scientists returned, followed in May 1968 by convoys carrying equipment to Rongbuk Monastery, 15,000 feet up the mountainside. By September large caves in the surrounding hills, their outlets carefully camouflaged from aerial reconnaissance, were reported to be linked by tunnels wide enough for jeeps and trucks to pass one another. Their dimensions were such that whole regiments, according to refugees and Sherpas from Nepal, could be quartered within. More camps were set up on the surface, and by 1970 high ridges in the area began sprouting radar dishes. In 1973 a major radar complex was constructed in Rudok in western Tibet. Indian intelligence confirmed that the technology was designed not just for detecting incoming flights but, more critically, was capable of functioning as tracking stations for both satellites and missiles. The stations were further proof of what India had suspected since 1968: Peking's decision to locate its major nuclear facility at the very heart of Tibet.

The first report that China was shifting its principal nuclear base from Lop Nor in Xinjiang to Tibet was leaked to the press by Indian intelligence sources in the summer of 1969. In the previous year a gaseous diffusion plant, warhead assembly plant and research labs were said to have been moved to an undisclosed area in Tibet. Lop Nor, despite China's great manpower in Xinjiang, had apparently been deemed vulnerable to a Soviet assault. Besides Tibet's added security and protected supply lines, two natural factors combined to work in its favor: the sparse population on the *changthang* or northern plains made it an ideal test site, and the extensive cloud cover for much of the year would hamper detection by spy planes and observation satellites. In 1970, the French air force periodical *Forces Aériennes Francaises* confirmed the Indian report, stating that the move had been detected by American satellites, though facilities had been left functioning at Lop Nor, it surmised, to confuse observérs. By 1976, the actual site of the transfer was revealed: Nagchuka, 165 miles north of Lhasa on the southern border of Amdo, already a major truck stop on the Xining-Lhasa highway.

Refugee reports soon brought further details to light. The entire county of Amdo Hsien, in which Nagchuka lay, had been declared off limits to both Tibetans and civilian Chinese, with only a few select PLA units permitted to remain. A way-stop called Changthang Kormo, three days by horseback from Nagchuka and previously containing only a single nomad's dwelling, was turned into a "new town" filled with Chinese workers. Further reports detailed extensive underground work. With the tracking station in Dhingri completed, now clearly in place to support Nagchuka, the western base at Rudok received a number of missiles, whether IRBM or MRBM (the former with a range of 1,500 to 2,500 miles, the latter with one of 400 to 600 miles) was not known. By 1978, Nagchuka was believed to be ready for its own complement of warheads, intelligence experts in India predicting that it would "come to occupy a place of importance rivaled only by the Nevada testing range in the United States." While the Dalai Lama appealed for Tibet to be left a "nuclear-free zone," it was not conclusively known whether the new installation had actually tested a weapon (though there was one eyewitness report of a mushroom cloud). By 1980, however, the Hong Kong *Times* reported the stockpiling of seventy medium-range and twenty intermediate-range missiles at the facility. Thus, New Delhi and twenty major Indian cities, as well as Irkutsk and Soviet population centers in both Central Asia and Siberia, came within range of the nuclear weapons. With Tibet high and secure at 14,000 feet, far above its neighbors, it seemed that the PRC's dream of transforming the region into its ultimate redoubt had finally been realized. Yet at this very moment, in many ways the climax of all of China's efforts in Tibet, the country's fate was once more to be opened to question—this time, ironically, by the Chinese leaders themselves.

V

II

Return

1977–1984

ON JANUARY 8, 1976, Zhou Enlai died. His demise was followed early in July by that of Chu The and on September 9, Mao Zedong himself passed away, completing, in nine months, a clean sweep of the triumvirate that had ruled China's Communist Party for almost four decades. Three and a half weeks later, the Peking garrison, led by two of the PLA's most venerable marshals, moved into the old imperial quarters at night and arrested what was soon to be known as the Gang of Four: the leaders of the extreme left wing of the Party who, under Mao's wife, Jiang Qing, had run the country from behind the mask of an ill and aging Chairman since the death of Lin Biao in 1971. Despite the initial visibility of Mao's designated successor, Hua Guofeng, within two years Deng Xiaoping, leader of the Party moderates, had effectively assumed power.

To many observers the shift appeared to be merely the inevitable swing of the pendulum—this time from the left back to the right wing of the party—that had pulled China through internal upheaval for thirty years. But to Tibetans, it constituted a far more significant threshold. In the early seventies the Nechung Oracle had predicted a decline in China. A second prophecy stated that Mao's death would be followed by the rapid dissolution of all that he had built. The successive deaths of the PRC's top leaders, complemented by the Tangshan earthquake occurring at the end of July less than a hundred miles from Peking and claiming from 150,000 to 800,000 lives (depending on the estimate), signaled to the Tibetans an irrevocable turn in the fate of nations, one, they believed, presaged the end of an era in China and with it the possibility of a new beginning for Tibet.

The first political indication came the following spring. At the end of April 1977, in a meeting with a Japanese delegation in Peking, Ngabo Ngawang Jigme stated that China "would welcome the return of the Dalai Lama and his followers who fled to India. . . ." Within little more than a week, Peking permitted older Tibetans in Lhasa to circumambulate both the Lingkhor and the Barkhor on Saka Dawa—the anniversary of Buddha's birth, enlightenment and death. Soon after, families with relatives abroad were told to invite them home "now that conditions are so good." The "good conditions" were formalized by Hua Guofeng himself, who in mid-1977 called for a full-fledged revival of Tibetan customs. Local cadres, either unaware of the new policy or simply unwilling to grant such freedoms, introduced instead a new "three antis," entailing a nationwide wave of mass executions. Before other mixed signals could occur, the Dalai Lama replied to China's confused but clearly conciliatory moves. In comments made to the Indian press during a trip to greet the newly elected Janata Party in New Delhi, he stated that the problem of Tibet was not that of his or the exiles' cause alone, but the happiness of all the Tibetan people. If they did not feel "happy and satisfied," he pointed out, there was no possibility of his returning. If he were to venture home before his country's plight was remedied, he added humorously, "the Tibetans themselves might push me out."

China's new leaders, however, were plainly bent on effecting a major change in Tibet's status. On February 25, 1978, after fourteen years, Peking suddenly released the Panchen Lama. He appeared at a meeting of the Chinese People's Political Consultative Conference, at which, as reported by the New China News Agency, he said, "For a period of time I discarded the banner of patriotism and committed a crime. Guided by Chairman Mao's revolutionary line, I have corrected my errors." Only a year later, and then by chance, did news of where the Panchen Lama had been held for so long leak out. At that time, Wei Jinsheng, one of China's leading dissidents, hung a twenty-page big-character poster on Democracy Wall. The poster stated that he had been imprisoned with the Panchen Lama in Qin Cheng Prison No. 1, China's elite jail for top party members, located an hour and a half northeast of Peking. Life had been so intolerable there, Wei reported, that in the midst of torture the Panchen Lama (known only by his number) attempted to commit suicide. Without detailing why the attempt failed, Wei's poster described how the Panchen Lama had refused to eat, saying to prison officials, "You can take my body to the Central Committee." Now that he was full, the Panchen Lama had obviously agreed to work with the Party's new leadership, but to what extent remained to be seen. For Tibetans everywhere, it was sufficient just to know that he was alive.

While the Panchen Lama's reappearance was further proof of Peking's intention to find a solution to the problem of Tibet, a more significant event occurred in secrecy. Through private channels, a personal emissary of Deng Xiaoping contracted Gyalo Thondup, the Dalai Lama's elder brother, at his business office in Hong Kong. Deng's message was plain: he wanted direct communication with the Dalai Lama. After nineteen years of open hostility, China was offering an unconditional truce. To prove his good will, Deng invited Gyalo Thondup to Peking so that he could personally relate what he wished to tell the Dalai Lama. Gyalo Thondup, though, refused to go without first obtaining his brother's approval. "On receiving this news, my brother immediately came to visit me," recounted the Dalai Lama. "After listening to him I said, 'Very good. We are not followers of a foreign power and we do not have personal or hidden motives but are acting sincerely and for a just cause. So there is no problem in discussing things face to face with China. But,' I pointed out, 'I have nothing to say—no offer to make—beyond explaining the real situation in and outside of Tibet. After seeing the Chinese leaders and listening to their views, we will consider the next step.' Then my brother went to China and met some Chinese, including Deng Xiaoping. And at that time Deng admitted that China had made many mistakes in Tibet. He also said that he was very much concerned about the future of the country. And finally, besides discussing the general problem, he specifically asked for my return. He mentioned that I would be most welcome to come back —that the Dalai Lama should work not only for the welfare of the Tibetan people but for the whole People's Republic of China. Very good, I thought. I decided these talks and discussions were good."

Though Tenzin Gyatso knew that much of the refugee community would oppose compromise with China, he had always considered it to be the most practical means of regaining Tibetan freedom. Since the early sixties he had stressed Tibet's human rights over its political status, portraying his country's dilemma not as one of opposing ideologies but as one of a people's suffering. In fact, he often told correspondents that Marxism and Buddhism could, theoretically, be integrated, both sharing an egalitarian social ideal. By removing the issue from a strictly political arena, he had allowed room for Peking to admit its mistakes without contradicting its own dogma. Now that it had done so, he felt confident there was a base for negotiations.

Such was the situation from the Dalai Lama's standpoint. That of China's, however, was far more complex. To begin with, Deng Xiaoping's overture had to be appraised in light of his general policies and beliefs. By 1978, following almost fifteen years of turmoil under the radical left line, a major liberalization was occuring in the People's Republic. Behind it lay the goal of a modernized China that had always been crucial to the right line and now, after the failure of the radical experiment, remained the sole means for the Party to recoup its credibility. As part of this the PRC's new foreign policy was geared to play down international tensions while the economy grew. In Tibet's case, the international legacy of China's invasion remained entirely negative. What had once been a tranquil border now pitted Asia's two giants, India and China, against one another in a confrontation that not only sapped vast reserves of men and capital, but also held the potential, however remote, of a renewed conflagration which could embroil almost half of the human race. More immediately, a strong opposition abroad continued to threaten legitimization of Chinese rule in Tibet and, in Peking's viewpoint, remained a dangerous weapon in the hands of New Delhi. Finally, the question of Tibet cast a shadow over China's most troublesome foreign concern—the Nationalist government on Taiwan. Disagreements with the Soviet Union, India and Vietnam centered in large part on border disputes, were secondary when compared with the potentially fatal legacy of a China divided against itself. Unlike his left-wing predecessors, Deng recognized that Taiwan could not—in the foreseeable future—be subdued by force. Tibetan refugees speculated that Peking's overtures to them were part of its attempt to convince Taiwan that reunification was possible. Inversely, they surmised that China wished to destabilize the Tibetan diaspora by removing the object of its antagonism—an intractable Chinese government. Whatever its ulterior aims, it was evident that the cost of Peking's occupation of Tibet had become prohibitive. While annexing Tibet had successfully closed China's "back door" and given it a dominant position in Central Asia, the CCP's leadership now seemed aware that it had not come near to fulfilling the invasion's other goals. The great resources of *Xizang*, "The Western Treasure House," were there; their exploitation remained elusive. In three decades, China had been able to obtain only what it could take with little effort—the rich skim of wealth coating the barrier of permafrost protecting the even greater treasure below; liquid currency from centuries of accumulated wealth in Tibet's monasteries; lumber from Kham; livestock from Amdo. No matter how badly the PRC coveted the vast mineral reserves of the plateau, its new leaders had to ask themselves when and how would they ever obtain it. Unless subsidized at tremendous expense, large-scale settlement was out of the question. Even after a decade of living in Tibet many Han immigrants continued to suffer from severe health problems due to the altitude: the instance of heart failure, high blood pressure, miscarriage and stillbirth was far higher than in the homeland. The administrative structure running Tibet had stalled as well. China's 80,000 Tibetan cadres—10,000 to 40,000 of whom, by varying estimates, belonged to the party—were, despite every effort at indoctrination, both suspect and inefficient. In its most sacred task of winning a broad base of popular support, the Party itself had unquestionably failed. The figureheads of the "patriotic upper strate," such as the Panchen Lama and Ngabo Ngawang Jigme, were also unsuited for a governing role. Who then could lead Tibet, in a way that the Tibetans would follow, save the Dalai Lama? And just how necessary it was to have an acceptable accepted leader, if China indeed was to relinquish control, was clear from the most recent record of revolts.

Looked at plainly, "class enemies" abounded. Following the massive 1972 revolt, minor outbreaks had continued without stop. The eighteen districts of Kham that had turned into battlefronts overnight during the Cultural Revolution, along with the still fierce Goloks in Amdo, presented such a headache for the Chinese that the likelihood of ever fully subduing the wild inhabitants of eastern Tibet seemed small. As recently as 1977 a convoy of over a hundred PLA trucks had been ambushed on the Yunna–Tibet highway, looted and burned. In Central Tibet as well trouble continued. In a seven-month period between January and August 1976, Radio Lhasa issued twenty-six broadcasts—almost one a week—condemning subversive activity in the TAR. Sabotage by Tibetan cadres of senior rank was also on the increase, as evidenced by the severing in 1976 of a top secret underground cable linking the tracking station at Dhingri with Dakmar in southwestern Tibet. To discourage such acts, terror was consistently employed, primarily through executions. The "three antis" of May 1977—condemning "petty business, pilferage and bad elements"—resulted in thousands of arrests followed by a wave of executions, 20 alone reported to have been publicly executed in Lhasa on August 1 (PLA day). In the long run Tibet's instability presented more of a problem than that of merely policing its six million inhabitants. Despite their small numbers, Tibetans occupied almost a quarter of the PRC's land mass. China's other minorities, most of whom, like the Tibetans, occupied sensitive border regions, continued to chafe under Han domination and would, given the chance, eagerly follow a Tibetan bid for greater freedom.

With the Dalai Lama's return, perhaps Tibet could rebuild itself and begin to offer its abundant resources to the mainland. For internal as well as external reasons then, Peking's desire for a dialogue appeared to be the only untried course remaining to it.

Having considered the situation in depth, the Dalai Lama entered the delicate game at hand. Little more than a week after the Panchen Lama's reappearance, he tested China's avowed leniency by calling, as part of his regular March 10 speech, for free travel in and out of Tibet. His appeal was heeded. In June 1978, Peking made the stunning announcement that for the first time since 1959 Tibetans would be permitted to contact and then actually visit their relatives abroad. In exile, Tibetans waited anxiously for letters informing them whether their parents, brothers and sisters were alive or dead. Before the mail began, Tien Bao himself led the first trade delegation to Nepal since 1954, to start the process of opening the sealed region.

On November 4, the Chinese took their next step. A grand "Release Meeting" was held in Lhasa at which thirty-four Tibetan prisoners were displayed. The so-called "last of the rebel leaders," most of them were officials of the old Tibetan government, confined since the 1959 revolt. In photographs taken to publicize the meeting, the men sat weeping, incongruously dressed in new clothes and fur-lined Tibetan hats, with rolls of money and certificates of freedom clutched in their hands. Chinese periodicals reported that, having taken a month-long tour of the "new Tibet," they were now to be assisted in obtaining jobs and even going abroad if they so chose. After thanking the People's Republic for "educating them," they addressed the real purpose of the meeting, that of inviting home, "with no digging up the past," all "Tibetan brethren in exile." The refugees' reaction to this event was measured. Perceiving it as an example of the PRC's penchant for blithely disavowing the past by the mere announcement of a change in policy, they nevertheless praised the move, hoping for their own people's sake to encourage further liberalization. And so 1978 came to a close.

The new year opened with a carefully orchestrated series of events. Early on January 1, the People's Republic was officially recognized by the United States. Wang Bingnan, a senior party member, publicly stated that, as a means of reuniting Taiwan with the motherland, "a Tibet-like solution" was possible. Simultaneously, the Panchen Lama called for the Dalai Lama and other exiles to return. "If the Dalai is genuinely interested in the happiness and welfare of the Tibetan masses, he need have no doubts about it," said the Panchen Lama. "I can guarantee that the present standard of living of the Tibetan people in Tibet is many times better than that of the 'old society.'" A week later, on January 8, the invitation was reaffirmed as Radio Lhasa announced that a meeting of five hundred officials of the TAR had decided to form a "reception committee" to greet visiting Tibetans from abroad. The news that China would fulfill its six-month-old pledge to permit open travel was joined, the following day, by

an announcement from the newly formed Lhasa Reception Committee—
an unlikely amalgam of all the chief collaborators, both people's activists
and members of the upper strata. It stated, referring to the period of
Tibetan compromise in the fifties: "We would like to tell the Dalai frankly
that he has done good historical work." China, it seemed, was not only
proving its "good intentions," but hoping thereby to force reciprocal
gestures on the Dalai Lama's part, lest he appear intransigent.

On the last day of January 1979, while in Calcutta, Tenzin Gyatso
responded by commenting to reporters that he was "trying to contact the
Chinese embassy." His intent, he revealed, was to open a channel to the
small group of original Tibetan Communists. Concurrently, he sanctioned
a plan—initiated by fifteen young men, including Tempa Tsering—to test
China's travel offer by applying for visas to Tibet. While the Chinese
embassy in New Delhi worked out the details of their applications with
Peking, the authorities in Lhasa granted permission for Tibetans to visit
their relatives abroad for the first time since 1959. Once out, they revealed
that people were allowed to circumambulate the Tsuglakhang, that meat
and butter could be purchased in excess of the ration quota and that the
Potala had been repainted, Tibetan workers secretly mixing sugar in with
the whitewash as a traditional offering. Even the crows had returned to the
desolate city, Lhasans having enough food now to place *tormas* or offering
cakes on their rooftops for the birds to eat. In his speech on March 10, 1979,
the Dalai Lama urged the Chinese to "accept their mistakes, the realities,
and the right of all people of the human race to equality and happiness."
"Acceptance of this," he said, "should not be merely on paper; it should
be in practice." Peking responded a week later, on March 17, by removing
the "black hat" designation of 6,000 "class enemies," while releasing 376
more prisoners—the first group, apparently, not having been the "last" of
the incarcerated rebels. Though the fifteen exiles' requests for visas were
turned down, due to their having written, on the line requesting the
applicant's nationality, "Tibetan" rather than "Chinese," a refugee living
in Switzerland entered Tibet from Nepal in early May, the first exile to
officially visit his home in two decades. His trip, though, was soon over-
shadowed by a far more dramatic development.

After almost two and a half years of contact, Dharamsala and Peking
reached a breakthrough. At the Dalai Lama's request, China agreed to
receive an official fact-finding delegation to examine conditions in Tibet
and reestablish contact between the exile government and its people in the
homeland. Comprised of two Cabinet ministers, the Vice-Chairman of the
Tibetan People's Deputies, a department secretary and the Dalai Lama's
immediate elder brother, Lobsang Samten, the delegation was, if all went

well, to be followed, in time, by three more. Between them, they were to crisscross every region, except the far west, of Tibet's three original provinces, conducting one of the most extensive inspection tours in the nation's history. Once their reports were received in India, the next stage in discussions would be considered.

On August 2, 1979, the first delegation left New Delhi for Hong Kong. At their arrival the five men were greeted by Chinese officials at the airport and driven to a guest house in the city. The next day they attended a luncheon at the Hong Kong bureau of the New China News Agency, the motherland's equivalent of a legation in the Crown Colony. With a glass of *mai tai* liquor in hand, their host rose to offer a toast. "Welcome," he began. "We are the great land of China and you are the minority people. For too long you have been separated from your motherland. We two peoples, the Han and the Tibetan—one of the most important minority groups—should never be apart. Now we are very happy that you have come back to visit. Once again you can see your own homes and birthplace. You must understand," he concluded, "that you have such a good opportunity only because of the enlightened policy and excellent qualities of the Communist Party leadership."

"We were very patient," said Lobsang Samten, recalling the delegation's reaction to what, over the five months their tour lasted, proved to be a standard speech. "But of course it was infuriating. Everything the man said was a lie. Yet he spoke as though we all agreed. We didn't return the toast but for the moment there was nothing else we could do."

A few days later, the delegation entered China proper. Greeted on the tarmac of the Canton airport by the city's deputy mayor and a bevy of officials, they were ushered into the terminal, where, beneath a colossal portrait of Mao Zedong and a giant-character slogan, stood clusters of Red Army soldiers. "It was very curious," continued Lobsang Samten. "The airport was completely empty except for ourselves, customs officials and the troops. This made all of us uneasy. We had fled our country because of the Communist Chinese and here we were right back among them. I couldn't help thinking, 'Now I've finally fallen into the hands of my enemies.'" Issued special permits noting their entry into China, without, however, stamps being affixed to their passports—thereby avoiding a dispute over citizenship—the delegates were driven on a tour of Canton and then returned to the airport for the flight to Peking. On landing in the capital at nine o'clock that evening, they were formally welcomed at the foot of the aircraft by thirty officials, among whom were the highest-ranking members of the Nationalities Affairs Commission of the PRC. Their presence reassured the delegation of its elite status. Nevertheless, the sense of being intentionally isolated soon returned. After a long ride into Peking's suburbs, they were driven through a locked gate past rifle-bearing sentries to the entrance of a lone twelve-story building. Within, each man was shown to a small room, where a snack of yogurt and biscuits waited by a bed, and then left to what, for most, proved an uneasy sleep. The following morning they were escorted through a ground-floor dining hall to a breakfast room. En route they caught a glimpse of the guest house's other occupants: hundreds of high-ranking officers and adjutants of the People's Liberation Army. Having lost so many relatives and friends to the PLA, the delegates could not help but feel that the Chinese were attempting to intimidate them. As Lobsang Samten related, "Of course, army guest houses are among the better residences in China. But in our case, the choice of one to stay in had particular significance. It was meant to let us know who held the power."

Two weeks of planning followed. Each day after breakfast—Mr. Kao, a senior official in the Nationalities Affairs Commission, arrived at a conference room in the company of a dozen assistants bearing detailed maps of Tibet. Gradually a three-and-a-half-month itinerary covering roughly 2,500 miles and 50 stops was settled on. Mr. Kao offered a virtual carte blanche, insisting that, except for areas without roads and bridges, the country was open. Between sessions he also sought to persuade the delegation to accede to China's aims for Tibet. "There's no use in staying outside any longer," he repeated throughout their first days together. "You must come back to live in the motherland. We should be friends and work together. Please tell the Dalai that every suitable arrangement will be made for him if he returns."

On a tour of the Peking Institute of National Minorities, the delegates met their first compatriots. As they strolled across the campus in the company of a few young Tibetans, free, temporarily, of surveillance, each man gingerly broached the topic of the Chinese occupation of Tibet. "It was very revealing," said Lobsang Samten. "All the students we spoke with were extremely nationalistic. They had been born under alien rule. They had never known an independent Tibet. Yet every one was against the Chinese. We were amazed. These students, after all, are being trained as cadres." A second encounter with Tibetans came after leaving Peking, once more at a Minorities Institute, this time in Langzhou, capital of Gansu Province, the last stop before entering northeast Tibet. Again breaking into small, unobtrusive groups, the delegates managed to speak with prominent Tibetans from adjacent Amdo, now called Chinghai Province. Walking through the tall fir trees and buildings of the campus, Lobsang Samten was told by one man, just released after nineteen years in prison: "Whatever the Chinese say or do, don't trust them. Whatever they say about us Tibetans, don't believe it. We are all united against them. There are underground groups across the whole country and even in the prisons. The young people in particular are very committed."

Early on the morning of August 28 the delegation left Langzhou in two white Toyota minibuses. Escorted by six army jeeps containing twenty local officials plus ten who had accompanied them from Peking, they drove due west toward the foothills of the Hsi-ching Mountains. At the edge of the plain of China, the column paused for lunch in a small Moslem village. Afterwards, it began the two-hour ascent to the first pass, which, at an altitude of 10,000 feet, gave onto the far eastern rim of the Tibetan Plateau. Their mood increasingly expectant, the delegation stared at the countryside until a swarthy middle-aged nomad, dressed in a thick sheepskin robe, his single braid topped by a bright blue piece of turquoise, came into view by the side of the road. But it was the black-and-white animal standing next to him that brought forth an immediate outburst. "There's a yak! A yak!" cried Lobsang Samten. "Stop the car!"

The column came to an abrupt halt and the delegates ran out, calling to the perplexed nomad who returned a polite but vacanat smile. Once informed that the men had been sent by the Dalai Lama, his face fell into a look of utter disbelief, whereupon he clasped both hands in prayer, bowed his head and said simply, "Thank you." From a nearby field a group of women and children raced over. Sharing apples with them, the delegates insisted on taking their picture again and again with the yak. "We didn't care what the Chinese thought about us," said Lobsang Samten, laughing. "It might seem silly, but you can't imagine how it felt just to see a yak after all those years." Before returning to the buses, the men learned that their destination was now close by: Labrang Tashikhiel, the largest city in Amdo, renowned, since the eighteenth century, for its resplendent monastery of over 5,000 monks.

Yaks, fields and haystacks passed in increasing numbers. The sun began to dip behind the mountains and then, once more, the cars stopped. A group of Chinese officials stood in the center of the road, their jeep parked to one side. After a hurried conference, one of the cadres approached the delegation and, speaking through their interpreter, said, "You are two kilometers from Tashikhiel now. We are concerned, though, about your safety. There are thousands of people waiting up ahead. We don't know how they heard that you were coming. Please don't stop your bus, don't open the door or windows, don't put your hands out, keep everything closed. Whatever happens, you must not talk to the people."

"We were very surprised," recounted Lobsang Samten. "But at that juncture, we tried to compromise. Later, we learned that Tibetans in Langzhou had sent word to Tashikhiel saying that a delegation from the Dalai Lama was coming and that even a brother of His Holiness, myself, was in the group."

In a few more minutes the outskirts of Tashikhiel came into view with more than 6,000 people lining the road on either side. As the first jeep slowed, the crowd began to clap and shout. Then, seeing the delegation, it closed in on the column. "We opened our windows," continued Lobsang Samten. "It was unbelievable. Everywhere people were shouting, throwing scarves, apples and flowers. They were dying to see us. They broke the windows of all the cars. They climbed on the roofs and pushed inside, stretching out their hands to touch us. The Chinese were screaming, 'Don't go out! Don't go out! They'll kill you! They'll kill you!' All of the Tibetans were weeping, calling, 'How is the Dalai Lama? How is His Holiness?' We yelled back, 'He is fine. How are you?' Then, when we saw how poor they were, it was so sad, we all started crying, too."

With freedom of assembly banned for over twenty years, the demonstration was almost inconceivable to the Chinese. "Mr. Kao was sitting next to me in the bus," Lobsang Samten related. "He was terrified. 'You are the representative of the Dalai Lama,' he shouted, 'and the people are trying to get blessings even from you. What would happen if the Dalai himself came? We cannot control it. We cannot be responsible. These people are just crazy!' I had to talk to him like a child. 'Don't worry,' I said. 'We are used to it. They love the Dalai Lama. They've missed him for so many years, and when his people visit, they like it.' "

As Tashikhiel's few electric lights came on an hour and a half later, the column, immersed in a sea of people, reached the gates of a PLA guest house. There, a troop of white-jacketed police held the Tibetans back until, disembarking inside the tall iron fence surrounding the complex, the delegates calmed the crowd by promising to see them in the morning. Hundreds, however, refused to depart and instead camped before the gates. Inside, the Chinese officials were in an uproar. The delegation tried to appease them, but at the moment their own feelings took precedence. As Lobsang Samten explained, "That night we were all very upset. We were so proud of our people. The way they received us—their strength—was so encouraging. But it was also very sad. Their poverty was extreme. Most were just in rags, like beggars. And then, too, the situation was very difficult. We Tibetans were back together again, but we weren't free. The Chinese were still there between us."

The next morning, Lobsang Samten was disturbed soon after rising, by a knock on his door. One of the two doctors traveling with the group, accompanied by a translator, stepped into his room. "How are you feeling?" the doctor asked. "I expect you are not feeling well at all." "I feel fine," Lobsang Samten replied. "You must take care of yourself," the physician continued. "Please do not exert yourself unduly and don't become overexcited. The altitude can be very dangerous." After taking blood pressure and temperature, the doctor departed, leaving Lobsang Samten laughing in spite of himself. "The Chinese are so careful when they go up to Tibet," he reflected. "During the entire trip we Tibetans felt well, but the people from Peking constantly suffered headaches, nausea and nosebleeds. Their faces swelled up and every day they were forced to stop once or twice to vomit by the roadside." Each jeep was equipped with four three-foot-long sausage-shaped rubber oxygen pillows with a tube protruding from one end. These were primarily used by the officials from Peking, who were soon breathing from them, slumped in their seats throughout the day. In some cases altitude sickness because so severe that the pillows had to be carried continually. The sight of the Chinese walking slowly about at rest stops, a long tube stuck in one nostril, an ungainly pillow tucked under an arm, more than offset the delegates' own informal behavior.

After breakfast a meeting of forty of the cadres was convened. "It is our duty to protect you," said the local party secretary to the delegation. "We don't know who these people are and we can't control them. To avoid being troubled, you must visit Tashikhiel Monastery by car today. You must stay together and not separate or mix with the people." Lobsang Samten replied on the delegation's behalf. "We are Tibetan," he said. "The people greeting us are also Tibetan. Thus there is no problem. Whatever occurs, we will assume full responsibility." The assurance, though, proved unsatisfactory. The party secretary replied, "Now, it is impossible for you to go out—unless you do so in the manner I've said." Lobsang Samten paused before answering and then stated, "The Dalai Lama has informed the authorities in Peking that he has sent his people for the express purpose of discovering the feelings and conditions of the Tibetans in Tibet. This was agreed upon by the Peking government and the Dalai Lama. Therefore, we will not avoid the crowd but are going to walk directly through it and meet the people." To diffuse the confrontation Mr. Kao intervened. "It is true," he said. "This was agreed between Peking and the Dalai. Whatever they want we must let them do it." "At that point everyone fell silent," said Lobsang Samten. "We won this argument, but the same fight came up at every single stop. In general, the officials who traveled with us from Peking were patient, polite and diplomatic. On the other hand, the local authorities were terrible—short-tempered and narrow-minded. They behaved crudely, ordering and pushing us here and there. This is one thing we learned, that has made life very difficult for our people over the years."

At ten o'clock, the delegation left the guest house and walked to the gate. The Tibetans who had slept the night beside it were waiting. Behind them, lining the road to Ashikhile Monastery a mile and a quarter away, stood almost 10,000 people. While a Chinese official filmed and took notes (a task he performed every day of the trip), the delegates walked eagerly through the gates to greet the crowd. As they did a nearby police officer ordered his waiting detachment to surround them. Simultaneously, the officials from the meeting converged on the five men hoping as well to block them off. The attempt lasted no more than a moment. Like a wave, the Tibetans surged in from all sides straining to reach the delegation. "It all happened just like before," said Lobsang Samten. "Everyone rushed at us, weeping and calling for His Holiness. People were crying hysterically. There were some who just collapsed in tears on the ground. The others pulled our hair and tore our clothes for mementos—blessings in fact. From that time on, I lost so much hair, my hands were always cut and my voice was constantly hoarse from shouting to crowds. Altogether one over-coat, a raincoat, two shirts and a cap were torn off my back during the trip."

The delegation had brought a few hundred small photos of the Dalai Lama, as well as a number of red protection cords personally blessed by him. After the second stop on their tour, the supply of both was exhausted, compelling the men to distribute their own rosaries, a bead at a time. On this first morning, the forty pictures they carried disappeared well before reaching the entrance to Tashikhiel Monastery. Lobsang Samten had seen the cloister in 1955, while returning with the Dalai Lama from his trip to China. Then, its massive gold-roofed assembly hall had presided over a city of whitewashed hostels and shrines, whose streets were filled with a caval-cade of monks and pilgrims. Now 90 percent of the monastery was gone, razed to the ground, with only a few fenced-in buildings remaining. On a vacant field, newly created before the surviving structures, a few hundred elderly Tibetans had arranged themselves into a long line. Holding white scarves and flowers, they wept profusely as the delegation walked by. "God! They were crying so much," recounted Samten. " 'Now we have nothing left,' they kept saying. 'Everything has been destroyed!' What could we say? Once Tashikhiel was a fantastic, a beautiful place. Now everything is finished. The Chinese just tore it all down."

Eleven aged monks, dressed in brand-new robes, welcomed the delegates before the main building. Shown within, the men were surprised to find butter lamps burning, religious paintings neatly arranged on the walls and fresh offerings before the images. Then, over tea and biscuits in a reception room, a well-dressed cadre who had been waiting at the monastery stood up and made a speech. "You can see from these temples how the Communist Party ensures freedom of religion," he began. "In the old society there was no such freedom. The monks never worked. They only exploited the people. But now, after land reform and the Party's rule, all of that has been abolished. Conditions have become extremely good." One of the Cabinet ministers in the delegation asked, "What happened to all the buildings?" "Unfortunately, under the left-deviationist policies of the Gang of Four, some excesses occurred," replied the cadre. "And where are the five thousands monks?" inquired the minister. "Following the 1959 uprising, they voluntarily chose to leave and take up new lives as farmers. Today none wish to return."

In reality, as Lobsang Samten knew from talking quietly to a monk during the tour, Labrang Tashikhiel had been destroyed a full decade before the Cultural Revolution. Prior to the 1959 revolt its riches had been shipped to China, its scholars, physicians and artists sent to prison camps, from which only a handful returned alive. Only the empty buildings had been demolished during the Cultural Revolution. A month earlier, the eleven monks present had been collected from various communes in the neighboring countryside, along with images, scriptures and butter lamps scavenged from other ruins. Brought to the abandoned monastery, they had been ordered to create a facsimile of its previous state in time for the exiles' visit.

The delegates spent four days in Tashikhiel. On the second day Tibetans began to collect by the guest house, asking Chinese guards for permission to speak with the visitors. From them came the first broad sampling of the Tibetan people's sentiments. "Whenever we asked people what had happened since the revolt," related Lobsang Samten, "they would just start crying. Then, after composing themselves, they'd reply, 'Our country has nothing now. Everthing is finished. But we Tibetans who are still alive, our spirit is strong. We'll never lose it. As long as His Holiness the Dalai Lama is not in the hands of the Chinese we have hope. Please let him know whatever he is doing for our freedom, we are grateful.' This is all they said, over and over again. Very few wanted to discuss their personal problems." On one occasion, though, an old friend of Lobsang

Samten's came to visit. Formerly an important tribal leader in Amdo, he had been arrested after the uprising and imprisoned for twenty years at hard labor. He had been released, in a limited amnesty, only a few days before the delegation's arrival. "He looked unbelievable," said Samten. "He had been such a strong, heavily built man. Now I could barely recognize him. The fellow was just broken. He said everything he owned, his land, his home and possessions, were taken. His family had been separated. He had never seen them again. He had just heard a few days before that his son had died in prison. 'Look at me, Lobsang,' he said. 'I have nothing left except this one suit of clothes they gave me.' It was very upsetting. When we finally did get people to talk about themselves," concluded Lobsang Samten, "there wasn't a single family without some kind of story like this one."

Between visitors, the delegation toured Tashikhiel itself. Here they found two entirely separate worlds: the original city, still inhabited by Tibetans, and a Chinese "new town" surrounding it. The Tibetan section was little better than an open grave. Its buildings were in total disrepair, its streets muddy and impassable. The people lived in dark, decaying rooms with barely any furniture or utensils and no running water and only intermittent electricity. On the other hand, the Chinese quarter, though itself showing signs of neglect, was newly built, its inhabitants far better fed and clothed than the Tibetans. Seeing one impoverished home after another, the delegates began to find themselves overwhelmed.

"We were so shocked that after a few days none of us could eat or sleep," related Lobsang Samten. "We remembered life in the old Tibet. We thought of our freedom in India and we compared this to what had occurred in our country. All the while, the Chinese kept shamelessly repeating propaganda about improved conditions and how joyful the people were. We were furious about this, and on top of it all we had this mixed feeling of joy and sadness on seeing our people again. It was too much. When I reached Hong Kong at the end of the tour, I actually slept day and night for a week."

The delegation remained in Amdo for three weeks more. Twenty towns and dozens of villages, communes and nomad stations, spanning thousands of square miles, were visited. Drives lasting an entire day were common, always across barren windswept tundra, a network of Chinese military roads and telegraph lines having replaced the old caravan routes. Somehow, word of the delegation's approach preceded it, and invariably resulted in tumultuous greetings. By mid-September, after only a month in Tibet, the exiles had been mobbed by tens of thousands of Tibetans. The necessity of appearing liberal prevented the Chinese from calling on the

PLA to suppress the near-riots, yet it was clear that some action had to be taken. As a result, word was sent by Mr. Kao to the leaders of the Tibet Autonomous Region in Lhasa concerning the difficulties being encountered. Following this, last-minute efforts were made to prevent the flood inundating the countryside from pouring into the capital itself.

At Lhasa's nightly meetings Chinese cadres departed from their policy of secrecy, and announced that representatives of the Dalai Lama would soon arrive in the city. The men were *logchoepas*—"reactionaries"—it was said. Nevertheless, the facades of the buildings lining Lhasa's major thoroughfares were to be washed and the streets kept free of puddles and rubble. Lhasans were to wear their best clothes and if, by chance, they encountered visitors, were to maintain a cheerful demeanor. They were to talk only if spoken to first, and then in a firm, convincing tone, they should relate how good life was under the new order. Families whom the authorities thought might be visited by the delegation were issued coupons for new worker's suits as well as gaudy pink and blue ribbons to be braided in the women's hair. Tea thermoses, blankets and quilts were given to the most important and their rooms were inspected to make sure that portraits of Mao and Party Chairman Hua Guofeng were prominently displayed on the walls. A few days before the delegation's arrival, Chinese officials conveyed a final set of instructions. It was now revealed that the delegation had already been in Amdo. Tibetans there, unable to suppress their natural hatred for all *logchoepas*, had, it was claimed, openly attacked the group. Wherever the men appeared, hundreds turned out to throw dirt and stones and denounce and spit on them. Party workers were adamant: similar behavior would not be tolerated in the capital—though it seemed this was precisely what was being sought. As a gesture to the delegation itself, the Revolutionary Committee that had administered Tibet since 1968 was abruptly replaced by a new People's Government of the Autonomous Region of Tibet, headed by Tien Bao, a Tibetan. Ren Rong, however, retained his position as first party secretary of the regional CCP, the true repository of power in Tibet.

On the morning of September 26, the delegation left Langzhou on a three-hour flight to Central Tibet. At Gongkar Airport they were met by new minibuses and two hours later, entering the western end of the Lhasan Valley, they caught their first glimpse of the Potala's golden rooftops shining in the distance. "I always believed that one day I would see my home again," recalled Lobsang Samten. "When I did, I was overwhelmed by memories. My whole childhood, living with His Holiness in that beautiful building, came into my mind. Then it was full of life; people worked in the offices, prayed in the chapels, walked on the outside stairways and on the rooftops and at night its windows were always lit by hundreds of butter lamps. Now it looked completely dead—empty and cold. All of its dignity was gone." Before reaching the Potala, the delegation was surprised to find itself routed away from the city and driven to a remote guest house four miles west of Lhasa. "This is the best residence available," local officials informed the party on their arrival. "Everything here is quiet and clean. Whatever you need we'll be happy to bring to you." The group demanded to be taken to Lhasa immediately, where the Tibetan people could see them, but were refused. A standoff ensued, until Lobsang Samten attempted to ease the tension with a joke. "Actually, my home is in Lhasa," he mentioned wryly. "I don't need to stay in a military guest house. I am just going over to stay in my mother's place right now." "The Chinese all had a good laugh when I said that," he remarked. "Then they said, 'Lobsang, your home doesn't exist anymore. Now it belongs to the public.' 'What public?' I couldn't help asking. 'Tibetans or Chinese?' 'Oh, just the ordinary public,' they said. After that everyone was quiet."

Three days later the delegation was transferred to Guest House No. 2 in the old city itself. By then it was amply clear that a new level of discord had been reached. On September 29, the delegates' first morning in Lhasa, 17,000 Tibetans stormed the Central Cathedral, where the group had come to worship. Chinese security personnel were trampled, the cathedral's front gates broken open and the delegates mobbed in a wild frenzy that profoundly shocked Tibet's highest authorities. That night meetings were convened and a strict warning issued to the city's population not to engage in demonstrations. Regardless, the very next day Lhasans openly defied the orders, taking to the streets by the thousands whenever the delegates ventured out. Before dawn each morning long lines formed in the courtyard of Guest House No. 2. Many of those waiting were close friends whom the men hadn't seen since 1959. From them, they learned that despite the general mood of defiance, hundreds of people were still too frightened to appear. Thereafter, they took long walks through Lhasa's narrow streets, where the size of the accompanying crowds made surveillance difficult. In this way they were able to visit many people directly in their homes.

On October 1, China's liberation day, officials of the Tibet Autonomous Region insisted they attend a celebration at the Norbulingka or "People's Park." The event was a crucial test for Ren Rong, Tien Bao and the TAR's other chief administrators. Having failed to check an increasingly unstable situation, they hoped under controlled conditions and on the most important holiday of the year to present a convincingly different view of Tibet. Accordingly, scores of Tibetan cadres and their families were instructed

to picnic at the Jewel Park, their best clothes, thermoses, radios and mah-
jong tiles prominently on display. By 10 a.m., however, almost 8,000 unin-
vited guests had gathered in the park. Like all the others, the crowd
erupted and a phalanx of police was required to clear the way to a building
beside the Takten Mingyur, the Dalai Lama's residence, built, under Lobsang Samten's own supervision, in 1956. There, greeted by the TAR's
leading officials, the exile group was served tea and biscuits, and requested
not to venture into the gathering; as one of their hosts put it, they "might
get lost."

The delegation had already toured the Norbulingka a few days before.
Its gardens, save for the immediate area surrounding the Takten Mingyur,
were a jungle. Among the ramshackle shells of old temples and pavilions,
the only improvement had been an odd zoo of artificial rocks and monkey
cages. Guided by a Chinese man and woman through the Dalai Lama's
modest two-story residence, they had been treated to a description, given
to the palace's few visitors, of the Tibetan leader's lifestyle. "This is where
the Dalai slept. This is where he ate. This is where the Dalai met his
mother. This is his record player and his electric fan," they were told.
Finally, Lobsang Samten interjected, "I understand very well what you are
saying, but don't you think I should tell you people where you are? I built
this palace and worked here every day." "Oh yes, Lobsang knows better
than we do," they replied, laughing, before going on with their account.
Shortly afterwards the delegation had walked past the Kalsang Phodrang,
a large palace in the Norbulingka, once used for state occasions. Finding
the front doors locked, they mounted the building by exterior steps and
peered through a bay of broken windows into the main hall. Inside, the
temple was filled to a height of twenty-five feet with a mass of shattered
heads, limbs and pedestals, the mangled remains of centuries-old statuues.
"We saved these from the people," the guides explained. "It was the people
themselves who destroyed them, not us, during the Cultural Revolution.
They robbed the jewels and gold. In fact, if we hadn't protected these
statues, they would have been stolen as well."

Recalling the wreckage in the Kalsang Phodrang, Lobsang Samten left
the official reception and contrary to an understanding with the Chinese
—never to make a public speech—strode to the palace's front steps to
address the crowd.

Thousands of Tibetans had jammed into the flagstone yard in front of
the building. A single line of police, their arms interlocked, held them
back, while plainclothes cadres filmed and took notes. The moment Lobsang Samten appeared, the crowd started to chant, "Long live the Dalai
Lama!" A man waving a stick with a white scarf tied to its end pushed

forward crying, "This scarf is for you from the people of Tibet." On accepting it, Samten gestured for silence and then began to speak. "His Holiness the Dalai Lama misses you," he said. "And he knows how you have suffered. We hope that one day he will come to see you. In the meantime, we are here to view the progress that has been made as well as the mistakes. Whatever we do, when we return to His Holiness we will report the truth."

Lobsang Samten walked inside, and as he did, hundreds of Tibetans broke through the police cordon and stormed the building. Seeing them, he ignored the Chinese officials within who, terrified, forbade him to go back out, and immediately rejoined the gathering. Ten young men linked arms to protect him from the commotion. In their midst he spent the next five hours walking back and forth across the Jewel Park. Several times, the whole group was inadvertently pushed over, once waist-deep into a pond. "It was so chaotic that I only managed to sit down and picnic with people in a few spots," Lobsang Samten remembered. "When I did, after only a few minutes of polite conversation, the people's real feelings would pour out and they would start to cry uncontrollably. I'd try to get up to move on, and they would beg me to stay. Then they'd insist that we all have just one dance. So, for a little while, everyone, old men, women and children would join arms and try to do a few of our own Tibetan steps, laughing, singing, crying and dancing all at once."

Halfway through the afternoon, a voice in the crowd called out, "Lobsang! Dr. Tenzin Choedrak is here. He's looking for you." In the next moment Dr. Choedrak appeared and the two men met each other for the first time since the mid-fifties. "You must be very tired" is all Dr. Choedrak said. It was he, though, as Lobsang Samten recalled, who looked "half dead." Having asked the Chinese to find the doctor, Lobsang Samten now resolved to test their sincerity by requesting that Tenzin Choedrak be permitted to leave Tibet and come to India.

A few days after October 1, the delegates were informed of something else that had happened that day. Carried away by the excitement, a fifty-six-year-old woman named Tsering Lhamo, the wife of one of the Norbulingka's gardeners and a mother of seven, had yelled, "Tibet is independent!" Arrested on the spot, she had been taken to a commune hall in southern Lhasa and held for three days. Between interrogation sessions, she was brought before the six hundred people in her neighborhood and given *thamzing*. Despite the beatings, she persistently said that her words were not an act of defiance but merely a simple mistake. Seeing Lobsang Samten standing on the steps of the Takten Mingyur, she was sure that he would soon be followed by the Dalai Lama and with him would come

Tibet's independence. She had only called out what she believed was obvious to all. Her account failed to satisfy the Chinese. Determined to make an example of Tsering Lhamo, the Public Security Bureau threw her in prison, where, according to many accounts, she was tortured with electric shock. "As soon as we heard this," related Lobsang Samten, "we decided that there was no point in going on with our trip. We realized that our presence could only bring trouble for these poor people. That day, we did not go out. We canceled all our plans and told Mr. Kao that we wished to return as soon as possible to Peking and from there to India." Fearful of the consequences of cutting the trip short, Mr. Kao swiftly secured the woman's release. By way of explanation he stated that hers was a "very serious case": her arrest had occurred "because the people themselves demanded it."

On October 6, the delegation arrived at Shigatse, Tibet's second largest city. Shigatse, however, was empty. The entire city, save for a few frightened and infirm old people, had been sent to the fields before dawn. The same held true for Sakya, the next stop, and then Gyantse as well. It was only as the delegates were making their way out of the country, through the less closely administered mountainous areas of Kham, that they were able to meet people freely once more. Lobsang Samten recalled one incident in particular on this final stage of the journey. "One day we stopped in a small village for lunch," he related. "A crowd gathered before the guest house, but Chinese guards kept them out. We were waiting to eat when a young Tibetan man somehow got in the door. He was very young, about twenty, and very strongly built. A great robust fellow—a real Khampa—bare-chested, in a sheepskin robe, with long hair. He didn't give a damn about the Chinese. He walked right past them up to our table, stopped and just stared at me. He was trembling violently all over. Then he burst into tears. Tears, I mean, were just rolling out of his eyes. I tried to console him. 'Don't worry,' I said. 'I know how you feel.' He didn't say a word. He squeezed my hands tightly, stared at me, then just turned around and walked out."

Leaving Tibet in the first week of November, the delegation flew from Chengdu to Peking, where they spent ten days meeting with high-ranking officials in both the Great Hall of the People and the Minority People's Hall. During the discussions, those in charge of the new relations with the Tibetan exiles candidly asked the delegates what they thought of conditions in Tibet. "We decided beforehand that there was no use in antagonizing the situation by telling the whole truth," recalled Lobsang Samten. "But we did say that Tibet was much poorer now than it had ever been in the past. 'Education, health care, decent housing and employment, these things don't exist,' we told them. 'Your people don't even speak the language—and they treat the Tibetans very badly,' 'Yes, yes,' they replied. 'It's all true. We are sorry. In the future we promise to improve conditions.' I couldn't believe it. I was so angry. They have done such terrible things in our country. So many atrocities for so many years. What could the Chinese possibly do to compensate for our tragedy? Finally I said, 'We have been very upset by what we saw but now it's finished. In the future, these things will be discussed directly between His Holiness and Peking. We will wait and see what happens.' "

Flying to New Delhi via Hong Kong, the delegation returned to Dharamsala on December 21, 1979. They brought with them eleven hours of film, seven thousand letters written to relatives in exile, countless requests for the Dalai Lama to mention personal names in his prayers and a number of rare scriptures and relics secretly preserved during the destruction of the monasteries. They were met, though, by a somewhat confused, if expectant mood. To forestall a potentially divisive debate, their departure five months before had been kept strictly secret. The highest policy-making organ of the exile government, the National Working Committee, had been informed of the journey only a day before the group left Dharamsala. Two days later, on August 3, the Cabinet released a carefully worded circular, stating that, other than assessing "true conditions in Tibet," the delegation had no "authority to decide any issue." Despite this, fears of a sellout to China, mixed with indignation at the undisclosed departure, resulted in hundreds of letters pouring into Thekchen Chöling, most begging the Dalai Lama himself not to go to Peking.

The Tibetan leader, however, had already left India late in July on a trip to Europe and the United States, having visited the U.S.S.R. and Mongolia a month before. Undoubtedly, the specter of a Soviet-backed pan-nationalities front, led by the Dalai Lama, troubled Peking, just as did the renewed publicity Tibet received as the Dalai Lama toured Asia and the West. Yet, while applying pressure in this manner, Tenzin Gyatso, on receiving the delegation's report after their return, refused to release its condemnatory findings to the world press, believing that to do so would only cause Peking to curtail its liberalization and harm the Tibetans themselves. Instead, the Dalai Lama, on March 10, 1980, called for China to accept exile youth as teachers in Tibet, a step designed to broaden the growing contact. Though no response was forthcoming, it was announced in April that a second delegation would visit Tibet. It was to leave in May, to be followed by a third group a month later. Meanwhile, as a two-hour film showing crowds of destitute people, destroyed monasteries, and small children working in labor gangs circulated refugee settlements, the controversy over the value of "delegation diplomacy" paled, even the Youth Congress declaring its support for the government so long as it settled for nothing less than full independence in future negotiations.

In Tibet, the Chinese spent the winter of 1980 busily preparing for the next delegation's visit. On April 15, meetings were held identifying members of the second delegation as "agents of the Dalai's false government" whose mission it was to advocate Tibetan independence. Tibetans were forbidden to meet with them. If they were encountered by accident, the people were not to smile, cry, shake hands, stand up if seated, remove their hats, offer scarves or invite them to their homes. The *logchoepas*, it was said, would hand out "independence badges," small medals bearing the Tibetan flag. These should be thrown on the ground and stamped on. Pamphlets were then issued, outlining approved answers to questions the visitors might ask, while party cadres were given a crash course in Tibet's history as an integral part of China.

On May 22, CCP General Secretary Hu Yaobang, accompanied by Vice-Premier Wan Li, paid a visit to Tibet, the highest-ranking officials ever to come there in thirty years of Chinese occupation. During an inspection tour, Hu publicly expressed shock at the Tibetans' living conditions. As a result, Ren Rong lost his post as the regional CCP's First Secretary and was replaced by Yin Fatang, another military man who had been in Tibet since the arrival of the first occupation forces in 1950. A two-year six-point plan, intended to revitalize the area, was then announced. In it, withdrawal of 85 percent of the Chinese settlers was promised, as well as tax exemption, the right to engage in private enterprise and the lifting of the requirement to plant winter wheat instead of the more successful but, for the Chinese, unappetizing native barley.

In contrast to these conciliatory gestures, last-minute preparations to discourage public displays were carried out. Police in Lhasa and other major cities received shipments of arms, manacles and electric stunning equipment. Tibetan collaborators, posing as Khampas, attempted to rekindle regional animosities in a series of brawls staged in the Barkhor. Permission to consume alcohol was granted for the first time since 1959, it apparently being a local party officer's hope that the Tibetans would become too inebriated to care about the visit. Finally, on the eve of the second delegation's arrival, the case of Tsering Lhamo, the woman who had advocated Tibetan independence at the Norbulingka, was brought up at nightly meetings. As soon as the first delegation had departed, she had been thrown back in prison, where, it was now disseminated, she had been turned into "a vegetable" from electric shock. The names of those who had greeted the first delegation were on file, it was said; if they appeared again, they could expect a similar fate after the delegations had left. "The clouds of summer float by," stated Han cadres—quoting an old Tibetan proverb —"but the sky stays where it is forever." "The frog lives in the well all year round while the white crane comes briefly and then flies away."

In the first week of May the second delegation arrived in Peking. Unlike the first delegation, they were lodged in civilian quarters. Nonetheless, on their first major outing they were taken to a large field in the capital's suburbs to witness a military parade. For an hour and a half tanks rolled in formation past the reviewing stand, wheeled around and engaged in mock battle. The point was not missed. As Tenzin Tethong, head of the Office of Tibet in New York and the group's leader, put it, "It was obvious that the Chinese wanted to intimidate us, but in reality, I think we threatened them." Comprised of the Dalai Lama's representatives in the United States, Japan and Switzerland, the head of the Tibetan community in Great Britain and the president of the Tibetan Youth Congress, the five delegates—all in their early thirties—had been chosen to demonstrate that the question of Tibetan independence would not pass with time. "The Chinese took one look at us and realized we were not the type of Tibetans they were used to dealing with," explained Tenzin Tethong. "We were very outspoken. We challenged every statement they made, pointed out all their lies and mistakes. On top of that, they couldn't understand us. The fact that we were so well educated yet still had faith in our religion and traditional culture was incomprehensible to them. It didn't fit in with their dogma. Because of all this, there was a lot of tension between us."

On May 17 the delegation left Chengdu, the capital of Sichuan, for southern Amdo. As they entered the Tibetan highlands, people defiantly greeted them all along their route. In the next weeks, blockades of carts and bicycles pulled across roads deep in the countryside and continually forced their eight-car convoy to stop. When the Chinese attempted to clear the way, hundreds of people, collected from remote villages, appeared out of hiding to mob the party. Smaller groups prostrated in the road, bringing the speeding cars to a sudden halt. Everywhere the delegation was asked for "independence badges," which they did not have, while, as emissaries of the Dalai Lama, their own persons were treated as though sacred. Both they and the third delegation repeatedly saw people collect dirt from the roads over which their cars passed. In Chamdo, where hair cuttings from the first delegation had been scooped up for blessings from a barbershop floor, they were met with scores of requests to name babies, an act normally performed only by a high lama. Even seven- and eight-year-old children sought their blessings, begging to be touched by the friends of "Chairman Dalai."

On June 1, as the second delegation headed across Kham toward Central Tibet, the third delegation entered Canton. Sent to investigate educational standards, its seven members were led by Pema Gyalpo, the Dalai Lama's younger sister and head of the Tibetan Children's Village in Dharamsala. "You can't imagine what our first sight of China was like," she recalled, describing the negative impressions which beset her group from the start of its journey. "It was a miserable rainy day. Outside our train hundreds of people were queued up behind a high wire fence in the Canton train station. A line of policemen held them back, and they were all pushing to get out of the country. I mean, as Tibetan refugees we've learned so many bad things about the Chinese Communists and now the very first thing we saw in China, after all these years, was crowds of people trying to escape. It put a chill into all of us."

The third delegation's personal discomfort was accented by a pronounced shift in the behavior of their hosts. Aware of the second delegation's tumultuous greeting in Tibet, officials of the Nationalities Affairs Commission's "Third," or Tibetan, department dropped the veneer of hospitality the earlier hosts had assumed. Quartered in the same military guest house that the first delegation had stayed in, the third delegation was maneuvered away from foreigners in Peking's streets, taken on circuitous routes to their destinations—to discourage them, they assumed, from venturing out on their own—and on the few occasions they did take unguided walks, openly trailed by undercover police. "From the start the Chinese were studying us," observed Pema Gyalpo. "In the guest house in Peking, the Tibetan interpreters who worked for them came one at a time to our rooms, knocked on the door, stepped inside and said, 'How are you today?' Then, without waiting for an answer, they would just sit down and begin asking questions. 'How do the Tibetans in India live? What are their feelings about the Dalai Lama? How are they employed? What are their schools like? What are the children studying?' It was clear that their intentions were not good." On receiving answers from one delegate, the interpreters would go to a second, ask the same questions, and then, if the replies varied, return to the first to inquire why he had given one answer while his colleague employed another. As Pema Gyalpo explained, "Because of this cross-examination they soon knew each of our characters perfectly. I'm a very blunt, straightforward person. Not at all diplomatic. They couldn't get anything but an argument out of me, but with the others they directly tried to manipulate some of them and cause trouble." On one occasion, a Swiss-raised Tibetan photographer with the group was missing for three hours. When he returned the other delegates discovered that he had been subjected to an intensive grilling. "Our photographer didn't understand what the Chinese were getting at when they asked if the Tibetans in exile were disunited," said Pema Gyalpo. "He just answered candidly concerning the differences that do exist, which is exactly what they sought in order to make trouble." At the time, the questions themselves created dissension among the delegates, as the pressure of appraising different responses led to divisiveness. The photographer's replies became the subject of a heated argument and he was finally told "just to take photos and keep quiet."

But though all the delegates from then on behaved with the utmost care, the questions never ceased. "By the time our stay was coming to an end," said Pema Gyalpo, "they were trying to get as much information from us as possible. The cadres from Peking would go so far as to have teachers in schools we visited ask exactly how much aid the refugees receive from the government of India. What the budget for individual schools are, and who gives money to them. I couldn't believe how devious their thinking was."

In this strained atmosphere, the first untoward occurrence inevitably produced a breakdown in relations. Shortly after entering Tibet, while driving to a destination near Tashikhiel, in Amdo, the delegation suddenly found the road blocked by 7,000 people. In a rage, one of the officials from Peking leaped from the lead car, in which Pema Gyalpo was sitting, and began to beat the Tibetans back. Deluged by their numbers, he soon retreated to the jeep, locked the door and pushed Pema Gyalpo between himself and a Chinese woman cadre, who in turn forbade her to open the windows. "It took us three hours to get out of that crowd," Pema Gyalpo related. "The people were tearing bits of canvas from the jeep's roof. They were calling to meet me, but the Chinese kept me like a prisoner in the jeep. I was furious. A while after lunch we came to another large crowd on the road, and this time I opened the window myself. The Chinese woman ordered me to close it, and then I really blew my top. I told the interpreter in the front seat to translate every word I said and I let her have it. I told her that if I chose to greet my own people, that was my wish, and that I would not tolerate her dictating to me. His Holiness the Dalai Lama had sent us to meet the people and if she persisted in blocking this, I said that I would return to India immediately. Then everything I thought finally came out. There were our people in rags, half starving, in tears, calling out all around the jeep, and I said to this lady, 'Everywhere we've gone you've claimed that you've made so much progress. Look at these people. Is that progress? I want you to ask them when they had their last taste of meat like we had for lunch. What have you achieved in twenty years but this?' Then all she said was: 'Why are these people acting so wildly? Do the Tibetans in India behave like that?' I couldn't believe it. I said, 'Of course not.' And she said, 'Why?' I said, 'In India we are free. These people are acting like this because you have suppressed them too much. This is the result of your cruelty.' Then they just kept quiet. I was really in tears. When the Tibetan interpreter tried to calm me down, I turned on him and shouted, 'What are you doing for your people? Just look at them!' "

That evening Pema Gyalpo decided to cancel the tour. Apprised of her decision, the Chinese approached Rabten Chazotsang, the rector of the Mussoorie school, and tried to apologize. The woman, they explained, suffered from arthritis and could not bear a draft on her shoulder. For this reason—and no other—she had ordered Pema Gyalpo to keep the jeep's window closed. Promised that henceforth they would not be interfered with, the delegation continued its tour. From that time on, though, a state of open hostility threatened to break relations at any time.

After traveling for almost two months, the second delegation entered Lhasa in the last week of July 1980. On the morning of July 25, they were mobbed by 10,000 people while en route to the Central Cathedral. It took half an hour to drive the few blocks from the guest house and an hour to cross the short distance from where the bus stopped to the cathedral's entrance. Offered a white scarf by the temple's caretaker (fired that same day for his action), the delegation toured the interior and emerged on the roof to make a brief speech to the crowd, which had quietly seated itself in Tsuglakhang front courtyard. During their talk a group of young Tibetan men shouted in unison three times, "Tibet is fully independent!" The Chinese took no action, nor did they the next day, when, during a speech to a gathering of 3,500 at the base of the Potala, a man stood up and again yelled, "Tibet is independent!" On the following day, however, July 27, the most volatile demonstration to date exhausted their restraint.

Driving out of Lhasa at nine in the morning, the delegation crossed the Kyichu River and headed northeast. Thirty miles up the valley, they rounded the end of a long scarp in the mountains and began to climb upwards. At the first turn in the road a Tibetan family stood waiting to greet them holding sticks of incense, scarves and a thermos of tea. After halting their minibus for a brief talk, the delegation proceeded to the next turn, where two more groups waited. Stopping again, they then resumed driving until, turning a final bend, they caught sight of their destination: Ganden Monastery. Thirty-two years before, on the eve of the Chinese invasion, the renowned Tibetan scholar Giuseppe Tucci had described the traveler's first view of Ganden as "a sight out of this world." Its "freshly whitewashed walls framing the blazing red of the temples and the garish

gold of the roofs . . . looked bodiless," he had written, "a mere outline
silhouetted against the spotlessly blue sky." Now, where over a hundred
great buildings had once stood, only long lines of jagged ruins remained.
Ganden had literally been blown to pieces. "We'd heard about Ganden's
destruction before," recalled Tenzin Tethong, "but no words could ever
describe the sight. Ganden means 'the Joyful Paradise,' and it truly used
to be a shining city on a hill. Now it's a blasted, bombed-out hulk. It looks
as though it was destroyed five hundred years ago, not twelve."

At the last turn, more than eighty trucks, parked up to the first of the
broken walls, blocked the road. Five thousand people waited beside them.
"The moment we arrived, the crowd simply couldn't contain itself,"
related Tenzin Tethong. "Everyone came running down the hill, crying
and calling out. I remember a few young boys and girls, teen-agers, grabbing on to my jacket. They were practically howling in tears. They refused
to let go. People beside them were saying, 'Please, you mustn't cry so
much,' but then they started crying as well, pointing up the hill and saying,
'Look. There is our Ganden. See what they've done to it!' "

The Tibetans had gathered at Ganden not merely to welcome the
delegation but to undertake the seemingly impossible task of reconstructing it. Using stones and lumber pilfered from construction sites around
Lhasa, groups of volunteers had begun to work a few weeks before. Before
dawn each Sunday they would assemble at designated spots to be picked
up by Tibetan truck drivers. With their materials piled on board Chinese
trucks, they set out on what, with repeated stops for new groups,
amounted to a four-hour drive to the ruins of the monastery. Arriving at
the foot of the hill below Ganden, all would dismount and help to push
the overladen vehicles up the slope. Their labor, on the one free day in the
week, continued until after dark. Supervised by a group of monks, carpen-
ters and masons, the workers had already begun to rebuild a residence for
the Dalai Lama and the temple which once housed Je Tsongkhapa's tomb.
Not merely a defiance of Chinese ideology, the effort represented the
essence of the Tibetan people's will to pursue their own vision of life, and,
on the day of the delegation's visit—the 571st anniversary of Ganden's
founding—the underground meant to mark it as such, by openly escorting
the exiles through the demolished monastery to three tents in which
monks, wearing robes they had kept hidden for decades, waited to conduct
religious services before outdoor altars fashioned from images preserved
until then in secret caches. After reciting the Dalai Lama's prayers for a
free Tibet, the delegates made lengthy, impassioned speeches, during
which thousands, emboldened by both the moment and the distance from
Lhasa, raised their hands in clenched fists, shouting for Tibet's freedom.

Receiving reports of the day's event, Chinese authorities in Lhasa finally decided to act—regardless of its effect on relations with the Dalai Lama. Rumors of a demonstration at which the Tibetan flag was to be raised were circulating through the capital. Moreover a group of twenty-one Western correspondents, each representing a major periodical and only the second such party permitted into Tibet, were staying at the same guest house as the delegation. So far they had successfully been kept away from the visitors. Their presence, though, plainly threatened to turn an as yet unknown internal disturbance into an international publicity disaster.

At 4:00 p.m. on July 28, a few reporters noticed Tibetans beginning to gather in the courtyard of Guest House No. 2. Within an hour, over 2,000 people were standing shoulder to shoulder in the yard. As the sun set, the familiar white minibus appeared and the crowd went wild. Men raised clenched fists; women and children cried. Those closest to the bus stormed its occupants, placing their hands on top of their own heads in blessing, embracing them, tearing their clothes. Amazed, the correspondents began photographing while Phuntso Wangyal, chairman of the Tibetan community in Great Britain, addressed the gathering from the steps of the Guest House, "May the Dalai Lama's hopes and aspirations be fulfilled," he began, but before he could continue, a young man leapt up crying, "Long live His Holiness, the Dalai Lama," a call the crowd began to chant in unison, raising their fists with each repetition. As the delegation retired indoors, correspondents rushed to speak with them, but were prevented from doing so by the Chinese.

The next morning the bus failed to arrive as usual. By 11:30, a meeting of sixteen officials was convened in the sitting room of the guest house. Here, the second delegation was informed that its tour had been canceled. They were to pack immediately and return to Peking. "By your actions," Sonam Norbu, a Tibetan vice-chairman of the TAR, stated, "you have deliberately incited the Tibetan people to break with the motherland, and to sever their ties with their elder brothers, the Han Chinese. This amounts to a grave breach in relations between the Dalai and Peking and will not be tolerated." Hustled three hours later out the building's back door, having, in the interim, been detained in their rooms, the second delegation was driven from Lhasa. Their route was watched over by cadres of the Public Security Bureau, soon to be reinforced by PLA squads, who had been meticulously held on their bases until now. Taken to Gongkar Airport, the delegation spent the night, and the next day was flown out of the country to Chengdu and thence to Peking.

On hearing of the second delegation's expulsion, the third delegation cabled Dharamsala from Shigatse. They received instructions to complete the remaining six weeks of their tour. A fourth delegation, however, scheduled to depart in August, never left India. Put off by Peking until the spring of 1981, it was then told that, although Ngabo Ngawang Jigme had replaced Tien Bao as the head of the TAR government (a further gesture of Chinese conciliation), their visit was postponed indefinitely. Nothing substantial occurred for another year until, in April 1982, a three-member team—comprised of Juchen Thubten Namgyal, the senior minister in the Dalai Lama's Cabinet; P. T. Takla, Minister of Security; and Lodi Gyaltsen Gyari, Chairman of the renamed Assembly of the Tibetan People's Deputies—flew to Peking. There they met with Xi Zhongxun, Secretary of the Party Central Secretariat, Ulanfu, longtime head of the Nationalities Affairs Commission, and Yang Jiren, a Vice Premier. In several weeks of discussion, the highest level exchange to date, both sides sought to clarify their positions on Tibet's status while exploring possible compromise solutions. Unfortunately, these talks ended in a stalemate. Their contents, though, were kept secret until a November editorial in *Beijing Review* claimed that the exiles had requested China to incorporate all Tibetan areas into a "unified big Tibetan Autonomous Region" which would be granted the same status offered by the PRC to Taiwan in its 9-point reunification proposal of October 1, 1981. It also noted that the most recent entreaty from the Tibetans had been automatically rejected since Tibet had been "liberated for more than three decades." Ongoing calls for its independence were, it said, nothing more than "a dirty allegation of imperialist aggression . . . opposed by the Chinese people and most strenuously by the Tibetan people."

On May 9, 1983, Dharamsala finally responded. Not bothering to address the claim that the Tibetans had, in the manner of supplicants, initiated contact with China, the Kashag nevertheless refuted virtually every other point in the *Beijing Review*'s editorial. The Tibetan delegation had not asked for the status offered to Taiwan nor had it suggested the creation of a new autonomous region. Instead, while presenting a detailed brief on Tibet's racial, cultural and historic independence, the delegation had noted the correct boundaries of the region (of which the TAR was only one third) and concluded, as an aside, that any concessions from Peking must entail "a far greater degree of freedom" than that presented to Taiwan.

The contrasting versions of the talks underscored how far the two sides actually were from a negotiated settlement. Although the Panchen Lama had been permitted to visit Lhasa during the summer of 1982—where tens of thousands of people greeted him—a new wave of mass arrests, the imposition of a curfew in Lhasa and the public execution of a number of "counterrevolutionaries" occurred as late as the autumn of 1983. The attempt to find a solution to Tibet's problems had, it seemed, collapsed, only a few years after it had begun. One single benefit continued to accrue, keeping alive the hopes of individual Tibetans: permission, granted warily and to a chosen few, to travel abroad.

LATE IN OCTOBER 1980—a year after the first delegation's visit to Lhasa—Dr. Tenzin Choedrak's "black hat" was removed before 3,000 inmates of Sangyip Prison and he was proclaimed a free man. He was then informed that Lobsang Samten's request had been granted. He would be permitted to go to India. Aware of his imminent departure, hundreds of people came to visit, bearing letters for the Dalai Lama. Unable to carry them, Dr. Choedrak promised instead to relate in person to the Dalai Lama how bad conditions in Tibet were. Meanwhile, at a tea party given for him by prison authorities on the eve of his departure, Tenzin Choedrak dutifully swore to abide by the Party's newest maxim, that of "seeking truth from facts." The next day he went by jeep to Shigatse and from there to the Nepalese border. On the Tibetan side stood a PLA guardhouse, the red five-starred flag of China displayed beside a single sentry standing rigidly at attention. Across the Nepal-China Friendship bridge, which spanned the fast-flowing Nyanang river, flew the blue and maroon double pennant of the kingdom, Nepalese soldiers relaxing over a cup of tea by a customs house beneath it. Dr. Choedrak walked in company with another Tibetan, and as he stood on the red line dividing the bridge, turned to face the PLA for the last time. The first real feeling of freedom he had experienced in twenty-one years surged up, and with the realization that he was beyond the control of his guards forever, he yelled, "Now all of you Chinese can go to hell, and may I never see you again!" Then smiling, but somewhat confused, he walked across the remainder of the bridge and stepped onto the free soil of Nepal.

Dr. Choedrak continued his story: "A friend of Lobsang Samten's picked me up at the border. He owns a restaurant and he drove me into Katmandu. When we arrived, there was so much noise and commotion that I didn't feel settled. I wanted to relax, but I couldn't help thinking, 'When will there be a problem in this place? When will there be an unsettled period? When will trouble come here? Katmandu is such a small city and Nepal so little in comparison to Tibet that the Chinese could topple the whole country in just one or two hours if they wanted.' That's the feeling I had because of all the confusion. Nothing seemed secure."

Tenzin Choedrak stayed in Katmandu for almost a week before flying to India. During his first days of freedom the conflicting impressions continued.

"When I entered Katmandu I was surprised by how much people possessed," he said. "It was a shock to realize that the merchandise in the stores and that all the cars and scooters on the streets were privately owned. In all of Tibet there is not a single good cooking pot that a person can buy or sell individually. I asked the man who was my host, 'Are these cars made in Nepal, or do they come from India?' He replied, 'No. These cars are made mostly in Japan.' So I asked him, 'How much does a car cost?' And he said, 'Oh, about fifty to sixty thousand rupees.' And then I was completely overwhelmed, because if all the families in Lhasa put their money together, they still couldn't afford to buy one car, and here many people actually owned their own."

Following his arrival in India Dr. Choedrak's disorientation grew stronger. "I flew from Katmandu to New Delhi at night," he said. "All I could think about was how anxious I was to see His Holiness. But the next morning, when I walked through the city, again I became completely confused. There was so much more prosperity than even in Nepal, that I couldn't help thinking, 'This world really is unfair. In Tibet a person struggles just to eat and here they have so much!' I remember seeing a store that sold silverware and another that sold meat. When I watched people shopping in them, I realized, 'Oh, this really is a free country. If you have money you can buy as much as you want and no one can stop you.' In Tibet, there is nothing to buy, there are no products and no one has money. Then I saw Indian ladies strolling about, well dressed and doing nothing. 'This really is a free world,' I thought. 'People can just be idle if they choose to.' And I wondered, 'How can they have so much improvement if the people are not working all the time?' In Tibet everyone works constantly. The women, especially, work all the time, day and night. But still there is no improvement. While here in India no one was working but there was so much of everything. This development must somehow result from freedom, but how it does is very confusing to me."

Arriving in Dharamsala on November 19, 1980, Tenzin Choedrak was reunited with Lobsang Samten and given a room in Meunkay Khangsa, the government guest house, in McLeod Ganj. Though he wished to meet the Dalai Lama in the traditional manner, on an astrologically auspicious day, he was summoned almost immediately to Thekchen Chöling. Dressed in a new *chuba* with leather shoes replacing the blue sneakers he had been issued in Lhasa, he walked through McLeod Ganj's main street and out the far end of town. Reaching the Dialectical School behind the exiles' own

Central Cathedral, he passed a group of young monks, lined up in pairs for their morning debate class. Then, met by a secretary at the green and white canopied gate of the Dalai Lama's compound, he was ushered past turbaned Indian guards up the hillside to the Tibetan leader's office. Holding a white scarf, he walked nervously down a flower-lined veranda and into a large room hung with bright *thankas*. The Dalai Lama stood waiting for him, smiling broadly. "The moment I saw His Holiness," recounted Dr. Choedrak, "I couldn't say a word. I just started to cry. He led me to a chair and sat beside me. He called for tea. I tried to speak but I couldn't. Every time I began to talk I would break into tears again. His Holiness just sat patiently, and finally, when the tea came, I felt composed. While we talked I noticed how much older he looked. Of course, he was a young man when I saw him last and now he has grown into middle age. But he also looked very well, and I could tell that he has learnt so much about the world, very different from how we were in Tibet before. I was happy because I found that after all my doubt and concern, he was living quite comfortably. Everything was well kept and clean. This was the most important thing to me—that His Holiness was well."

After meeting with the Dalai Lama, Tenzin Choedrak visited the Cabinet. Here, however, the changes between the old and new Tibetan society reinvoked his sense of disquiet.

"The Kashag appeared to be working in better quarters than His Holiness. Their office seemed more decorative, richer," he explained. "I became quite upset, quite angry. 'Now the world has gone upside down,' I thought. 'Our leader is sitting on a small cushion and the members of his Cabinet have fat mattresses with beautiful Tibetan rugs on them.' I know I'm from the old Tibet now, but I think that this new equality is not right. And also, when I looked around at all the large buildings in Dharamsala, the library, the government buildings, the medical center, I wondered if the Tibetans in exile are really planning to go back to Tibet at all. I asked them, 'Have you bought these buildings?' And when they said, 'Yes,' I couldn't help thinking that the money should have been saved to use in Tibet when we are free. But now my ideas are gradually changing. I realize that over twenty years something had to be done. And perhaps the Tibetan question won't be resolved all that quickly. So naturally the Tibetans in India need some place to settle. And I realize that there is much for the government officials to do as well. It is with those outside of Tibet that the hope for our freedom really lies."

Despite Dr. Choedrak's difficulties in adjusting to life outside prison and Tibet, he was soon absorbed in his duties as the newly designated head of the Tibetan Medical Center's hospital and pharmacy. Appointed to be the Dalai Lama's chief personal physician, he walked to Thekchen Chöling just after dawn every other day to examine the leader's pulse. With the Dalai Lama's support, he undertook the manufacture of *tsother*, one of Tibetan medicine's most powerful drugs, whose ingredients had been unknown in exile until his arrival. Having received the medicine's formula directly from Kenrab Norbu, the Master of Mendzekhang, Dr. Choedrak was eager to pass on his knowledge before it was lost. Under the Dalai Lama's insistence, the drug was made—by a staff of eighteen pharmacists working twenty-four hours a day for three months—in Thekchen Chöling itself, where he could observe the preparation. Successfully completed, it was the largest quantity of *tsother* to be manufactured in the history of Tibetan medicine and once combined with other compounds, vastly enhanced their efficacy. In light of the achievement, Dr. Choedrak looked back over both his own fate and that of Tibet as a whole. "Of the 76 men in my group who went to China only four are now alive," he said. "I have survived and so the lineage of this important medicine, *tsother*, has too. This is true for Tibet as well. We came very close to losing everything, but we have not. We have endured. In his last testament the Thirteenth Dalai Lama warned us of what lay ahead. He plainly said that if people behaved according to the precepts of religion and ceased to deceive one another, acting out of self-interest alone, the disaster could be averted. But the Tibetan people ignored his advice and as a result Tibet became a land of beggars. Now Tibetans in and out of Tibet are following closely the white way, the religious path. Our faith has been strengthened. For the future, we are placing all our hope in it and the guidance of His Holiness."

DHARAMSALA, JANUARY 21, 1983, 4:00 A.M. An alarm clock rings in the Dalai Lama's hilltop cottage. Tenzin Gyatso wakes, rises from his bed, washes and, once dressed, moves through an adjoining room to the center of the house. Outside the night is overcast. The Central Cathedral looms dark against the mountains. A lone Indian sentry, rifle by his side, guards the canopied gate of Thekchen Chöling. As lights come on in the Dalai Lama's cottage, his attendants stir in the staff quarters below and a kettle is set atop the stove for the day's first pot of butter tea.

In a large, windowless room Tenzin Gyatso stands before a golden statue of Avalokiteshvara. Folding his palms in prayer, he prostrates three times and then, sitting on a cushion to the left of the image, briskly polishes the surface of a small, copper tray with his right sleeve. Upon it, he doles out handfuls of rice, gradually building, along with prayers and visualizations, a three-tiered cone. Buttressed by circular bands, crowned by a solar and lunar disk, the mandala represents an image of the cosmos. When it is complete, the Dalai Lama offers it to the assembly of Buddhas, together with a request that they continue to alleviate the suffering of all sentient beings. At 5:30 sharp, he leans to his left, uncovers a large shortwave radio and tunes in the international news on BBC World Service. President Mitterand of France is in Bonn to mark the twentieth anniversary of the West German–French friendship treaty. A nuclear-powered satellite belonging to the Soviet Union is due to fall to earth two days hence. President Reagan has called for the establishment of "Democracy Institutes" around the world. After listening, he continues to meditate. At 6:00 he walks to his study, a narrow room carpeted in a maroon rug at the rear of the cottage. Its windows are lined with pink and white flowers tinged now by a soft gray light. It is dawn. Sparrows and finches dart between the fir trees of the garden and a wooden birdhouse the Dalai Lama has hung close by. Their singing fills his room. Seated beneath a portrait of the Thirteenth Dalai Lama, a color postcard of Bodh Gaya stuck in the corner of its frame, Tenzin Gyatso glances across the way at a neatly arranged altar case. A doorway to its left opens on his workroom where a pile of broken watches waits to be repaired. There is a low murmur at the front of the study and Lobsang Gawa, the Dalai Lama's chief attendant, enters, setting a breakfast tray of toast, tea, cornflakes and *tsamba* on a low table. He returns the Dalai Lama's greeting and departs, as the Tibetan leader opens a clothbound scripture to read while he eats.

At seven o'clock Tenzin Gyatso leaves his residence and descends a steep flight of stairs to a beige Range Rover. After bidding farewell to the Cabinet, which is lined up to see him off, he is driven past his greenhouse and office complex, before which wait two Ambassadors filled with nine members of his party. Together the cars leave Thekchen Chöling, bypass the Cathedral beyond and, turning right at the edge of McLeod Ganj, drive gingerly down the precipitous back road, past Gangchan Kyishong, the Secretariat Compound, and through the silent streets of Katwali Bazaar. Despite a run of foul, winter weather the day is pleasantly mild. Ngari Rinpoché, riding in the second car with Dr. Tenzin Choedrak and Delhi's new liaison officer, Mr. A. N. Khanna, notes that Dharamsala itself is particularly warm. The closer the car comes to the plains, the colder the temperature turns. Emerging from the foothills to battle Pathankot's perennial snarl of traffic, he rolls up his window against the chill, barely heeding the familiar sight of dust-encrusted buildings, their cockeyed balconies melting, it seems, off the insipid mud of their walls. Then Pathankot is gone and a grueling drive across the Punjab begins, ending, after one flat tire and a thorough assault from the local roadworks, at the Amritsar airport two and a half hours later.

Flight IC-424, a small jet which makes the daily run from New Delhi up to Srinigar and back, takes off for the capital at 3:15. On board, the Dalai Lama sits beside a Kashmiri Moslem with whom he converses until the sari-clad stewardess appears with a basket of candies and the plane lands at Palam Airport. Tenzin Gyatso bids his companion farewell, disembarks and is welcomed on the tarmac by officials from the Ministry of External Affairs, North Division. On the far side of the terminal, three hundred Tibetans wait around the school band of the Majnu-ka Tilla refugee camp. Flutes and drums play beneath the Indian and Tibetan flags, and the children sing "Channa Palmo," Holder of the Lotus, a paean to Tibet's patron saint, Avalokiteshvara and the favorite anthem of Tibet's old regimental bands. The Dalai Lama then drives to the Ashoka Hotel, the Indian Tourist Ministry's state-owned complex where, for the next two days, he conducts audiences from a suite on the fourth floor of the large sandstone annex.

At 10:30 on the morning of January 24, Tenzin Gyatso leaves the Ashoka to fulfill the purpose of his stop in New Delhi. A police car leads the way from the hotel's grand, arched doorway, down the capital's wide, tree-lined avenues to its Parliament building, which, half a mile in circumference, stands entirely ringed by an open colonnade. Arriving beneath the massive portico, the Dalai Lama enters the building and, turning right, is led into the office of the Prime Minister's special assistant, adjacent to the chamber of the Lok Sabha or lower house. There he is greeted by Indira Gandhi who ushers him through an adjoining door into her wood-paneled office overlooking the rose gardens and fountains in the Parliament's interior. Their talk is strictly confidential. It is plain, however, that matters of some significance are being discussed. Of late, India and China have begun to negotiate a resolution to their border differences. This is rejected as a possible topic by Tibetans who know of the meeting. So is the likelihood of a bid by the Dalai Lama to have Tibet's plight addressed at the seventh summit of non-aligned nations to be held in New Delhi in little over a month. Only one thing seems plausible—a development in relations between Dharamsala and Peking critical enough to warrant informing the Indian Prime Minister. This is heady stuff, but when the Dalai Lama leaves an hour later, as expected, no explanation is given, not even a rumor slips out. Instead, the party departs the Ashoka the following morning, drives to Palam Airport and, after a two-hour delay, boards IC-489 bound east to Patna, capital of Bihar.

Late Afternoon: In the distance, the rocket-like capstan of Bodh Gaya's temple comes into view. Its massive stone flanks, coated in a ruddy, pastel light, grow in size until they loom over the plain. Then, as the lead car of the Dalai Lama's column passes before the Japanese Monastery on the right, the sound of two Tibetan long horns thunders off its roof, reverberates ahead and is picked up by relaying pairs at the Thai, Chinese and finally the Tibetan *gompa* itself. Welcome gates grace the way and abruptly the cars slow to a near halt. Khatas, incense and flowers in hand, almost thirty thousand Tibetans stretch in two long lines down either side of the road. Among them stand five hundred pilgrims from Tibet, noticeable not just for the ragged condition of their robes but, as the Dalai Lama's car passes, an almost universal weeping. Dressed in crested yellow hats, holding rainbow-hued victory banners, and playing cymbals, horns and drums, Bodh Gaya's monks welcome the Dalai Lama at the monastery's threshold. He is shown to his usual quarters on the second floor and while the entourage adjourns to the dining room for a meal, the great crowd sees to its own dinner in the adjacent tent city.

At 8:30 in the morning of February 1, the Dalai Lama leaves the Tibetan monastery. Behind a phalanx of khaki-clad police he walks to the precincts of the temple, enters at the west gate, circumambulates the highest, outer ring and, descending at the shrine room, rounds the monument to the site of the Bodhi Tree. The entire crowd rises as he comes before them, palms pressed together at his chest, smiling broadly. The weather is bright and warm, the flowering gardens filled with birdsong, the Bodhi Tree itself a ship of green sails hung in pennants and prayer-flags. The Dalai Lama prostrates quickly, dons his yellow teaching robe and mounts the brocade-draped throne beneath its red and blue cotton canopy. As he places his wristwatch face upwards on the table to his right, the assembly completes its prostrations, thousands of heads bobbing up for a final time before settling into a motionless sea. The preliminary prayers, led by the *umze* or chant master, begin. At their conclusion, hundreds of white puffs, like a silent cannonade, advance on the tree and throne from the rear of the audience. Coming closer, they focus into a wave of *khatas*, bunched and hurled forward, bunched again and hurled again by each tier of listeners. When the fusillade ends five minutes later, the high lamas in the front row appear to be floating in a cloud of white cotton descended to earth. Clearing little islands around their knees, they lean forward attentively as the Dalai Lama starts to speak. As always, he prefaces his teaching with remarks on the usefulness of religious practice in daily life. Today, however, he delivers a piece of news which, more than explaining his meeting with Indira Gandhi, amounts to one of the most significant statements he has made since coming into exile twenty-four years before.

"If conditions permit," he says informally in the middle of his talk, "I am thinking of paying a visit to Tibet sometime in 1985. I am not likely to fall into any traps," he quickly adds to reassure the crowd. "I've had thirty years' experience dealing with the Chinese."

The Dalai Lama's announcement, which he has chosen to deliver at the center of his faith, signals a quantum leap to the Tibetan refugees. After three years of stalemate between Dharamsala and Peking, the Tibetan diaspora once more comes alive with anticipation. Despite the torrent of speculation, Tenzin Gyatso seems almost unconcerned with the nuances of the present political maneuvering. Already, following his return from Bodh Gaya, he is thinking of the future, toward the day when Tibet once more will control its own destiny. Sitting behind his desk, piled high with government reports, he reflects on that time. "During our stay in India we have prepared some sort of solution for the future of Tibet based on our own draft constitution," he explains. "We practice according to it as much as we can in a foreign land. In the future, from this side, we will make a presentation to our people inside. Now, you see, we will discuss it, but the ultimate decision will be made by Tibetans in Tibet itself. Those people have really suffered. It is their determination which inspires us. The younger ones in particular have gone through tremendous difficulties and have gained useful experience. I am quite sure that they will take the right path."

And for the distant future, the Dalai Lama reveals that he has long considered retiring, though doing so in a manner which would radically alter the nature of his position and, with it, Tibet's government. "There are many prophecies which indicate that I will be the last Dalai Lama," he continues, matter-of-factly. "The world is changing so dramatically, that there may no longer be a need for the lineage. Even if the institution of the Dalai Lama does remain, the method of choosing the new Dalai Lama may not be the old, traditional way. I may pick the next Dalai Lama myself. Theoretically, this is possible, and for practical reasons it may be more sound. Then, once I have chosen him I can become an extra Dalai Lama. Just a simple Buddhist monk," he adds, laughing. "In any event, the future is very open, very large. Anything can happen. In general, if we handle our situation carefully and act in accordance with our beliefs it is possible that things will turn out well in the end. Certain of the predictions concerning Tibet's future make this point and I myself have always been convinced of it."

Afterword

On December 16, 1984, six days after the return from Peking of a second negotiating team, the Dalai Lama stated that he would not visit Tibet in 1985. The latest round of talks, which had lasted for a month, served once more only to highlight the differences between Tibet and China. During the course of the discussions, Chinese newspapers publicized five conditions for the Dalai Lamai's return. Among them were stipulations that he live in Peking, not Tibet, and that he and his representatives should not "beat around the bush . . . quibbling over the deeds of 1959." The terms were capped by a final point stating that if the Dalai Lama chose to "come back" he could give "a brief statement to the press" in which it would be "up to him to decide what he would like to say."

While the Tibetan diaspora reacted with outrage to the Chinese points, the Dalai Lama's own statement was mild. It noted that once again China had either failed to grasp or deliberately distorted the critical issue of Tibet's fate by addressing only that of his own status. "The question of my return does not arise at all," it said, "as long as the Tibetan people are not fully satisfied." The Dalai Lama concluded, in the latest step in the developing relationship, by stating that, although a 1985 visit was no longer possible, in the future he still hoped "to make a short visit to Tibet."

—John F. Avedon
1985

Chronology of Major Tibet-Related Events: 1984–1994

1984

MAY   60,000 Chinese settlers join 50,000 already dispatched in 1983 to "develop" Tibet.

JUNE   China launches 43 projects, costing $160 million, to upgrade the Tibet Autonomous Region (TAR).

OCT. 17   The Dalai Lama cancels 1983 plans to visit Tibet.

DEC. 26   Beijing announces that 200 tons of Buddhist "relics," taken to China during the Cultural Revolution, are being returned to Tibet. 32 tons collected from 5 provinces are, in fact, shipped.

1985

APR. 28   China and Nepal open Himalayan passes to travel.

JULY 24   91 members of U.S. Congress send letter to Chinese President Li supporting direct talks between Beijing and Tibetan Government-in-Exile.

AUG. 9   The Dalai Lama criticizes Chinese population transfer totaling 230,000 Chinese from 20 provinces to date. 30,000 Tibetan workers in Lhasa's 16 labor units are replaced by Chinese.

SEPT. 1   Twentieth anniversary celebration of the founding of the TAR curtailed after 3 unexploded bombs found in Lhasa.

1986

NOV.   Border skirmishes between India and China in Sikkim and Arunachal Pradesh.

DEC.   30,000 tourists said to have visited Tibet in 1986.

1987

MAY 19   Representatives Gilman and Rose introduce H.R. 2476 in the U.S. Congress condemning China's human rights abuses in Tibet.

JUNE 18   U.S. Congress unanimously expresses "grave concern" to China over Tibetans' suffering in Foreign Relations Authorization Act.

SEPT. 21   The Dalai Lama presents Five Point Peace Plan before Congressional Human Rights Caucus calling for "1) Transforming of the whole of Tibet into a zone of peace; 2) Abandonment of China's population transfer policy which threatens the very existence of the Tibetans as a people; 3) Respect for the Tibetan people's fundamental human rights and democratic freedoms; 4) Restoration and protection of Tibet's natural environment and the abandonment of China's use of Tibet for the production of nuclear weapons and dumping of nuclear waste; 5) Commencement of earnest negotiations on the future status of Tibet and of relations between the Tibetan and Chinese people."

SEPT. 22   Congressional letter to Premier Zhao Ziyang supporting Five Point Peace Plan.

SEPT. 24   15,000 Tibetans assembled by Chinese in Lhasa's Triyue Trang Stadium for sentencing of 8 Tibetan nationalists and public execution of 1 in response to the Dalai Lama's presence in Washington.

SEPT. 26   Second Tibetan nationalist executed.

SEPT. 27   21 monks from Drepung Monastery, joined by 200 bystanders, lead demonstration in Lhasa protesting executions and calling for Tibetan independence.

OCT. 1   30 monks, joined by 300 bystanders, lead demonstration in Lhasa. When the monks are arrested, 3,000 Tibetans burn Public Security Bureau jail. 19 Tibetans, followed by 20 more, die from Chinese police fire on protesters.

OCT. 6   Third demonstration by 90 monks from Drepung Monastery.
            U.S. Senate votes 98–0 to condemn China for violent response to demonstrations.

OCT. 9	Phone and telex lines cut. Foreign correspondents expelled from Lhasa.
OCT. 15	Chinese crackdown begins, including 5,000 arrests and propaganda campaign conducted by 600 squads.
OCT. 15	West German Bundestag unanimously passes resolution condemning Chinese human rights violations in Tibet.
DEC. 22	Foreign Relations Authorization Act becomes U.S. law, including congressional findings that China invaded and occupied Tibet.

1988

FEB. 16	Panchen Lama disputes Beijing's claim that police did not fire on unarmed Tibetans during October demonstrations.
FEB. 28	BBC reports thousands of special Chinese security forces have occupied Lhasa.
MAR. 5	300 monks call for independence in Central Cathedral at conclusion of Monlam Chenmo, or Great Prayer Festival. 2,000 police attack monks. 16 hours of riots result in deaths of at least 18 Tibetans and 1 Chinese policeman.
APR. 5	Beijing states the Dalai Lama can live in Tibet if he gives up call for independence.
APR. 6	The Dalai Lama rejects Chinese offer.
JUNE 15	The Dalai Lama presents Strasbourg Proposal at European Parliament, offering Beijing control of foreign relations and defense in exchange for Tibetan self-government "in association" with China.
JULY	Qiao Shi, China's top security official, calls for a policy of "merciless repression" against Tibetan nationalists.
JULY 27	Cabinet of Tibetan Government-in-Exile names 5-member negotiating team for future talks with China.
AUG.	Winston Lord is first U.S. Ambassador to China to visit Tibet. China conducts chemical warfare maneuvers in Tibet.
SEPT. 16	U.S. S.R. 129 calls for Chinese to act on the Dalai Lama's proposals and Reagan administration to support them.
SEPT. 21	China offers negotiations on Tibet's future at a venue of the Dalai Lama's choosing, but refuses to negotiate with the Tibetan Cabinet or discuss issue of Tibetan independence.
SEPT. 23	Tibetan Cabinet states that it would like talks to commence in Geneva, Switzerland, in January 1989.
OCT. 14	European Parliament resolution calls on China to respect human rights in Tibet.

DEC. 7	Wu Jinghua, First Party Secretary in Tibet, replaced by Hu Jintao.
DEC. 10	Demonstration in Lhasa on International Human Rights Day results in estimated 20 Tibetan deaths and 130 injuries from Chinese security forces.
DEC. 19	60 Tibetan students march in Beijing, protesting police shootings in Tibet.

1989

JAN.	United Nations World Food Program starts agricultural project to boost crop production in Tibet. China fails to participate in Geneva talks.
JAN. 2	Hundreds of students demonstrate in Lhasa.
JAN. 27	Panchen Lama dies.
MAR. 5–8	3 days of demonstrations in Lhasa see 80–150 Tibetans and 1 Chinese policeman killed in most serious disturbances since 1959 uprising. Martial law declared in Tibet.
MAR. 9	Thousands of Chinese troops occupy Lhasa; tourists and journalists expelled.
MAR. 15	European Parliament resolution calls for lifting martial law. U.S. S.R. 82 calls for U.N. observers in Tibet.
APR. 20	The Dalai Lama offers to send representatives to meet Chinese counterparts in Hong Kong to remove obstacles to talks.
MAY 6	H.R. 63 urges China to allow international monitors in prisons; Bush administration to raise human rights issues as part of U.S. China policy.
JUNE 4	Tiananmen Square massacre.
JULY	China airlifts 14,000 troops into Tibet, demonstrating People's Liberation Army's new rapid deployment capacity on the Indian front.
SEPT. 2, 22, 30	Protests by nuns in Lhasa.
OCT. 6	The Dalai Lama awarded Nobel Peace Prize.
DEC. 11	The Dalai Lama accepts Nobel Peace Prize in Oslo, Norway.

1990

| FEB. | U.S. State Department Human Rights Report cites China for violations in Tibet. |

APR. 24   European Parliament hearings on Tibet.

APR. 25   The Dalai Lama announces plan for broadening democratic structure of the Tibetan Government-in-Exile.

APR. 30   Martial law lifted in Tibet.

MAY   China announces new plan for birth control in Tibet, underscoring ongoing reports of forced abortion and sterilization of Tibetan women as well as infanticide.

Chengdu, Szechuan office responsible for managing Chinese entry into Tibet, announces a rate of 2,000 travelers per day.

MAY 23   European Parliament decides to dispatch a human rights mission to Tibet.

MAY 29   Asia Watch issues its first report exclusively on conditions in Tibet.

JUNE   TAR Governor Dorje Tsering replaced by hard-liner Gyaltsen Norbu.

JULY 8   Parliamentarians from 17 nations call for Tibetan self-determination at a Tibet conference in London.

SEPT.   Demonstrations resume in Lhasa.

NOV. 29   Foreign aid bill signed by President Bush providing humanitarian assistance for Tibetan refugees.

1991

MAR. 2   China orders much of the Barkhor, Lhasa's central marketplace, to be demolished.

MAR. 10   Start of International Year of Tibet, refugee effort to draw attention to Tibet's cause.

APR.   Greenpeace exposes Chinese plan to ship toxic waste from U.S. to Tibet.

APR. 16   The Dalai Lama meets President Bush in the White House in first reception by a U.S. President.

APR. 17   The Dalai Lama addresses Congress in the Capitol Rotunda. Senate adopts S.R. 107 supporting Tibet.

MAY 25   Construction of Yamdrok Tso hydroelectric station begins despite Tibetan protests over ecological damage to central Tibet's principal lake.

JUNE 4   Demonstrations in Lhasa.

AUG.   Ongoing demonstrations in Lhasa.

AUG. 23   U.N. Human Rights Sub-Commission resolution criticizes China's violations in Tibet.

SEPT. 2   Tibetan Government-in-Exile announces the Dalai Lama is no longer bound by Strasbourg Proposal.

SEPT. 24	Foreign Relations Authorization Act bill finds that "Tibet is an occupied country under international law whose true representatives are the Dalai Lama and Tibetan Government-in-Exile."
OCT. 9	In address at Yale University, the Dalai Lama states his wish to visit Tibet on a fact-finding mission.
OCT. 10	Chinese Foreign Ministry says the Dalai Lama must "stop his activities aimed at splitting China" before he can visit Tibet.
NOV.	128 party cadres sent to Tibet to "strengthen national unity," reflecting Beijing's concern over loyalty in the region's bureaucracy.
NOV. 1	Chinese "White Paper" on Tibet begins new effort to justify occupation.
NOV. 26	U.S. House of Representatives includes Tibet provision in its vote to condition China's most favored nation trading status.
DEC. 2	The Dalai Lama meets with British Prime Minister John Major.

1992

JAN. 6	China reported to relocate its nuclear test site from Lop Nor in Xingjiang to Alar on the Xingjiang-Tibet border.
FEB.	Xinhua news agency reports record profits from gold and timber extraction in Tibet.
MAR. 18	U.S. S.R. 271 urges Bush administration to support Tibetan human rights at U.N.
APR. 1	U.S. H.R. 2621 grants $1.5 million in assistance to Tibetan refugees.
APR. 6	China denies Senators Pell and Boren visas to visit Tibet.
MAY	Contracts for Yamdrok Tso station's turbines awarded to 2 Austrian firms.
MAY 14	1,000 Tibetan refugees begin to be admitted to U.S.
MAY 21	Demonstrations in Lhasa.
JUNE 21	Widespread unrest across Tibet.
SEPT.	Chen Kuiyuan, TAR Communist Party Deputy Secretary, calls on Tibet to open its job market to Chinese.
OCT. 3	Wei Jingsheng, China's foremost democracy advocate, writes letter to Deng Xiaopeng condemning his Tibet policy.
DEC. 1	Hu Jintao replaced by Chen Kuiyuan as First Secretary of Communist Party in Tibet.
DEC. 5	Regional military headquarters moved to Lhasa.

1993

JAN.   Checkpoints on roads into Tibet removed, promoting unrestricted Chinese influx.

FEB. 14   Chen Kuiyuan calls for purge of officials who do not take a strong stand against the Dalai Lama.

MAR.   Beijing announces plans for Zhikong hydroelectric project on Kyichu River, even larger than Yamdrok Tso project now costing $40 million and suspected by Tibetans to be a mining project, due to its massive tunnel excavations.

MAR. 4   U.S. Secretary of State Warren Christopher says Chinese treatment of Tibet is improper.

MAR. 10   Conference on Work of External Propaganda on the Question of Tibet held in Beijing. Plans developed to disrupt Tibetan exile community.

MAR. 15   15 Tibetan monks arrested in Lhasa protest.

APR. 28   President Clinton and Vice President Gore meet the Dalai Lama in White House.

MAY 22   Largest protest in Lhasa since 1989, following celebration of forty-second anniversary of Tibet's "peaceful liberation" through 17 Point Agreement.

MAY 28   President Clinton issues executive order conditioning 1994 renewal of China's most favored nation trading status on 7 areas of "overall significant progress," among them "protecting Tibet's distinctive religious and cultural heritage." The order represents the first time since China invaded Tibet 43 years before that a foreign government has based its relations with Beijing on conditions in Tibet.

SEPT.   Beijing loses Olympic bid over human rights record, including extensive lobbying by Tibet groups.

OCT.   Demolition of old Lhasa increases.

OCT. 16   China allows a U.S. consul in Lhasa in concession to help renew most favored nation trade status.

OCT. 28   European Parliament passes motion calling for Beijing to disclose information on political prisoners in China and Tibet.

NOV. 4   The Dalai Lama received at French National Assembly.

NOV. 10   General Secretary Jiang Zemin assures Chinese leaders that unrest by ethnic minorities will be crushed.

NOV. 16   The Dalai Lama meets French President François Mitterrand.

NOV. 19   President Clinton urges Jiang Zemin to negotiate with the Dalai Lama.

1994

JAN. 23   Secretary of State Christopher urges Chinese Foreign Minister Qian to negotiate with the Dalai Lama.

APR. 28   The Dalai Lama meets with President Clinton and Vice President Gore in White House and receives pledge for continued U.S. support of Sino/Tibetan talks.

APR. 29   State Department Authorization Bill mandates annual report on developing relationship between U.S. and Tibetan Government-in-Exile, establishes U.S. Information Agency office in Lhasa, and requests State Department to list Tibet under a separate state heading in all of its reports.

A Note on Sources

The oral sources for this book are roughly a hundred people met with during a four-year period in the United States and India. Though principal informants were interviewed repeatedly over a period of weeks and months and others on only one occasion, their first-hand accounts together provide the basis of the book. The key contributors are mentioned in the Acknowledgments. Among the written sources, certain authors and periodicals, listed in the bibliography, were invaluable. For a portrait of Tibetan society at its apogee, the classics of Tibetan studies, written by Bell, Richardson, Shakabpa and Stein were fundamental, including a small but unique text on the discovery of the Fourteenth Dalai Lama by Sonam Wangdu, a member of the search party. For their firsthand accounts of Tibet in its declining days, the works of Heinrich Harrer and Robert Ford were indispensable as, for the Tibetans' own view of their nation's invasion and fall, were those of Rinchen Dolma Taring, Thubten Jigme Norbu and the Dalai Lama's own autobiography, *My Land and My People*. Much of the Tibetan revolt was revealed in the history of Chushi Gangdruk, written by Gompo Tashi Andrugtsang, as well as by Noel Barber's account of the fighting in Lhasa in March 1959. For information on the Tibetan refugees' quarter century in exile I am beholden to the various reporters of India's chief newspapers and above all to the *Tibetan Review*, which, published in New Delhi, is essential reading for any student of Tibetan affairs. Main sources for the period covering China's unabridged occupation of Tibet include the Union Research Institute's Tibetan documentation, *Tibet 1950–1967*, and the personal accounts of Kunsang Paljor, Tsering Dorje Gashi and Dhondub Choedon, all of whom, as Tibetan cadres working in the region's administration, had access to its interior functions. Peking's numerous publications issued to present its achievements in Tibet have been of value, including the English-language staples, the *Beijing Review* and *China Reconstructs*. For an overview of the PRC's Minority Policy since its inception I am indebted to June Teufel Dreyer's definitive study, *China's Forty Millions*. Special thanks to John Ackerley of the International Campaign for Tibet, and to the International Committee of Lawyers for Tibet for the Chronology of Major Events from 1984–1994.

Acknowledgments

In varying ways, many people contributed time and effort to this book. To begin with, Pema Thonden, of New York City, the third Tibetan to visit Lhasa following the 1978 liberalization, provided a vivid description of life in the previously sealed capital. Her account, originally to have been a chapter unto itself, ranked with those of the principal figures in the book: Tempa Tsering, Gendun Thargay, Dr. Yeshi Dhonden, Lobsang Jigme and Dr. Tenzin Choedrak. I am grateful to all of them for their patience during long work sessions and for their generosity in permitting their lives to be singled out as emblematic.

For memories of the old Tibet, prior to 1950, I am obliged to numerous experts, among whom Nechung Rinpoché, abbot of Nechung Monastery, and the foremost authority on Tibet's State Oracle, was of inestimable assistance. Over a protracted series of interviews, he offered the first public explanation of the oracle's role and function in both spiritual and temporal terms, after which he took considerable care in checking every detail of the transcripts. I wish to thank Kesangla, lifelong companion of Lobsang Jigme, the Nechung Kuden, as well as Tenzin Wangdrak, current medium of the Gadong oracle for their help. Taktser Rinpoché, the Dalai Lama's eldest brother, offered one-of-a-kind background on both his family and present-day Tibet, which he visited in 1980. For illuminating the unique place of religion in Tibet's government I am most thankful to Serkhong Rinpoché, one of the Dalai Lama's seven *tsenshap* or debate instructors and particularly to the senior and junior tutors of the Dalai Lama, Kabjé Ling Rinpoché and Kyabjé Trijang Rinpoché. Tsepon W. D. Shakabpa, who accompanied Reting Rinpoché, the regent of Tibet, on his visit to the sacred lake of Lhamo Lhatso, whereafter he helped arrange Lhasa's reception for the newly discovered Dalai Lama, furnished an impeccable account of life in the capital up to the Chinese invasion. Mr. Thubten Tharpa Liushar, Tibet's last Foreign Minister as well, gave his kind assistance to the project. For the hard work of elucidating minute points of religious and historical detail I have also to thank the following: Khensur Rinpoché—ex-abbot of Gyudme, the Lower Tantric College, Thubten Jamyang and Kalsang, respectively, master of ceremonies and *umze* or chant master for Namgyal Dratsang, the Dalai

Lama's private monastery; Sangay Samdup, a Swiss monk in training at Dharamsala's School of Buddhist Dialectics and Yeshi Khedup, an ex-monk of Drepung monastery currently residing in New York. For their views on Tibetan medicine's introduction to the West I am grateful to doctors Gerald Goldstein and Donald Baker of the University of Virginia, as well as to Herbert Benson and Richard Selzer of Harvard and Yale. I am equally appreciative of Mr. William Schneider's kind help in permitting his meeting with Dr. Yeshi Dhonden to be recounted. Lobsang Rabgay, a student of Tibetan medicine, offered essential aid in confirming my presentation of the topic.

Those who assisted me most in chronicling the experience of Tibetans from 1959 through the present often did so under conditions of some delicacy. Jamyang Norbu, current head of the Tibetan Institute of Performing Arts in Dharamsala was at the core of the refugees' more volatile intramural conflicts. His aid, however, was both candid and objective. So was that of someone I may only identify as KN, a key player in the tense relations between Katmandu and the Tibetan guerrillas in Mustang. Lobsang Chonzin of Byllakuppe Camp Number 1 and Khentrul Rinpoché, an inmate at the Buxa Lama Ashram, were instrumental in describing the refugees' early days in India. Mr. N. N. Nowrojee, proprietor of Nowrojee and Sons, McLeod Ganj, deserves my deepest thanks for his captivating description of the history of Dharamsala from its beginning. Bikku Gian Jagat, caretaker of the *stupa* at Bodh Gaya, was a gracious host who inspired me with his singlehanded efforts at preservation and renovation of the great shrine. Mr. Om Prakesh Dawan, New Delhi's liaison officer to the Dalai Lama, not only has my gratitude for elucidating his government's remarkable record of aid to the Tibetan refugees, but for his warmth of spirit and unqualified assistance in carrying out my research.

Most of those Tibetans, recently permitted to visit abroad, who gave critical aid to this book have now returned home. For obvious reasons, they must remain nameless. I was honored by their courage in speaking up, given the ongoing existence of prison camps and frequent reprisals exacted on family members. I can only indicate two of those who have remained in exile: DL, a trader from Amdo, recently released after twenty-one years in five Chinese prisons; DY, a woman of Lhasa now residing in Dharamsala. Suzette Cook, an Australian student of more than normal enterprise, was, with her companion Christina Jengen, the first Westerner in decades to travel overland from Chengtu to Lhasa; she patiently submitted to close questioning. The members of the Tibetan Government-in-exile's three fact-finding missions, sent to Tibet in 1979 and 1980, each deserve their own acknowledgment both for copious notes taken during their tours and the lucid presentation of the facts on their return. In particular, I wish to thank the Dalai Lama's immediate elder brother and head of the Tibetan Medical Center, Lobsang Samten, without whose assistance my comprehension of the personal dimension of the relations currently underway between Peking and Dharamsala would be nil. By the same token I am indebted to Pema Gyalpo, the Dalai Lama's sister and the director of the Tibetan Children's Village, for her penetrating depiction of the current social atmosphere in China and Tibet. I am also obliged to Lobsang Jinpa, President of the Tibetan Youth Congress, who rendered an exact and valuable account of his delegation's travels.

It was the special necessity of this project to rely heavily on translators. Without their exhaustive work in refining points and definitions, whatever degree of accuracy has been achieved herein would be far less. I am most thankful to Namgyal Lhamo Samten for her painstaking but marvelously fluid translation of Dr. Tenzin Choedrak's life in prison, delivered within weeks of his release. I am equally grateful to Marya Schwabe who gave a truly herculean performance, worthy of a book unto itself, not just in translating but also in perfecting, with Nechung Rinpoché, essential background to the chapter on Tibet's State Oracle. No less thanks go to Professor Jeffrey Hopkins of the University of Virginia, the Dalai Lama's chief Western translator and a peerless scholar of Tibetan Buddhism. Professor Hopkins's help has for years been a mainstay of my own limited research into Tibetan medicine and religion, which could never have been undertaken without it. I am beholden to Alexander Berzin and Glenn H. Mullin, members of the Tibetan Library of Works and Archives Translation Bureau, and among the first Westerners to settle permanently in Dharamsala in order to study with Tibetan teachers. Prof. Robert Thurman of Amherst, a pioneer of Tibetan Buddhist studies in the West, has been consistently gracious and forthcoming in his assistance. Sangay Rabten, currently posted to the exile government's bureau in Switzerland, and Phuntso Thonden, the Dalai Lama's second representative in New York, also generously offered their services as translators. The results of every interview were transcripts, thick piles of which accumulated early on. Those who transcribed had no simple task, due to accents, as well as the frequent, spontaneous exchange of Tibetan and English equivalents in conversation. They were Rinchen Khando, Pema Dorje, Joyce Murdoch and Diane Short in Virginia. I am particularly obliged for both transcription and a bevy of other tasks to Ngoudup Tesur of the Dalai Lama's Private Office. I am no less appreciative of the daunting task undertaken by the typists who submitted to much painstaking revision: Shirley Baker, Carol Atkinson, and Jane Freeman. Nora Paul and Neesha Sethi also graciously contributed time to the project.

Certain friends and colleagues have provided substantial assistance to me from the inception through the end of work on this book. Jann Wenner, publisher of *Rolling Stone*, was the first to recognize the present significance of Tibet's story and support its telling. Lodi Gyaltsen Gyari, ex-Chairman of the Assembly of the Tibetan People's Deputies, not only added much to my understanding of the Tibetans' fledgling democratic experiment, but in his present capacity as additional secretary in the Information Office of the Tibetan government-in-exile oversaw the vast task of corroborating the accuracy of my research. Sonam Topgyal, General Secretary of Information, Samphel Dy and other members of the staff who assisted with checking, as well as Lhamo Tsering, an ex-officer of Chushi Gangdruk, and P. T. Takla, retired minister of the Kashag all have my thanks. Tenzin Geyché Tethong, for sixteen years the Dalai Lama's chief foreign secretary and now a member of his cabinet, has offered me precious insights at every juncture of the project. The combined services of the Library of Tibetan Works and Archives under Gyatso Tsering, aided by Tashi Tsering, in addition to those of the Bureau of H.H. the Dalai Lama in New Delhi under Tashi Wangdu, were consistently appreciated. Most helpful has been the staff of the Office of Tibet in New York City: Frances Thargey, Tinley Akar and Tenzin Choedrak. Their assistance has for many years contributed in every capacity, from turning up rare sources to keeping open the somewhat difficult lines of communication with India. I owe them much. Tenzin Namgyal Tethong, the Dalai Lama's representative in New York, has, besides detailing the experiences of the second delegation sent to Tibet, which he led, worked long and hard to verify the accuracy of material, assemble maps and photos and bring me together with certain sources, emanating directly from Peking, which otherwise I would have been unable to contact. Valrae Reynolds, curator of the Newark Museum's collection of Asian art, was extremely generous in allowing the use of photos, as were George Patterson, Khedroob Thondup, Dolma Ladenla and most especially Nicholas Vreeland. Michael Van Walt Van Praag and Peter Brown, friends and students of Tibet, proved excellent sounding boards for plumbing the depths of Sino-Tibetan relations through the ages. Kunga Wangdrak, Anila Kungsang and Roberta Mullin all provided munificent hospitality in India. John Brzostoski, an instructor at the New School of Social Research, afforded me with a stimulating introduction to Tibetan iconography. Above all my good friend and mentor in all things Tibetan has been Khyongla Rato Rinpoché, a preeminent lama of Rato, Drepung and Gyudto monasteries and currently president of the Tibet Center in New York City. He has given me, through years of generous help, the basic vocabulary for comprehending Tibetan culture and religion without which I would have been unable to understand the overall terms let alone the present day particulars of the Tibetans' world view.

Final thanks are due to those closest to the project. Lee Goerner, my editor at Alfred A. Knopf, had the wisdom to cut the manuscript by more than half and thus save it from a morass of secondary material. It was Andrew Wylie, my literary agent, who conceived the idea of the book. To him I owe gratitude for a constant infusion of enthusiasm during the tedium of day-to-day work and for fulfilling the writer's greatest need, that of an objective observer and a subjective collaborator in one. Ngari Rinpoché, presently chief foreign secretary of the Dalai Lama's Private Office, in his own ever truthful words worked "his tail off" from day one of my research. He arranged innumerable interviews, provided a plethora of superlative personal information, and energetically coordinated most aspects of production. RCA and EFA, throughout, offered their loving support.

My wife Elizabeth has been my ultimate resource. She has aided every phase of the project, consistently taking time off from her own work to evaluate, instruct and offer guidance through the various obstacles encountered. She has offered the assistance of many in one, and she has done so unfailingly.

Finally, I am indebted to the Dalai Lama. Through long hours of probing interviews, he frankly related his personal reaction to historic events, thereby revealing the heart of the issue. His concern for and interest in this book stemmed not so much from the understandable desire to see Tibet's story told, but from a genuine motive to assist however he could. It was this spirit that made possible my other work and for which I owe my greatest thanks.

Bibliography

Andrugtsang, Gompo Tashi. *Four-Rivers-Six Ranges: A True Account of Khampa Resistance to Chinese in Tibet.* Information Office of His Holiness the Dalai Lama, Dharamsala, India, 1973.

Avedon, John F. *An Interview with the Dalai Lama.* Littlebird Publications, New York, 1980.

Barber, Noel. *The Flight of the Dalai Lama.* Hodder & Stoughton, London, 1960.

———. *From the Land of Lost Content.* Houghton Mifflin Co., Boston, 1970.

Bell, Sir Charles. *Tibet Past and Present.* Oxford University Press, London, 1968 (first published 1924).

———. *The People of Tibet.* Oxford University Press, London, 1968 (first published 1928).

———. *The Religion of Tibet.* Oxford University Press, London 1968 (first published 1931).

———. *Portrait of the Dalai Lama.* Collins, London, 1946

Bhushan, Shashi. *China: The Myth of a Superpower.* Progressive People's Sector Publications Ltd, New Delhi, 1976

Bonavia, David, and Magnus Bartlett. *Tibet.* The Vendome Press, New York, 1981.

Buddha, Sakyamuni. *The Ambrosia Heart Tantra.* Library of Tibetan Works and Archives, Dharamsala, India, 1977.

Bull, Geofrey T. *When Iron Gates Yield.* Hodder & Stoughton, London, 1964.

Burman, Bina Roy. *Religion and Politics in Tibet.* Vikas Publications, New Delhi, 1979.

Butterfield, Fox. *China: Alive in the Bitter Sea.* Times Books, New York, 1982.

Carrasco, Pedro. *Land and Polity in Tibet.* The University Press of Kentucky, Lexington, 1976.

Central Intelligence Agency. *People's Republic of China Atlas.* United States Government Printing Office, Washington, D.C., 1971.

Chang-hao, Hsi, and Kao Yuan-mei. *Tibet Leaps Forward.* Foreign Languages Press, Peking, 1977.

China's Inner Asian Frontier. The Peabody Museum of Archaeology and Ethnology, Harvard University, Cambridge, Mass., 1979.

China's Minority Nationalities. Modern China Series No. 3, Red Sun Publishers, San Francisco, 1977.

Choedon, Dhondub. *Life in the Red Flag People's Commune.* Information Office of His Holiness the Dalai Lama, Dharamsala, India, 1978.

Choephel, Gendun. *The White Annals.* Library of Tibetan Works and Archives, Dharamsala, India, 1978.

Clark, Leonard. *The Marching Wind.* Hutchinson, London, 1955.

Constitution of Tibet. Bureau of His Holiness the Dalai Lama, New Delhi, 1963.

Dalai Lama, the Third. *Essence of Refined Gold.* Gabrial/Snow Lion, Valois, N.Y., 1982.

Dalai Lama, the Seventh. *Songs of Spiritual Change.* Gabrial/Snow Lion, Valois, N.Y., 1982.

Dalai Lama, the Fourteenth. *My Land and My People.* McGraw-Hill, New York, 1962.

Dalai Lama, the Fourteenth. *The Buddhism of Tibet and the Key to the Middle Way.* Harper and Row, New York, 1975.

Dalai Lama, the Fourteenth. *The Opening of the Wisdom Eye.* The Theosophical Publishing House, Wheaton, Ill. 1972.

Dalai Lama and India. The Institute of National Affairs, New Delhi, 1959.

Dalvi, Brig. J.P. *Himalayan Blunder.* Thacker and Company Ltd, Bombay, 1969.

Dhargey, Geshé Ngawang. *Tibetan Tradition of Mental Development.* Library of Tibetan Works and Archives, Dharamsala, India, 1974.

Dreyer, June Teufel. *China's Forty Millions.* Harvard University Press, Cambridge, Mass., 1976.

Ford, Robert. *Wind Between the Worlds.* David McKay, New York, 1957.

Fraser, John. *The Chinese: Portrait of a People.* Summit Books, New York, 1980.

From Liberation to Liberalisation. Information Office of His Holiness the Dalai Lama, Dharamsala, India, 1982.

Fundamentals of Tibetan Medicine. Tibetan Medical Center, Dharamsala, India, 1981.

Gashi, Tsering Dorji. *New Tibet.* Information Office of His Holiness the Dalai Lama, Dharamsala, India, 1980.

Ginsburgs, George, and Michael Mathos. *Communist China and Tibet.* Martinus Nijhoff, The Hague, 1964.

Glimpses of Tibet Today. Information Office of His Holiness the Dalai Lama, Dharamsala, India, 1978.

Gould, B.J. *The Jewel in the Lotus.* Chatto & Windus, London, 1957.

Great Changes in Tibet. Foreign Languages Press, Peking, 1972.

Harrer, Heinrich. *Seven Years in Tibet.* E. P. Dutton, New York, 1954.

International Commission of Jurists. *The Question of Tibet and the Rule of Law.* Geneva, 1959.

————. *Tibet and the Chinese People's Republic.* Geneva, 1960.

Jain, Girilal. *Panchsheela and After.* Asia Publishing House, Bombay, 1960.

Karan, Pradyumna P. *The Changing Face of Tibet.* The University Press of Kentucky, Lexington, 1976.

Lang-Sims, Lois. *The Presence of Tibet.* Cresset Press, London, 1963.

Lati Rimbochay, and Jeffrey Hopkins. *Death, Intermediate State and Rebirth in Tibetan Buddhism.* Rider, London, 1979.

Lehmann, Peter-Hannes, and Jay Ullal. *Tibet: Das Still Drama auf dem Dach der Erde.* GEO, Hamburg, 1981.

Ling, Trevor. *The Buddha.* Temple Smith Ltd, London, 1973.

Mele, Pietro Francesco. *Tibet.* Oxford and IBH Publishing Co., Calcutta, n.d.

Migot, Andre. *Tibetan Marches.* Rupert Hart-Davis, London, 1955.

Mitter, J.P. *Betrayal of Tibet.* Allied Publishers Private Ltd, Bombay, 1964.

Moraes, Frank. *The Revolt in Tibet.* Sterling Publishers, New Delhi, 1966 (first published 1960).

Murphy, Dervla. *Tibetan Foothold.* John Murray, London, 1966.

Nanporia, N.J. *The Sino-Indian Dispute.* The Times of India, Bombay, 1963.

Norbu, Dawa. *Red Star over Tibet.* Collins, London, 1974.

Norbu, Jamyang. *Horseman in the Snow.* Information Office of His Holiness the Dalai Lama, Dharamsala, India, 1979.

Norbu, Namkai. *The Necklace of Gzi.* Information Office of His Holiness the Dalai Lama, Dharamsala, India, 1981.

Norbu, Thubten Jigme, and Heinrich Harrer. *Tibet Is My Country.* E. P. Dutton, New York, 1961.

Norbu, Thubten Jigme, and Colin M. Turnbull. *Tibet.* Simon and Schuster, New York, 1968.

Paljor, Kunsang. *Tibet: The Undying Flame.* Information Office of His Holiness the Dalai Lama, Dharamsala, India, 1977.

Patterson, George N. *Tragic Destiny.* Faber and Faber, London, 1959.

––––––. *Tibet in Revolt.* Faber and Faber, London, 1960.

Peissel, Michel. *Cavaliers of Kham.* Heinemann, London, 1972.

Rahul, Ram. *The Government and Politics of Tibet.* Vikas Publications, New Delhi, 1969.

Rato, Khyongla Ngawang Losang. *My Life and Lives.* E. P. Dutton, New York, 1977.

Richardson, H.E. *Tibet and Its History.* Oxford University Press, London, 1962.

Rockhill, William Woodville. *Notes on Tibet.* Asian Publication Services, New Delhi, 1977.

Rowland, John. *A History of Sino-Indian Relations.* D. Van Nostrand, Princeton, New Jersey, 1967.

Shakabpa, Tsepon W.D. *Tibet: A Political History.* Yale University Press, New Haven, 1967.

Shantideva, *A Guide to the Bodhisattva's Way of Life.* Library of Tibetan Works and Archives, Dharamsala, India, 1979.

Sharma, Parmanand. *People of the Prayerwheel.* Ambika Publications, New Delhi, 1979.

Shen, Tsung-lien, and Shen-chi Liu. *Tibet and the Tibetans.* Stanford University Press, Stanford, Cal., 1953.

Sinha, Nirmal C. *An Introduction to the History and Religion of Tibet.* Ambica Charan Bose, Calcutta, 1975.

Snellgrove, David, and Hugh Richardson. *A Cultural History of Tibet.* Prajna Press, Boulder, Colo. 1980 (first published 1968).

Stein, R.A. *Tibetan Civilization.* Stanford University Press, Stanford, Cal., 1972 (first published 1962).

Strong, Anna Louise. *When Serfs Stood Up in Tibet.* Modern China Series No. 1, Red Sun Publishers, San Francisco, 1976 (first published 1959).

Suyin, Han. *Lhasa, the Open City.* Triad Panther Books, London, 1979 (first published 1977).

Tada, Tokan. *The Thirteenth Dalai Lama.* The Center for East Asian Cultural Studies, Tokyo, 1965.

Taring, Zasak J. *Lhasa Tsug-lag Khang Gi Sata and Karchag.* J. Taring, Dehra Dun, India, n.d.

Taring, Rinchen Dolma. *Daughter of Tibet.* John Murray, London, 1970.

Thomas, Lowell Jr. *Out of This World.* Greystone Press, New York, 1950.

Thubtob, Rev. Ngawang. *Tibet Today*. Bureau of His Holiness the Dalai Lama, New Delhi.

Tibet. McGraw-Hill, New York, 1981.

Tibet Fights for Freedom, Orient Longman's, Bombay, 1960.

Tibet in the United Nations. Bureau of His Holiness the Dalai Lama, New Delhi, 1961.

Tibet: 1950–1967. Union Research Institute, Hong Kong, 1968.

Tibet: No Longer Medieval. Foreign Languages Press, Peking, 1981.

Tibet: The Sacred Realm. Philadelphia Museum of Art/Aperture, New York, 1983.

Tibet Today. Foreign Languages Press, Peking, 1974.

Tibet Under Chinese Communist Rule. Information Office of His Holiness the Dalai Lama, Dharamsala, India, 1976.

Tibetans in Exile: 1959–1969, Information Office of His Holiness the Dalai Lama, Dharamsala, India, 1969.

Topping, Audrey. *The Splendors of Tibet*. Sino Publishing Company, New York, 1980.

Tsongkhapa, Je. *Compassion in Tibetan Buddhism*. Ed. Kensur Lekden and Jeffrey Hopkins. Gabrial/Snow Lion, Valois, New York, 1980.

———. *The Yoga of Tibet: The Great Exposition of Secret Mantra Nos. 2 and 3*. George Allen and Unwin, London, 1977 and 1981.

Tucci, Giuseppe. *To Lhasa and Beyond*. Instituto Poligrafico Dello Stato, Libreria Dello Stato, Rome, 1956.

———. *The Religions of Tibet*. Routledge and Kegan Paul, London, 1980.

Tung, Rosemary Jones. *A Portrait of Lost Tibet*. Thames and Hudson, London, 1980.

Van Walts Van Praag, M.C. *Tibet and the Right to Self-Determination*. Information Office of His Holiness the Dalai Lama, Dharamsala, India, 1979.

Waddell, Austine L. *Tibetan Buddhism*. Dover Publications, New York, 1972 (first published 1895).

Wangdu, Sonam. *The Discovery of the Fourteenth Dalai Lama*. Khett Thai Publications, Bangkok, 1975.

Wrath of the Serfs. Foreign Languages Press, Peking, 1976.

PAMPHLETS AND PERIODICALS

Beijing Review, 1957–1983. Peking, China.

Bobb, Dilip. *Blunting the Edge*. India Today, Dec. 1–15, 1980.

Brief Survey of History and Present-Day Conditions in Tibet. Information Office of His Holiness the Dalai Lama, Dharamsala, India, 1977.

China Reconstructs, 1951–1983. Peking, China.

Choedrak, Tenzin. *Seventeen Years in a Chinese Prison*. Spearhead, New York. Autumn 1981.

Dalai Lama, the Fourteenth. *An Introduction to Buddhism*. Library of Tibetan Works and Archives, Dharamsala, India, 1965.

———. *Short Essays on Buddhist Thought and Practice*. Library of Tibetan Works and Archives, Dharamsala, India, n.d.

———. *The Key to the Madhyamika*. Library of Tibetan Works and Archives, Dharamsala, India, 1974.

Dhonden, Dr. Yeshi. *Introductory Lectures on Tibetan Medicine*. University of Virginia, 1980 (class notes).

Dreyer, June Teufel. *China and Tibet: A Thirty Year Assessment*. Spearhead, New York, Autumn 1981.

Far Eastern Economic Review, 1946–1983. Hong Kong.

Gyalpo, Pema. *Three Months in Tibet.* Metok, Tibetan Children's Village, Winter 1980.

Introduction to Tibetan Medicine. Tibetan Review, New Delhi, 1976.

Life magazine, 1950–1959. New York.

Long, Jeff. *Going After Wangdu.* Rocky Mountain Magazine, July/Aug., 1981.

National Geographic, Vol. LXVIII, no. 4; VOL. XC, no. 2; Vol. CVIII, no. 1; Vol. 157, No. 2.

National Integration (Tibet Issue), New Delhi, 1964.

News Tibet, 1965–1983. The Office of Tibet, New York.

Rabten, Geshé. *The Preliminary Practices.* Library of Tibetan Works and Archives, Dharamsala, India, 1974.

Rangdzen, 1972–1983. Magazine of the Tibetan Youth Congress, Dharamsala, India.

Reiter, Elmer R. *How Tibet's Weather Affects Other Countries.* Natural History, Vol. 90, no. 9, New York, 1981.

Ripley, S. Dillon. *Tibet: The High and Fragile Land Behind the Ranges,* Smithsonian, Washington, D.C., Jan. 1981.

Schaller, George B. *Tibet: Behind the Clouds a Troubled Ecosystem.* Animal Kingdom, Dec. 1980–Jan. 1981.

———. *The Dusty Road to China's Wild West. Asia,* Vol. 4, no. 5, Feb. 1982.

Schell, Orville. *Journey to the Tibetan Plateau.* Natural History, Sept. 1982.

The Hindustan Standard, 1959–1983.

The Hindustan Times, 1959–1983.

The Indian Express, 1959–1983.

The New York Times, 1959–1983.

The Statesman, 1959–1983.

The Sunday Standard, 1959–1983.

The Tibet Journal, Dharamsala, India, 1975–1983.

The Times of India, 1959–1983.

The Truth About Tibet, Bureau of His Holiness the Dalai Lama, New Delhi.

Thogs-med bzang-po. *The Thirty Seven Practices of All Buddhas' Sons.* Library of Tibetan Works and Archives, Dharamsala, India, 1973.

Tibet News Review, London, 1980–1983.

Tibet: A Sovereign Nation for Centuries. Tibetan Youth Congress, Dharamsala, 1977.

Tibetan Bulletin, 1968–1983. Information Office of His Holiness the Dalai Lama, Dharamsala, India.

Tibetan Medicine, Series nos. 1 & 2. Library of Tibetan Works and Archives, Dharamsala, India, 1980–81.

Tibetan National Uprising—20th Anniversary of the 10th March, 1959. Information Office of His Holiness the Dalai Lama, Dharamsala, India, 1979.

Tibetan Review, 1968–1983. New Delhi.

Miscellaneous Reports from the Bureau of His Holiness the Dalai Lama, New Delhi, and the Information Office of His Holiness the Dalai Lama, Dharamsala, India.

Index

John F. Avedon was born in New York and educated at Sarah Lawrence College. He has written for the overseas edition of *Newsweek* and his articles have appeared in *GEO*, *Rolling Stone*, *The New York Times Magazine*, and *Macleans*. He lives in New York City with his wife and family.